Contract Law in South Africa

Contract Law in South Africa

Sixth Edition

Louis F. Van Huyssteen
Catherine J. Maxwell

This book was originally published as a monograph in the International Encyclopaedia of Laws/Contracts.

Founding Editor: Roger Blanpain
General Editor: Frank Hendrickx
Volume Editor: Jacques Herbots

Wolters Kluwer

Published by:
Kluwer Law International B.V.
PO Box 316
2400 AH Alphen aan den Rijn
The Netherlands
E-mail: international-sales@wolterskluwer.com
Website: lrus.wolterskluwer.com

Sold and distributed in North, Central and South America by:
Wolters Kluwer Legal & Regulatory U.S.
7201 McKinney Circle
Frederick, MD 21704
United States of America
Email: customer.service@wolterskluwer.com

Sold and distributed in all other countries by:
Air Business Subscriptions
Rockwood House
Haywards Heath
West Sussex
RH16 3DH
United Kingdom
Email: international-customerservice@wolterskluwer.com

Printed on acid-free paper

ISBN 978-94-035-1334-8

e-Book: ISBN 978-94-035-1381-2
web-PDF: ISBN 978-94-035-1404-8

Printed in the United Kingdom.

The Authors

Prof. Dr Louis F. van Huyssteen obtained his LLB from the University of Stellenbosch, South Africa, the Drs. Jur. from the University of Leiden, the Netherlands and LLD from the University of Cape Town, South Africa. He has taught Law of Contract and related subjects for more than twenty-five years. He is the author of several books on the law of contract and has published extensively in local and international journals on this topic and on legal history. He was also a member of a specialist committee on unfair contracts of the South African Law Commission which ultimately led to new legislation on consumer protection. He has retired from full-time teaching and is now practising in Cape Town, South Africa as an attorney of the High Court and consultant and arbitrator, specializing in Contract Law and aspects of Commercial Law. He has also been appointed as a Mellon Senior Research Fellow in the Faculty of Law, University of the Western Cape and has now been appointed as Research Mentor there.

Dr Catherine J. Maxwell graduated from the University of Cape Town, South Africa, BA LLB (cum laude) and obtained an LLM degree from the University of Cambridge, followed by an LLD from the University of Cape Town. Until 2009, she was an Associate Professor at the University of the Western Cape, where she taught Law of Contract, Law of Unjustified Enrichment, Law of Delict, Property Law, Family Law and Legal History. She has been admitted as an Advocate of the High Court of South Africa.

The Authors

Table of Contents

Table of Contents

List of Abbreviations

A	Appellate Division
AD	Appellate Division Reports (with respect to pre-1947 law reports)
All ER	All England Law Reports
BCLR	Butterworths Constitutional Law Reports
BGD	Bophuthatswana General Division
Bpk	Beperk (Limited)
BSC	Bophuthatswana Supreme Court
Buch	Buchanan's Supreme Court Reports (Cape)
C	Cape Provincial Division
CC	Constitutional Court
Co.	Company
CPD	Cape Provincial Division Reports (with respect to pre-1947 law reports)
D	Durban and Coast Local Division
E	Eastern Cape Provincial Division
ECB	Eastern Cape High Court Bisho
ECG	Eastern Cape High Court Grahamstown
ECM	Eastern Cape High Court Mthatha
ECP	Eastern Cape High Court Port Elizabeth
ed.	Editor
EDL	Eastern Districts Local Division Reports (with respect to pre-1947 law reports)
Edms	Eiendoms (Proprietary)
FB	Free State High Court Bloemfontein
GSJ	South Gauteng High Court Johannesburg
GNP	North Gauteng High Court Pretoria
GW	Griqualand-West Local Division Reports (with respect to pre-1947 law reports)
Hertzog	Hertzog's High Court Reports (*Transvaal*)
HHA	*Hoogste Hof van Appèl* (Supreme Court of Appeal)

List of Abbreviations

ILJ	Industrial Law Journal
Inst	*Institutiones* in the *Corpus Iuris Civilis*
J	Judge
JA	Judge of Appeal
KPA	*Kaapse Provinsiale Afdeling* (Cape Provincial Division)
KZD**	KwaZulu-Natal Local Division Durban
KZP**	KwaZulu-Natal Division Pietermaritzburg
LP**	Limpopo Division Polokwane (operating in the Gauteng Division since August 2013)
LRHL	Law Reports, House of Lords
LRQB	Law Reports, Queen's Bench
LT	Law Times Reports
LT.**	Limpopo Local Division Thohoyandou (operating in the Gauteng Division since August 2013)
Ltd	Limited
MN**	Mpumalanga Division Nelspruit (operating in the Gauteng Division since August 2013)
N	Natal Provincial Division
NCK**	Northern Cape Division Kimberley
NJ	*Nederlandse Jurisprudentie*
NWM**	North West Division Mahikeng
O	Orange Free State Provincial Division
OPD	Orange Free State Provincial Division Reports (with respect to pre-1947 law reports)
Pty	Proprietary
QB	Queen's Bench
SA	South Africa/South African Law Reports
SALJ	South African Law Journal
SC	Supreme Court Reports (Cape)
SCA	Supreme Court of Appeal
SR	Southern Rhodesia High Court
Stell LR	Stellenbosch Law Review
s.v.	*sub verba* (under the word)
T	Transvaal Provincial Division
THRHR	*Tydskrif vir Hedendaagse Romeins-Hollandse Reg*
TPD	Transvaal Provincial Division Reports (with respect to pre-1947 law reports)
TS	Transvaal Supreme Court Reports
TSAR	*Tydskrif vir Suid-Afrikaanse Reg*
vol.	Volume

W	Witwatersrand Local Division
WCC**	Western Cape Division Cape Town
ZACC	South Africa Constitutional Court
ZAECGHC	South Africa Eastern Cape Grahamstown High Court
ZAGPJHC	South Africa Gauteng Province Johannesburg High Court
ZAKZDHC	South Africa KwaZulu Durban High Court
ZANCHC	South Africa Northern Cape High Court
ZASCA	South Africa Supreme Court of Appeal
ZAWCHC	South Africa Western Cape High Court

** The Superior Courts Act 10 of 2013 created a single High Court with various divisions.

List of Abbreviations

General Introduction

§1. The General Background of the Country

I. Geography

1. The Republic of South Africa is a large country of approximately 1.2 million km^2 and is situated in the southernmost part of the African Continent.[1] To the north and east, South Africa borders Namibia, Botswana, Zimbabwe, Mozambique, and Swaziland, while also encircling Lesotho. South Africa has a coastline of about 3,000 km, on the South Atlantic and southern Indian Oceans. On the whole, it is a dry country with a warm and temperate climate. The average rainfall is 450 mm per annum, compared to the world average of 860 mm per annum. It is predicted that the western and central parts of the country will become drier and the eastern parts will become wetter as a result of climate change. This has already occurred with devastating droughts and resultant crop and livestock losses and water shortages in many provinces, particularly in the Western Cape and Cape Town itself.

II. Population

2. The total population of South Africa is now 57.5 million, composed of heterogeneous people, of which 30% are younger than 15 years of age and 51% are female. The life expectancy for males is 61.2 years and for females it is 66.7 years. A significant factor in the growth of the population is the influx of refugees from other African countries, notably Zimbabwe and the Democratic Republic of the Congo.

3. About 80% of the population classify themselves as black and are regarded as indigenous people. Four main groups may be distinguished by language and cultural differences, with further identifiable sub-groups. The main groups are the Nguni people (the sub-groups being the Xhosa, the Zulu, the Swazi, and the Ndebele), the Sotho-Tswana people, the Venda people, and the Tsonga people.

---

1. The main sources of reference are the official yearbook, Govt. Commun. & Info. Sys. *South Africa Yearbook 2014/15*, http://www.gcis.gov.za/content/resourcecentre/sa-info/yearbook/2016-17.htm and *Statistics South Africa*, http://www.statssa.gov.za.

4. South Africans of European origin are about 4.6 million (9%) and classify themselves as white. Their ancestors arrived here as colonists, and later immigrants, from the seventeenth century onwards. Mainly, their countries of origin are the Netherlands, France, the United Kingdom, Germany, and Portugal.

5. South Africa has a large population of Eastern extraction. In the Dutch colonial period, many people were brought to the country as slaves from present-day Indonesia and Malaysia. In the latter half of the nineteenth century, large number of Indians arrived to work on the sugar plantations. They were eventually followed by others, mainly traders. The country now has a population of about 1.3 million people who classify themselves as Asian or Indian.

6. About 4.6 million South Africans are people of mixed race; they classify themselves as coloured – a hybridization of all the above as well as the original inhabitants of South Africa, the Khoisan people.

7. It is important to note that the South African population is essentially a hybrid one, not only genetically, but also, and more importantly, culturally.[2] This last aspect will be discussed below.

8. A notable feature of the present South African population is rapid urbanization. More than one-third of the inhabitants live in the metropoles of Tshwane (Pretoria)-Witwatersrand-Vereeniging (Gauteng), Cape Town, e-Thekwini (Durban) and Nelson Mandela Bay (Port Elizabeth-Uitenhage).

III. Economy, Labour Relations, and Infrastructure

9. South Africa is the 38th largest economy in the world. The country's gross domestic product (GDP) has increased annually since 1996 until recently, showing a markedly slower growth of 1.3% in 2017 falling to -2.2% for the first quarter of 2018. This is largely due to a decrease in agricultural production (as a result of the devastating drought), mining and manufacture. Foreign direct investment is currently low (0.7% of GDP, due to lack of skills, visa restrictions and land expropriation), but is expected to increase, in line with the trend to invest more heavily in Africa. This is particularly true since the very recent BRICS (*see* below) conference in Johannesburg where, for example, China pledged to invest USD 15 billion directly. The trade deficit on the current account is extremely volatile due mainly to fluctuating exports of commodities and is currently 2.3% of GDP.

An important feature of the economy is a new commitment to macroeconomic stability, strong growth in foreign trade and an increase in the export of manufactured goods, a problem being price inflation. This goes hand-in-hand with an increasingly positive role in world and regional economic organizations, expansion of the trade network to the 'new' economies (e.g., trade agreements with Brazil,

2. Cf. R.E. van der Ross, *Myths and Attitudes: An Inside Look at the Coloured People* 30 et seq. (Tafelberg 1979).

China (our biggest trading partner), India, Russia and various African countries; South Africa is now a member of the BRICS organization and the BRICS bank), the rise of South African multinational corporations and direct participation in international financial markets. South Africa is considered to be one of the world's promising emerging markets but has unfortunately, due to political uncertainty exacerbated by the previous government, decreased its ranking from 47th in the previous Global Competitiveness Report to 61 out of 137 in 2017/2018. In the latest report, however, progress in the labour market, infrastructure, better use of talent and quality of primary education and healthcare are mentioned as positive. A positive aspect is that South Africa was placed as 57th in the Global Innovation Index as the most innovative in Sub-Saharan Africa. Considering the youth of the population and a marked increase in the award of degrees by our tertiary education institutions, it bodes well for the advent of the so-called Fourth Industrial Revolution. It is interesting to note that the South African economy has not been as greatly affected by the global economic downturn (recession) of 2008–2009 as were some developed countries in North America and Europe. This is, to some extent, because of fiscal policy and lending controls through legislation. Our main trading partners are China, the United States of America, Japan, Germany, and the United Kingdom.

The main economic problems in South Africa presently are poverty, lack of skills, unemployment (27.2% despite creating 74,000 new jobs in the formal sector in the first quarter of 2018), labour unrest and pressure on the infrastructure (particularly electricity supply) resulting from growth and urbanization. Concerns about crime, corruption and political instability locally and in neighbouring countries are also factors that are presently influencing investment negatively, and that are being actively addressed by the government. In recent times many criminal cases have been instituted against officials in local and national government and particularly in state-owned enterprises.

The thrust of the government's economic policy is free trade, international competitiveness, privatization, and stimulation of the small-business and informal sectors aimed at growth and job creation. In this regard, training and skills development, the creation of opportunities, and black economic empowerment are regarded as crucial, to be attained through active partnership with the private sector. These aspects are now supported by various laws, government agencies, and formal agreements between the government and the private sector, including the New Growth Path, supported by the budget. Capital investments in infrastructure (particularly the generation of electricity), transportation, the road network and urban renewal are of the highest priority, in spite of slow economic growth – for example, more than 80% of the population now have formal housing, access to piped water and electricity. To expedite the development of infrastructure, the President has very recently announced the creation of a fund of ZAR 400 billion. A burning and emotive issue now is the provision of agricultural land to emerging farmers by expropriation (sometimes without compensation), despite the land restitution process that has been in operation since 1994. This process has been marked with failure largely due to the lack of support and financing by government. An even greater issue is the provision of urban land for (informal) housing which has caused a spate of sometimes violent protests throughout the country. This is relatively easy to solve providing there is political will and administrative capacity in the municipal structures with support by central government.

Labour relations legislation is based on the principle of free association and provides the usual range of protective measures and worker benefits. Legislative progress has been made in the field of employment equity and the fixing of basic conditions of employment as well as a minimum wage. There is a strong and vociferous labour-union movement. It appears that the collective bargaining and dispute-resolution mechanisms are working reasonably well in creating stable and mature labour relations. Nevertheless all industries are annually subject to strikes and work stoppages, mostly legitimate and peaceful. A negative factor impeding growth is over-regulation in some fields.

South Africa has a sophisticated and well-developed financial services industry, including every type of institution needed in a modern economy, as well as a busy and effective stock exchange, which is now linked with the London Stock Exchange. The Johannesburg Stock Exchange is one of the top twenty in terms of market capitalization.

The country has a good infrastructure: a road network of about 232,000 km, of which 55,000 km are tarred (the tenth longest network in the world); an extensive rail network (of which 2,300 km are electrified); a good freight-container service; a national air carrier providing service to all continents, as well as a number of local airlines; and two large harbours that provide all necessary port services, as well as a number of specialized (bulk commodities) and smaller harbours. However, as indicated above, the infrastructure is under pressure, and thus maintenance, renewal, and expansion are regarded as priorities. A long-term infrastructure programme was introduced by the government in 2012 to invest ZAR 4,000 billion over the next fifteen years, consisting of 645 projects in eighteen key areas, such as transport, energy, water, sanitation, skills development, education, health care, and mining.

IV. Political System

10. After intense negotiations among most political groups in the country at the Multi-Party Negotiating Process in 1992–1993, a new interim Constitution was agreed to, creating a single sovereign democratic South Africa,[3] based on universal franchise for all citizens over the age of 18 years, separation of powers and a government of national unity. Nine provinces were established, instead of the previous four. In 1996, the envisaged (final) Constitution of the Republic of South Africa (Act 108 of 1996) was adopted. In general, it further entrenches the principles of democracy and human rights contained in the interim Constitution. It appears that a quasi-federal State is established in terms thereof.

3. The self-governing territories and independent states created in terms of the ideology of separate development have been re-incorporated into the boundaries of the country.

11. The Constitution provides for an executive State President and a Deputy President, a bicameral Parliament (the National Assembly and the National Council of Provinces, with a provision for joint sittings for certain matters), and a national cabinet. A National House of Traditional Leaders was also established to advise Parliament on customary law, and it has representatives in the National Assembly.

The Constitution operates in a multi-party system, with proportional representation, and a national and regional list system. The Constitution establishes itself as supreme law, with all government actions and laws subject to it, and it also provides for an independent judiciary. The Constitutional Court, with the power to decide on the constitutionality of Acts of Parliament, any executive or administrative act as well as now any arguable point of law of general public importance if it is in the interests of justice[4] was created, as were higher courts (headed by the Supreme Court of Appeal) and lower courts. A chapter containing a charter of fundamental rights is entrenched in the Constitution. A unique feature of the Constitution is the creation of various bodies and courts to protect the interests of citizens and to redress the inequalities of the past. A further notable feature is that it requires a cooperative government and the advancement of inter-governmental relations.

12. At the second tier of government, legislative authority is vested in the nine provincial legislatures, and executive authority is vested in the premiers and executive councils. Parliament has concurrent powers with respect to some functional areas falling within the jurisdiction of the provinces. These matters include health, welfare, education, tourism, trade, and culture. There are extensive provisions regarding conflicting laws in these areas. Further, there are a number of functional areas of exclusive provincial legislative competence. Parliament may intervene in these areas in certain special circumstances. A province may draw up its own constitution and provide for legislative and executive structures that are different from those provided for in the Constitution, but not inconsistent with it.

The Constitution provides for different categories of municipalities charged with local governance.

V. Cultural, Social, and Economic Values

13. As pointed out above, South African culture, to a large extent, is a hybrid of many cultures. The dominance or strength of a particular culture or aspect of a culture depends, *inter alia*, on the socio-economic status of the particular cultural group. In this respect, rapid change as a result of increased urbanization and the rise of a strong and economically powerful black middle class is taking place, so that it is even more difficult than before to attempt to make generalizations – the percentage of the population with school-leaving and tertiary qualifications has increased significantly and most South Africans are now in the middle ranges of the Lifestyle Index. Accordingly, in very broad terms, South African society does not differ much from any other modern semi-industrialized society.

4. Section 167 (3) (b) (ii) of the Constitution as amended. Cf. *Paulsen and Another v. Slip Knot Investments 777 (Pty) Ltd* 2015 3 SA 479 (CC).

Information about some of the important determinants of South African culture may give a rough indication of the diversity, as well as of the homogeneous nature, of the cultural and social values of South Africans. Eleven major languages are spoken, but none of these is spoken by a majority of the population. These languages are all official languages, but English is the language understood by most of the people in the country (the *lingua franca*), and also being the second language of the majority of people. IsiZulu, isiXhosa, Afrikaans, and English in this order are the dominant languages as far as first (home) languages are concerned. With respect to religion, about 80% of the population is Christian. South Africa is a secular democracy which protects freedom of religious beliefs. A large part of the population adheres to traditionalist indigenous religions, although, often, not to the exclusion of the Christian faith. Other important religions are Islam, and the Hindu and Jewish (mainly Orthodox) religions. As a very general rule, the adherents of particularly the Hindu and Muslim faiths tend to preserve some of the more traditional values associated with their religions, although by no means to the extent of being fundamentalist. The Constitution actively promotes the protection of diverse languages and cultural rights, for example, by the establishment of a Pan-South African Language Board. The promotion of tolerance, freedom of religion and speech and the recognition of diversity are important ingredients of the movement to build a South African nation united in its loyalty to the country, as evidenced by the 'Proudly South African' campaign regarding manufacturing and consumer trade.

14. It may be stated[5] with a measure of impunity that the primary social and economic values reflected in the formal dogma, principles, and rules of South African law of contract are those of individualism (autonomy) and self-interest. Thus, freedom of contract is a basic value which expresses the Constitutional value of dignity and equality, and, in principle, a promise that has been agreed is sacrosanct and should be enforced. However, and importantly so, the more generalized values of social and community responsibility, altruism, respect for the interests of others and of society are by way of the concepts of good faith, fairness, reasonableness and ubuntu, (also reflective of the Constitutional values of dignity, equality, and freedom) again strongly influencing the development of existing principles and rules of the law of contract, and perhaps the creation of new principles and rules in specific circumstances, particularly recently in the context of the enforcement of contracts which have been judged to be contrary to public policy and the values of the Constitution in particular circumstances.[6] To some extent, this is possibly the result of

5. Cf. Van Huyssteen, Lubbe & Reinecke, *Contract General Principles*, para. 1.41 et seq., *ch. 9 I* (Juta 2016); *Barkhuizen v. Napier* 2007 5 SA 323 (CC); *Bredenkamp v. Standard Bank of South Africa Ltd* 2010 4 SA 468 (SCA); *Phumelela Gaming and Leisure Ltd v. Grundlingh* 2007 (6) SA 350 (CC); *Silent Pond Investments CC v. Woolworths (Pty) Ltd* 2011 6 SA 343 (D); *Everfresh Market Virginia (Pty) Ltd v. Shoprite Checkers (Pty) Ltd* 2012 1 SA 256 (CC; *Uniting Reformed Church, De Doorns v. President of the Republic of South Africa and Others* 2013 5 SA 205 (WCC) where inequality of bargaining power was held to be against the public interest and thus unconstitutional and unenforceable.
6. *See* the cases referred to above and *Combined Developers v. Arun Holdings and Others* 2015 3 SA 215 (WCC); *Botha and Another v. Rich NO and Others* 2014 4 SA 124 (CC) paras 24, 28, 45–46; *Paulsen and Another v. Slip Knot Investments 777 (Pty) Ltd* 2015 3 SA 479 (CC) paras 71, 72,

the rapid socio-economic changes that are taking place in the country and, as indicated above, are reflected in the recognition and entrenchment of fundamental human rights in the Constitution. This trend is in keeping with the jurisprudence of the indigenous (customary) law of contract, which more recently has seemed to place greater emphasis on group interests than on individual interests – in this regard the concept of ubuntu may well play a pivotal role.[7] Islamic law has had no direct influence on the principles and rules of the law of contract, but some of the

---

113,119; *W v. H* 2017 1 SA 196 (WCC) (unilateral waiver of right to claim maintenance unenforceable); *Bondev Midrand (Pty) Ltd v. Madzhie and Others* 2017 4 SA 166 (GP) (repurchase clause grossly unfair and infringing the right to housing); *Beadica 231 CC and Others v. Trustees, Oregon Unit Trust and Others* 2018 1 SA 549 (WCC) (enforcing of cancellation and eviction clauses in lease disproportionate and against public policy in the particular circumstances); *Four Wheel Drive Accessory Distribution CC v. Rattan NO* 2018 3 SA 204 (KZD) (terms in standard contract too small to read and unenforceable against public policy). In *Cool Ideas 1186 CC v. Hubbard and Another* 2014 4 SA 474 (CC) the majority of the Constitutional Court warned that fairness could not be invoked to circumvent the plain meaning of a statute which is rationally connected to legitimate purpose. In the result the applicant was legitimately deprived of its property. The minority applied an interpretation which did not have this result. In *Mohamed's Leisure Holdings (Pty) Ltd v. Southern Sun Hotel Interests (Pty) Ltd* 2018 2 SA 314 (SCA), the appeal court overturned the decision of the high court (based on public policy and ubuntu) and decided that the circumstances did not warrant a departure from *pacta servanda sunt,* consequently enforcing a cancellation and eviction clause in a lease. The appeal court in *Roazar CC v. The Falls Supermarket CC* 2018 3 SA 76 (SCA) refused in the particular circumstances (the requirement of certainty and absence of a deadlock-breaking mechanism) to develop the common law to import a term to compel parties to negotiate a renewal of a lease in good faith: '*It is difficult to conceive how a court, in a purely business transaction, can rely on "ubuntu" to import a term that was not intended by the parties, to deny the other party a right to rely on the terms of the contract to terminate it' (para 24).*

7. In *Everfresh Market Virginia (Pty) Ltd v. Shoprite Checkers (Pty) Ltd* 2012 1 SA 256 (CC) para. 71 *ubuntu* has been described in an obiter dictum as that it 'emphasises the communal nature of society and "carries in it the ideas of humaneness, social justice and fairness" and envelopes "the key values of group solidarity, compassion, respect, human dignity, conformity to basic norms and collective unity"'. These values, as affirmed by the Constitutional Court 'inspire much of our Constitutional compact'. Cf. also *Barkhuizen v. Napier* 2007 5 SA 323 (CC) para. 51.

   Also, in many systems of indigenous law in southern Africa, binding *contracts* are not based solely on a mutual intention to be bound and agreement thereanent, but are real contracts that become finally binding only upon performance by one of the parties. Also, should the other party not perform, the first party is entitled to restitution only and not to damages. *See* M. Gluckman, *The Ideas in Barotse Jurisprudence* 175, at 182 et seq. (Manchester U. Press 1972); cf. M.W. Prinsloo & L.P. Vorster, *Indigenous Contract in Bophuthatswana* 10 (Ctr. Indigenous L. U. S. Afr. 1990); *The Law of South Africa* vol. 32, paras 230 et seq. (W.A. Joubert ed., 2d ed., Lexis Nexis 2009); *Southern Cross Civil and Common Law in South Africa* 12 et seq. (R. Zimmermann & D.P. Visser eds., Juta 1996). It is important to note that indigenous law will also be affected by the horizontal application of the chapter on fundamental rights in the Constitution, and further that indigenous law must be taken into account in the development of the law and must be applied when relevant. In this regard, also cf. *S v. Makwanyane* 1995 3 SA 391 (CC); *Bhe v. Magistrate, Khayelitsha (Commission for Gender Equality as Amicus Curiae); Shibi v. Sithole; South African Human Rights Commission v. President of the Republic of South Africa* 2005 1 SA 580 (CC); *Fosi v. Road Accident Fund* 2008 3 SA 560 (C), where the claim for damages by a parent for the death of his child was extended in terms of customary law; *Shilubana v. Nwamitwa* 2009 2 SA 66 (CC); also *Seleka v. Road Accident Fund* 2016 4 SA 445 (GP) in which Tswana law was applied regarding the duty of support by children; *Gongqose and Others v. Minister of Agriculture and Others* 2018 5 SA 104 (SCA) which dealt with the limitation of traditional fishing rights.

basic tenets of *Shari'a* are sometimes adhered to in commercial practices (some banks have Shari'a account facilities), such as the prohibition against charging interest on monetary loans.

On the whole, one can say that the cultural and social values of most South Africans are compatible with an open-market economy, with the necessary social controls, and that the principles and rules of the law of contract regulate economic transactions accordingly.

§2. South African Law Belongs to the Civil Law Legal Family

15. In very general terms, one can say that South African law is a part of the civil law legal family, as distinguished from the common law (or Anglo-American) legal family or any other legal family. If one subscribes to further classification, it belongs to the Romanist branch of the civil law family. The categorization of South African law as a 'mixed system'[8] has the merit of immediately drawing attention to the various sources of modern South African law.

16. The common law of South Africa (as distinguished from law contained in statutory enactments), especially the field of private law, is rooted in Roman-Dutch law, particularly as it was expounded by those institutional writers who were regarded as being most authoritative during the seventeenth century,[9] when Roman-Dutch law first found application at the Cape of Good Hope, on the southern tip of Africa. In general, however, it appears that, in practice, the entire *jus commune* [10] of Western Europe of the time was and is still accepted and applied as the dominant common law of South Africa.

It was not certain to what extent the above position would hold true in cases of conflict between the views of authoritative Dutch writers and the views of other authoritative civil law writers, or in cases in which the views of the old authorities appear to conflict with modern notions of reasonableness and fairness. The Appellate Division of the Supreme Court of South Africa (renamed the Supreme Court of Appeal in 1996), in the past, on a number of occasions, took a rather strict and mechanical historical – analytical approach to such questions.[11] However, the view that the Court should follow a wider approach and apply the equitable principles that are to be found in the common legal heritage of civil law (including Roman

8. *See Southern Cross Civil Law and Common Law in South Africa* (R. Zimmermann & D.P. Visser eds., Juta 1996); *Mixed Legal Systems in Comparative Perspective* (R. Zimmermann, D.P. Visser & K. Reid eds., Juta 2004).
9. The most well-known of these writers are Voet, de Groot, van Leeuwen, van der Keessel and van der Linden.
10. Writers on the law in the other provinces of the Netherlands (e.g., Sande, Damhouder and A. Mattheus II) are cited by the courts as authorities, as well as French writers (e.g., Cujacius, Faber, and Pothier) and German writers (e.g., Brunneman, Leyser, Wesenbeckius, von Savigny, and Windscheid).
11. Cf. *Tjollo Ateljees (Eiens) Bpk v. Small* 1949 1 SA 856 (A) regarding the doctrine of *laesio enormis; Gerber v. Wolson* 1955 1 SA 158 (A); the majority judgment in *Bank of Lisbon & South Africa Ltd v. De Ornelas* 1988 3 SA 580 (A) regarding the question of whether the *exceptio doli generalis* of Roman law formed part of Roman-Dutch law and thus of modern South African law.

law – even when the Roman law on the issue was, strictly speaking, not incorporated into Roman-Dutch law) has received strong support from the Appeal Court and divisions of the High Court, as well as from academic commentators.[12] One can say that this wider approach was prevalent, if not dominant, in legal thinking in the recent past until the advent of the Bill of Rights, the horizontal application thereof, and the positive duty of the courts to develop common law where appropriate. It now appears that in cases in which issues of reasonableness and fairness are raised, the Bill of Rights and public policy (or the public interest) are often the first points of reference, rather than equitable rules and principles of South African common law, such as good faith and even the *exceptio doli generalis*. This trend has limitations and may lead to jurisprudence that is too generalized in the context of contracts. On the other hand, however, it seems that the same practical and generally applicable rules and criteria for fairness, reasonableness, and good faith are increasingly being fused and used in respect of both approaches.[13]

English law has markedly influenced the development of certain areas of South African law and its procedures, even though, technically, English law may not have been incorporated into South African law. Mercantile law (and particularly company law), the law of evidence, and constitutional law are outstanding examples. Even in the field of private law, English law has enriched and supplemented existing law – trusts, the doctrine of estoppel by representation, and the acceptance of undue influence and repudiation as part of the law of contract are prominent examples.

17. Apart from more subtle influences on the development of law already referred to, it must be noted that indigenous law is an independent and original source of law subject only to the Constitution. [14] However, in the context of private law, it operates mainly on a subsidiary or voluntary level and is of particular importance in the law of persons and the family and in the law of succession. In the future, a greater synthesis of common law and indigenous law in these fields will probably

---

12. Cf., for example, *Kommissaris van Binnelandse Inkomste v. Willers* 1994 3 SA 283 (A) 332–335; the minority judgment in *Bank of Lisbon & South Africa Ltd v. De Ornelas* 1988 3 SA 580 (A); *Rand Bank Ltd v. Rubinstein* 1981 2 SA 207 (W); the important and persuasive minority judgment in *Eerste Nasionale Bank van Suidelike Afrika Bpk v. Saayman* 1997 4 SA 302 (SCA); S. van der Merwe, G.F. Lubbe & L.F. van Huyssteen, *The Exceptio Doli Generalis: Requiescat in Pace – Vivat Aequitas*, S. African L. J. 237 (1989); R. Zimmermann, *Synthesis in South African Private Law: Civil Law, Common Law and Usus Hodiernus Pandectarum*, S. African L. J. 259 (1986).
13. *See* Van Huyssteen, Lubbe & Reinecke, *Contract General Principles*, para. 1.41–1.59 ch. 9 I (Juta 2016); Para. 16 above and the cases referred to there; Cf. *Bredenkamp v. Standard Bank of South Africa Ltd* 2010 4 SA 468 (SCA) para. 39. *See* now *Uniting Reformed Church, De Doorns v. President of the Republic of South Africa and Others* 2013 5 SA 205 (WCC); *Combined Developers v. Arun Holdings and Others* 2015 3 SA 215 (WCC); *Botha and Another v. Rich NO and Others* 2014 4 SA 124 (CC) paras 24, 28, 45–46; *Paulsen and Another v. Slip Knot Investments 777 (Pty) Ltd* 2015 3 SA 479 (CC) paras 71, 72, 113–119. *See* further the discussion below on good faith and the influence of the Constitution, and the cases cited there.
14. *Bhe v. Magistrate, Khayelitsha (Commission for Gender Equality as Amicus Curiae); Shibi v. Sithole; South African Human Rights Commission v. President of the Republic of South Africa* 2005 1 SA 580 (CC); *Gongqose and Others v. Minister of Agriculture and Others* 2018 5 SA 104 (SCA) paras 22, 23 & 50.

take place.[15] This development may well be accelerated by the fact that the Constitution determines that in the development of both common law and indigenous law, the fundamental rights entrenched in the Constitution must be taken into account.

18. Compared to most other civil law systems, very little statutory codification has taken place in South African law.

19. In summary, one can say that South African common law is a living and developing system of law, as expressed and applied in the decisions of the courts. It is traditionally based mainly on Roman-Dutch law but also draws on indigenous law, English law, and all modern comparable notions of jurisprudence, always taking into consideration the values ensconced in the Constitution, so as to be in accordance with the spirit, purport, and objects of the Bill of Rights.[16]

20. It is still appropriate to note that Roman-Dutch law as such, more than seventy years ago, was already aptly described as 'a virile living system of law, ever seeking, as every such system must, to adapt itself consistently with its inherent basic principles to deal effectively with the increasing complexities of modern organized society'.[17]

§3. Primacy of Legislation

21. South Africa now has a regime of constitutional supremacy, and all legislation (and, indeed, all law)[18] is ultimately justiciable by the Constitutional Court in light of the Constitution and the fundamental rights entrenched in it.[19] Any law or provision found to be inconsistent with the Constitution must be declared invalid to the extent of its inconsistency.[20] This power also applies to laws passed before the commencement of the Constitution and, in special circumstances, to bills before Parliament or provincial legislatures.

15. *See*, for example, *The Law of South Africa* vol. 32, paras 7–12, 79 et seq., 204 et seq. (W.A. Joubert ed., 2d ed. Lexis Nexis 2009). Cf. *Seleka v. Road Accident Fund* 2016 4 SA 445 (GP) in which Tswana law was applied regarding the duty of support by children.
16. *See* s. 39(1) and (2) of the Constitution, where, Courts are specifically empowered to consider foreign law.
17. Per Lord Tomlin in the Privy Council decision of *Pearl Assurance Co. v. Union Government* reported in 1934 AD 560–563.
18. *See Bredenkamp v. Standard Bank of South Africa Ltd* 2010 4 SA 468 (SCA) para. 39; *Paulsen and Another v. Slip Knot Investments 777 (Pty) Ltd* 2015 3 SA 479 (CC).
19. Where the Supreme Court of Appeal or a division of the High Court finds legislation unconstitutional, the decision must be referred to the Constitutional Court for confirmation – s. 15 of the Superior Courts Act 10 of 2013. In *Public Servants Association obo Ubogo v. Head, Department of Health, Gauteng and Others* 2018 2 SA 365 (CC) the Constitutional Court found that the Labour Court had jurisdiction to declare legislation unconstitutional.
20. This power of the Constitutional Court is not precluded or limited by the doctrine of separation of powers (which is accepted in our constitutional order); *Paulsen and Another v. Slip Knot Investments 777 (Pty) Ltd* 2015 3 SA 479 (CC) paras 71, 72, 113–119.

22. Compared to many other systems of law, legislation plays a relatively minor role in South African law, at least as far as its general principles are concerned, subject to, of course, the horizontal application of the Constitution. In the fields of public law, labour relations, and commercial law (particularly company law and negotiable instruments), however, specific legislation virtually completely regulates some areas of the law. In the field of private law, legislation plays a limited but nevertheless important role in the law of persons and the family, of property, and of succession. With respect to consumer protection, South Africa now has very comprehensive legislation in which all consumer rights are set forth and protected.

23. Where legislation does exist and has to be interpreted, it is presumed that the legislature did not intend to alter the common law.

§4. Position of the Judiciary

I. Role and Function of the Judiciary

24. In terms of the Constitution, the courts are independent and subject to only the Constitution.[21] The decisions of the superior courts are, as mentioned above, a particularly important source of South African law. In the pre-constitutional era, the courts themselves often maintained that their function was merely to 'find' or 'state' the law and not to 'make' it, the arguments being that lawmaking was the exclusive function of Parliament, and, more importantly, that judicial creativity would lead to too much uncertainty.[22] In this context, the courts have sometimes expressly refused to consider matters of policy and socio-economic circumstances.[23]

While this might have been a valid approach in the rare difficult case for which existing principles gave no guidance and provided no basis for development, superior courts increasingly, and overtly, developed and extended the existing principles of common law to meet the practical requirements and equities of a particular case.[24] Thus, for example, the Supreme Court of Appeal (at that time called the Appellate Division) stated in the context of the law of unjustified enrichment that: 'This being the nature of our system, the Courts should not hesitate to adapt a principle which is found not to be in line with present-day developments in the particular branch or other branches of the law.'[25] If, in such a case, the *ratio decidendi* was stated sufficiently generally, it could then, as a result of the principle of stare decisis and within the system of precedent as discussed below, become a rule of general

21. *See* now specifically the Preamble to the Superior Courts Act 10 of 2013.
22. For an example, *see Kommissaris van Binnelandse Inkomste v. Willers* 1994 3 SA 283 (A).
23. Cf., for example, *Martin v. Murray* (1995) 16 ILJ 589 (C).
24. Cf., for example, *Sasfin (Pty) Ltd v. Beukes* 1989 1 SA 1 (A); *ST v. CT* 2018 (5) SA 479 (SCA).
25. Per Hefer JA in *Willis Faber Enthoven (Pty) Ltd v. Receiver of Revenue* 1992 4 SA 202 (A) 220; *see* also a subsequent endorsement of this approach in *Kommissaris van Binnelandse Inkomste v. Willers* 1994 3 SA 283 (A) 332–335.

application. Sometimes, however, a court still – usually for unexpressed reasons of policy – took a conservative approach in terms of its perceived function when refusing to develop the law.[26]

Since the adoption of the 1996 Constitution,[27] the courts have come to interpret the Constitution as applying to all law, as binding on the judiciary,[28] and, additionally, as requiring courts to develop common law in light of fundamental constitutional values.[29] This latter duty is considered to be a general obligation and not purely discretionary.[30] Where common law is found to be deficient in light of the Constitution, it must be developed to bring it in consonance with the Constitution. In fact, the common law is only valid if it complies with or is congruent with the Constitution.[31] In the field of the law of contract, fundamental rights and the values of the Constitution will most probably in the first instance be given effect by way of the existing common law doctrine of legality, which requires that contracts should be in accordance with public policy.[32] However, there may be cases where the values in the Bill of Rights may be directly applied, such as cases of discrimination where the rights to equality and dignity are applicable.[33] Also, the enforcement of contractual obligations is increasingly subject to compliance with Constitutional values, reasonableness, fairness and good faith.[34] Thus, matters of policy and socio-economic factors can no longer be ignored and passed over as being the exclusive

26. Cf., for example, *Bank of Lisbon & South Africa Ltd v. De Ornelas* 1988 3 SA 580 (A).
27. Act 108 of 1996.
28. Section 8.
29. Section 39(2).
30. *See*, for example, *Carmichele v. Minister of Safety and Security (Centre for Applied Legal Studies Intervening)* 2001 4 SA 938 (CC) paras 33–56; *Brisley v. Drotsky* 2002 4 SA 1 (HHA) paras 88–95; *Afrox Healthcare Bpk v. Strydom* 2002 6 SA 21 (HHA) paras 14–30; *Napier v. Barkhuizen* 2006 4 SA 1 (SCA) para. 6; *Paulsen and Another v. Slip Knot Investments 777 (Pty) Ltd* 2015 3 SA 479 (CC) paras 71, 72, 113–119.
31. *See*, e.g., *Bredenkamp v. Standard Bank of South Africa Ltd* 2010 4 SA 468 (SCA) para. 39; *Paulsen and Another v. Slip Knot Investments 777 (Pty) Ltd* 2015 3 SA 479 (CC) paras 71, 72, 113–119.
32. *Brisley v. Drotsky* 2002 4 SA 1 (HHA) para. 91; *Afrox Healthcare Bpk v. Strydom* 2002 6 SA 21 (HHA) para. 18; *Napier v. Barkhuizen* 2006 4 SA 1 (SCA) paras 7–8; *Barkhuizen v. Napier* 2007 5 SA 323 (CC) paras 28–30; *Bredenkamp v. Standard Bank of South Africa Ltd* 2010 4 SA 468 (SCA) para. 39: 'Public policy and the boni mores are now deeply rooted in the Constitution and its underlying values. This does not mean that public policy values cannot be found elsewhere. A constitutional principle that tends to be overlooked, when generalized resort to constitutional values is made, is the principle of legality. Making rules of law discretionary or subject to value judgments may be destructive of the rule of law.' In this regard, *see* the specific warning by the Supreme Court of Appeal in *Potgieter v. Potgieter N O* 2012 1 SA 637 (SCA) para. 34 that 'the reason why our law cannot endorse the notion that judges may decide cases on the basis of what they regard as reasonable and fair, is essentially that it will give rise to intolerable legal uncertainty'. And … 'reasonable people, including judges, may often differ on what is equitable and fair. The outcome in any particular case will thus depend on the personal idiosyncrasies of the individual judge'. The role of good faith in this context will be discussed below.
33. Sections 9 and 10. With regard to the possible direct application of s. 22 (Freedom of trade, occupation and profession) *see* the discussion on the topic below. Cf. also the minority judgment of Langa C J in *Barkhuizen v. Napier* 2007 5 SA 323 (CC) para. 186.
34. E.g., *Combined Developers v. Arun Holdings and Others* 2015 3 SA 215 (WCC); *Botha and Another v. Rich NO and Others* 2014 4 SA 124 (CC) paras 24, 28, 45–46; *Paulsen and Another v. Slip Knot Investments 777 (Pty) Ltd* 2015 3 SA 479 (CC) paras 71, 72, 113,119; *W v. H* 2017 1 SA 196 (WCC) (unilateral waiver of right to claim maintenance unenforceable); *Bondev Midrand (Pty) Ltd v.*

domain of the legislature. These aspects will have to be overtly dealt with in the process of finding a fair balance between the interests of the parties (including the binding force of contracts), against the background of the interests of the community.[35]

However, the Constitutional Court itself has, on a number of occasions, warned against overzealous law reform by the courts and has stated that the major engine for law reform is still the legislature and not the judiciary.[36]

All in all, it would seem that common law is increasingly regarded as the law expressed in the decisions of the courts.

II. System of Precedent

25. In South African law, previous decisions of the South African courts do not merely have persuasive or comparative value, but they are, in fact, generally speaking, of binding authority on lower courts and courts of the same standing that are confronted with a similar question at a later stage: *stare decisis et non quieta movere*. This principle is now regarded as '... a manifestation of the rule of law itself, which in turn is a founding value of our Constitution'.[37] More specifically stated, it is the *ratio decidendi* of the previous decision that is subsequently binding in a case with similar material facts. The distinction between a binding principle or authoritative reasons and *obiter dicta*, which can be of greater or lesser persuasive value only, is sometimes a fine one since the concept of *ratio decidendi* is necessarily an abstraction based on a number of considerations.[38] A further complicating factor is the possibility of distinguishing the facts of the case currently before the court from those of the previous case, thereby ousting the operation of the rule of stare decisis. In this connection, practitioners show considerable ingenuity.

Madzhie and Others 2017 4 SA 166 (GP) (repurchase clause grossly unfair and infringing the right to housing); *Beadica 231 CC and Others v. Trustees, Oregon Unit Trust and Others* 2018 1 SA 549 (WCC) (enforcing of cancellation and eviction clauses in lease disproportionate and against public policy in the particular circumstances); *Four Wheel Drive Accessory Distribution CC v. Rattan NO* 2018 3 SA 204 (KZD) (terms in standard contract too small to read and unenforceable against public policy). But in *Mohamed's Leisure Holdings (Pty) Ltd v. Southern Sun Hotel Interests (Pty) Ltd* 2018 2 SA 314 (SCA) the appeal court overturned the decision of the high court (based on public policy and ubuntu) and decided that the circumstances did not warrant a departure from *pacta servanda sunt*, consequently enforcing a cancellation and eviction clause in a lease. The appeal court in *Roazar CC v. The Falls Supermarket CC* 2018 3 SA 76 (SCA) refused in the particular circumstances (the requirement of certainty and absence of a deadlock-breaking mechanism) to develop the common law to import a term to compel parties to negotiate a renewal of a lease in good faith: '*It is difficult to conceive how a court, in a purely business transaction, can rely on "ubuntu" to import a term that was not intended by the parties, to deny the other party a right to rely on the terms of the contract to terminate it*' *(para 24)*. Van Huyssteen, Lubbe & Reinecke, *Contract General Principles*, para. 7.16 et seq. and ch. 9 I (Juta 2016).

35. *See* the more detailed discussion in paras 95–99 below.
36. *See*, for example, *Carmichele v. Minister of Safety and Security (Centre for Applied Legal Studies Intervening)* 2001 4 SA 938 (CC) para. 36.
37. *See Camps Bay Ratepayers' and Residents' Association v. Harrison* 2011 4 SA 42 (CC) para. 28. *See* however para 29 below for circumstances in which the principle of *stare decisis* is departed from.
38. If a court decides more than one issue in the course of arriving at a final disposition, those decisions are not *obiter dicta*. *Camps Bay Ratepayers' and Residents' Association v. Harrison* 2011 4 SA 42 (CC) para. 30.

III. Hierarchy of Courts and Law Reporting

26. A system such as the one described above depends on a clear hierarchy of courts. In South Africa, a distinction is made between superior and lower courts. The Constitutional Court has jurisdiction as the Court of Final Instance in constitutional matters and matters of general public importance if in the interests of justice,[39] and its decisions are binding upon all courts.[40] In some constitutional matters, the Constitutional Court has exclusive jurisdiction, such as where the arms of government have specific duties in terms of the Constitution which have allegedly not been complied with. [41] This, of course, raises the difficult issue (which appears globally in constitutional democracies) of the separation of powers and the authority of the judiciary. Presently in South Africa, the courts (particularly the Constitutional Court) are carefully willing, as empowered by the Constitution, to intrude and to determine whether the particular arm of government has in substance and fact fulfilled its Constitutional obligations.[42]

The superior courts consist of the Supreme Court of Appeal, having appellate and constitutional jurisdiction, and the High Court, which is divided into provincial divisions, some of which have more than one seat of the court.[43] The provincial divisions have principally original or inherent jurisdiction within a defined geographical area to determine all matters between litigants, including also constitutional jurisdiction. Within the structure of the High Court, a number of special courts have been created to deal with specialized matters, such as tax appeals, water cases, patents, competition appeals in terms of the Competition Act 89 of 1998, and land claims appeals in terms of the Restitution of Land Rights Act 22 of 1994. The National Credit Act 34 of 2005 provides for a tribunal that also has jurisdiction to hear consumer matters in terms of the Consumer Protection Act 68 of 2008. The various provinces may also create consumer courts. The High Court derives admiralty jurisdiction from the Admiralty Jurisdiction Regulation Act 105 of 1983, which replaced the English Colonial Courts of Admiralty Act of 1890. Although the matter is not beyond doubt, it seems that the admiralty law to be applied by the High Court is

---

39. *See* para. 13 above.
40. *See* the Superior Courts Act 10 of 2013 which rationalised the laws relating to these courts and made provision for all administrative matters. *See also* the Legal Practice Act 28 of 2014: *To provide a legislative framework for the transformation and restructuring of the legal profession in line with constitutional imperatives so as to facilitate and enhance an independent legal profession that broadly reflects the diversity and demographics of the Republic;* and to further provide for a host of administrative matters
41. *See Economic Freedom Fighters v. Speaker, National Assembly and Others* 2016 3 SA 580 (CC) paras 39–40, 45.
42. *Economic Freedom Fighters v. Speaker, National Assembly and Others* 2016 3 SA 580 (CC) para 93: *That is the sum total of the constitutionally permissible judicial enquiry to be embarked upon ... Courts ought not to blink at the thought of asserting their authority, whenever it is constitutionally permissible to do so, irrespective of the issues or who is involved. At the same time, and mindful of the vital strictures of their powers, they must be on high alert against impermissible encroachment on the powers of the other arms of government.*
43. The objective of the Superior Courts Act is to consolidate and rationalize the various laws pertaining to superior courts and to bring the structure of these courts in line with the Constitution. It provides for new divisions of the High Court with new seats of court, and various important provisions regarding the constitution and operation of courts, rules of procedure, appeals and access to courts.

English admiralty law, as of 1 November 1983.[44] Labour legislation has created a Labour Court and Labour Appeal Court which have jurisdiction to declare legislation unconstitutional. The legislative framework for a system of Divorce Courts has also been established.

Lower courts (Magistrates' Courts) were created by statute with limited jurisdiction, both as far as area and subject matter are concerned.[45] Apart from these Courts, a system of Small Claims Courts has been established. Customary law is applied by the Courts when it is applicable in particular cases.

The Constitution, which enjoins courts to develop common law in accordance with the spirit, purport, and objects of the Bill of Rights,[46] has not affected the operation of the principle of stare decisis, at least as far as post-constitutional decisions are concerned.[47]

In constitutional matters, all other courts are, in terms of the Constitution, bound by the decisions of the Constitutional Court. In principle, this Court probably considers itself bound by its own previous decisions, except when the social and policy considerations surrounding a certain fundamental right that may be at issue have substantially changed, or when other circumstances, as mentioned below, apply.

In terms of the principle of stare decisis (which is not applicable in distinguishable cases, as explained above) and the system of precedent, provincial and local divisions of the High Court, and, of course, lower courts, are bound by the decisions of the Supreme Court of Appeal. However, in cases in which the Supreme Court of Appeal handed down a decision before the Constitution came into being and the High Court is convinced that the rule of common law as laid down by that decision is in conflict with a provision of the Constitution, the High Court must deviate from that decision – the Constitution is the highest law and must prevail.[48] Also, when, prior to the establishment of the Constitution, the Supreme Court of Appeal made a decision based on public interest or the *boni mores*, and the High Court is convinced that that decision no longer correctly reflects the public interest in light of the Constitution, it is obliged to deviate from it.[49] However, when such a prior decision of the Supreme Court of Appeal does not fall within the two categories just discussed, the High Court is bound to follow that decision in terms of *stare decisis.*[50]

The Supreme Court of Appeal considers itself bound by its own previous decisions, except, of course, when the application of the Constitution requires a deviation or when (as stated above) the case can be distinguished or the *ratio decidendi*

---

44. *See*, in general, on shipping law, *The Law of South Africa* vol. 25 part 2, 1st re-issue, paras 5 et seq., generally para. 29 (W.A. Joubert ed., Butterworths 2006).
45. In terms of amendments to the Magistrates' Court Act 32 of 1944, there are district and regional courts, the latter having extended jurisdiction to hear also murder trials and divorce matters.
46. Section 39(2).
47. *Afrox Healthcare Bpk v. Strydom* 2002 6 SA 21 (HHA) para. 26; *Camps Bay Ratepayers' and Residents' Association v. Harrison* 2011 4 SA 42 (CC) para. 29.
48. *Afrox Healthcare Bpk v. Strydom* 2002 6 SA 21 (HHA) para. 27.
49. *Afrox Healthcare Bpk v. Strydom* 2002 6 SA 21 (HHA) para. 28.
50. *Afrox Healthcare Bpk v. Strydom* 2002 6 SA 21 (HHA) para. 29.

does not apply, or when the previous decision is *clearly* wrong.[51] Provincial divisions of the High Court are not bound by decisions of other provincial or local divisions, but such decisions do, of course, have persuasive value, particularly if they emanate from a bench consisting of more than one judge. A court consisting of a single judge is bound by the decision of a full bench in its own division. Also, a judge of the High Court is bound by the previous decision of a judge in the same division, unless it is *clearly* wrong.[52]

To support the system of precedent, an extensive system of law reporting exists. Most noteworthy decisions of the Constitutional Court and the High Court, as well the other special courts of the same status as the High Court, are reported on a monthly basis, providing the full text of the decisions as well as the orders of the Courts. A headnote, giving a summary of the judgment, and prepared by the publisher of each report, is included. There are also separate reports of criminal cases and the decisions of the Labour Court. The decisions of the Constitutional Court are published in the ordinary reports just mentioned, and they also are published monthly in specialized constitutional law reports. Some of these reports are available in printed and CD-ROM formats, and also online. The Southern African Legal Information Institute (Saflii) also provides legal databases, including law reports, for various African countries.[53]

§5. Distinction Between Public Law and Private Law

27. The traditional distinction between public and private law is made in South African law. The law of contract as part of the law of obligations is private law. The values of individual autonomy and self-determination play a basic role in the principles and rules of the South African law of contract, and freedom of contract has often, also with reference to the Constitution, been held to be a basic component of the public interest.[54] However, other competing aspects of the public interest and

51. *Patmar Explorations (Pty) Ltd and Others v. Limpopo Development Tribunal and Others* 2018 4 SA 107 (SCA) para 3: *A decision will be held to have been clearly wrong where it has been arrived at on some fundamental departure from principle, or a manifest oversight or misunderstanding, that is, there has been something in the nature of a palpable mistake. This court will only depart from its previous decision if it is clear that the earlier court erred or that the reasoning upon which the decision rested was clearly erroneous.*
52. *Patmar Explorations (Pty) Ltd and Others v. Limpopo Development Tribunal and Others* 2018 4 SA 107 (SCA) paras 7–8*: The test for departing from a judgment from one's own court is set high so that it is only done in few cases and then only after anxious consideration.*
53. *See* in more detail paras 118–120 below.
54. *See*, for example, *Brisley v. Drotsky* 2002 4 SA 1 (HHA) paras 31, 94–95; *Barkhuizen v. Napier* 2007 5 SA 323 (CC) paras 30, 57, 70, 73; *Bredenkamp v. Standard Bank of South Africa Ltd* 2010 4 SA 468 (SCA) paras 38, 40; *Uniting Reformed Church, De Doorns v. President of the Republic of South Africa and Others* 2013 5 SA 205 (WCC).Cf. also *Paulsen and Another v. Slip Knot Investments 777 (Pty) Ltd* 2015 3 SA 479 (CC) paras 71, 72 113–119.

other broader community values, as also reflected in the Constitution, must be carefully weighed to find a balance between these competing interests. In this process, concepts such as good faith and public policy come into play at all stages of the contracting process.[55]

28. The division between private law and public law in regard to the law of contract is, of course, most blurred in cases of contracts with the State or its organs, particularly when a contract may be classified as the so-called administrative-law agreement.

§6. Distinction Between Civil Law and Commercial Law

29. In South African law, 'commercial' or 'mercantile' law is a branch of the common law of the country, and the appellation does not indicate any different body of substantive law or of procedure. There is no specific commercial code or special general commercial or market court in South Africa, except for a number of regulatory institutions and ombuds in various specialized fields of commerce.[56]

Historically, English law (in particular, the law merchant) played an unusually important role in the development of South African common law relating to commerce, although the influence of the *lex mercatoria* as a part of Roman-Dutch law is not to be underestimated. The influence of English law is particularly noticeable in company law and the law of negotiable instruments, whereas Roman-Dutch law forms the root of (by way of example) the law of partnership, insurance, and representation (agency). Insofar as admiralty law may be termed commercial law, it is of interest to note that our law on the subject is mainly English law.[57]

In modern South African law, the term 'commercial law' is used as a convenient collective concept to denote various fields of law that are relevant to commerce and trade, whether they can be classified as private law or public law, or display elements of both. Relatively new fields of law in South Africa that are usually classified as commercial law are international trade, business, economic law, intellectual property (IP) and IT law. Many principles of the international law merchant are also principles of South African domestic law (e.g., the principle of *pacta sunt servanda*) or are in the process of being recognized as such (e.g., the principles of reasonableness, fairness or good faith).

55. E.g., *Paulsen and Another v. Slip Knot Investments 777 (Pty) Ltd* 2015 3 SA 479 (CC) paras 71, 72, 113–119.
56. E.g., in the related fields of competition regulation (Competition Act 89 of 1998), income tax (Income Tax Act 58 of 1962), and consumer affairs Consumer Protection Act 68 of 2008, National Credit Act 34 of 2005, rental housing, financial services and short – and long-term insurance
57. *See* s. 6 of the Admiralty Jurisdiction Regulation Act 105 of 1983.

Chapter 1. Introduction to the Law of Contract

§1. Definition of a Contract

I. A Contract as a Juristic Act

30. When defining a contract in South African law, commentators usually stress as a point of departure that a contract is a legal fact, a juristic abstraction from proven facts that create a contract in terms of legal norms, principles, and rules.

II. Agreement or Reliance as Facts Creating a Contract

31. The facts (or events), that form the basis of the conclusion that, juristically, a contract has come into being, are a legally relevant agreement, in the sense of a meeting of the minds (consensus) between at least two parties or, in the absence of such an actual agreement, the reasonable belief on the part of one of the parties that there is an actual agreement.

These basic principles would also have to apply to what are often called 'smart contracts' if they are to have any legal force. Generally and globally it appears that these 'contracts' are indeed defined as agreements in the above sense, often written in computer code, running on a blockchain system and automatically executed, and that general principles of law are applicable. [58] In South Africa these contracts presently take the form of an ordinary underlying contract (mostly concluded electronically) which is then automatically executed via blockchain. [59] Presently the automatic execution is simple relating only to the transfer of funds and currency tokens or receipts. However, the generally acknowledged problem is how to provide in computer code for pre-agreed instances of legitimate cancellation, non-enforcement and other legal principles and rules. This is particularly difficult in the South African context where the principles of legality, public policy and Constitutionality are paramount, including the right of access to a court or tribunal.

III. Intention to Create a Contract, Consideration, and Legality

32. The intention of the parties to create obligations by their agreement, or the reasonable belief that such intention exists, is the crucial element that distinguishes a legally relevant agreement from a legally irrelevant agreement. When an agreement is reached, but without the requisite intention to create an obligation, there can be no contract – an expression of will that has been made without the intention of

58. *See*, e.g., R de Caria 'Defining Smart Contracts-the Search for Workable Legal Categories' *Oxford Business Law Blog* 25 May 2018; P Paech' What is a Smart Contract?' *Oxford Business Law Blog* 9 July 2018.

59. In practice this occurs mostly in contracts to trade in cryptocurrency (e.g., Bitcoin) entered into with a trading platform on the internet where typically the parties agree to a very detailed contract, often containing various exclusion clauses in favour of the dealer; or in loan agreements with banks. *See* S Roux 'Smart Contracts' *without prejudice* (vol 17.2 2017).

it eventually becoming legally binding cannot be an offer in law. In a broad sense, however, this means that a simple promise is binding according to South African law – an agreement need not entail a bargain. Thus, an agreement may be relevant even when no discernible transfer of economic performances has taken place – valuable consideration is not required.

33. An agreement must also comply with the opposite norms of society before it will create obligations – hence the requirement of legality (public policy). This requirement obviously also entails that the agreement must be in accordance with the Constitution.

IV. Civil and Natural Obligations

34. As in many other legal systems, a contract is generally regarded as a source of civil (as distinguished from natural) obligations in the sense that the law attaches enforceable consequences to contracts. The obligations created by a contract must be distinguished from their source. When a breach occurs, it is therefore the obligation that is infringed and not the contract that is breached. Similarly, when a qualification, such as a condition, is agreed upon, the operation of the obligation, and not the contract, is qualified. In practice, however, the terms 'breach of contract' and 'conditional contract' are commonly used.

Natural obligations may also be created by an agreement (such as an agreement entered into by a minor without the required consent, or a wagering agreement, which is generally said to be a natural obligation). Although a natural obligation is not directly enforceable, it does have some legal effect in that it can be discharged or set-off, and it may serve as the basis for an accessory contract.

V. A Contract Distinguished from Other Legally Relevant Agreements

35. A contract, being a source of obligation, is distinguished from other legally relevant agreements, such as agreements extinguishing obligations (e.g., release and novation), agreements by which rights are transferred (real agreements), and agreements causing a change in status.

VI. A Contract Is a Multilateral Legal Act

36. By its nature, a contract is a multilateral (usually bilateral) legal act. When only one of the parties has a duty to perform, however, such as in the case of a donation, the contract is often called a 'unilateral contract'.

VII. A Contract Creates Personal Rights and Duties

37. The obligation that is created by a contract entails a right to claim that the content of the obligation be rendered and a corresponding duty to do so. In principle, the right may be enforced only against the party who has undertaken the duty. Consequently, as in many other legal systems, it is called a personal right. Privity of contract is thus a basic principle in South African law. Real rights (rights to physical things), however, may, in principle, be enforced against any person who has the thing at issue.

VIII. Bases of a Contract in Brief: Definitions

38. It will have become apparent that, in South African law, a contract rests on one of the two bases: the existence of a legally relevant actual agreement or, in the absence of an actual agreement (with resultant *dissensus*), a reliance on the existence of an actual agreement insofar as the law deems the reliance worthy of upholding.

39. On the basis of actual consensus, a contract (being an obligationary agreement, in other words, an agreement that creates an obligation or obligations) is an agreement in terms of which the parties specifically intend to create an obligation and which complies with all the other requirements (such as legality, contractual capacity of the parties, and prescribed formalities) set by the law for the creation of enforceable obligations by agreement.[60]

40. Reasonable reliance on consensus has long been advanced in various guises by courts and writers as an alternative basis to an actual agreement (the term 'quasi-mutual assent' is sometimes used in this context). However, it has only recently been clearly and unambiguously acknowledged as such by the Appeal Court. (Some of these decisions were made by the Appellate Division (previously so-called) and others by the Supreme Court of Appeal).[61] In practice – at least in cases in which a person has signed a document indicating his or her assent but subsequently, on the basis of his or her mistake, denies being bound – a reasonable reliance on consensus is upheld indirectly: there is usually no direct enquiry into the presence of reasonable reliance on the part of the contract assertor; rather, the contract denier is required (by an onus of rebuttal) to show that his or her mistake was reasonable (that he or she had made an *iustus error* as it is sometimes put) and had not created a

60. Often, however, a contract is defined merely as an agreement made with the intention of creating an obligation. This approach does not accord with the universally accepted view, which is followed in this work, that a contract is a legal fact. *See* further Van Huyssteen, Lubbe & Reinecke, *Contract General Principles*, para. 1.31–1.33 (Juta 2016).

61. *See*, for example, *Sonap Petroleum (SA) (Pty) Ltd (formerly known as Sonarep (SA) Pty Ltd) v. Pappadogianis* 1992 3 SA 234 (A); *Steyn v. LSA Motors Ltd* 1994 1 SA 49 (A); *Investec Bank Ltd v. Lefkowitz* 1997 1 SA 1 (A); *HNR Properties CC v. Standard Bank of SA Ltd* 2004 4 SA 471 (SCA); *Constantia Insurance Co. Ltd v. Compusource (Pty) Ltd* 2005 4 SA 345 (SCA); *Pillay v. Shaik* 2009 (4) SA 74 (SCA) and the discussion below.

reasonable reliance on the existence of consensus in the mind of the other party In this connection, reference has often been made to the English case of *Smith v. Hughes*,[62] but more recently, the so-called reliance theory has been applied more directly as just explained.[63] It is now clear that the reasonable reliance doctrine and that of reasonable mistake have been integrated.[64]

§2. Historical Background of the Law of Contract

I. Roman-Dutch Law

41. The law of contract has the same general historical background as the common law of South Africa. It is rooted in Roman-Dutch law, which was introduced at the Cape as the applicable legal system by the Dutch East India Company, probably in 1657, although 1652 is the date of the first Dutch settlement at the Cape.[65] From there, it spread to the other regions of South Africa, and towards the mid-nineteenth century, it was introduced as the applicable system in Natal and the two Boer Republics. At the time of the formation of the Union of South Africa, Roman-Dutch law was indisputably the dominant force in common law.[66]

II. Concepts of Roman and Roman-Dutch Law in the Modern Law of Contract

42. Of particular importance to the modern South African law of contract is the fact that the Roman law concept of obligation (Inst 3 12 *pr*) and the distinction between civil and natural obligations have been taken virtually intact into South African law. It seems also as if Roman law was not merely a subsidiary system of law, but rather occupied a more important position in legal practice at the Cape until

62. (1871) LR 6 QB 597, where J. Blackburn, said at 607: 'If, whatever a man's real intention may be, he so conducts himself that a reasonable man would believe that he was assenting to the terms proposed by the other party, and that other party upon that belief enters into the contract with him, the man thus conducting himself would be equally bound as if he had intended to agree to the other party's terms.' This dictum has on occasion been referred to in support of the doctrine of estoppel by representation as a manner of approaching the problem of mistakes, as well as in connection with the so-called doctrine of quasi-mutual assent.
63. *See* in particular the *Sonap* and *Steyn* cases, and now also the *Constantia Insurance* case; *Pillay v. Shaik* 2009 (4) SA 74 (SCA); *Slip Knot Investments 777 (Pty) Ltd v. Du Toit* 2011 2 SA 72 (SCA); cf. also *Spenmac (Pty) Ltd (formerly Bobcart (Pty) Ltd) v. Tatrim CC* 2015 3 SA 46 (SCA); *Botha v. Road Accident Fund* 2017 2 SA 50 (SCA) para 10.
64. *See* Van Huyssteen, Lubbe & Reinecke, *Contract General Principles*, paras 2.127–2.133 (Juta 2016).
65. For a detailed exposition and analysis of the law at the Cape, *see* G.G. Visagie, *Regspleging en Reg aan die Kaap van 1652 tot 1806* (Cape Town: Juta, 1969).
66. *See* in general *Southern Cross Civil Law and Common Law in South Africa* 33–64 (R. Zimmermann & D.P. Visser eds., Juta 1996).

at least 1828.[67] A striking example of direct Roman law influence in present-day law is to be found in the application of the aedilitian actions in the law of sale which have even been extended to trade-in exchanges. In general, this branch of the law displays much Roman law influence.

43. Of basic importance to modern South African theory and practice is the concept of a contract – as it was finally received in Roman-Dutch law (influenced by Germanic and Canon law) towards the seventeenth century – as being an agreement that is seriously and deliberately made and that creates an obligation.[68] The meaning in modern South African law of the requirement of *justa causa*, which was established by many of the institutional writers, was a particularly vexing question in the early decades of the twentieth century. This was mainly the result of uncertainty as to whether *justa causa* was to be equated with the concept of valuable consideration in English law. The latter concept is, of course, inimical to the idea, as it is espoused in the civilian tradition, that, in principle, mutual promises are a binding force. In 1919, the Supreme Court of Appeal (then called the Appellate Division) decided that *justa causa* was not the equivalent of valuable consideration. Since that decision, it has been generally accepted that the requirements for a contract in modern South African law leave no room for additional elements over and above the elements described by the old authorities and is discussed below.[69] A survey of textbooks on the modern law of contract and judgments of the High Court with regard to almost all aspects of the law of contract still, but to a much lesser degree, indicates the authority of the Roman-Dutch institutional writers for the law of contract, subject to the judicial function and the Constitution, which are now dominant factors [70]

III. The *Jus Commune*

44. Although one may say that, in general, the South African law of contract is very strongly rooted in Roman-Dutch law, the influence of the *jus commune*[71] of Western Europe must not be underestimated.[72] Apart from frequent references in

67. *See* L.F. van Huyssteen, 'Some Notes on Roman-Dutch Law at the Cape under British Rule. Evaluation of a few General Principles of the Law of Contract as applied by the Court of Justice between 1806 and 1827', *Tijdschrift voor Rechtsgeschiedenis* (1994), 357.
68. *See*, for example, the definition of contract given by Vinnius *Institutionum Commentarius ad Inst.* 3 14 2.
69. *See Southern Cross Civil Law and Common Law in South Africa* 166–173 (R. Zimmermann & D.P. Visser eds., Juta 1996).
70. E.g., *Paulsen and Another v. Slip Knot Investments 777 (Pty) Ltd* 2015 3 SA 479 (CC).
71. *See* in general the interesting discussions on the contributions by the late Prof. J.C. de Wet in A Man of Principle/'n Man van Beginsel (J. du Plessis & G. Lubbe eds, Juta 2013), for example G. Lubbe, 'Die Laaste Pandektis? – J.C. de Wet in Metodologiese Perspektief' 105.
72. Cf. in general, R. Zimmermann, *The Law of Obligations: Roman Foundations of the Civilian Tradition* 546 et seq. (Juta 1990); *Southern Cross Civil Law and Common Law in South Africa* (R. Zimmermann & D.P. Visser eds., Juta 1996). *See also* L.F. van Huyssteen, 'Some Notes on Roman-Dutch Law at the Cape under British Rule: Evaluation of a Few General Principles of the Law of

modern case law to early writers from provinces of the Netherlands other than Holland, writers from other European countries played an important role. The French writers Domat and Pothier are of particular importance. For example, considerable weight is still given by the courts to Pothier's views on liability for damages for breach of contract, even though these views tend to obscure the proper application of the general principle concerned.[73] Writers of the German School of Natural Law (Pufendorf and Heineccius in particular) are important, but even more so are the writers of the historical school, or the pandectists. Of these, von Savigny, Windscheid, and von Jhering are the most important. In spite of the sometimes justified aversion to the excessive *Begriffsjurisprudenz* (conceptual jurisprudence) that members of this school have been accused of promoting, their contribution to South African law is a lasting one. An example that immediately comes to mind is von Savigny's contribution to the better understanding of the problem of mistake.

IV. English Law

45. As has been previously indicated, English law historically exerted an immense influence in general on the law in South Africa. Although from time to time there have been efforts, even judicially, to 'cleanse' South African common law of English law, it has been accepted on the whole that the English influence has been beneficial and has contributed to the development of South African law. To some extent, this holds true also for the law of contract.[74]

A number of external historical factors, related, of course, to the various British occupations of the territories of South Africa from the first occupation of the Cape in 1795 to the annexation of the South African Republic (Transvaal) in 1900, may serve as the background against which this influence must be viewed. In accordance with general British colonial policy, the existing common law in occupied territories was not expressly replaced by English law. Rather, a policy of gradual assimilation was espoused. One of the factors that decidedly advanced this policy was the importation of the English system of procedure and evidence into the Cape Colony by the Charter of Justice in 1828, and its subsequent application in the other territories. A court of equity was never established, perhaps because it was reported to the British government that equitable jurisdiction already appeared to be a part of the law of Holland.[75]

There are many examples in the law of contract in which the common law of South Africa has indeed been enriched by the acceptance of concepts from English law. The doctrine of estoppel by representation played an important role in the development and ultimate acceptance of the notion that a reasonable reliance on

---

Contract as applied by the Court of Justice between 1806 and 1827', *Tijdschrift voor Rechtsgeschiedenis* (1994): 357 for a discussion of the law at the Cape.

73. Cf., for example, *Shatz Investments (Pty) Ltd v. Kalovyrnas* 1976 2 SA 545 (A); *Holmdene Brickworks (Pty) Ltd v. Roberts Construction Co. Ltd* 1977 3 SA 670 (A).
74. *See* in general *Southern Cross Civil Law and Common Law in South Africa* Chs 5–11 (R. Zimmermann & D.P. Visser eds., Juta 1996); cf. in general also *Mixed Legal Systems in Comparative Perspective* (R. Zimmermann, D. Visser & K. Reid eds., Juta 2004).
75. *See* G. McC. Theal, *Records of the Cape Colony* vol. 28, 10 (Public Record Office 1905).

consensus is an alternative basis of a contract. The acceptance in South African law of aspects of the doctrine of undue influence as grounds for rescinding a contract has contributed in no small way to the development of a general principle relating to rescission. There is also the adoption of the so-called innocent-bystander test with respect to tacit terms; the adoption of the notion of time being 'of the essence' with respect to a right to cancel because of *mora* (delay) by a party in the performance of his or her contractual duties; and the acceptance of repudiation as being a breach of contract, which has necessitated an endeavour to explain theoretically the nature of breach of contract in general.

V. Indigenous Law

46. Indigenous contract law has had no direct influence on the existing principles and rules of modern South African contract law, and indeed, it may be said to be basically different in approach with regard to freedom of contract and the creation of an enforceable contract (in this respect, it more closely approximates English common law). Nevertheless, this very difference in approach may in future contribute to the justifiable limitations that are increasingly placed on private autonomy in the conclusion and enforcement of contracts. In this regard the incorporation of the value of ubuntu which emphasizes the communal nature of society and the values of social justice and fairness as a standard of conduct in the law of contract may very well contribute to this development.[76]

§3. Classification of Contracts

I. 'Consensual', 'Real', and 'Solemn' Contracts

47. Since, in South African law, a contract is principally based on and defined in terms of consensus or a reliance on consensus, the concepts of 'real' or 'solemn' contracts, as they are used in other systems of law to denote contracts based on legal facts other than agreement or reliance, form no part of the South African law of contract. Indeed, such concepts would be self-contradictory and meaningless. The term 'consensual contract', however, would be merely tautologous.

48. The concept of a 'real agreement' (as distinct from a contract as an 'obligationary agreement') is well-known in South African law as an agreement by which rights are transferred. Thus, for example, when A donates and hands a thing to B, who immediately accepts it, the following agreements are present, albeit they have been concluded simultaneously: first, a contract creating a duty for A to deliver the thing to B; second, an agreement that extinguishes the obligation in terms of which the duty arose; and, third, an agreement in terms of which delivery as a

76. *See* paras 16 above and 97 et seq. below; *Everfresh Market Virginia (Pty) Ltd v. Shoprite Checkers (Pty) Ltd* 2012 1 SA 256 (CC) para. 71–72; cf. *Combined Developers v. Arun Holdings and Others* 2015 3 SA 215 (WCC) paras 38–39, quoting with approval from *Everfresh passim.*

method of transferring ownership takes place – the real agreement. Again, when A wishes to sell and transfer to B a personal right that A has against Z, he or she may conclude with B a contract of sale of the right to B and then transfer or cede the right to B by way of a real agreement of cession. The contract and the real agreement are often concluded simultaneously.

49. Although in South African law, a contract cannot be created merely by compliance with a specific form, some specific agreements cannot be contracts if they fail to comply with formalities that are required for their validity (see the definition of 'contract' above). Writing is the most common formal requirement, but failure to render the agreement in writing does not necessarily result in invalidity. Examples of agreements that would be invalid if not rendered in writing are alienations of land, executory donations, and suretyship agreements. The requirement of writing creates particular problems relating to rectification and the proof of the contents of a written contract. Prospecting contracts and mining leases are examples of contracts that have to be executed before a notary public. Some contracts are valid *inter partes* without having to conform with formalities, but they must be notarially executed and registered to acquire validity as against third parties, such as antenuptial contracts and mortgages securing loans. In this sense, one may speak of 'solemn contracts' if one must, but the term is best avoided.

II. Unilateral, Multilateral, and Reciprocal Contracts

50. The distinction among unilateral, multilateral, and reciprocal (synallagmatic) contracts in South African law has the same function and consequences as in other civil law systems.

A unilateral contract remains a bilateral juristic act, but only one of the contractants has the duty to perform. A donation is the prime example. In this respect, South African law differs substantially from English law, with its doctrine of consideration.

A multilateral contract imposes duties to perform on more than one contractant, and more than one obligation flows from such a contract.

A reciprocal (synallagmatic, or mutual) contract is a particular type of multilateral contract in that one performance is undertaken in exchange for another – the one obligation is thus created only because the other is created, and it follows that performance of one is a prerequisite for the enforceability of the right in terms of the other obligation. Normally, therefore, a party who is sued for performance may refuse to do so unless the claimant has himself or herself performed properly in terms of the principle of reciprocity.[77] This right to withhold performance is often expressed in terms of the *exceptio non adimpleti contractus*.

---

77. However, when the strict application of this principle will lead to disproportionate loss and unfairness to a contractant it will be relaxed: *Botha and Another v. Rich NO and Others* 2014 4 SA 124 (CC) paras 45–51.

III. Express and Tacit Contracts

51. An important classification, at least as far as proof of existence and content is concerned, is that of express and tacit contracts or terms of a contract. In principle, there is no difference in quality between the two types of contracts. However, proving a tacit contract can be difficult, since it depends on inferences from surrounding facts and circumstances, and a court will not readily accept such inferences. In this regard, the courts have adopted the so-called innocent-bystander test as it was expressed in the English case of *Reigate v. Union Manufacturing Co. (Ramsbottom).*[78] This test is applied by ascertaining whether the parties, as reasonable people, would have agreed to the alleged tacit contract or term if they had thought about it – the so-called presumed or inferred intention of the parties with reference to the express terms of the contract and the surrounding circumstances.

IV. Nominate and Innominate Contracts

52. It will be clear that, as a matter of principle, the classification of contracts as nominate and innominate has no consequences in South African contract law. In principle, every contract is created in the same way and may have any content, irrespective of whether it can be classified as one of the *numerus clausus* of Roman consensual contracts, provided that the contract is not illegal. The concept of a nominate contract may be relevant when a contract is to be classified as being of a particular type, largely so as to ascertain whether it contains certain *ex lege* terms or *naturalia.* The contract must then contain the characteristics or essential terms *(essentialia)* that will allow the classification. A typical example of such a nominate contract is the contract of sale, of which most of the *ex lege* terms originated in Roman law,[79] such as warranties against latent defects and eviction. The *naturalia* of a contract are not fixed and may, with certain exceptions, be limited or extended by agreement in response to particular circumstances.

V. Standard Form Contracts

53. Standard form contracts and contracts of adhesion are very much phenomena of modern business practices, in South Africa as well as in other countries. The possible abuse of these contracts is controlled by statute in a piecemeal way. An important example is the National Credit Act 34 of 2005, which protects consumers who enter into credit transactions. There is also legislation prohibiting the formation of cartels and monopolies. Other significant protective measures relate to the protection of tenants by the Rental Housing Act 50 of 1999, as well as laws protecting consumers in the financial services and insurance (short-and long-term)

78. 118 L T 479 483.

79. Cf. *GrainCo (Pty) Ltd v. Van der Merwe and Others* 2014 5 SA 444 (WCC), which deals with a naturale adopted from English law. In the appeal the court did not deal with the issue as being irrelevant: *GrainCo (Pty) Ltd v. Van der Merwe and Others* 2016 4 SA 303 (SCA).

industries. Consumers who enter into electronic contracts are protected by the Electronic Communications and Transactions Act 25 of 2002.[80]

The entire field of consumer protection was under consideration by the government for a number of years, following reports by the South African Law Commission, including a proposal that a general 'good faith/fairness and reasonableness clause' be enacted. Finally, the Consumer Protection Act 68 of 2008 (operational since 31 March 2011) was passed, which consolidates previous measures provided for in various acts (which were repealed) and provides for wide-ranging protection of consumers.[81] It identifies 'fundamental' consumer rights and attempts to protect these rights in various ways. For example, it prohibits false or misleading representations and proscribes unfair or unjust contracts[82] as well as unconscionable conduct.[83] The Act provides for various methods of redress.[84] Also, the provinces have jurisdiction over consumer affairs and may pass appropriate legislation, such as, for example, the Western Cape Consumer Affairs (Unfair Business Practices) Act 5962 of 2002.

As far as common law is concerned, a number of general principles may be applied to protect contractants in situations that commonly occur in connection with standard form contracts. For example, the rules relating to consensus or non-disclosure would apply when a contractant agreed to certain terms without being aware of or fully understanding them (despite having signed a document containing the terms of a contract), with the result that no contract would ensue or that the contract may be rescinded, or that a particular term would not form part of the contract.[85] An abuse of bargaining power during the negotiating process may result in the contract being rescinded because consent was obtained improperly; or an agreement may be illegal if the terms are so unreasonably protective of the interests of one contractant at the expense of the other contractant's interests that it is against the public interest; or an agreement may be held to be unenforceable as being against public policy for other reasons, for example the text in a standard form agreement being too small to read.[86] The concepts of fairness, reasonableness or good faith also play an important role in this regard.

---

80. *See* para 31 above regarding smart contracts. It seems clear that these contracts, including the underlying one, will be subject to the controls referred to as well as the rules and principles of the law of contract.
81. The Act applies in principle to agreements for the supply of goods and services to consumers for consideration. 'Supply' includes to sell, rent, hire, perform services in the ordinary course of business, including financial services. It does not apply to contracts concluded outside the area of 'continual marketing', for example, 'once-off' contracts between natural persons or even between a natural person and a corporation.
82. In this regard the following aspects should be taken into account: the fair value of the goods or services; the circumstances of the contract; the nature of the parties; their relationship to each other; and their relative capacity, education, and bargaining position.
83. This includes undue influence and probably abuse of circumstances.
84. These include various forms of administrative action controlled by the Commission established by the Act, alternative dispute-resolution (e.g., referral to an ombud), and approaching the Consumer Tribunal, a provincial consumer court, or the ordinary courts.
85. A common example is the treatment of exemption clauses in the law – *see* below and *Mercurius Motors v. Lopez* 2008 3 SA 572 (SCA). Such clauses are often also restrictively interpreted. *See*, for example, *Masstores (Pty) Ltd v. Murray & Roberts Construction (Pty) Ltd* 2008 (6) SA 654 (SCA).
86. *Cf. Four Wheel Drive Accessory Distribution CC v. Rattan NO* 2018 3 SA 204 (KZD).

VI. Onerous and Gratuitous Contracts

54. The distinction between onerous and gratuitous contracts has no effect in principle in South African law, although it does have some practical consequences. An executory donation, for example, will be valid only if it is in writing and signed by the donor or his or her agent (section 5 of Act 50 of 1956). This enactment is criticized by some as unnecessary, because the courts will not readily infer an intention to donate and also because the wording of the section causes uncertainty. A donation is a 'disposition ... not for value' in terms of insolvency legislation and may be set aside in certain circumstances. It is uncertain whether the rule that a gratuitous depositary is burdened with a lesser degree of care than a depositary for reward is still part of South African law, as well as whether a gratuitous mandatory's duties in terms of the contract are less than those of a mandatory who is rewarded for his or her services.

VII. Aleatory Agreements

55. The classification of a contract as an aleatory agreement for which performance is dependent on some uncertainty is known to South African law. Examples are the contract of insurance and certain wagers. Not all aleatory agreements are enforceable contracts; however, some wagers are unenforceable, whereas others are even completely void for being against the public interest.

In this context, the National Gambling Act 7 of 2004 must be considered.

VIII. Accessory Obligations

56. The concept of an accessory obligation that is created by contract is part of South African law and is applied in contracts of suretyship, mortgage, and pledge. Central to this concept is that the accessory obligation cannot exist without a main obligation, even though the latter may be a natural obligation.

IX. Collateral Contracts

57. The common law concept of a collateral contract as it is used in connection with the parol evidence rule is not often used in South Africa, where the problem of admissibility of evidence extrinsic to a document is approached rather with reference to the concept of integration. In fact, serious doubt has been expressed as to the need for the continued existence of the parol evidence rule.

X. *Pacta de Contrahendo*

58. The classification of contracts as *pacta de contrahendo* is an important one in South Africa. Option contracts by which an offeror's capacity to revoke an offer is restricted and contracts of preference creating a preferential right to contract with another, should the latter decide to contract at all, are classified as *pacta de contrahendo*. These contracts are construed as ordinary contracts, which immediately create enforceable rights and duties for the parties, subject to the normal rules governing contracts.

So-called agreements in principle and letters of intent generally have no consequences in South African law, largely because of the lack of the requisite intent, but in modern commercial practice they play an increasingly important role where an intent to be bound to basic terms is clearly incorporated.

The equivalent of the continental concept of an obligationary agreement that binds one or both of the parties eventually to conclude a contract as contemplated by them (the *voorovereenkomst* or *Vorvertrag*) is not unknown to South African law, but its usefulness is limited by the requirement of certainty. Recently, however, there is increasing support by the courts to enforce 'agreements to agree' or to negotiate further in certain circumstances (such as where there is a deadlock-breaking mechanism) based on the Constitutional principles of *ubuntu* and good faith. [87]

XI. Contracts in Favour of Third Parties

59. Contracts in favour of third parties are a part of the South African law, as is the case in some other civil law systems. The construction of the *stipulatio alteri* in South African law is not certain. In principle, it should be construed as a contract by which a right for the third party is created immediately, but the courts tend to favour the construction[88] that the contract is intended to enable the beneficiary to eventually step in as a party to a contract with one of the original contractants by 'accepting' the benefit.

§4. Contracts and Delicts (Torts)

I. Law of Delict and Tort

60. The South African law of civil wrongs resembles the law of delict as it is found in civil law systems much more closely than it resembles the law of torts in common law systems, although there has been some English law influence in this branch of the law. The South African law of delict is applied and developed in terms of general requirements for liability, namely wrongful conduct, fault, causation, and harm. When patrimonial loss has been suffered, the Aquilian action for compensation may apply, and when a *solatium* is claimed, an *actio iniuriarum* or an action

87. *See, e.g., Everfresh Market Virginia (Pty) Ltd v. Shoprite Checkers (Pty) Ltd* 2012 1 SA 256 (CC); *Makate v. Vodacom Ltd* 2016 4 SA 121 (CC); *Roazar CC v. The Falls Supermarket CC* 2018 3 SA 76 (SCA) paras 19, 21–22.

88. There are at least three constructions, differing in detail.

for pain and suffering may be instituted. Contributory negligence on the part of the claimant does not oust his or her claim, and damages may be apportioned in terms of statute.

II. Blurring of Distinction Between a Contract and a Delict

61. In broad terms, one may say that the traditional distinction between a contract and a delict is in the process of becoming blurred in South African law, although not to the extent that the 'death' of either is imminent. Rather, it seems that, together with the concept of good faith or reasonableness and fairness, the delictual concepts of wrongfulness, fault, and harm will provide a stimulus and offer practical guidelines for the development of uniquely contractual standards for the conclusion and execution of contracts and the enforcement of contractual remedies, while respecting the basic value of private autonomy. Also, of course, the focal point of the distinction is at the level of conduct causing harm, which encompasses the entire concept of a delict. A contract, however, exists in a more extended sphere, relating not only to its conclusion but also to its execution.

An interesting development broadly along these lines took place recently when the Supreme Court of Appeal held that the duty to inform during pre-contractual negotiations and the duty to inform in the context of a delict had been synthesized into a general test for liability based on the legal convictions of the community.[89] This general test, it was held, entails that a contracting party need not tell the other party all that he or she knows about anything that may be material – he or she is expected to speak when the information falls within his or her exclusive knowledge (when, in a practical and business sense, he or she is the only source) and when the information is such that the right to have it communicated would be mutually recognized by honest people in those circumstances.[90] Clearly, the contractual context and the concept of good faith would result in the construction of a duty to speak that would differ in its practical application from that of a delict, albeit both are based on the same principle.

62. 62 The recognition, after a long period of development, that a contract may also, in the absence of consensus, be based on a reasonable reliance on consensus illustrates the above point.[91] The reasonableness of the reliance is not dependent on the wrongfulness, in the delictual sense, of the other party's conduct – although, if the conduct is wrongful, the reliance would, at least prima facie, be reasonable. Fault is also not a decisive factor in this context.

89. The legal convictions of the community are to be determined with reference (also) to the Constitution (particularly the Bill of Rights). *See Du Plessis v. Road Accident Fund* 2004 1 SA 359 (SCA); *Phumelala Gaming and Leisure Ltd v. Gründlingh* 2007 6 SA 350 (CC).

90. *See ABSA Bank Ltd v. Fouche* 2003 1 SA 176 (SCA) and the discussion of the duty to inform below.

91. *See* Van Huyssteen, Lubbe & Reinecke, *Contract General Principles* ch. 2 and in conclusion para. 2.127 et seq. (Juta 2016).

III. *Culpa in Contrahendo*

63. In South African law, there is yet no comprehensive approach to the issue of relations between parties *in contrahendo*. It is generally assumed that negotiating parties have complete freedom to break off negotiations. Here, the doctrine of *culpa in contrahendo* may play a role, although the development of standards of conduct based on good faith would be preferable. Such a development, however, is not imminent. For the time being, an extension of the element of wrongfulness as it applies in the law of delict will more probably be practical in this context.[92] Of course, one may say that the recent decisions on negligent misstatements *in contrahendo*, which is referred to below, could pave the way for a more comprehensive development of a doctrine of *culpa in contrahendo*.

IV. Rescission of a Contract and Delict

64. The grounds for rescinding a contract in South African positive law are based, at least in part, on a delict. Misrepresentation in the form of fraud and negligent misrepresentation, as well as duress, are clearly regarded as delictual in nature, and all the relevant elements of a delict have to be proved. Undue influence, and, of course, innocent misrepresentation as grounds for rescission cannot readily be classified as a delict. However, despite judicial pronouncements to the contrary, South African law is in the process of developing general grounds for rescission of contracts on the basis of improperly obtained consensus, when wrongfulness in the delictual sense is clearly a guideline to the unacceptability of the conduct in question, but when norms more directly appropriate to a contract should be applicable and are capable of development.[93]

V. Delictual Damages and Contract

65. When, in the context of an improperly obtained consensus, the aggrieved contractant claims damages, the claim will generally be a delictual one, and the usual measure of damages is the claimant's negative interest and not his or her positive interest, which is the normal contractual measure. However, there is support for the view that the measure of damages should be expressed in terms of the single objective of compensating a victim for his or her loss. This approach would obviate the necessity of making the sometimes artificial and arbitrary distinction between the 'delictual' measure and the 'contractual' measure,[94] with the result of the fact

92. *See* Van Huyssteen, Lubbe & Reinecke, *Contract General Principles*, para. 3.58 et seq. (Juta 2016); *Olitzki Property Holdings v. State Tender Board* 2001 3 SA 1247 (SCA); *Transnet Ltd v. Sechaba Photoscan (Pty) Ltd* 2005 1 SA 299 (SCA).

93. On the development of a general ground and the application of improperly obtained consensus, *see* the discussion below and Van Huyssteen, Lubbe & Reinecke, *Contract General Principles* ch. 4 and in particular paras 4.6–4.12 and 4.93–4.104 (Juta 2016).

94. Cf. the minority and majority judgments regarding damages for *dolus incidens* in *Ranger v. Wykerd* 1977 2 SA 976 (A).

that the loss was caused by a misrepresentation or by a breach of contract would be relevant mainly to the question of causation.

VI. Delictual Damages for Negligent Misstatements in Contrahendo

66. The question of a basis for liability for damages in the case of a negligent misstatement inducing a contract when purely economic loss has been suffered is particularly an interesting one from the comparative point of view. The Supreme Court of Appeal's decision in *Bayer South Africa (Pty) Ltd v. Frost* [95] indicates clearly that South African law has come down squarely in favour of a delictual basis for a claim for such damages.[96] The Court found no distinction in principle between misstatements made without or within the context of contractual negotiations. It is significant to note, however, that the fact that contractual negotiations had been conducted and that a contract had resulted, were particularly important factors regarding the presence of wrongfulness (or, as it was expressed, a duty to ensure that the statement was 'correct') and causation. In light of the need to guard against casting the net of liability too wide, it is doubtful in the extreme that a court would construe a general duty to speak the truth *in contrahendo*. More probably, the courts will develop a duty not to make statements that, in the circumstances of a particular case, are unreasonably harmful.[97]

67. The impact of the decision in the *Bayer* case on product liability and consumer protection[98] in general is uncertain. It would certainly provide greater scope for claiming damages when privity of contract does exist, but, as that is not the case in most instances, a consumer is still faced with the daunting task of proving the elements of a delict, in particular, negligence.[99] In the field of advertising, the courts may well construe a specific duty to make correct statements.

VII. Breach of Contract and Delict

68. Whether a breach of contract in South African law is a particular form of a delict is a moot question.[100] There are certainly similarities, but since fault is now

95. 1991 4 SA 559 (A).
96. *See* L.F. van Huyssteen, S. van der Merwe & J.H. Herbots, 'Onzorgvuldige en Onjuiste Informatie bij de Contractsluiting in het Zuidafrikaans Recht', *Tijdschrift voor Privaatrecht* 1 (1993): 61.
97. Cf. *Delphisure Group Insurance Brokers Cape (Pty) Ltd v. Dippenaar* 2010 5 SA 499 (SCA). In *Cape Empowerment Trust Ltd v. Fisher Hoffman Sithole* 2013 5 SA 183 (SCA) (a case where the plaintiff had suffered pure economic loss due to a grossly negligent misstatement by an auditor) the court warned against conflating negligence and wrongfulness and considered various facts which in the circumstances and as a matter of policy would constitute wrongfulness or not.
98. The Consumer Protection Act 68 of 2008 provides the consumer with a range of protective measures in this context.
99. *See Ciba-Geigy (Pty) Ltd v. Lushof Farms (Pty) Ltd* 2002 2 SA 447 (HHA).
100. *See* Van Huyssteen, Lubbe & Reinecke, *Contract General Principles* ch. 10 A & B (Juta 2016).

authoritatively regarded as not being a requirement to constitute a breach of contract the view that a breach of contract is not a delict is current.[101] Rather, it can be described as conduct that is unacceptable for being contrary to the norms that protect the contractual interests of one contractant against certain conduct of the other contractant. In this regard the principle of good faith as informed by the legal convictions of the community is the decisive criterion to establish breach of contract.[102] Also the courts have refused to apportion damages in claims based on a breach of contract.[103]

The approach that a breach of contract is not a delict also probably influences the refusal by the courts to grant damages for non-patrimonial loss caused by a breach,[104] such as for inconvenience or disappointment (cf. the English 'holiday cases'). The one possible exception to this approach is a sui generis action, in which a financial institution wrongfully refuses to honour a cheque, and the client claims consolation in conjunction with a claim for patrimonial loss.

VIII. Concurrence of Actions

69. The question of whether, as a matter of policy, a free choice of actions should be allowed when the facts of a particular case can provide the basis for an action for a breach of contract as well as for an action in delict (the question of concurrence of actions) is a problematic one in South African law.

The matter usually arises for decision when a litigant institutes a delictual action rather than a contractual action, because his or her contractual action has prescribed or because the contract excludes a contractual claim for damages. Apart from the question of proof, which might in many cases make a contractual claim more practicable, there are no procedural considerations favouring the institution of one claim or the other. Indeed, it has been stressed by the Appeal Court that the mere fact that a claimant has framed his or her claim in a contract will not per se debar him or her from attempting to claim in delict.[105] On the substantive question of concurrence of actions, the Appeal Court in 1985 seemed to have accepted in principle the 'alternative' system in permitting a choice of actions.[106] That this is indeed the approach

101. *Scoin Trading (Pty) Ltd v. Bernstein NO* 2011 (2) 118 (SCA); *Loureiro and Others v. Imvula Quality Protection (Pty) Ltd* 2014 3 SA 394 (CC) para. 42; Van Huyssteen, Lubbe & Reinecke, *Contract General Principles* ch. 10 B (Juta 2016).
102. Van Huyssteen, Lubbe & Reinecke, *Contract General Principles* ch. 10 A (Juta 2016).
103. *Thoroughbred Breeders' Association v. Price Waterhouse* 2001 4 SA 511 (SCA).
104. *See*, for example, *Administrator, Natal v. Edouard* 1990 3 SA 581 (A).
105. *See Lillicrap, Wassenaar & Partners v. Pilkington Brothers (SA) (Pty) Ltd* 1985 1 SA 475 (A) 496; *see also NSC Carriers & Forwarding CC and Others v. Hyprop Investments Ltd and Others* 2013 1 SA 340 (GSJ) where the problem of issue estoppel arose where a contractual claim had previously been decided against claimant.
106. In the *Lillicrap, Wassenaar & Partners v. Pilkington Brothers (SA) (Pty) Ltd* 1985 1 SA 475 (A) 496, the Court put it as follows: 'Our law also acknowledges that the same facts may give rise to a claim for damages *ex delicto* as well as one *ex contractu*, and allows the plaintiff to choose which he wishes to pursue.'

of the Supreme Court of Appeal has been specifically confirmed by later decisions.[107] What is still a matter of some uncertainty, however, is the application by the Supreme Court of Appeal of the element of wrongfulness, and the effect of such an application on the freedom of choice that was acknowledged in principle. Upon analysis, it appears that the Court in the *Lillicrap* case[108] went no further than to decide that a breach of a contractual duty to perform (professional) work with due diligence, which caused purely economic loss, should not as a matter of policy be allowed to form the basis of a claim in delict. The complainant should rather claim for breach of contract – in effect, then, no choice exists in such a case. However, in cases in which a contractual claim, as well as a delictual claim for purely economic loss exists *independently* of the contract, or in cases of damage to persons or property, a free choice exists.[109]

Clearly, what is essentially an issue here is the problem of the extent to which a legal system should allow the recovery of damages for purely economic loss. Since the Appeal Court in 1991, with reference to many of the same policy considerations that moved the Court in the *Lillicrap* case to act restrictively, extended delictual liability for negligent misstatements *in contrahendo* causing purely economic loss (see the discussion above), the next step could have been to extend delictual liability and to acknowledge a free choice of action in cases in which a negligent breach of a contractual duty to render professional services has caused purely economic loss. A recent tentative step in this direction has been to espouse a flexible approach and to allow an action in delict in the case of a negligent breach of a contract to render quasi-professional services – *in casu*, offering financial services and providing investment advice.[110]

However, the Supreme Court of Appeal has now clearly put a stop to such a possible development by holding that the restrictions imposed by the Court in the *Lillicrap* case were valid as a matter of policy[111] and were not limited to contracts for professional services only: a negligent breach of a contractual duty causing purely

107. Cf. *Bayer South Africa (Pty) Ltd v. Frost* 1991 4 SA 559 (A); *see Cathkin Park Hotel v. J D Makesch Architects* 1993 2 SA 98 (W) 100; *see* now in particular *Holtzhausen v. ABSA Bank* 2008 5 SA 630 (SCA).

108. *Lillicrap, Wassenaar & Partners v. Pilkington Brothers (SA) (Pty) Ltd* 1985 1 SA 475 (A) 496.

109. Cf. *Van Wyk v. Lewis* 1924 AD 438, a case of medical malpractice, and *Cathkin Park Hotel v. J D Makesch Architects* 1993 2 SA 98 (W) 100, in which a fireplace was allegedly badly designed, causing actual physical damage to the property; cf. *Holtzhausen v. ABSA Bank Ltd* 2008 5 SA 630 (SCA), in which the claim was framed in a delict based on negligent misstatements by a bank official causing purely economic loss, and not on negligent breach of contract.

110. *See Pinshaw v. Nexus Securities (Pty) Ltd* 2002 2 SA 510 (C). But see *Alfa Laval Agri (Pty) Ltd v. Ferreira* 2004 2 SA 68 (O).

111. In *AB Ventures Ltd v. Siemens Ltd* 2011 4 SA 614 (SCA) the court with reference to *Lillicrap* emphasized 'that there was no call for the law to be extended when the existing law provided adequate means for the plaintiff to protect itself against loss'. (paras 19–21). In *Nortje v. Fakie* 2013 1 SA 577 (KZP) the court applied the *Lillicrap* case rather widely by finding that the appellant had effective remedies in terms of the contract and '... to accord to the appellant a cause of action based in delict would have the effect of eliminating provisions, in the agreement, which the parties considered necessary or desirable for their own protection'.

economic loss cannot per se found a claim in delict.[112] Recently it was again emphasized by the Supreme Court of Appeal that to be successful in delict when claiming for pure economic loss wrongfulness, as considered in light of public policy, must be proved, and if the conduct was negligent, specifically the requirement of foreseeability.[113]

70. Regarding the co-existence of contractual and delictual liability, South African law clearly accepts that, when a breach of contract (e.g., between A and B) amounts at the same time to a delict with respect to a third party (C), the latter may claim damages from the party who breaches the contract.[114] Of course, all the elements of a delict must be present. In this regard, the Supreme Court of Appeal emphasized the elements of indeterminacy (raising the spectre of indeterminate liability) and the non-vulnerability of the claimant who could have taken alternative steps to recover the loss.[115]

§5. Contracts and Quasi-Contracts

I. 'Quasi-Contract' Is Not a Term of Art in South African Law

71. The classification of an obligation as a 'quasi-contract' as it was used in the common law of South Africa to describe obligations that were akin to obligations *ex contractu* [116] is seldom used in modern South African law, where the term has, in any event, not developed as a term of art. Rather, the prime example of such an obligation, unjustified enrichment, has developed as a separate substantive source of obligation with its own distinct requirements or elements.

II. No General Enrichment Action: Development of Liability

72. Despite the fact that Roman-Dutch law recognized a general enrichment action,[117,118] in 1966, the Appeal Court, in the case of *Nortje v. Pool,* [119] declined to

112. The court in *Holtzhausen v. ABSA Bank Ltd* 2008 5 SA 630 (SCA) found that the decision in the *Pinshaw v. Nexus Securities (Pty) Ltd* 2002 2 SA 510 (C) was incorrect, and that the decision in the *Lillicrap* case was not applicable because the delictual claim was not based on breach of contract but on an independent duty of care.
113. *See Country Cloud Trading CC v. MEC, Department of Infrastructure Development* 2014 2 SA 214 (SCA); *Country Cloud Trading CC v. MEC, Department of Infrastructure Development* 2015 1 SA 1 (CC).
114. *See S. M. Goldstein & Co. (Pty) Ltd v. Cathkin Park Hotel (Pty) Ltd* 2000 4 SA 1019 (SCA).
115. *See Country Cloud Trading CC v. MEC, Department of Infrastructure Development* 2014 2 SA 214 (SCA); *Minister of Safety & Security v. Scott & Another* 2014 6 SA 1 (SCA) where the court again warned against indeterminate liability and strictly applied the elements of delictual liability. Also *Country Cloud Trading CC v. MEC, Department of Infrastructure Development* 2015 1 SA 1 (CC).
116. *See*, for example, D 44. 7. 1 *pr*, Voet 12. 6. 1.
117. For an overview of the development of this branch of the law in South Africa and the various influences thereon, *see* R. Zimmermann & D. Visser, *Southern Cross Civil Law and Common Law in South Africa* 523 et seq. (Juta 1996). For more detail, *see* Daniel Visser *Unjustified Enrichment* Part

recognize the existence of a general enrichment action in South African law, prompted mainly by the fear of unlimited liability, the lack of guidelines, and the view that the laying down of general guidelines was the prerogative of the legislature. The subsequent approach of the courts has been generally conservative, although in a number of instances they have been willing to extend the scope of a specific enrichment action on an ad hoc basis (e.g., it was decided that an excusable mistake of law should, on the basis of fairness, no longer be a bar to an enrichment claim).[120] In general, however, a claimant wishing to claim on the basis of unjustified enrichment has had to bring his or her claim within the confines of one of the specific enrichment actions recognized by law.[121]

Trenchant criticism has been levelled against the generally conservative and piecemeal approach of the courts to the development of enrichment liability, and strong support for a general enrichment action has been voiced, not only mainly by commentators,[122] but also on occasion by the judiciary.[123] It is argued that a number of core elements for liability have come to be identified, and that these would adequately serve to limit enrichment liability and thus pave the way for the recognition of a general enrichment action in modern South African law.

While the Appeal Court in the past expressed support for its decision in *Nortje v. Pool*,[124] in 2001, it held that that case had been incorrectly decided.[125] The Supreme Court of Appeal went so far as to say that, while it did not need to do so in the case before it, it would in principle favour the recognition of a general action in a case in which the extension of an old action would be insufficient, but that this general action should preferably not displace the old remedies but rather fulfil a subsidiary role.[126] In due course, the Court may well expressly recognize the general action.[127] However, it is still emphasized that there is as yet no general enrichment action in South African law.[128]

1 (Juta 2008). On the nature of the right to restitution on the basis of unjustified enrichment, *see National Credit Regulator v. Opperman and Others* 2013 2 SA 1 (CC) at para. 15.

118. *See*, for example, J.E. Scholtens, *The General Enrichment Action That Was*, S. African L. J. 391 (1966).

119. 1966 3 SA 96 (A).

120. *See Willis Faber Enthoven (Pty) Ltd v. Receiver of Revenue* 1992 4 SA 202 (A). *See also Bowman, De Wet and Du Plessis NNO and Others v. Fidelity Bank Ltd* 1997 (2) SA 35 (A).

121. Cf. *Mndi v. Malgas* 2006 2 SA 182 (E).

122. *See*, for example, W. de Vos *Verrykingsaanspreeklikheid in die Suid-Afrikaanse Reg* (Cape Town: Juta, 1987), 328 et seq.; S. Eiselen & G. Pienaar, *Unjustified Enrichment: A Casebook* 22 et seq. (Butterworths 1999); Daniel Visser, *Unjustified Enrichment* 7–13, at 27–54 (Juta 2008); G.T.S. Eiselen 'Herlewing van die Algemene Verrykingsaksie', *Tydskrif vir Hedendaagse Romeins-Hollandse Reg* (1992): 124; D.P. Visser, *Error of Law and Mistaken Payments: A Milestone*, S. African L. J. 177, at 185 (1992).

123. *See*, for example, *Rulten v. Herald Industries (Pty) Ltd* 1982 3 SA 600 (D) 606–607; *Blesbok Eiendomsagentskap v. Cantamessa* 1991 2 SA 712 (T) and, most importantly, *McCarthy Retail Ltd v. Shortdistance Carriers CC* 2001 3 SA 482 (SCA).

124. *See*, for example, *Kommissaris van Binnelandse Inkomste v. Willers* 1992 4 SA 202 (A).

125. *McCarthy Retail Ltd v. Shortdistance Carriers CC* 2001 3 SA 482 (SCA) 488 (para. 9).

126. *See* the judgment 488–489. Since then, the court has more often considered the general requirements for enrichment liability alongside the traditional requirements for the specific remedies: *see*, for example, *Trustees, Estate Whitehead v. Dumas and Another* 2013 3 SA 331 (SCA); *Absa Bank Ltd v. Lombard Insurance Co Ltd* 2012 6 SA 569 (SCA).

III. Specific Enrichment Actions

73. A brief overview of the specific enrichment actions follows, with particular reference to those rules that most directly relate to aspects of contracts.[129]

A. Condictio Causa Data Causa Non Secuta

74. 74 The *condictio causa data causa non secuta* has a limited scope in modern South African law and may only be used to recover that which was transferred to another on the basis of an assumption relating to the future which did not materialize, or that which was transferred subject to a modal clause that was not complied with or was frustrated. It now seems to be generally accepted that a claim for the return of performance subsequent to cancellation of a contract is not an enrichment claim, but a contractual one.

B. Condictio Ob Turpem Vel Iniustam Causam

75. The *condictio ob turpem vel iniustam causam* finds application when a performance that was rendered in terms of an illegal agreement is reclaimed. The claim for return is subject to a limitation imposed for reasons of policy: the law will usually not assist a person who participated in an illegality, except when public policy and the need to ensure a fair result for the parties involved dictate otherwise. This matter will be discussed further below.

C. Condictio Indebiti

76. The *condictio indebiti* is available to reclaim what was paid or delivered to another in error, in the reasonable belief that the performance was due when it was

---

127. Recent examples of the courts' more relaxed approach include, for example, *McCarthy Retail Ltd v. Shortdistance Carriers CC* 2001 3 SA 482 (SCA); *First National Bank of Southern Africa Ltd v. Perry NO and Others* 2001 3 SA 960 (SCA) 969–970; *Besselaar v. Registrar, Durban and Coast Local Division and Others* 2002 1 SA 191 (D) 197–198; *Financial Services Board and Another v. De Wet NO and Others* 2002 3 SA 525 (C) 622 B–J (paras 290 and 291); but cf. *FirstRand Bank Ltd (formerly First National Bank of SA Ltd) v. ABSA Bank Ltd* 2001 1 SA 803 (W) 805 J–806 A. *See also Bowman, De Wet and Du Plessis NNO and Others v. Fidelity Bank Ltd* 1997 (2) SA 35 (A) 40 and *Nissan South Africa (Pty) Ltd v. Marnitz NO* 2005 1 SA 441 (SCA). *See* further the analysis of Daniel Visser, *Unjustified Enrichment* 7–13, at 27–54 (Juta 2008).

128. *See St Helena Primary School v. M E C, Department of Education, Free State Province* 2007 4 SA 16(O); *Laco Parts (Pty) Ltd t/a ACA Clutch v. Turners Shipping (Pty) Ltd* 2008 1 SA 279 (W); *Watson NO v. Shaw NO* 2008 1 SA 350 (C).

129. For a useful short statement of the law of enrichment, *see* F. du Bois (gen. ed.), *Wille's Principles of South African Law* ch. 39 (Juta 2007); for a detailed exposition, *see* W. de Vos, *Verrykingsaanspreeklikheid in die Suid-Afrikaanse Reg* (Cape Town: Juta, 1987); Daniel Visser *Unjustified Enrichment* (Juta 2008). *See also*, *The Law of South Africa* vol. 9 (W.A. Joubert ed., 2d ed., Butterworths 2005).

in fact not due. The error may be one of fact or of law. A distinction must be drawn between a case of so-called duress of goods, which is to be regarded as a case of improperly obtained consensus resulting in the rescission of the contract and the return of the performance, and a situation in which, for example, money has been paid to avoid loss or harm to property, and the payment is subsequently reclaimed. The latter claim will be in terms of the *condictio* and must comply with the requirements set for it.[130]

D. Condictio Sine Causa Specialis

77. The *condictio sine causa specialis* is still part of South African law. It is applicable when money or other property has been transferred to another for a valid *causa* that subsequently falls away, for example, when performance has been made in terms of a reciprocal contract and supervening objective impossibility of performance extinguishes the other obligation. The *condictio* is also available in certain circumstances when property has been alienated or consumed by the person who was in possession of it. Whether this *condictio* has any further application in South African law, and what the scope of such application is, are uncertain.[131]

E. Action for Improvements

78. An enrichment action is available when improvements to property of another have been made by the possessor of the property without the consent of the other. The amount by which the value of the property has been enhanced may be claimed.

F. Negotiorum Gestio

79. Negotiorum gestio is an important basis of liability in South African law. In general, a person who manages the affairs of another without his or her consent or knowledge is entitled to recover from the latter any necessary or useful expenses that he or she has incurred while doing so. Usually, the action for recovery of expenses is not an enrichment action. In exceptional circumstances, namely when the requirements of the normal *actio negotiorum gestorum* have not been met, however, the action will only apply for the amount by which the *gestor* has been enriched.

---

130. *Commissioner for Inland Revenue v. First National Industrial Bank Ltd* 1990 3 SA 641 (A); *Shuttleworth v. SA Reserve Bank and Others* 2015 1 SA 586 (SCA).
131. *See*, further, the discussion in Part II of this work, and the references cited there.

G. Claim Against a Minor

80. When a person of full capacity enters into an agreement with another who has limited capacity to act (e.g., a minor) and who is not assisted, the first person may reclaim whatever he or she has performed (or its value) insofar as the latter remains enriched.

H. Alienation of Land: Statutory Enrichment Action

81. A statutory enrichment action was created by the Alienation of Land Act 68 of 1981 to provide for the recovery of interest and reasonable compensation when performance has taken place in terms of an agreement of alienation of land, which is of no force because of failure to comply with the required formalities.

I. Claim for Reduced Performance

82. When a party to a reciprocal contract retains his or her own performance because of inadequate performance by the other party, the latter may be allowed by the court in its discretion to claim reduced performance in certain circumstances. This claim for reduced performance, often a reduced contract price, such as that of a building contract, has long been typified as a quantum meruit based on enrichment. The Supreme Court of Appeal has held that such a claim is not based on enrichment but is a 'contractual' claim.[132] The precise nature of this claim is not clear, but at least it is certain that the reduced performance is calculated with reference to the performance agreed upon in the contract.

When, however, the contract is cancelled by one party because of the serious degree to which the other party's performance was insufficient, the latter may have an enrichment action. Thus, when a builder completes only a part of the building that he or she has contracted to erect and the building owner cancels the contract, the contractor will have an enrichment claim against the owner.

§6. Contract and Law of Property

I. Real Rights and 'Equitable Ownership'

83. Essential to the understanding of the relationship between a contract and the law of property in South Africa is an understanding of the nature of and distinction between the rights created by a contract and the rights with which the law of property is concerned. The type of right created by a contract is a personal right, whereas the rights that form the subject matter of the law of property are real rights.

132. *See BK Tooling (Edms) Bpk v. Scope Precision Engineering (Edms) Bpk* 1979 1 SA 391 (A) 422–423.

This distinction has been discussed above, but it merits re-emphasis that personal rights are closely connected with a person other than the holder of the right and may, in principle, be enforced only against the person who has a duty to the holder to render a performance, whereas a real right is a right in a thing, which confers on the holder a right that is legally indefeasible by any other person and which, in principle, may be vindicated against all persons whatsoever.

In the context of certain contracts, there are important limitations on real rights. For example, in the case of a 'double' sale, the doctrine of notice may have the result that a second buyer who had knowledge[133] of, the first sale becomes liable to transfer to the first buyer the property that the second buyer bought, and of which he or she became the owner. In certain cases, the ownership of a buyer of leased property is subject to the right of the tenant to remain in occupation of the property in terms of the lease, by virtue of the rule *huur gaat voor koop*, that is, 'lease takes preference over sale'.

This description and classification of rights conforms in essence to the position in other civil law systems and leaves no room for a notion of equitable ownership. By the operation of the doctrine of estoppel by representation, however, a possessor of property may, as against the representor, be regarded as if he or she were the owner, but as the law stands, it would seem that he or she is not regarded as the owner in law.

II. Creation of Real Rights and Kinds of Real Rights

84. There is no *numerus clausus* of real rights in South African law. A new particular real right in a contracting party's property may be created by the usual methods, for example, by registration, as agreed upon by the parties to a contract. To determine whether the right in question is personal or real (in terms of the Deeds Registries Act 47 of 1937, only real rights are registerable in the Land Register), the courts have, in the context of rights to land, developed the following practical criteria: the intention must be to bind not only the present owner of the land, but also his or her successors in title; and the nature of the right must be such that its registration diminishes the right of ownership in the land against which it is registered. Section 25 of the Constitution protects the right to hold 'property' against arbitrary deprivation and provides for expropriation in certain circumstances in the public interest subject to just and equitable compensation.

The most common kinds of real rights in South Africa are ownership, in the sense of *dominium plenum*, and *iura in re aliena*, such as long lease, mortgage, servitude (praedial and personal), perpetual quitrent, leasehold, and mineral rights. In principle, possession is not a real right. However, a possessor is protected against a variety of other persons to the extent that, in practice, possessors often come close to enjoying the benefits of a real right.

---

133. Or foresaw the possibility of the existence of a prior sale: *see Meridian Bay Restaurant (Pty) Ltd and Others v. Mitchell NO* 2011 4 SA 1 (SCA), paras 17–18.

III. Transfer of Real Rights and Registration

85. The transfer of real rights, in particular, ownership, is accomplished by various means, according to whether the real right in question relates to movable, immovable, or incorporeal property.

Ownership in *corporeal movable property* is transferred by way of delivery. Delivery has a mental and a physical element. The transferor by agreement intends to relinquish the possession of the thing and to transfer it to the transferee, who in turn intends to take over the possession. This is the mental element, which is coupled with the transfer itself, actually or constructively, of the physical control of the thing. These coinciding intentions constitute an agreement (a 'real agreement') but not a contract; the agreement is a part of the process of transfer and cannot alone effect transfer. In principle, real rights in movables cannot be conferred by registration. There are some anomalous exceptions to this principle.

The only registration in South Africa that effectively creates or transfers a real right in *immovable property* is registration in the Land Register in terms of the Deeds Registries Act. Every piece of land in South Africa is surveyed, described in a diagram, and registered in a deeds office. Thus, ownership in immovable property is transferred by registration, which in principle is conclusive proof of ownership. Most other real rights in land are transferred by an agreement to transfer attested by a notary public and registered in a deeds office, although in the case of a mortgage bond, notarial attestation is not necessary. An agreement of transfer is a real agreement and not a contract.

IV. A Contract Does Not Transfer Rights

86. As will be clear from what has been said above, a contract is more often than not the reason or *causa* for the creation or transfer of real rights, but it does not by itself create a real right, nor is it by itself a transfer or method of transfer of a real right. The following examples are typical illustrations of this basic principle in South African law: a real right of long lease of land only comes into being upon registration of the contract – otherwise the lease creates a mere personal right; the sale of a movable, even though *perfecta* for the purposes of passing the risk to the buyer, only creates a personal right for the buyer to claim delivery of the movable (an *ius* in personam *ad rem adquirendam*). Only by delivery can the buyer become the owner. In this respect, the relationship between a contract and the law of property in South Africa (where the abstract system of transfer is applied) differs materially from the position in some other systems of law where the causal system is applied.

§7. CONTRACTS AND TRUSTS

I. Relationship Between a Contract and a Trust: Nature of a Trust

87. In South African law, the trust is a particularly useful and adaptable legal concept, notwithstanding anomalies in the theory of trust law and trust practices, and uncertainty about the legal nature of a trust, including the question of whether a trust is a legal person.[134]

The relationship between a contract and a trust can only be understood once the basic characteristics of a trust in South African law have been explained.

Analytically and for comparative purposes, the South African law of trusts may broadly be described as typically South African, being an amalgam that emanates from strong English influences adapted in the mould of the *jus commune* and further developed by the courts and the legislature to suit modern concepts and needs. For example, the idea that trusteeship is a public office has been taken from English law but has been applied in terms of Roman-Dutch institutions such as tutorship and administratorship; the creation and revocation of trusts are governed by the rules and institutions of the common law of South Africa, such as the *stipulatio alteri*; and the rights of trust beneficiaries to the trust property and against the trustee have been developed by the courts and statute law in terms of the general principles of personal and real rights and of delictual and contractual liability, without making use of the English concept of equitable interests.[135]

II. Definition of a Trust

88. Although it is very difficult – if not impossible – to give an exhaustive definition of a trust, there are various definitions formulated for various purposes. For example, a trust has been defined in the Trust Property Control Act 57 of 1988 for the purposes of administrative control of the trust property, and there are various judicial definitions, mainly in the context of the duties of a trustee. The definition or description of a trust in the Hague Convention on the Law Applicable to Trusts and their Recognition of 1986 is not a part of domestic law, since South Africa is not a party to the convention, although the main features of the South African trust conform to that definition. However, the following general definition of a South African trust appears to cover all aspects of the institution as approved by the courts: 'A

134. The standard work on trust law in South Africa is E. Cameron et al., *Honoré's South African Law of Trusts* (Juta 2002); P. A.Olivier et al., *Trust Law and Practice* (Lexis Nexis loose-leaf). An interesting short exposition on the anomalies of trust law and practice is to be found in M.J. de Waal, 'Anomaliëe in die Suid-Afrikaanse Trustreg', *Tydskrif vir Hedendaagse Romeins-Hollandse Reg* (1993): 1. Extensive use has been made of these publications in writing this paragraph. *See also* M.J. de Waal, *The Core Elements of the Trust: Aspects of the English, Scottish and South African Trusts Compared*, S. African L. J. 548 (2000).

135. For a more detailed description of the development of trust law in South Africa, *see* R. Zimmermann & D. Visser, *Southern Cross Civil Law and Common law in South Africa* 849 et seq. (Juta 1996).

trust is a legal institution in which a person, the trustee, subject to public supervision, holds or administers property separately from his or her own, for the benefit of another person or persons, or for the furtherance of a charitable or other purpose.'[136]

III. Main Features of a Trust

89. A brief summary of the main features of a trust will be given with reference to the applicable rules of the law of contract and the most important areas of uncertainty about or divergence between trust theory and practice.

A. *Creation of a Trust*

90. To create a trust, the founder must have intended to do so in such a way that he or she is legally bound and must have transferred the trust property to a trustee or a beneficiary and must hand over or be bound to hand over its control to the trustee. The so-called resulting trust of English law or a unilateral declaration of an *inter vivos* trust is therefore not a part of South African law.

The usual ways in which a trust is formed are by will or by contract. As far as a contract is concerned, the creating act is usually a *stipulatio alteri.* This means, mainly, that the benefit of a trust property must be accepted and that the law of contract applies to the revocation of a trust.[137] The trust cannot usually be classified as a donation (except in the case of a 'bewind' trust), but for estate duty and tax purposes, it is treated as such. Because it involves the creation of an office of trusteeship, a trust cannot convincingly be classified simply as a contract subject to certain modalities, such as condition or modus.

B. *Transfer of Trust Property*

91. he transfer of trust property usually takes the form of a transfer of ownership to the trustee. The founder may, however, remain a co-owner of the property in his or her capacity as trustee. In South African law, a trust is also created when the founder transfers the trust assets to the beneficiary but vests the control of those assets in a trustee. This arrangement corresponds to the 'bewind', as it is known, for example, in modern Dutch law. That the trust is, in South African law, a single institution irrespective of the location of the assets has been confirmed in the Trust Property Control Act 57 of 1988.

---

136. E. Cameron et al., *Honoré's South African Law of Trusts* 1 (Juta 2002).
137. *See Potgieter v. Potgieter N O* 2012 1 SA 637 (SCA) para. 18, 29.

C. A Trust Is Not a Legal Person

92. It has often been stated that a trust in South Africa is not a legal person, and that consequently the ownership of trust assets cannot be vested in the trust as such.[138] The trust is therefore not analogous to the foundation, or *stigting*. While it is true that at this stage of the development of the trust, it does not have a juristic personality, many rules and practices (e.g., the method of registration of trust assets, taxation practices, and the rules referred to below) point in the direction of construing such a personality. For now, it is, however, probably correct in terms of the positive law to describe a trust as 'a separate aggregate of assets and liabilities'.[139]

D. Separation of the Trust Estate

93. In practice, the most important consequences of the separation of a trust estate are the following:

- upon insolvency of the trustee, the trust assets do not form part of his or her personal estate, except insofar as he or she is entitled to it as a trust-beneficiary; and
- creditors of the trust may only look to the trust assets for fulfilment of their claims and not to the personal estate of the trustee – the trustee is cited in his or her capacity as trustee. This position differs from that in England and probably makes a trust in South Africa a more desirable vehicle to conduct a business, although there are obvious disadvantages for creditors that might have to be addressed in the future;

In recent years, in practice, the 'business trust' and the 'family trust' have become popular. Concomitant with this, however, it has increasingly occurred that the founder, for all practical purposes, and resulting from the flexibility of the trust instrument, has treated the trust assets as his or her own. This has led to a number of court decisions that have warned that the enjoyment and control of trust assets should be functionally separate,[140] and that regard will be given to the de facto situation, even if the trust deed on the face of it appears to require this.[141]

---

138. *See*, for example, *Commissioner for Inland Revenue v. MacNeillie's Estate* 1961 3 SA 833 (A); *Kohlberg v. Burnett* 1986 3 SA 12 (A); *Land and Agricultural Bank of South Africa v. Parker* 2005 (2) SA 77 (SCA)
139. *See* E. Cameron et al., *Honoré's South African Law of Trusts* 9–10 (Juta 2002).
140. *See*, for example, *Land and Agricultural Bank of South Africa v. Parker* 2005 2 SA 77 (SCA), in which it was warned that non-compliance with this principle could lead to invalidity of the trust and claims for breach of trust against the trustees. In cases in which the trustees were all beneficiaries and related to each other, the court recommended that the Master of the High Court should insist on the appointment of an independent outsider as trustee as a requirement for registration of the trust in terms of the Trust Property Control Act. (In practice, now the Master in all cases requires at least three trustees, of which one should be independent.) *See also Raath v. Nel* 2012 5 SA 273 (SCA) paras 13 & 14 where the separate identity of a family trust was emphasized. In *Van Zyl and Another NNO v. Kaye NO and Others* 2014 4 SA 452 (WCC) the court recognized that where a trustee had abused the trust form by using the trust as his alter ego (and did not keep the trust assets functionally separate from his own) an equitable remedy for an affected third party

E. Office of Trustee

94. A trustee, as a holder of an office, is subject to a fiduciary obligation to manage the trust in accordance with the terms in which the trust was created and is also subject to public control in this regard. The main civil remedy against the trustee for a breach of trust is a delictual remedy. When a trust has been created by contract, it might be argued that a contractual remedy for a breach of contract will be available. It is highly doubtful that this will be the case, however, since a trust is not a contract but might merely have been created by one. In any event, a choice of actions will most probably not be allowed.

§8. Good Faith and Fair Dealing

I. The Development of a General Doctrine of Good Faith in South African Common Law: Ubuntu

95. As far as South African common law is concerned,[142] the concept of good faith[143] (or any equivalent) has not yet been recognized or developed to the extent that it can be said to be an all-pervasive, objective, and directly enforceable norm or general rule relating to all aspects of obligations, or, in particular, to all phases and aspects of contracts, particularly that of the enforcement of contractual terms. Very recently however the Constitutional Court and other courts have paved the way for the future acceptance of a general principle of good faith (and the related concept of ubuntu[144]) to be concretized in specific instances in order to ameliorate the consequences of an application of the current rules of law.[145]

---

existed allowing the court to go behind the trust form and hold the trustee personally liable for an obligation ostensibly undertaken as trustee. *In casu*, however, the applicants had failed to prove such abuse. *See also REM v. VM* 2017 3 SA 371 (SCA) paras 19–20, where it was emphasised that the 'piercing of the trust veneer' would only be allowed in clear circumstances of unconscionable abuse by a trustee.

141. *See Badenhorst v. Badenhorst* 2006 2 SA 255 (SCA).

142. *See* in general *Ubuntu Good Faith & Equity: Flexible Legal Principles in Developing a Contemporary Jurisprudence* (F. Diedrich ed. Juta 2011).

143. There seems to be a general consensus that good faith in contracts in South African law would require that one party show a minimum respect for the interests of the other – in practical terms, this means that one party may not over-protect his or her own interests at the unreasonable expense of the other – *see* Van Huyssteen, Lubbe & Reinecke, *Contract General Principles* ch. 9 I (Juta 2016).

144. This value has been described in *Everfresh Market Virginia (Pty) Ltd v. Shoprite Checkers (Pty) Ltd* 2012 1 SA 256 (CC) para. 72 as follows: 'It emphasises the communal nature of society … "carries in it the ideas of humaneness, social justice and fairness" and envelopes "the key values of group solidarity, compassion, respect, human dignity, conformity to basic norms and collective unity."' *See Combined Developers v. Arun Holdings and Others* 2015 3 SA 215 (WCC); *Botha and Another v. Rich NO and Others* 2014 4 SA 124 (CC) para. 46: 'Bilateral contracts are almost invariably cooperative ventures where two parties have reached a deal involving performances by each in order to benefit both. Honouring that contract cannot therefore be a matter of each side pursuing his or her own self-interest without regard to the other party's interests. Good faith is the lens through which we come to understand contracts in that way.' *Paulsen and Another v. Slip Knot*

The Supreme Court of Appeal has on occasion stated that the South African legal system is an equitable one, and that contracts are *iudicia bonae fidei*. The recognition of the *exceptio doli generalis* of Roman law as a part of South African law, which seemed probable at one stage, could, of course, also have provided the stimulus for the development of a doctrine of good faith. In 1988, however, the Appeal Court expressly denied that the *exceptio doli generalis* had been received in Roman-Dutch law, or that it had ever formed part of modern South African law.[146] This decision has been criticized as being too technical and restrictively historical-analytical, instead of taking into consideration the values underlying the Roman remedy and applying them so as to reach an equitable result.[147] However, the decision must be accepted as a decisive statement of positive law.[148] The doctrine of *laesio enormis* (as an expression of the idea of a reasonable balance between performance and counter-performance), which formed a part of South African law until it was finally abolished by statute in 1952, might also have stimulated the development of a doctrine of good faith.

Nevertheless, good faith has been referred to in various cases from time to time as a basis on which enforcement of a contract could be refused. The most notable decision was a minority judgment in *Eerste Nasionale Bank van Suidelike Afrika*

Investments 777 (Pty) Ltd 2015 3 SA 479 (CC) paras 71, 72, 113–119. Cf. also *Barkhuizen v. Napier* 2007 5 SA 323 (CC); *S v. Makwanyane* 1995 3 SA 391 (CC);

145. *See Everfresh Market Virginia (Pty) Ltd v. Shoprite Checkers (Pty) Ltd* 2012 1 SA 256 (CC) para. 72; Van Huyssteen, Lubbe & Reinecke, *Contract General Principles*, para. 9.264–272 (Juta 2016); cf. *Silent Pond Investments CC v. Woolworths (Pty) Ltd* .2011 6 SA 343 (D). Cf. also *Indwe Aviation (Pty) Ltd v. Petroleum Oil and Gas Corporation of South Africa (Pty) Ltd (No 1)* 2012 6 SA 96(WCC) paras 27, 28 where the court uses the concept of the *arbitrio boni viri* to import considerations of reasonableness, good faith and honesty into a duty to negotiate; *Combined Developers v. Arun Holdings and Others* 2015 3 SA 215 (WCC); *Botha and Another v. Rich NO and Others* 2014 4 SA 124 (CC); *Paulsen and Another v. Slip Knot Investments 777 (Pty) Ltd* 2015 3 SA 479 (CC) paras. 71, 72, 113,119; *W v. H* 2017 1 SA 196 (WCC) (unilateral waiver of right to claim maintenance unenforceable); *Bondev Midrand (Pty) Ltd v. Madzhie and Others* 2017 4 SA 166 (GP) (repurchase clause grossly unfair and infringing the right to housing); *Beadica 231 CC and Others v. Trustees, Oregon Unit Trust and Others* 2018 1 SA 549 (WCC) (enforcing of cancellation and eviction clauses in lease disproportionate and against public policy in the particular circumstances); *Four Wheel Drive Accessory Distribution CC v. Rattan NO* 2018 3 SA 204 (KZD) (terms in standard contract too small to read and unenforceable against public policy). *See also* below.
146. *See Bank of Lisbon & South Africa Ltd v. De Ornelas* 1988 3 SA 580 (A).
147. *See*, for example, S. van der Merwe, G.F. Lubbe & L.F. van Huyssteen, *The Exceptio Doli Generalis: Requiescat in Pace: Vivat Aequitas*, S. African L. J. 235 (1989); cf. also the minority judgment in the *Bank of Lisbon & South Africa Ltd v. De Ornelas* 1988 3 SA 580 (A) 612–617. In *Crown CC v. Gold Reef City Theme Park (Pty) Ltd* 2008 4 SA 16 (CC), it was argued that the *exceptio doli generalis* should be re-introduced as part of South African law since it accorded with the requirements of the Constitution. The Constitutional Court declined to deal with this argument since it was irregularly raised for the first time in that Court.
148. This was confirmed by the Supreme Court of Appeal in *Bredenkamp v. Standard Bank of South Africa Ltd* 2010 4 SA 468 (SCA).

Bpk v. Saayman NO,[149] in which a general role for good faith as a basis for interfering in contractual relations was espoused. This judgment was subsequently applied as persuasive authority, with reference also to the application of the Constitution, in a number of cases.[150]

More recently, however, the Supreme Court of Appeal delivered a number of judgments in which it spelled out its views on the role of good faith in contracts.[151] Good faith, it was held, being an abstract concept, forms the basis and reason for the existence of legal rules (and can also lead to the formation of new rules and the changing of existing ones), but it is itself not a rule of law.[152] Thus, good faith cannot (yet) be applied by a court as the general basis to set a contract aside or to refuse its full performance.[153] In practice, and for the time being at least, it seems that the requirement of legality, which entails that a contract may not offend against public policy (or the public interest), will mostly be applied and adapted to give effect to the values of reasonableness and fairness,[154] as well as the requirements of the

149. 1997 4 SA 302 (HHA) 318 et seq. per Olivier JA.

150. E.g., *Combined Developers v. Arun Holdings and Others* 2015 3 SA 215 (WCC).

151. *Brisley v. Drotsky* 2002 4 SA 1 (HHA) 12–19; *Afrox Healthcare Bpk v. Strydom* 2002 6 SA 21 (HHA) 40–41; *Bredenkamp v. Standard Bank of South Africa Ltd* 2010 4 SA 468 (SCA); cf. *African Dawn Property Finance 2 (Pty) Ltd v. Dreams Travel and Tours CC* 2011 3 SA 511 (SCA); *Potgieter v. Potgieter NO* 2012 1 SA 637 (SCA) para. 32.

152. It is interesting to note that the Court in *Nedcor Bank Ltd v. SDR Investment Holdings Co. (Pty) Ltd* 2008 3 SA 544 (SCA) called good faith a 'principle' in the context of inferring a tacit term. However, one cannot take this any further.

153. *See Mohamed's Leisure Holdings (Pty) Ltd v. Southern Sun Hotel Interests (Pty) Ltd* 2018 2 SA 314 (SCA) where the appeal court overturned the decision of the high court (based on public policy and ubuntu) and decided that the circumstances did not warrant a departure from *pacta servanda sunt*, consequently enforcing a cancellation and eviction clause in a lease. The appeal court in *Roazar CC v. The Falls Supermarket CC* 2018 3 SA 76 (SCA) refused in the particular circumstances (the requirement of certainty and absence of a deadlock-breaking mechanism) to develop the common law to import a term to compel parties to negotiate a renewal of a lease in good faith: '*It is difficult to conceive how a court, in a purely business transaction, can rely on "ubuntu" to import a term that was not intended by the parties, to deny the other party a right to rely on the terms of the contract to terminate it*' *(para 24)*.

154. In recent years this requirement was given content by the Appeal Court by applying the notion that an agreement may be so unreasonably protective of the interests of one party to the detriment of the other that the particular term or even the whole agreement will be considered to be illegal because it offends the public interest. *See Sasfin (Pty) Ltd v. Beukes* 1989 1 SA 1 (A). The case concerned a cession agreed to by a medical practitioner to secure a loan from a financial enterprise. Seen as a whole, the contract had the effect of subjecting the borrower to the lender to the extent that the borrower could not freely exercise his profession and was reduced to the position of a 'slave' of the lender. In *Ex Parte Minister of Justice: In Re Nedbank Ltd v. Abstein Distributors (Pty) Ltd & Donelly v. Barclays National Bank Ltd* 1995 3 SA 1 (A), the Appeal Court interpreted the *Sasfin* case as having decided, in connection with a so-called conclusive proof clause in a certificate of balance clause, that when, in terms of the clause, the creditor was to be the author of the certificate of balance, such clause was, in any agreement and regardless of the context of the agreement, *contra bonos mores* and thus void. The Court did not employ the concept of good faith as such, but made use of the notion of 'simple justice between man and man', probably because the latter notion had been applied previously by the Appeal Court in the context of illegality. *See*, for example, *Jajbhay v. Cassim* 1939 AD 537. This case concerned the application of the *par delictum* rule in connection with a claim for the return of performance made pursuant to an illegal agreement.

Constitution, in the law of contract.[155, 156] In this context, good faith and ubuntu may well contribute significantly towards giving concrete content to the concept of the public interest, and may in due course be accepted as a substantive enforceable principle giving rise to the development of specific rules of the law of contract.[157]

All told, South African law places a high premium on freedom of contract and the principle of *pacta sunt servanda*, but at once, as it always has, recognizes its limits and the need to control its excessive, oppressive and unfair use. Freedom of contract, shorn of its excesses, is considered to be a reflection of the broader constitutional values of freedom, dignity, and equality.

II. 'Subjective' Good Faith: Doctrine of Notice

96. The concept of so-called subjective good faith, as it is known in some continental legal systems, is reflected in South African law by the doctrine of notice. An example of the application of the doctrine relevant to contracts is a case in which

155. Here the constitutional values of human dignity and equality are of importance. Cf. *Brisley v. Drotsky* 2002 4 SA 1 (HHA) 18, at 34–36; *Afrox Healthcare Bpk v. Strydom* 2002 6 SA 21 (HHA) 40–41; this approach was again applied in *Napier v. Barkhuizen* 2006 4 SA 1 (SCA), in which it was emphasized that when the value of autonomy is weighed against those of dignity and equality, the excesses of contractual freedom may well be struck down. Inequality of bargaining power is an example of a situation in which the court may find an agreement to be illegal and thus unenforceable. *See also Barkhuizen v. Napier* 2007 5 SA 323 (CC) 341–342; *Bredenkamp v. Standard Bank of South Africa Ltd* 2010 4 SA 468 (SCA) para. 38; *Uniting Reformed Church, De Doorns v. President of the Republic of South Africa and Others* 2013 5 SA 205 (WCC); *Botha and Another v. Rich NO and Others* 2014 4 SA 124 (CC); *Paulsen and Another v. Slip Knot Investments 777 (Pty) Ltd* 2015 3 SA 479 (CC).

156. Where parties to a contract agree to observe the utmost good faith, that requirement applies to the overall implementation of the contract and the conduct of the parties, and will be enforced as such to the extent that one party is not entitled to advance its own interests at the expense of the other – *see Silent Pond Investments CC v. Woolworths (Pty) Ltd* .2011 6 SA 343 (D).This approach was taken even further, albeit in an obiter dictum in *Everfresh Market Virginia (Pty) Ltd v. Shoprite Checkers (Pty) Ltd* 2012 1 SA 256 (CC) para. 72 to the effect that where there 'is a contractual obligation to negotiate, it would be hardly imaginable that our constitutional values would not require that the negotiation must be done reasonably, with a view to reaching an agreement and in good faith.' Cf. also *Indwe Aviation (Pty) Ltd v. Petroleum Oil and Gas Corporation of South Africa (Pty) Ltd (No 1)* 2012 6 SA 96(WCC) paras 27, 28; *Makate v. Vodacom Ltd* 2016 4 SA 121 (CC): oral agreement to negotiate in good faith may be enforceable; but in *Roazar CC v. The Falls Supermarket CC* 2018 3 SA 76 (SCA) the appeal court refused in the particular circumstances (the requirement of certainty and absence of a deadlock-breaking mechanism) to develop the common law to import a term to compel parties to negotiate a renewal of a lease in good faith: '*t is difficult to conceive how a court, in a purely business transaction, can rely on "ubuntu" to import a term that was not intended by the parties, to deny the other party a right to rely on the terms of the contract to terminate it" (para 24).*

157. *See* Van Huyssteen, Lubbe & Reinecke, *Contract General Principles*, para. 1.50, ch. 3, 9 I, 10.14, 10.92 et seq., 11.52 and 11.181. (Juta 2016).

an acquirer of property who knows[158] that the property is the subject matter of a prior sale is, in terms of the doctrine, obliged to re-transfer the property upon a claim by the prior purchaser.[159]

III. Rescission and Good Faith

97. Although the courts have, on a few occasions, mostly indirectly, referred to good faith in the context of the rescission of contracts,[160] it is doubtful whether that concept as such will develop significantly or be expressly recognized as being the norm against which conduct that justifies rescission should be measured.[161]

The type of conduct that is presently recognized as grounds for rescission is construed either as a wrongful act or as a delict, where the elements of wrongfulness (or the *boni mores*) and fault are crucial, such as fraud and duress or as conduct transgressing the bounds of what is *proper* in the circumstances, such as misrepresentation without fault (so-called innocent misrepresentation, undue influence[162] and other cases that cannot be classified as falling within the grounds already mentioned, for example, bribery.[163]

Any future development of general grounds for rescission of contracts will, in all probability, take place along these lines and not with reference to good faith. Such a development should not be limited to the elements of a delict in the strict sense. Factors that could be considered as justifying rescission might indeed be the recognized elements of a delict; they may, however, include factors more appropriate to a contractual setting, such as abuse or improper exploitation of circumstances, harm in the wide sense, or an intention to gain an unreasonable advantage or to induce the other party to contract.[164] All these factors are now often dealt with in

158. Or perhaps it suffices if he foresaw the possibility of the prior sale: *see Meridian Bay Restaurant (Pty) Ltd and Others v. Mitchell NO* 2011 4 SA 1 (SCA), paras 17–18.
159. *See Meridian Bay Restaurant (Pty) Ltd and Others v. Mitchell NO* 2011 4 SA 1 (SCA).
160. Cf., for example, *Meskin v. Anglo-American Corporation of SA Ltd* 1968 4 SA 793 (W); *Tuckers Land & Development Corporation (Pty) Ltd v. Hovis* 1980 1 SA 645 (A); *Mutual & Federal Insurance Co. Ltd v. Oudtshoorn Municipality* 1985 1 SA 419 (A); *Bank of Lisbon & South Africa Ltd v. De Ornelas* 1988 3 SA 580 (A).
161. *See BOE Bank Bpk v. Van Zyl* 2002 5 SA 165 (C) 182–184; *Brisley v. Drotsky* 2002 4 SA 1 (HHA) 12–19; *Afrox Healthcare Bpk v. Strydom* 2002 6 SA 21 (HHA) 40–41.
162. *See* Van Huyssteen, Lubbe & Reinecke, *Contract General Principles* ch. 4 D & E (Juta 2016); *Gerolomou Constructions (Pty) Ltd v. Van Wyk* 20111 4 SA 500 (GNP).
163. *See Plaaslike Boeredienste (Edms) Bpk v. Chemfos Bpk* 1986 1 SA 819 (A); *Extel Industrial (Pty) Ltd v. Crown Mills (Pty) Ltd* 1999 2 SA 719 (SCA).
164. *See* further below and Van Huyssteen, Lubbe & Reinecke, *Contract General Principles* ch. 4 A & E (Juta 2016). Cf. now also ss 48 and 40 of the Consumer Protection Act 68 of 2008, which prohibit the use of manifestly unfair, unreasonable, or unjust terms (excessively one-sided or inequitable) in certain contracts, and unconscionable conduct (which includes coercion, undue influence, pressure, duress, and unfair tactics) in the negotiation, conclusion, execution, or enforcement thereof. It can be expected that the application of these provisions will result in an extension of common law.

terms of the concept of improperly obtained consensus.[165] In this regard, the probable development of South African common law would be similar to the development that has taken place in Dutch law, particularly with respect to abuse of circumstances.

IV. No Duty to Negotiate in Good Faith

98. It is quite possible that the courts may now recognize or further develop a duty *in contrahendo* to negotiate or to continue negotiating in good faith or to have regard in general to the reasonable expectations of the other party, particularly where the parties have specifically agreed to do so, or even where there is an agreement to negotiate in future, for example regarding the renewal of a lease.[166] Insofar as good faith may require a party who has created the reasonable impression that a contract exists to keep to the terms of what appears to be a contract, but where there is in fact no consensus, South African law will protect the other party by accepting his or her reasonable reliance on consensus as an adequate basis for the creation of a contract. This development has, however, not taken place with reference to good faith. It has, rather, occurred with reference to reasonable reliance or expectation, previously mainly in the context of the concept of *iustus error* or quasi-mutual assent (cf. the English case of *Smith v. Hughes*,[167] and the doctrine of estoppel by representation). It is also now very probable that South African law may accept delictual liability upon a wrongful termination (breaking off of negotiations or withdrawal of an offer) of pre-contractual negotiations.[168]

165. *See*, e.g., Van Huyssteen, Lubbe & Reinecke, *Contract General Principles* ch. 4 (Juta 2016); Hutchison & Pretorius (eds) *The Law of Contract in South Africa* ch 4, 4.6 (OUP 2017).

166. *See* Van Huyssteen, Lubbe & Reinecke, *Contract General Principles ch. 3 D* (Juta 2016). *See Silent Pond Investments CC v. Woolworths (Pty) Ltd* .2011 6 SA 343 (D), *Everfresh Market Virginia (Pty) Ltd v. Shoprite Checkers (Pty) Ltd* 2012 1 SA 256 (CC) para. 72. Cf. *Indwe Aviation (Pty) Ltd v. Petroleum Oil and Gas Corporation of South Africa (Pty) Ltd (No1)* 2012 6 SA 96 (WCC) paras 27, 28 (preliminary agreement to negotiate further); *Makate v. Vodacom Ltd* 2016 4 SA 121 (CC): oral agreement to negotiate in good faith may be enforceable if it provides a deadlock-breaking mechanism. In *Roazar CC v. The Falls Supermarket CC* 2018 3 SA 76 (SCA) the appeal court refused in the particular circumstances (the requirement of certainty and absence of a deadlock-breaking mechanism) to develop the common law to import a term to compel parties to negotiate a renewal of a lease in good faith: *It is difficult to conceive how a court, in a purely business transaction, can rely on "ubuntu" to import a term that was not intended by the parties, to deny the other party a right to rely on the terms of the contract to terminate it" (para 24)*. For the position regarding administrative contracts – *see* paras 630 et seq. below and Van Huyssteen, Lubbe & Reinecke, *Contract General Principles*, para. 3.65 et seq. (Juta 2016).

167. (1871) LR 6 QB 597.

168. *See* Van Huyssteen, Lubbe & Reinecke, *Contract General Principles*, para. 3.62 et seq. particularly para. 3.65 (Juta 2016).

V. Good Faith with Respect to Content, Execution, and Enforcement of a Contract

99. As set out above,[169] the main principle that is applied in South African law with respect to the content, execution, and enforcement of contracts is that the agreement must not offend against public policy or the public interest. However, good faith, being a value and principle consonant with the Constitution, may very well influence the content of public policy. It may also lead to the creation of new rules regarding the enforcement of contracts in cases of a duty to negotiate in specific circumstances, changed circumstances, the exercise of contractual discretions, enforcement of terms that would lead to gross unfairness and injustice, the enforcement of the principle of reciprocity and breach of contract.

A. Interpretation

100. Although the courts have not directly employed the concept of good faith with respect to the interpretation of contracts,[170] it may be tentatively stated that its application could well influence the extent to which effect is given to the ordinary meaning of the words used by the contractants. When the words of a contract are ambiguous, a court will lean towards an interpretation that is equitable in the sense that one party will not be given an unreasonable advantage over the other.[171]

B. Supplementing Function

101. An example in South African law of the judicial acceptance of the supplementing operation (*aanvullende werking*) of good faith is to be found in the recognition of a so-called duty placed on a contractant not to commit an anticipatory breach of contract in the form of repudiation.[172] The conduct that allegedly amounts to repudiation must, objectively seen, lead a reasonable person in the position of the other contractant to believe that the contract will not be performed – in other words, that his or her reasonable expectations will not be met. Further examples are the creation of a duty to negotiate in specific circumstances and the exercise of contractual

169. Paragraph 97.
170. In regard to the use of the process of interpretation to prohibit the enforcement of a term in the contract for a purpose for which it was not really intended, *see* C. Lewis, *The Demise of the Exceptio Doli: Is There Another Route to Contractual Equity*?, S. African L. J. 60, 26 (1990).
171. Cf. *Van der Westhuizen v. Arnold* 2002 6 SA 453 (SCA) 469; *South African Forestry Co Ltd v. York Timbers Ltd* 2005 3 SA 323 341 B-E; Van Huyssteen, Lubbe & Reinecke, *Contract General Principles para.* 9.217 and ch. 9 I.
172. *See Tuckers Land & Development Corporation (Pty) Ltd v. Hovis* 1980 1 SA 645 (A). For criticism of this construction, *see* Van Huyssteen, Lubbe & Reinecke, *Contract General Principles* para. 10.106 et seq. (Juta 2016).

discretions as set out above; as well as the role of good faith in the enforcement of the principle of reciprocity and the classification of conduct as breach of contract.[173]

C. Derogating Function: Illegality

102. As set out above, there are some examples of the application of good faith as it operates to detract or derogate (*derogerende werking*) from the terms of a contract as they have been agreed upon. However, as has also been explained, good faith may well play an important role in the process of giving content to the requirement that an agreement may not offend against the public interest or public policy and may well become a substantive principle.[174]

D. Changed Circumstances

103. With regard to the effect of changed circumstances on the execution and enforcement of contracts, the present state of the law is that, unless the circumstances amount to objective impossibility of performance (which is determined with reference to a standard of commercial reasonableness), the contract will in principle be enforced fully.[175] To some extent, the *exceptio doli generalis* found application in this context during its 'illegitimate' lifespan. The Court would refuse to enforce a term when its enforcement would amount to 'unconscionable conduct' and would result in 'some great inequity'[176] (which was the generally accepted test for the granting of the defence). A typical example was a case in which a widely drafted term was sought to be enforced with respect to circumstances that arose after the conclusion of the contract and that were not contemplated by the parties at the time of such conclusion.[177]

Some academic commentators suggest that good faith is an appropriate norm to apply so as to determine which party should bear the risk of changed circumstances. The court may then give consideration to factors such as which party is the better risk bearer in terms of an economic analysis, the reasonable expectations of the parties, and the social circumstances against the background of which the agreement between the parties must be considered.[178]

---

173. Van Huyssteen, Lubbe & Reinecke, *Contract General Principles* ch. 10 A, and para. 11.52 (Juta 2016).
174. Paragraph 98.
175. *See*, however, now s. 40 of the Consumer Protection Act 68 of 2008, which prohibits unconscionable conduct also in the enforcement of an agreement to supply goods or services.
176. *See Zuurbekom Ltd v. Union Corporation Ltd* 1947 1 SA 514 (A) 537.
177. *See*, for example, *Paddock Motors (Pty) Ltd v. Igesund* 1976 3 SA 16 (A); *Rand Bank Ltd v. Rubinstein* 1981 2 SA 207 (W). The facts of some of the cases referred to in para 27 & 98 border on a change of circumstances.
178. *See* L.F. van Huyssteen & S. van der Merwe, *Good Faith in Contract: Proper Behaviour Amidst Changing Circumstances*, Stellenbosch L. Rev. 244 (1990); Van Huyssteen, Lubbe & Reinecke, *Contract General Principles* paras 13.62–13.68 (Juta 2016).

E. Rechtsverwerking (Limitation of Enforcement of Rights) and Estoppel by Representation

104. In some civil law systems, the doctrine of *rechtsverwerking* is related to the operation of the requirement of good faith[179] so as to prevent a contractant from exercising his or her contractual 'good right' in certain circumstances. In this respect, the doctrine of estoppel by representation fulfils much the same function in South African law. Briefly stated, when a contractant has, by his or her conduct or silence, created a reasonable impression in the mind of the other party that he or she will in future not exercise a contractual right, and the other party acts on that belief to his or her detriment, the first party will be prevented from exercising that right.[180] Although the courts often state that the representation must be one of fact, it appears that any representation that is of such a nature that, in law, it is regarded as being unreasonably misleading, will suffice as grounds for an estoppel, provided that the other elements of estoppel are also present. Concerning the vexing question of whether prejudice is required and in what form, it seems reasonably clear that the courts presently require proof that some form of probable (future) patrimonial prejudice will result if the estoppel is not granted. Fault on the part of the representor is no longer a general requirement for the operation of estoppel.

F. Future Development

105. Since the Supreme Court of Appeal judgments in *Brisley v. Drotsky* 2002 4 SA 1 (HHA), *Afrox Healthcare Bpk v. Strydom* 2002 6 SA 21 (HHA), *Napier v. Barkhuizen* 2006 4 SA 1 (SCA), and the Constitutional Court judgment in *Barkhuizen v. Napier* 2007 5 SA 323 (CC) referred to above, from which it appeared that good faith would probably not be directly applied as a rule or remedy in the field of contracts,[181] there have been further developments. It now appears that good faith is accepted as a principle (rather than a free-floating value) consonant with public policy and the Constitution creating new legal rules, determining the application of, and extending existing ones. This would apply particularly to the requirement of legality, the duty to negotiate in good faith, the exercise of contractual discretions, the enforcement of contractual terms, reciprocity and the determination of breach of contract.[182]

---

179. Cf. the judgment of the Hooge Raad of The Netherlands, 7 Jun. 1991, N. J. 1991 no. 708.

180. A typical example of this kind of operation of the doctrine of estoppel in South Africa is to be found when a lessor of property is prevented from exercising a cancellation and ejectment clause in a lease (*see*, for example, *Whitfield v. Phillips* 1957 3 SA 318 (A).

181. *See also Potgieter v. Potgieter NO* 2012 1 SA 637 (SCA) para. 32.
Good faith was not raised by the parties or discussed as an issue in *Bredenkamp v. Standard Bank of South Africa Ltd* 2010 4 SA 468 (SCA).

182. *Everfresh Market Virginia (Pty) Ltd v. Shoprite Checkers (Pty) Ltd* 2012 1 SA 256 (CC); *Uniting Reformed Church, De Doorns v. President of the Republic of South Africa and Others* 2013 5 SA 205 (WCC); *Combined Developers v. Arun Holdings and Others* 2015 3 SA 215 (WCC); *Botha and Another v. Rich NO and Others* 2014 4 SA 124 (CC) paras 45–46; *Paulsen and Another v. Slip Knot Investments 777 (Pty) Ltd* 2015 3 SA 479 (CC) paras 71, 72 113–119; *Makate v. Vodacom Ltd*

This trend accords in broad terms with the history of the development of good faith in some comparable legal systems. As has been pointed out, the Bill of Rights and the values of the Constitution will certainly further influence this development, as will, on a more indirect level, the provisions of the Consumer Protection Act of 2008.

VI. Direct Legislation

106. There is as yet no legislation that generally requires adherence to the norm of good faith or any other similar norm. Certain specific statutes do, in effect, require it, in particular, labour legislation by way of the concept of unfair labour practices.

Previously, the South African Law Commission[183] had submitted to the government draft legislation with regard to the introduction of fairness and reasonableness[184] as general principles in the law of contract, alongside that of *pacta sunt servanda.*

Apart from the usual criticism that the introduction of such general norms would undermine contractual certainty, it was also argued that legislation should rather be specifically aimed at protecting the consumer as such, preferably as part of wide-ranging measures covering all aspects of consumer protection. The resultant Consumer Protection Act 68 of 2008[185] aims to do just that. It identifies nine fundamental consumer rights, including the right to fair and honest dealing and the right to fair, just, and reasonable terms. Accordingly, unconscionable conduct (section 40) and unfair terms (section 48) are prohibited. The Act applies to all consumer transactions for the supply of goods and services in the ordinary course of a supplier's business, that is, where continual marketing takes place. Thus, for example, the Act will not apply to one-time transactions between natural persons. However, it is reasonably certain that it will lead to a wider application in common law of the grounds for rescission of a contract, illegality, and the enforcement of contracts, particularly when there are changed circumstances.[186]

2016 4 SA 121 (CC). *W v. H* 2017 1 SA 196 (WCC); *Bondev Midrand (Pty) Ltd v. Madzhie and Others* 2017 4 SA 166 (GP); *Four Wheel Drive Accessory Distribution CC v. Rattan NO* 2018 3 SA 204 (KZD); *Beadica 231 CC and Others v. Trustees, Oregon Unit Trust and Others* 2018 1 SA 549 (WCC). But in *Roazar CC v. The Falls Supermarket CC* 2018 3 SA 76 (SCA) the court declined to import a duty to negotiate in good faith in the circumstances; and in *Mohamed's Leisure Holdings (Pty) Ltd v. Southern Sun Hotel Interests (Pty) Ltd* 2018 2 SA 314 (SCA) the court declined in the particular circumstances not to enforce a term on the basis of public policy.

183. Project 47: Unfair contract terms and the rectification of contracts.

184. The choice of these terms rather than 'good faith' rested on the dubious grounds that they were more in accordance with South African legal heritage and conceptualization. However, in content and meaning, there is no difference. (Cf. the similar situation in The Netherlands.)

185. The Act came into operation in general on 29 Oct. 2010.

186. For an excellent discussion of the Consumer Protection Act often from a comparative perspective, *see* the looseleaf work of Naude & Eiselen (eds) *Commentary on the Consumer Protection Act* (Original service 2014 Juta).

§9. EFFECT OF THE CONSTITUTION ON LAW OF CONTRACT

I. Effect of the Bill of Rights on Private Law

107. Since the introduction of the (final) Constitution Act 108 of 1996, the questions raised by the interim Constitution regarding the application of the Bill of Rights to private law have largely been laid to rest. In general, the Bill of Rights applies to all law and binds the judiciary. It also binds natural and juristic persons (as well as, obviously, the state) to the extent that it is applicable.[187] In addition, the courts have a duty to promote the spirit, purport, and objects of the Bill of Rights when developing common law or customary law.[188]

108. In the context of the law of contract,[189] too, it is now clear that any relevant fundamental right that is protected in the Bill of Rights may apply horizontally when a court considers the legality and enforcement of a contractual right in a case between private persons.[190]

109. The duty of the courts to promote the values of the Bill of Rights when developing common law[191] is also of paramount importance to the law of contract.

---

187. Section 8.

188. Section 39. This application of the Bill of Rights is sometimes referred to as indirect horizontal application.

189. *See* Van Huyssteen, Lubbe & Reinecke, *Contract General Principles* paras 1.43–1.59 et seq. (Juta 2016).

190. *See Brisley v. Drotsky* 2002 4 SA 1 (HHA) 19–22, at 31–33 & 33–36. In this case, the Supreme Court of Appeal had to consider the application of s. 26(3) of the Constitution, which prohibits evictions from dwellings without an order of a court. Cf. also *Afrox Healthcare Bpk v. Strydom* 2002 6 SA 21 (HHA), in which the constitutional right of access to health care (s. 27(1)(a) of the Constitution) was considered in the context of an exclusion clause in a private hospital admission contract. *See also Napier v. Barkhuizen* 2006 4 SA 1 (SCA) and *Barkhuizen v. Napier* 2007 5 SA 323 (CC), in which the public policy requirements and the constitutionality of a time-bar clause in an insurance contract were considered. In this context, the rights to dignity, equality, and self-determination were at issue. *See* further *Bredenkamp v. Standard Bank of South Africa Ltd* 2010 4 SA 468 (SCA);*Uniting Reformed Church, De Doorns v. President of the Republic of South Africa and Others* 2013 5 SA 205 (WCC). Cf. *Reddy v. Siemens Telecommunications (Pty) Ltd* 2007 2 SA 486 (SCA) regarding restraints of trade; *Everfresh Market Virginia (Pty) Ltd v. Shoprite Checkers (Pty) Ltd* 2012 1 SA 256 (CC); *Combined Developers v. Arun Holdings and Others* 2015 3 SA 215 (WCC); *Botha and Another v. Rich NO and Others* 2014 4 SA 124 (CC) paras 45–46; *Paulsen and Another v. Slip Knot Investments 777 (Pty) Ltd* 2015 3 SA 479 (CC) paras 71, 72, 113–119; *Makate v. Vodacom Ltd* 2016 4 SA 121 (CC); *W v. H* 2017 1 SA 196 (WCC); *Bondev Midrand (Pty) Ltd v. Madzhie and Others* 2017 4 SA 166 (GP); *Four Wheel Drive Accessory Distribution CC v. Rattan NO* 2018 3 SA 204 (KZD); *Beadica 231 CC and Others v. Trustees, Oregon Unit Trust and Others* 2018 1 SA 549 (WCC). But in *Roazar CC v. The Falls Supermarket CC* 2018 3 SA 76 (SCA) the court declined to import a duty to negotiate in good faith in the circumstances; and in *Mohamed's Leisure Holdings (Pty) Ltd v. Southern Sun Hotel Interests (Pty) Ltd* 2018 2 SA 314 (SCA) the court declined in the particular circumstances not to enforce a term on the basis of public policy.

191. In *Carmichele v. Minister of Safety and Security (Centre for Applied legal Studies Intervening)* 2001 4 SA 938 (CC) (a case concerning delictual liability), the Constitutional Court set out the practical application of this duty: the first stage of the enquiry the court must make is to reconsider common law in light of the Constitution; if this indicates a need for development, the question then

It has been emphasized by the Supreme Court of Appeal that this duty does not entail free judicial discretion to change the law, but rather entails discretion to adapt the law when necessary in light of constitutional values, of which freedom of contract and the principle of *pacta sunt servanda* are important components. However, it is also clear that this freedom may not lead to excessive contractual oppression and unreasonableness, or the contravention of other societal values or interests that are judged to be of greater weight in the circumstances.[192]

II. Effect on Law of Contract: Restraint of Trade

110. The effect of the Bill of Rights on the law of contract has directly been brought to issue with regard to the enforceability of contractual restraints of trade. It has been argued that such restraints are contrary to the fundamental right to freely engage in economic activity (section 26 of the interim Constitution and section 22 of the 1996 Constitution), and that this right should be given preference over the principle of freedom of contract, which is not expressly mentioned as a fundamental right. The practical effect of this may, then, at least be that a restraint is invalid unless it is proved to be reasonable and, perhaps, also 'justifiable in an open and democratic society based on freedom and equality',[193] by the party attempting to enforce it.[194]

---

is how such development should take place to meet the requirements of the Constitution. Cf. *Crown CC v. Gold Reef City Theme Park (Pty) Ltd* 2008 4 SA 16 (CC), in which the Constitutional Court emphasized the importance of the role of the High Court and the Supreme Court of Appeal in the development of common law; *Everfresh Market Virginia (Pty) Ltd v. Shoprite Checkers (Pty) Ltd* 2012 1 SA 256 (CC) para. 72; *Paulsen and Another v. Slip Knot Investments 777 (Pty) Ltd* 2015 3 SA 479 (CC) paras 71, 72, 113, 119; *Bondev Midrand (Pty) Ltd v. Madzhie and Others* 2017 4 SA 166 (GP) (socio-economic rights).

192. *See* in general *Brisley v. Drotsky* 2002 4 SA 1 (HHA); *Afrox Healthcare Bpk v. Strydom* 2002 6 SA 21 (HHA); *Napier v. Barkhuizen* 2006 4 SA 1 (SCA); *Barkhuizen v. Napier* 2007 5 SA 323 (CC); *Bredenkamp v. Standard Bank of South Africa Ltd* 2010 4 SA 468 (SCA); *African Dawn Property Finance 2 (Pty) Ltd v. Dreams Travel and Tours CC* 2011 3 SA 511 (SCA); *Everfresh Market Virginia (Pty) Ltd v. Shoprite Checkers (Pty) Ltd* 2012 1 SA 256 (CC) para. 72; *Uniting Reformed Church, De Doorns v. President of the Republic of South Africa and Others* 2013 5 SA 205 (WCC); *Combined Developers v. Arun Holdings and Others* 2015 3 SA 215 (WCC); *Botha and Another v. Rich NO and Others* 2014 4 SA 124 (CC) paras 45–46; *Paulsen and Another v. Slip Knot Investments 777 (Pty) Ltd* 2015 3 SA 479 (CC) paras 71, 72, 113–119; *Makate v. Vodacom Ltd* 2016 4 SA 121 (CC). *W v. H* 2017 1 SA 196 (WCC); *Bondev Midrand (Pty) Ltd v. Madzhie and Others* 2017 4 SA 166 (GP); *Four Wheel Drive Accessory Distribution CC v. Rattan NO* 2018 3 SA 204 (KZD); *Beadica 231 CC and Others v. Trustees, Oregon Unit Trust and Others* 2018 1 SA 549 (WCC). But in *Roazar CC v. The Falls Supermarket CC* 2018 3 SA 76 (SCA) the court declined to import a duty to negotiate in good faith in the circumstances; and in *Mohamed's Leisure Holdings (Pty) Ltd v. Southern Sun Hotel Interests (Pty) Ltd* 2018 2 SA 314 (SCA) the court declined in the particular circumstances not to enforce a term on the basis of public policy. Cf. *Reddy v. Siemens Telecommunications (Pty) Ltd* 2007 2 SA 486 (SCA) regarding restraints of trade, as well as *Mozart Ice Cream Franchises (Pty) Ltd v. Davidoff* 2009 3 SA 78 (C).

193. Section 36 of the Constitution.

194. Placing of the onus to prove the reasonableness of the restraint on the party wishing to enforce it would conform to the position in South African law (which followed English law) before the Appeal Court decided differently in *Magna Alloys & Research (SA) (Pty) Ltd v. Ellis* 1984 4 SA 874 (A).

Thus far, the preponderance of the decisions of the courts support the view that the Constitution was not intended to affect the basic principle of freedom of contract directly in favour of protecting the right to trade freely, and that the balance between these principles that was struck by the Supreme Court of Appeal[195] should remain undisturbed. As a result, a restraint is enforceable, except if the party who does not wish to be bound by it proves it to be against the public interest and unreasonable.[196]

III. Freedom of Contract as a Leading Principle and Future Developments

111. It appears that freedom of contract has retained its proper position in the common law of South Africa as the leading principle *(leitsatz)* in the law of contract, in the face of potentially conflicting fundamental rights. In this regard, freedom to trade, freedom of association, the right to dignity and equality, and the right to access to justice as they are recognized in the Constitution are probably most relevant. The law of contract consists of detailed rules and principles that strive for, and often attain, a fair balance between the interests of the parties. Thus, it probably accords with the spirit, purpose, and objects of the Constitution. Moreover, the Constitution does not demand a radical break with the legal traditions of the past. Nonetheless, it is manifest that the horizontal application of the Bill of Rights does, and will in future continue to, have a marked influence on the law of contract. The courts are now required to take into consideration aspects of policy and social values,[197] which have up to now only rarely been overtly acknowledged.

The development of general rules from present specific applications in some areas may be accelerated, such as the overt judicial recognition of a concept of improperly obtained consensus. The content of public policy, and in particular the

195. In *Magna Alloys & Research (SA) (Pty) Ltd v. Ellis* 1984 4 SA 874 (A).

196. *See* the discussion in. Van Huyssteen, Lubbe & Reinecke, *Contract General Principles* paras 7.73–7.74, particularly n. 194 (Juta 2016). In *Reddy v. Siemens Telecommunications (Pty) Ltd* 2007 2 SA 486 (SCA), the Court side-stepped the issue on the basis that the question of onus is one of substantive law (and the substantive law was as laid down in the *Magna Alloys* case); that it was not necessary in the matter to decide whether the Constitution required a shift of onus, since the reasonableness of a restraint in essence entailed a value judgment for which the facts in the matter had been fully explored; and, even if the onus were shifted, the result would be the same (493–497). In practice, this would probably be true for most cases. In *Advtech Resourcing (Pty) Ltd t/a Communicate Personnel Group v. Kuhn* 2008 2 SA 375 (C), the Court was of the opinion that the duty of the courts to develop common law in light of the values protected in the Constitution should indeed result in a shifting of the onus to prove that the restraint is reasonable to the covenantee (employer) wishing to enforce the restraint. However, in light of the precedent set in *Reddy v. Siemens Telecommunications (Pty) Ltd* 2007 2 SA 486 (SCA), it could not make such a finding. In *Mozart Ice Cream Franchises (Pty) Ltd v. Davidoff* 2009 3 SA 78 (C), the Court did not address the issue of onus, but reiterated that the Constitution required that cases of restraint of trade essentially concern a balance between the bargain as phrased in the contract and the demands of public policy; so that, even if a protectable interest is prejudiced (*see* below for a fuller discussion of this concept), it must still be weighed against other interests.

197. *See* the cases referred to above and also *De Klerk v. Du Plessis* 1995 2 SA 40 (T) 50–51, in which, in somewhat flowery language, the Court expressed the opinion that the Constitution 'is intended to permeate our judicial approach to … the development of the common law with the fragrance of the values in which the Constitution is anchored' (at 50I).

interests of society, in relation to the legality of an agreement, will certainly be further influenced by the Bill of Rights. The negotiating process and consequences of a contract for the parties (and for society as a whole), with reference to also its content, may well have to be considered when the enforcement of the contract is at issue. The right to equality could provide the stimulus for further development of the concept of good faith, ubuntu or reasonableness in this respect,[198] which in turn may be applied to create new rules or adapt existing ones, and which may include recognition of the effect of changed circumstances on the enforceability of a contract. The inference of tacit terms and the construction of *ex lege* terms in a contract, as well the interpretation of contractual terms, stand to be influenced by the values protected in the Constitution. It may also be that specific or general legislation affecting the law of contract will be spawned by the recognition of fundamental rights, as is perhaps illustrated by the proposals with respect to the importation of good faith or reasonableness and fairness as standards applicable by the courts to all aspects of contracts.

§10. Style of Drafting

112. In general, it seems that South African drafters of contracts follow what may be called a comprehensive approach in an attempt to reflect the essentials of agreements and to provide for all aspects and contingencies that may affect the contractants. This approach will undoubtedly create major problems when attempting to encode terms for smart contracts.[199] This is so despite the fact that many terms are incorporated into contracts by law, such as warranties against latent defects in the subject matter of a sale. Often, particularly in standard form contracts (which are widely used), these *ex lege* terms are varied by way of exclusion clauses. Also, drafters often use elaborate and antiquated terminology, which unnecessarily mystifies and obfuscates the essence of what the parties have agreed on, despite a current call by the regulating bodies of the legal professions, law schools, and the public to use plain language.[200]

Practitioners make widespread use of commercially published forms and precedents and also of their own pre-drafted forms. This is probably one of the causes of the common incidence of contracts that unreasonably protect the interests of one party to the detriment of the other.[201]

198. As explained above, the courts are still wary of recognizing good faith as a rule or principle of law – it is kept at the subservient level of an underlying value, where of course, it may more easily be ignored in practice, or applied by rendering lip-service. However, as set out above, this approach is being slowly rejected. *See* the discussion above.

199. *See* para 31 above.

200. *See also* the plain language requirements in s. 22 of the Consumer Protection Act 68 of 2008.

201. Cf., for example, the contract in *Sasfin (Pty) Ltd v. Beukes* 1989 1 SA 1 (A) and in many of the cases referred to above.

§11. SOURCES OF LAW OF CONTRACT

I. Classification of Areas of South African Law

113. Although classifications of main areas of law are often not precise and do not represent exclusive categories, they are helpful in finding the sources of a particular area or rule of law. In general, South African law is not codified; it is accordingly not practical to distinguish generally between codified and unwritten law for the purpose of classification.

A very broad distinction is sometimes made between public law and private law. This distinction has little practical value for the purpose of finding the sources of South African law. More useful in this respect is the classification generally made for the purposes of teaching law. The following areas are usually distinguished:

1. Jurisprudence; legal history (Roman and Roman-Dutch law up to approximately the seventeenth century and other European schools of legal thought); comparative law, and indigenous law. These areas are sometimes integrated or combined with other areas of law.
2. Private law, which includes the law of persons and the family, property, succession, and delict and contract, as well as other applied fields of the law of obligations, such as trusts, estoppel, product liability, consumer protection, and the like. Private international law (conflict of laws) is usually included here. There are statutes dealing with important and often controversial aspects of the different fields of law in this category. Here, the Consumer Protection Act 68 of 2008 is particularly important.
3. Public law, which includes criminal law, constitutional and administrative law, human rights, international law, labour law (particularly aspects of constitutional and administrative law), and related and applied fields such as housing law, environmental protection, and social security law. In this category of law, statutes play a more important role than they do in private law.
4. Commercial or mercantile law, which includes company law, partnerships, close corporations and other business forms, negotiable instruments, tax law, financial institutions, labour law, international business law, insurance, immaterial property law, electronic communications (IT) law, and related and applied fields. In this category of law, statutes are an important source of law to the extent that some areas are, for all practical purposes, codified.
5. Procedural law, which includes criminal and civil procedure, the judicature, evidence, and legal aid. In this field of law, too, there is much legislation to the point of codification of some areas.

II. Sources of Law of Contract

114. Because of the emphasis on general principles in South African law, the law of contract is generally a coherent system of principles and rules, which allows further development to take place in terms of principle, rather than ad hoc.[202] This is so despite, or perhaps owing to, the fact that the law is not codified, and that the system of judicial precedent is a basic part of South African law.

115. The law of contract is to be found mainly in the principles and rules of South African common law, as developed in terms of the Constitution, and that have been applied, analysed, and developed by judgments in cases decided by the superior courts. Often, a comparative study is made by the courts with reference to other civil and also common law systems. In practice, textbooks and articles in legal journals are important descriptions of the positive law and are often cited as such in decisions of the courts. Legal writers also contribute to the further development of the law when their views and proposals are accepted by the courts in the course of a judgment. Reports by the South African Law Commission are important catalysts of change and lead to new law or statutes. In general, statute law is a minor source of the law of contract, although there is important legislation affecting certain specific contracts, as well as some areas of general principles.

III. Finding the Law

116. To find the law of contract, the following categories of materials may be consulted.

A. *Case Law*

117. In South Africa, mainly because of the system of precedent, the full text of those judgments of the High Court, Supreme Court of Appeal, and Constitutional Court that are reported is published.[203] (Unreported cases can be found in the ordinary court records.) A typical judgment usually commences with a recital of the facts that the court finds to have been proved on a balance of probabilities, often making reference to the pleadings and the evidence given. Quite often, this is followed by an exposition of the legal principles and rules that, in the opinion of the court, are relevant and applicable to the issues raised by the litigants and the facts. Finally, the court expresses a judgment on whether these elements support the order(s) sought by the plaintiff or defendant and then sets out the order of the court

202. A good example is to be found in *BK Tooling (Edms) Bpk v. Scope Precision Engineering (Edms) Bpk* 1979 1 SA 391 (A) with respect to the application of the principle of reciprocity and the *exceptio non adimpleti contractus*. *See also Benson v. SA Mutual Life Assurance Society* 1986 1 SA 776 (A) with respect to the right to specific performance in South African law as contrasted to the position in English law.

203. Also published are the reported judgments of the Labour Court of South Africa, the Labour Appeal Court, the Land Claims Court of South Africa, and the Competition Appeal Court of South Africa.

in specific terms. The first published case law reports commenced in 1828 with the publication of the judgments of the Supreme Court of the Cape Colony. These reports were later followed by reports in the other areas of South Africa. After the Union of South Africa came into being in 1910, the reports continued in separate series for the various divisions of the Supreme Court, as well as a series for the Appellate Division. Since 1947, the reports have been consolidated in *The South African Law Reports,* in which 'reportable' decisions of all divisions of the High Court and Supreme Court of Appeal[204] on all fields of law and decisions of the Constitutional Court are published monthly in book form.[205] These books are then often bound together in six (previously four) volumes per year. Decisions of the Constitutional Court are also published monthly in *Butterworths Constitutional Law Reports.* Also available now in book form are the *All South African Law Reports,* which sometimes contains reports of cases not in the other reports.

118. The law reports are published commercially but for all practical purposes have the status of 'official' reports. The reports are also available on CD-ROMs, which are updated every month. Since it usually takes a few months before a particular judgment is fully published in the reports, a digest of cases that are being considered for publication is available commercially. In the digest, concise details of these cases are given within weeks of delivery of the judgments. A photocopy of the unedited judgments is available to subscribers upon request.

Most reports are now available online free or by subscription through the websites of the major law publishers in South Africa, Juta Law, and LexisNexis. A very useful free addition to online reporting is to be found on the site of The Southern African Legal Information Institute: for Constitutional Court decisions go to www.saflii.org.za/za/cases/ZACC; judgments as from 1995 are fully reported and upda ted as the judgments are sent by the court; for Supreme Court of Appeal go to www.saflii.org.za/za/cases/ZASCA; these judgments are reported as from 1984. High Court judgments are also to be found on the saflii site, as well as those of special courts and of a number of Southern and East African courts. Also to be found are judgments of regional courts of justice, such as the SADC tribunal.

119. Indices of the cases reported in *The South African Law Reports* and the *All South African Law Reports* are published regularly in the appropriate volume of law reports under the following headings: 'Table of cases', 'Index' (alphabetical according to subject matter), and 'Case annotations' of Southern African and foreign cases.

---

204. Cases decided in the High Court of Namibia, the Supreme Court of Namibia, and the High and Supreme Courts of Zimbabwe are also reported in the *South African Law Reports.* Since 1990, separate *Namibian Law Reports* are published by Juta Law online.

205. Only 'reportable' decisions are reported. Normally, the judge who decided the case decides whether it merits reporting (although other interested parties may also suggest that it should be reported). A separate series of reports of criminal cases is now published in *The South African Criminal Law Reports*, besides the cases reported in *The South African Law Reports*. Cases decided by the Industrial Court and the High Court on labour matters are also published separately in the *Industrial Law Journal* and the *Butterworths Labour Law Reports*, although some High Court decisions on labour law are also published in *The South African Law Reports*. Judgments relating to patent law are published in *Burrell's Patent Law Reports*. There are also reports available for various other specialized fields, such as arbitration.

A consolidated index is published every few years. The judgments of the Constitutional Court are also indexed in the *Butterworths Constitutional Law Reports* cumulatively each year.

120. Discussions of particularly important cases in the form of 'case notes', usually written by academic lawyers, are published by most legal journals.

1. Method of Citation of Cases

121. The standard method of citation is illustrated by the following example:

South African Law Reports:
Brisley v. Drotsky 2002 4 SA 1 (SCA) – the names of the litigants, the year of publication, the volume (in this case, the fourth) of the reports for that year, the name of the report (SA being the abbreviation for the South African Law Reports), the page in the volume at which the report commences, followed by the abbreviation of the court in which the case was decided (SCA being the abbreviation for the Supreme Court of Appeal [HHA is the Afrikaans abbreviation]).
All South African Law Reports:
Die Dros (Pty) Ltd v. Telefon Beverages CC [2003] 1 All SA 173 (C) – the citation follows the same pattern as that for the South African Law Reports.

B. Legislation

122. Statute law is a less important source of the law of contract. Legislation of Parliament, regulations, and proclamations in terms thereof and official notices are published weekly in the official *Government Gazette.* Provincial legislation is published in the *Provincial Gazette.*

123. There are also a number of commercial legislation services in loose-leaf, CD-ROM and online format covering all legislation or specific legislation, and sometimes providing a table of cases that have been decided with respect to specific legislation. Important discovery aids are the indices to all legislation, both central and provincial. These provide an alphabetical subject index and a numerical index to published notices, proclamations, regulations, bills, and statutes. A weekly statutes bulletin is also available. The websites of the relevant government departments have some information on the legislative activity of the department. There is also a general government website for statutes and bills.

C. Books, Periodicals, and Encyclopaedias

124. The body of South African legal literature is amazingly large and comprehensive, considering the relatively small size of the market. Most writings are in English. For the law of contract, there are a number of textbooks written for practitioners and students on the general principles of contract, some including expositions on certain specific contracts. There are also many specialized books on particular contracts. Apart from these, there are casebooks and student editions.

125. The market offers many legal journals containing writings on every branch of the law, as well as a few specialized journals, mainly in the fields of business and public law. There is no specialized journal on the law of contract. Generally, the journals contain long articles, shorter notes, and case comments. Many journals are now available online at various sites, including saflii.

126. An encyclopaedic work, *The Law of South Africa*, is intended to cover the whole of South African law, systematically by title, with an index, a cumulative supplement, and table of cases, and a monthly updating service. This series is also available on CD-ROM and online. There is a separate title for the law of contract. A comprehensive and very helpful bibliographical index of the old authorities of South African common law is also available.

1. Method of Citation of Literature

127. A common method of the full citation of books is, by way of example, as follows: Van Huyssteen, Lubbe & Reinecke, *Contract General Principles* (5th edn 2016 Juta Cape Town). However, the usual practice now is to give less detail in footnote citations with fuller bibliographical details in a list of works or principal works cited.

128. The works of the well-known old Roman-Dutch authorities are often cited as follows: Van Leeuwen *C F* 1.1.13.7; (*Censura Forensis*); or de Groot *Inl* 3.48.6; (*Inleidinge tot de Hollandsche Rechtsgeleerdheid*). The standard editions of these works are referred to in this way. Full bibliographical details are usually provided only in academic theses, where other editions might be referred to.

129. The codification of Justinian is usually cited as follows: D 4.2.9.1 (*Digesta*); or C 4.10.5 (*Codex*).

130. There is no absolute standard method of citation of publications in journals. One common form of citation is the following: Beck, 1985 *SALJ* 660; (the author, the *South African Law Journal* of 1985, and the specific page of the article to which reference is made.) Sometimes the title of the article, the initials or first names of the authors, and the first page number of the publication are also given.

Part I. General Principles of the Law of Contract

Chapter 1. Formation

§1. Agreement, Quid Pro Quo (Reciprocity), and Reliance

I. Offer and Acceptance

131. A contract, being usually created by an agreement between the parties, entails the (eventual) formation of a common intention to be bound as a result of a reaction to prior declared intentions. To analyse this creative process, the declarations of intention are often characterized as an invitation to create obligations, namely the offer, and an affirmative response, namely the acceptance. However, since the crucial element of a contract is an agreement (consensus), South African law does not require that an offer and an acceptance must always be distinguished,[206] as long as an agreement, entailing the intention to be bound,[207] has come about and the other requirements for the creation of a contract are present. It is, in any event, not always possible to make such a distinction in practice, although it is often important to be able to do so, particularly in regard to establishing the exact time and place of contract.

132. In light of the prime importance of private autonomy and consensus in South African law, it should be stressed that, in principle, an offer, although accompanied by the requisite intention, does not in itself create rights and duties:[208] South African law does not accept that a unilaterally expressed intent creates obligations, even though reasonable expectations (falling short of a reasonable reliance on the existence of a contract) may have been raised.[209] In this respect, South African law differs markedly from some other comparable systems, and care must be taken when

206. Offer and acceptance are facts from which consensus may be inferred – *see Bourbon-Leftley v. WPK (Landbou) Bpk* 1999 1 SA 902 (C); *Lowe v. Commission for Gender Equality* 2002 1 SA 750 (W).
207. *See Lambons Edms (Bpk) v. BMW (Suid-Afrika) Bpk* 1997 4 SA 141 (SCA).
208. *See*, for example, *Hersch v. Nel* 1948 3 SA 686 (A); *Commissioner, South African Revenue Service v. Wyner* 2004 4 SA 311 (SCA); Van Huyssteen, Lubbe & Reinecke, *Contract General Principles* para. 3.7 (Juta 2016).
209. Of course, a reasonable reliance on the existence of a contract may have been created or delictual liability may have resulted – *see* the discussion of these matters below.

considering the practical effects of the South African approach, particularly in connection with the revocation of an offer by the offeror.

133. It also follows that, as a general rule, a contract is concluded where and when the offeror becomes informed that the offer has been accepted by a person entitled by law to do so.[210] The position relating to contracts entered into through the post (and perhaps by other methods traditionally associated with the post) is different and will be discussed below.

A. *Offer*

134. To qualify as an offer, the invitation to create obligations must contain sufficient terms so that an unqualified acceptance will bring about a contract with a content that is certain or objectively ascertainable to the extent that it complies with the requirement of certainty and can be enforced by law: the offer must be complete and definite.

135. An offer can be validly made not only to a specific addressee, but also to the public at large (such as an offer of reward) or to a particular class of person or a member of that class (such as at certain types of auctions).

As a general rule, an offer can be made in any form or manner determined by the offeror, and the offeror may prescribe the manner or form of acceptance of the offer, for example, that it should be in writing and signed. This freedom is limited by the general requirement of legality and by the provisions of particular statutes, such as statutes regarding the alienation of land and suretyship. Also, the Consumer Protection Act 68 of 2008 prohibits discrimination with respect to offers to supply goods or services[211] and sets out certain requirements regarding the offer.[212]

B. *Revocation of Offer, Option Contracts, and Lapse of Offer*

136. Since it does not have any obligationary effect in South African law,[213] an offer may be revoked or amended freely at any time before the contract is concluded, provided that the offeree is notified of the revocation.

---

210. *See*, for example, *Driftwood Properties (Pty) Ltd v. McLean* 1971 3 SA 591 (A); *Amcoal Collieries Ltd v. Truter* 1990 1 SA 1 (A); *Seeff Commercial & Industrial Properties (Pty) Ltd v. Silberman* 2001 3 SA 952 (SCA).

211. Section 8.

212. Section 22 – the notice, document or visual representation containing the offer must be in the prescribed form (if any) and in plain language; s. 25; Part E – right to fair and responsible marketing, for example, prohibition of bait marketing; Part G – prohibition of an offer at an unfair price or on unfair terms (s. 48).

213. The view has been advanced that an offer may not be revoked after the addressee has begun to make over his or her acceptance, even though no contract has yet come into existence. *See* J.C. de Wet & A.H. van Wyk, *Die Suid-Afrikaanse Kontraktereg en Handelsreg*, vol. 1 (Durban: Butterworths, 1992), 33, at *38*. The courts have not expressed a clear opinion on the matter, but this alternative

137. The offeror's capacity to revoke his or her offer may, however, be restricted by a contract called an option contract.[214] The option contract is construed in South African law as a *pactum de contrahendo* [215] and not as a preliminary contract,[216] as it is known in some comparable civil law systems; nor is it construed as a substantive contract qualified by a suspensive condition. The option contract, then, is a contract between the option grantor and the option holder that binds the option grantor to keep open (for a fixed time or a reasonable time) the substantive offer for the possible subsequent acceptance exclusively by the option holder. By exercising the option, the holder accepts the substantive offer, and a substantive contract arises. A unilateral declaration by an offeror that the offer is irrevocable has no effect.

138. The option contract must be distinguished from an offer with a limited duration when the offeror did not contract to entrench the offer, as well as from rights of preference, such as a right of pre-emption when the grantor of the right has the freedom to decide whether or not to sell.[217]

139. The breach of an option contract and the consequences of a breach are governed by the ordinary rules of contract. This means that the option holder may enforce his or her right in terms of the option, for example, by obtaining an interdict against the grantor to prohibit him or her from alienating the subject matter of the contract to another, or even to compel the option grantor to cooperate to enable the option to be exercised,[218] or he or she may obtain an award of damages to put him or her in the financial position that he or she would have occupied had he or she exercised the option.

140. Because of the nature of the offer as construed in South African law, it lapses upon the death of either party and can also not be transferred. This would, of course, not apply to the rights of an option holder in terms of an option contract. An offer also lapses when it is rejected by the offeree or when he or she makes a counter-offer. An offer lapses after a reasonable time or on expiry of any time stipulated in the offer for acceptance.

---

approach is not strictly in accordance with the principles of the information theory as such. *See* Van Huyssteen, Lubbe & Reinecke, *Contract General Principles* para. 3.8 (Juta 2016).

214. *See* in general. Van Huyssteen, Lubbe & Reinecke, *Contract General Principles* ch. 3 C et seq. (Juta 2016).
215. *See*, for example, *Hirschowitz v. Moolman* 1985 3 SA 739 (A); *Investec Bank Ltd v. Lefkowitz* 1997 3 SA 1 (A).
216. Depending of course on the intention of the parties. Cf. *Du Plessis NO and Another v. Goldco Motor & Cycle Supplies (Pty) Ltd* 2009 6 SA 617 (SCA) paras 14–17; *Van Aardt v. Galway* 2012 2 SA 312 (SCA).
217. *See* Van Huyssteen, Lubbe & Reinecke, *Contract General Principles* para. 3.46 et seq. (Juta 2016) for a full discussion of the distinction and the problems surrounding the exercising of a right of pre-emption.
218. This remedy can be criticized on conceptual grounds; *see* Van Huyssteen, Lubbe & Reinecke, *Contract General Principles* para. 3.43 (Juta 2016).

C. *Pre-contractual Fault*

141. Again, because of the nature of the offer and other factors, such as the primacy of private autonomy, South African law as yet does not recognize a doctrine of pre-contractual fault[219] in relation to pre-contractual conduct, such as the unreasonable revocation of an offer or withdrawal from negotiations. However, it is probable that the application of the Constitution and the acceptance of good faith as a substantive principle, as explained above, may limit the freedom to withdraw.[220]

Fault would be a necessary element of pre-contractual conduct that would justify a claim for damages.[221]

D. *Offer and Promise to Contract*

142. It will be clear that, in principle, so-called promises to contract,[222] unless entrenched in *pacta de contrahendo* or contained in another contract, will have no legal effect in South African law, neither, in general, are 'agreements to agree'. However, where there is a contractual obligation to negotiate in future (e.g., a renewal of a lease) in good faith, it may very well be enforceable and certain; or in the case of a preliminary agreement to negotiate a further agreement [223] Arrangements such as 'letters of intent' or 'agreements in principle' are merely memoranda recording the state of negotiations between prospective contractants.[224] In principle, agreements that have an effect that is ultimately similar to the preliminary contract, as it is known in some continental systems, are valid in South African law, but such

219. For a full discussion of the relations between parties in contrahendo, *see* Van Huyssteen, Lubbe & Reinecke, *Contract General Principles* ch. 3 D (Juta 2016).

220. There is a strong possibility that the content of the requirement of wrongfulness will be increasingly expanded so as to lead to the acceptance of a doctrine of *culpa in contrahendo.* This would certainly be the case in administrative contracts or contracts with the state on the basis of the right to administrative fairness; *see Olitzki Property Holdings v. State Tender Board* 2001 3 SA 1247 (SCA); *Transnet Ltd v. Sechaba Photoscan (Pty) Ltd* 2005 1 SA 299 (SCA).

221. An interesting development is the recognition that the use of confidential information obtained during negotiations may result in an Aquilian action for damages – *Union Shipping & Managing Co. SA v. Lina Maritime Ltd* 1998 4 SA 633 (N).

222. *See* Van Huyssteen, Lubbe & Reinecke, *Contract General Principles* para. 3.35 and ch. 3 D (Juta 2016).

223. *See Everfresh Market Virginia (Pty) Ltd v. Shoprite Checkers (Pty) Ltd* 2012 1 SA 256 (CC) para. 71; *Silent Pond Investments CC v. Woolworths* (Pty) *Ltd* 2011 6 SA 343 (D); *Indwe Aviation (Pty) Ltd v. Petroleum Oil and Gas Corporation of South Africa (Pty) Ltd (No1)* 2012 6 SA 96 (WCC) paras 27, 28 where the court uses the concept of the *arbitrio boni viri* to import considerations of reasonableness, good faith and honesty into a duty to negotiate; *Makate v. Vodacom Ltd* 2016 4 SA 121 (CC) para. 95 et seq. where it was held that an agreement to negotiate a further agreement in good faith was enforceable if it contained a deadlock-breaking mechanism. *See also Roazar CC v. The Falls Supermarket CC* 2018 3 SA 76 (SCA) paras 19, 21–22 where the court refused in the particular circumstances (the requirement of certainty and absence of a deadlock-breaking mechanism) to develop the common law to import a term to compel parties to negotiate a renewal of a lease in good faith: *It is difficult to conceive how a court, in a purely business transaction, can rely on "ubuntu" to import a term that was not intended by the parties, to deny the other party a right to rely on the terms of the contract to terminate it" (para 24).*

224. *See Murray & Roberts Construction Ltd v. Finat Properties (Pty) Ltd* 1991 1 SA 508 (A).

agreements will often not comply with the requirement of certainty.[225] For reasons of policy, the courts are also not eager to enforce an oral agreement to conclude a contract, which is required by law to be in writing.[226]

E. Offer or Invitation to Treat

143. Whether conduct by a person amounts to an offer that creates a contract upon acceptance, or whether it merely amounts to an invitation to do business or to treat, is determined in the first place with reference to the presence or absence of an intention to create an obligationary relationship with the other party, which was brought to the attention of the offeree so as to enable him or her to establish a contract by accepting the offer as it was made,[227] as well as with reference to whether the requirement of certainty is complied with. So, for example, an advertisement in a newspaper or on the internet, in a shop window,[228] or by way of leaflets or catalogues freely distributed to the public, or the display of goods in a self-service shop, will *usually* not amount to an offer.[229] The person who reacts to the advertisement or who presents the selected articles to the cashier makes the offer. However, on the other hand, an advertisement offering a reward[230] or a trade circular sent to listed regular customers may well amount to an offer.

144. In some respects, this state of affairs may justifiably be criticized as being undesirable from the point of view of protecting the consumer.[231] However, it must be pointed out that rules have been developed in common law that already serve that end. An example in the present context is the recognition of a duty to speak when a party, before the conclusion of the contract, created an impression (e.g., by a false advertisement) that is in conflict with the terms of the agreement that he or she subsequently wishes to enforce. Depending on the facts, the other party can rely directly on misrepresentation to rescind the contract, or, if that is not possible (e.g., because of an exclusion clause), he or she may rely on his or her reasonable material mistake to escape the agreement, even though he or she may have signed it.[232]

225. *See H Merks & Co. Ltd v. The B-M Group (Pty) Ltd* 1996 2 SA 225 (A). However, an agreement to render a certain or ascertainable performance in future, when required by the other party, is perfectly valid and enforceable.
226. *See*, for example, *Docrat v. Willemse* 1989 1 SA 487 (N).
227. *See* Van Huyssteen, Lubbe & Reinecke, *Contract General Principles* paras 3.4–3.6 et seq. (Juta 2016).
228. *See*, for example, *Crawley v. Rex* 1909 TS 1105.
229. Cf. the English case of *Pharmaceutical Society of Great Britain v. Boots Cash Chemists (Southern) Ltd* [1953] 1 QB 401 (CA), [1953] 1 All ER 482.
230. Cf., for example, *Bloom v. The American Swiss Watch Co.* 1915 AD 100.
231. *See* now the extensive measures aimed at protecting the consumer contained in the Consumer Protection Act 68 of 2008, in this context particularly in parts E (right to fair and responsible marketing) and F (right to fair and honest dealing).
232. *See*, for example, *Du Toit v. Atkinson's Motors Bpk* 1985 2 SA 893 (A) and further, the discussion below.

F. Acceptance of Offer

145. An acceptance of an offer is an expressed declaration of will, by way of a conscious reaction, to indicate assent, and made with the intention of creating obligations according to the terms set out in the offer.[233] Because of the consensual basis of a contract, an unexpressed or incidental decision to accept an offer is not effective. Thus, for example, there is no acceptance when the person purporting to accept is unaware of the offer.[234]

146. An acceptance must be unqualified; otherwise it amounts to a rejection or, at most, to a counter-offer. This has the effect of destroying the original offer.[235] In certain circumstances, an incomplete acceptance may be regarded as evidencing an intention to create a contract with a content that is certain, while negotiations on outstanding aspects continue.[236] The practical problem that arises when parties accept that there is a contract despite the absence of a final agreement as to incidental terms (e.g., in the so-called battle-of-forms situation), has not received much attention in South African law. It appears that there is a tendency to apply the rules of dissensus to such situations and to enquire the presence of a reasonable reliance, rather than applying the rules of offer and acceptance to ascertain the last declaration of intention, which would lead to a result similar to the so-called last-shot rule in English law.[237]

It also follows from the consensual nature of a contract that an offer can only be accepted by the person to whom it was made and with whom the offeror intended to contract.[238] An offer may be made to the public at large or 'to whomever accepts'.

147. The intention to accept may be made evident by any form of conduct, express or tacit, as long as it indicates unequivocal assent.[239] Failure to respond

233. The Consumer Protection Act 68 of 2008 gives the consumer the right to 'rescind' the contract within five days when it has been concluded as a result of direct marketing – a so-called cooling-off period (s. 16).

234. *See*, for example, *Volkskas Spaarbank Bpk v. Van Aswegen* 1990 3 SA 978 (A).

235. *See Gaap Point of Sale (Pty) Ltd v. Valjee and Others NNO* 2011 6 SA 601 (KZD); *Command Protection Services (Gauteng) (Pty) Ltd t/a Maxi Security v. South African Post Office Ltd* 2013 2 SA 133 (SCA).

236. *See CGEE Alsthom Equipments & Enterprises Electriques, South African Division v. GKN Sankey (Pty) Ltd* 1987 1 SA 81 (A); *Lambons Edms (Bpk) v. BMW (Suid Afrika) Bpk* 1997 4 SA 141 (SCA).

237. For a detailed discussion of this problem, *see* Van Huyssteen, Lubbe & Reinecke, *Contract General Principles* paras 3.13–3.15 (Juta 2016).

238. An offer made mistakenly by A to B, while A actually intends to contract with C, will not bring about a contract when the offer is 'accepted' by B – it is a case of a material error *in persona*. *See Levin v. Drieprok Properties (Pty) Ltd* 1975 2 SA 397 (A).

239. *See Withok Small Farms (Pty) Ltd v. Amber Sunrise Properties 5 (Pty) Ltd* 2009 2 SA 504 (SCA) for a case in which the circumstances gave rise to an inference that mere signature of the written contract by the offeree was enough to constitute a valid acceptance, without communication thereof with the offeror.

may, in exceptional circumstances,[240] be taken to have created a reasonable impression that the offer has been accepted, with the result that the offeree will be held bound.

148. An acceptance must comply with any formalities prescribed by law or by the offeror.[241]

G. *Contract by Correspondence and Other Methods When Parties Are Not in Each Other's Presence*

149. As a rule, the courts in South Africa accept that a contract is concluded at the time when and the place where the offeror becomes aware of the acceptance of the offer (also called the 'information theory'). Traditionally, this rule was applied to all contracts, regardless of the method of communication used by the contractants, except, of course, if the offeror had prescribed a different mode of acceptance.[242] In 1921, the Cape Supreme Court, for what it considered to be reasons of practical convenience and commercial certainty, adopted a different approach and decided that commercial contracts entered into *inter absentes* by post (to the extent that both the offer and acceptance were made by post) were concluded at the place and moment of posting the acceptance (the 'expedition theory').[243] This approach has been criticized both judicially and by commentators. In the first place, it is regarded as being at variance with the requirement of consensus. Second, the argument goes, where a reliable postal service exists; there are no good reasons of policy or equity to favour the offeree by placing the risk of loss of the communication on the offeror. Despite this justifiable criticism, the expedition theory is applied by the courts to commercial contracts entered into *inter absentes* by post[244] and by telegram (in so far as these rather antiquated methods are still relevant). Presumably, in the eyes of the courts, the same uncertainty surrounding the delivery of letters applies to telegrams.

240. An example is a previous course of dealing in a particular business relationship.

241. However, the offeree may by his or her conduct create the reasonable belief on the part of the offeror that the offer had been duly accepted according to the prescribed mode – in such a case the application of the doctrine of reasonable reliance would lead to a contract being extant. *See Pillay v. Shaik* 2009 4 SA 74 (SCA). On the doctrine, *see* below.

242. *See Driftwood Properties (Pty) Ltd v. McLean* 1971 3 SA 591 (A); *Seeff Commercial and Industrial Properties (Pty) Ltd v. Silberman* 2001 3 SA 952 (SCA).

243. *See Cape Explosive Works Ltd v. South African Oil & Fat Industries Ltd* 1921 CPD 244.

244. Except of course when there are indications to the contrary, such as in a statute, the offer itself or the nature of the transaction: *A to Z Bazaars (Pty) Ltd v. Minister of Agriculture* 1975 3 SA 468 (A); *SA Yster & Staal Industriële Korporasie Bpk v. Koschade* 1983 4 SA 837 (T).

The expedition theory has been rejected in the case of a contract concluded by telephone, the argument being that such communication was virtually instantaneous, and that there was thus no reason to depart from the general rule.[245] The courts would probably also reject the expedition theory with respect to contracts concluded by telex or telefax.[246]

When the offer is not posted but communicated in another way and the acceptance is communicated by post, the normal principle and not the expedition theory will apply. A number of recent cases have stressed the central role of the intention of the offeror in determining the mode of acceptance. It has even been suggested that the operation of the expedition theory can be neutralized if the offeree withdraws his or her acceptance by a speedier means of communication before the offeror has received the acceptance.[247]

The situation regarding computer-mediated communication has not yet been fully regulated by statute or considered by the courts.[248] However, The Electronic Communications and Transactions Act[249] provide rules regarding contract formation in the absence of regulation by the parties themselves. Contracts concluded by means of data messages are concluded at the time when and the place where the acceptance of the offer was *received* by the offeror.[250]

In summary, it may be said that the general principle reflected in the information theory should apply, except where the law or the parties themselves clearly prescribe otherwise.[251]

II. Intention to Create Legal Relations

150. As has been pointed out earlier, an agreement entered into without the accompanying intention to create legal relations by way of obligations (containing rights and duties enforceable at law) cannot be a contract. Whether such an intention is present is a question of fact, and if the intention has not been expressly articulated, it is to be inferred from all the facts and surrounding circumstances.[252] Thus, a social arrangement to take a friend to a train station in one's car will ordinarily not be a contract, but an arrangement to do so for a quid pro quo may well indicate

245. *See Tel Peda Investigation Bureau (Pty) Ltd v. Van Zyl* 1965 4 SA 475 (E).
246. *See*, however, the bald and unconvincing statement to the contrary in *Ex Parte Jamieson: In Re Jamieson v. Sabigo* 2001 2 SA 775 (W).
247. *See A to Z Bazaars (Pty) Ltd v. Minister of Agriculture* 1975 3 SA 468 (A).
248. For a full discussion of all the issues, *see* Van Huyssteen, Lubbe & Reinecke, *Contract General Principles* paras 3.28–3.32 (Juta 2016). Also see above regarding smart contracts.
249. Act 25 of 2002. The Act is based on the UNCITRAL Model Law on Electronic Commerce of 1996; cf. *Spring Forest Trading CC v. Wilberry (Pty) Ltd t/a Ecowash and Another* 2015 2 SA 118 (SCA) where the court interpreted sec 13 of the Act regarding the requirement of electronic signature.
250. Section 22(2). This is the so-called reception theory.
251. *See*, for example, *Millman v. Klein* 1986 1 SA 465 (C), in which the Court spoke of a presumption in favour of the general principle in cases in which the terms of the offer regarding the prescribed mode of acceptance are not clear (475).
252. The actual or constructive intention of the parties is ascertained 'in the context of the whole document, its purpose and all the relevant circumstances surrounding its creation,' *see* Van Huyssteen, Lubbe & Reinecke, *Contract General Principles* para. 9.218 et seq. (Juta 2016) and the cases cited there (e.g., *Novartis SA (Pty) Ltd v. Maphill Trading (Pty) Ltd* 2016 1 SA 518 (SCA)).

the presence of the requisite intention and may accordingly amount to a contract. Similarly, when parties purport to conclude a contract with a particular content but actually intend a different content (a simulated contract), the law will give effect to the actual intention of the parties and not to their simulated intention.[253] The presence of the requisite intention must be proved by the litigant who alleges that a contract exists, but, in practice, this onus will only arise when the other party denies the existence of the intention and has satisfied the need to rebut.

A. Consideration Is Not a Requirement

151. In a number of decisions at the end of the nineteenth century and at the start of the twentieth century, the Cape Supreme Court held that the requirement of *justa causa* set by some institutional writers on Roman-Dutch law for the validity and enforceability of a contract entailed that a valuable consideration, as required in English law, was also a requirement for a contract in South African law.[254] In 1919, the Appellate Division decided that the doctrine of valuable consideration was not part of South African law.[255] It has since been re-affirmed that for contracts in general, no additional elements beyond consensus (or a reasonable reliance on consensus) and legality are required to provide a just basis for a contract.[256] By way of exception, the Court was of the opinion that if a subsidiary agreement depends on the existence of a main agreement, the main agreement may be regarded as the *causa* for the subsidiary contract.[257]

B. Gratuitous Promises

152. A gratuitous agreement is an ordinary contract, provided that all the usual requirements for the creation of a contract are present. Executory donations are required by statute to be in writing and signed by the donor to be valid.[258]

---

253. To ascertain the true intention of the parties, the court will take into account all the relevant circumstances, including the manner in which the agreement is implemented – *see*, for example, *Michau v. Maize Board* 2003 6 SA 459 (SCA); *Unica Iron and Steel (Pty) Ltd v. Mirchandani* 2016 2 SA 307 (SCA); *Commissioner for the South African Revenue Service v. NWK Ltd* 2011 2 SA 67 (SCA) where it is said that 'the commercial sense' and 'the real purpose' of a transaction should also be considered in order to ascertain the intention and purpose of the parties; *Bosch and Another v. Commissioner, South African Revenue Service* 2013 5 SA 130 (WCC); *Roshcon (Pty) Ltd v. Anchor Auto Body Builders CC and Others* 2014 4 SA 319 (SCA) where the 'legitimate commercial purpose' was a factor indicating actual intention.
254. *See Alexander v. Perry* 1874 Buch 59; *Mtembu v. Webster* (1904) 21 SC 323.
255. *See Conradie v. Rossouw* 1919 AD 279.
256. *See Saambou-Nasionale Bouvereniging Bpk v. Friedman* 1979 3 SA 978 (A).
257. For a critical analysis of this decision, *see* S. van der Merwe & M.F.B. Reinecke, 'Usher v. AWS Louw Elektriese Kontrakteurs 1979 2 SA 1059 (O) en Saambou Nasionale Bouvereniging v. Friedman 1979 3 SA 978 (A)', *Tydskrif vir Hedendaagse Romeins-Hollandse Reg* (1979): 432.
258. Section 5 of Act 50 of 1956.

C. Natural Obligations

153. According to South African law, a natural obligation is a legal tie and not merely a moral relationship. It can be created by an agreement, which may establish either full or limited natural obligations. Although it cannot be enforced directly, a full (*plena*) natural obligation can be discharged validly and can be offset against a civil obligation. It can also be the basis of an accessory contract, such as suretyship or pledge. Whether it can be novated is a matter of controversy. In the case of natural obligations with limited effect (*minus plenae*), most of these consequences do not follow. It is often said that an obligation that requires performance by a minor who has acted without the necessary consent is a natural obligation. The position with respect to wagers and bets is particularly unclear, because of uncertainty in Roman-Dutch law and, of course, the changing mores of society.[259] From a practical point of view, it remains uncertain whether such agreements create full natural obligations,[260] and whether performance may be reclaimed subject to the *par delictum* rule. Other examples of natural obligations in modern South African law are of little practical importance.

III. Reasonable Reliance

154. As in other systems of law in which an agreement or consensus is generally regarded as the basis of a contract, South African law has not been prepared to hold that contractual liability can never result when there is dissensus or disagreement. Accordingly, the notion that a court may decide on objective grounds whether a party who laboured under a material mistake should nevertheless be held bound, and that a material mistake will only excuse liability if it was justifiable (*verschoonbaar*) to boot, is also part of South African law. This notion will be discussed in more detail below in the context of liability and negotiations, as well as with reference to mistakes and the consequences of mistakes.

Suffice it here to point out that the law has developed to the extent that the rules, which have been applied to solve this exceptional problem regarding mistakes, now form the substance of an alternative and supplementary basis for contract: in principle, a contract can come about in the absence of consensus when the will of one party coincides with the reasonable reliance created in his or her mind by the other party about the latter's will.[261] The doctrine of estoppel by representation, which has become a distinct doctrine in South African law via English law, has in the past been

259. Of course, some wagers and bets may be completely legal and enforceable, because they are not against the public interest or are sanctioned by law – *see* the National Gambling Act of 2004.

260. In *Nichol v. Burger* 1990 1 SA 231 (C), the Court was in favour of allowing set-off of a wagering debt.

261. *See* Van Huyssteen, Lubbe & Reinecke, *Contract General Principles* ch. 3 E and G. (Juta 2016); *Sonap Petroleum (SA) (Pty) Ltd (formerly known as Sonarep (SA) (Pty) Ltd) v. Pappadogianis* 1992 3 SA 234 (A); *Steyn v. LSA Motors Ltd* 1994 1 SA 49 (A); *Investec Bank Ltd v. Lefkowitz* 1997 1 SA (A); *HNR Properties CC v. Standard Bank of SA Ltd* 2004 4 SA 471 (SCA) 480–481; *Constantia Insurance Co. Ltd v. Compusource (Pty) Ltd* 2005 4 SA 345 (SCA); *Pillay v. Shaik* 2009 (4) SA 74 (SCA). Other terms have also been used to describe more or less the same principle, for

advanced as an alternative method for preventing a contract denier from escaping liability (even in the absence of consensus) when he or she has represented that he or she agrees and intends to be liable.[262]However, and importantly, the doctrine of reasonable mistake (*iustus* error) has been often applied in practice (e.g., where a party signs a contract without reading its contents but the other party who wishes to enforce it, due to his own conduct, did not reasonably believe that there was agreement) to reach the same result – the only difference being the location of the onus of proof. These two approaches have now merged to provide an alternative basis for contract. [263]

§2. Formal and Evidential Requirements

I. Formal Requirements

A. Contracts by Deed

155. From what has been said above, it follows that contracts under seal or by deed as they still appear in some common law systems (and particularly insofar as the concept may relate to the requirement of consideration) are not known in South African law. Insofar as the requirements relating to contracts by deed in these systems serve to protect either of the contractants or third parties and to effect publication, South African law achieves the same ends by requiring formalities such as writing, notarial execution, and registration in a public office for the validity or enforceability of certain contracts.

156. The regulation of donations in South African law has been eased substantially by a specific change to common law, with the result that, in principle, a donation no longer needs to be registered or notarially executed to be valid. An executory donation, however, must be in writing and signed by the donor.[264] This only applies to donations resting solely on the generosity of the donor; hence, a donation made

---

example, 'constructive consent', 'quasi-mutual assent'; cf. also the frequent references to the 'principle' formulated in the English case of *Smith v. Hughes* (1871) LR 6 QB 597. Previously, reference to the case of *South African Railways & Harbours v. National Bank of South Africa Ltd* 1924 AD 704 was made in this context. In that case, the Court also advanced some kind of objective approach to the conclusion of a contract, although many and varied interpretations have been put on the words of the Court.

262. All the other requirements for estoppel must be proved, including (probably) fault – cf. *Saambou-Nasionale Bouvereniging Bpk. v. Friedman* 1979 3 SA 978 (A).

263. Van Huyssteen, Lubbe & Reinecke, *Contract General Principles* ch. 3 F and G. (Juta 2016); *Slip Knot Investments 777 (Pty) Ltd v. Du Toit* 2011 4 SA 72 (SCA) paras 9–11; *cf. Spenmac (Pty) Ltd v. Tatrim CC* 2015 3 SA 46 (SCA).

264. *See*, for example, *Estate Phillips v. Commissioner for Inland Revenue* 1942 AD 35 for the previous position and *see* now s. 5 Act 50 of 1956.

in an antenuptial contract[265] is usually not affected by these requirements. A donation *mortis causa* must comply with the formalities required for wills.[266]

B. 'Solemn' Contracts

157. It was stated earlier that the term 'solemn contract' has no technical meaning in South African law, and, since it shifts the emphasis away from the central concept of consensus, it should best be avoided. When requirements such as writing, signature, or registration are set for the validity of a contract, they are construed as formalities and as constitutive elements for the contract (see the discussion on the definition of a contract in the General Introduction for a different approach to the 'place' of formalities in the theoretical structure of the concept of a contract).

C. Formalities Imposed by Parties and by Statute

158. Two broad classifications of formalities may be discerned, namely those imposed by the contractants themselves and those imposed by statute. Common law does not prescribe formalities.

1. Formalities Imposed by Parties

159. In exercising their freedom of contract, parties may agree that a particular formality, such as writing and signature, must be complied with as a constitutive element of their contract. They may subsequently also agree to dispense with the formality or may, after conclusion of the contract, cancel the contract orally, or, in principle, vary the terms informally. When the parties have included in the contract a so-called non-variation clause, which prescribes writing for any variation, it should depend on the intention of the parties whether an oral variation can be effective. In spite of criticism, it would seem that the courts, for policy reasons (including that of *pacta sunt servanda*), are inclined to interpret such a clause strictly, so as to uphold any entrenchment that the parties may have intended and will refuse to allow them subsequently to change their minds and effect an oral variation.[267] A waiver is said not to be subject to a non-variation clause. The distinction between

---

265. However, for the contract to be effective with respect to third parties, it must be registered in terms of ss 86–89 of the Deeds Registries Act 47 of 1937.
266. Wills Act 7 of 1953.
267. *See*, for example, *SA Sentrale Ko-op Graanmaatskappy Bpk v. Shifren* 1964 4 SA 760 (A). Recently, the Supreme Court of Appeal found that a non-variation clause was not unreasonable or against the good faith and came out strongly in favour of freedom of contract and *pacta sunt servanda* – *Brisley v. Drotsky* 2002 4 SA 1 (HHA); *Yarram Trading CC t/a Tijuana Spur v. Absa Bank Ltd* 2007 2 SA 570 (SCA); *Cecil Nurse (Pty) Ltd v. Nkola* 2008 2 SA 441 (SCA); *De Villiers v. Mc Kay* 2008 4 SA 161 (SCA) – even a prior inducing contract that varies from the main written contract is to be left out of consideration. Nevertheless, there is a limited scope for rendering such a clause ineffective on the basis of fraud or other unreasonable conduct – *see* Van Huyssteen, Lubbe

a waiver and agreeing not to apply a non-variation clause is a fine one, and it is not conducive to certainty in this context. Likewise, cancellation of a part of a contract has been said to be a form of variation, whereas cancellation of the entire contract is not.

Often, parties require writing only for purposes of proof and not as a constitutive requirement.

2. Formalities Imposed by Statute

160. In South Africa, there is no general legislation requiring formalities for contracts, but a number of statutes deal with particular types of contracts. Formalities may be imposed by statute for a variety of objectives (which may be relevant when interpreting the statute), and non-compliance may have different consequences.

1. Often, compliance with prescribed formalities is a prerequisite for the validity of the contract in question. The most important examples are the following:
   - sales, donations, and exchanges of land must be in writing and signed by both parties or their agents, acting upon written authority (Alienation of Land Act 68 of 1981);
   - contracts of suretyship must be in writing and signed by the surety (section 6 of the General Law Amendment Act 50 of 1956);
   - executory donations must be in writing and signed by the donor or his or her agent acting on written authority (section 5 of Act 50 of 1956); and
   - where legislation requires a document to be in writing, electronic declarations are regarded as equivalent, subject to certain provisions;[268]
2. Generally, non-compliance with such formalities results in complete nullity of the particular contract. However, when land has been transferred in terms of a defective alienation and when the alienee has performed in full, section 28 of Act 68 of 1981 accords full effect to the alienation as if it had been valid *ab initio*. Any performance that was made in terms of an invalid agreement may, in general, be reclaimed by an appropriate enrichment action, usually, the *condictio sine causa*. With respect to reclaiming performance in terms of a defective alienation of land that has not been fully performed, the statute permits recovery plus interest and compensation for necessary expenditures and certain useful improvements.
3. The National Credit Act 34 of 2005 is an example of legislation requiring compliance with certain formalities.[269]

& Reinecke, *Contract General Principles* para. 5.7 et seq. (Juta 2016). *See Nyandeni Local Municipality v. Hlazo* 2010 4 SA 261 (ECM) where the court refused to apply the so-called Shifren-principle in the interests of public policy.

268. Sections 11, 12, and 14–19 of the Electronic Communications and Transactions Act 25 of 2002. Section 13 deals with electronic signatures when such is required by law or the parties; cf. *Spring Forest Trading CC v. Wilberry (Pty) Ltd t/a Ecowash and Another* 2015 2 SA 118 (SCA) where the court interpreted sec 13.
269. *See also* s. 50 of the Consumer Protection Act 68 of 2008, which provides that certain consumer contracts may be required to be in writing.

4. By statute, certain contracts (many of them dealing with land) will only be valid against *third parties* if the contracts are notarially executed, registered against the title deed of the land concerned, or registered in an official registry. The following examples are the most important:
- long leases of land will not be binding for more than ten years against creditors or onerous successors in title, unless attested to by a notary and registered against the title deed of the land;
- antenuptial contracts must be attested to by a notary public and registered in a deeds registry within three months. Spouses whose matrimonial property is regulated by foreign law and who later become domiciled in South Africa need not register their foreign antenuptial contract for it to be valid against third parties;
- mortgages securing immovable property, if they are to provide a real right to the mortgagee, must be prepared by a conveyancer, executed in the presence of the Registrar of Deeds, and attested to and registered by him or her against the title deed of the property;
- a bond hypothecating movable property must be notarially executed and registered in a deeds registry. The bondholder does not obtain a real right to the property, but on the sequestration of the estate of the mortgagor, he or she has a preferential claim; and
- certain rights to mine and mining leases must be notarially executed and registered in the Mining Titles Registry or against the title deeds of the land to be effective against third parties;

D. Function of a Notary

161. In general terms, one may say that the function of a South African notary[270] is to serve as an expert and reliable adviser on the drafting of important contracts and authentication of documents, especially those that affect the rights of third parties. By law, a person may not practice as a notary without having been admitted as an attorney and without having passed a special practical examination;[271] a notary must preserve certain documents attested to before him or her and keep a protocol of them; the particularly high standard of professional conduct required of a notary in the execution of his or her duties provides protection to the public and some guarantee of skill and reliability, and certain favourable evidentiary assumptions are made with respect to notarially executed documents.

A notary does not have a monopoly on the drafting of contracts in general, and despite the fact that the office of notary is highly regarded, it is not the practice to instruct only legal advisers who are notaries to draft contracts. It seems that notaries are mainly used as such with respect to the drafting and attestation of those contracts that are required by law to be notarially executed and with respect to the noting of protests regarding bills of exchange as required by law. The preparation and

270. *See* in general M.J. Lowe et al., *Elliott: The South African Notary* (Juta 1987); F.E. van der Merwe, *Notarial Practice* (Butterworths 2001).
271. *See* s. 18 of the Attorneys Act 53 of 1979.

execution of some documents, notably deeds of transfer and mortgages of immovable property, must by law be done by another type of specialized advisor, a conveyancer.

162. Apart from the usual professional responsibilities of an attorney, a higher standard of care and the execution of certain more specific duties are required from a notary. Since a notary is a specialist in the drafting of documents, as evidenced by his or her having successfully completed a professional practical examination in that regard, the standard of care in drafting required from him or her will probably be higher than the standard required from an attorney. In general, the courts seem to require a higher standard of professional conduct by a notary. To warrant the solemnity and justify the public nature of a notarial document, the careful and exact execution of the following more specific duties are required:

- Before executing a deed or notarial instrument, the notary should satisfy himself or herself that he or she has the necessary jurisdiction; notaries are admitted in specific divisions of the High Court and in general may only practice as such within the area of jurisdiction of that Court.
- The notary must be adequately conversant in the language in which the document is to be drawn if he or she accepts the mandate.
- The document must be read aloud clearly and explained to the appearers.
- The notary must make sure that the document is complete and regular in every way; in particular, it should not be executed with any blank spaces.
- The notary must not allow a person to sign as a witness if that person did not actually see the appearer's sign, unless the signature is acknowledged to the witness by the appearer.
- The notary must be satisfied as to the competency of the appearers and the witnesses.
- The law with respect to form and other requirements, including stamp duties, relating to a contract or instrument, must be carefully observed.
- The notary must establish the identity of the appearers.
- The notary should not be an interested party.
- The notary must carefully preserve certain deeds and keep a proper protocol and register in the prescribed form.
- It is customary for a notary to have a seal.

II. Evidential Requirements

A. Ordinary Principles of Evidence Apply

163. In general, the ordinary principles of the South African law of evidence[272] apply to proof of the existence or the contents of a contract. At a trial, evidence may be adduced either orally by way of testimony or in documentary form supported by oral evidence or in any other admissible form. However, despite some liberalization

272. *See* in general D. Zeffertt et al., *The South African Law of Evidence* (Lexis Nexis 2017).

of the rules relating to proof (e.g., the admissibility of hearsay evidence in certain circumstances), South African courts are still to some extent more concerned with the application of formal and strict 'rules' of evidence (e.g., the so-called parol evidence rule, with respect to which, it must at once be noted, strong criticism has been raised, to the effect that the rule puts a serious restriction on a basic tenet of the law of contract, that is, so far as is reasonably possible, the subjective intention of the contracting parties should be carried out[273]) than with the main principle, namely the weight that a court may attach to particular evidence in the circumstances. To a large extent, the South African court procedure and law of evidence is derived from English law.

164. The standard of proof upon which a court will base its finding is that of a balance of probabilities – the litigant who bears the burden of proof must satisfy the court that the facts upon which he or she rests his or her case are probably correct, or more probable than those relied upon by his or her adversary.

B. Documentary Evidence

165. As a general rule, a litigant who presents documentary evidence must produce the *original* document by way of the testimony of the person who made or signed the document.[274] This rule is subject to some exceptions, such as that a copy or printout of an electronic contract may suffice.[275]

Such evidence could adequately prove only the authenticity and existence of the document. Contents of a document are admissible as evidence only if the authenticity of the document is proved or admitted, but the accuracy of the contents will still have to be proved in the ordinary way by other (usually oral) evidence. Reference to the document will, of course, make the task much easier.[276] A public document (made by a public official in the execution of his or her duties) may be tendered as proof of the accuracy of its contents, without further evidence.

166. When, for whatever reason, an agreement has been rendered in writing, the general approach of the courts is to deny the admissibility of any evidence beyond the document itself (so-called extrinsic evidence) to prove the terms of the contract

---

273. *See*, for example, Van Huyssteen, Lubbe & Reinecke, *Contract General Principles ch. 5 E* (Juta 2016).
274. This is often cited as one of the remaining examples in South African law of the common law rule of 'best evidence'.
275. Section 15 of Act 25 of 2002.
276. An interesting problem in this connection relates to the validity of a clause in a loan or suretyship agreement in terms of which the borrower or surety agrees that a certificate issued by an official of the creditor will be conclusive proof of the balance or amount owing at that time. The matter is dealt with as one of legality and public policy. The Appeal Court, after various conflicting provincial decisions, has now ruled that such a clause is *contra bonos mores* and thus void. *See Ex Parte Minister of Justice: In Re Nedbank Ltd v. Abstein Distributors (Pty) Ltd & Donnelly v. Barclays National Bank Ltd* 1995 3 SA 1 (A). Note, however, that in *Society of Lloyd's v. Romahn* 2006 4 SA 23 (C), the Court expressed the opinion that it might be time to reconsider this approach of the Appeal Court.

and that would tend to contradict the terms or would serve to support an interpretation beyond a simple linguistic one,[277] such evidence being regarded as irrelevant and misleading. This approach is based on the parol evidence rule that was incorporated into South African law from English law.

167. It will be appreciated immediately that the application of this rule is far from simple. Briefly put, nevertheless, one may say that the rule will prohibit extrinsic evidence when the parties intend the document to be the full and final reflection of their agreement (and, therefore, it is an 'integrated' document) and when the evidence tends to contradict the terms of the contract as they appear in the document. Thus, for example, when parties intended to document only a part of their whole agreement, extrinsic evidence may be presented to prove the rest of the agreement. Also, evidence proving that the agreement is void or voidable will not be contradictory to the terms and is admissible.

168. As pointed out above, the rule has been subjected to severe and cogent criticism to the extent that it does not serve the purpose for which it was intended but in fact creates uncertainty, and also that it unnecessarily undermines the principle of freedom of contract.

C. Probative Effect of Notarial Instruments

169. There is a prima facie assumption that declarations by the notary in a notarial instrument about its execution, the formalities complied with, and the documents and authorizations exhibited to him or her are correct. The assumption does not cover declarations for which the notary cannot vouch personally. The assumption can be refuted by contrary evidence.

D. Probative Effect of Signed and Unsigned Documents

170. Generally, the mere fact that a document has been signed does not prove the existence of any legal act reflected in the document or its contents sufficiently, nor is there any presumption or assumption in that regard.

---

277. *See* Van Huyssteen, Lubbe & Reinecke, *Contract General Principles* paras 5.45–5.47 for a discussion of the scope of the prohibition of extrinsic evidence. Also, in light of the new approach to interpretation that the literal meaning of the words is only the starting point of a unitary interpretation which takes into account all relevant context (whether background or surrounding), this limitation on extrinsic evidence may well be discarded in future *cf. North East Finance (Pty) Ltd v. Standard Bank of South Africa Ltd* 2013 5 SA 1 (SCA); *Bothma-Batho Transport (Edms) Bpk v. S Bothma & Seun Transport (Edms) Bpk* 2014 2 SA 494 (SCA); *Unica Iron and Steel (Pty) Ltd v. Mirchandani* 2016 2 SA 307 (SCA); *G4S Cash Solutions (SA) (Pty) Ltd v. Zandspruit Cash & Carry (Pty) Ltd and Another* 2017 (2) SA 24 (SCA); *GPC Developments CC v. Uys* [2017] 4 All SA 14 (WCC); *Auction Alliance (Pty) Ltd v. Wade Park (Pty) Ltd 2018 (4) SA 358 (SCA)* and the discussion below at para. 295 et seq.

171. In terms of the general principles of contractual liability, a person who signs a contractual document is usually (subject, however, to the rules relating to reasonable reliance and *iustus error*) taken to be bound to the terms of the document. Accordingly, the presentation of such a document by way of the evidence of the other party will be strong evidence and often sufficient proof on a balance of probability that the contract exists.

172. An unsigned document by itself is usually not sufficient proof of the existence of a contract on the terms contained in the document. Other and further evidence is necessary. In practice, when a ticket or receipt has been issued by one party, and the other party (usually a customer) denies liability and knowledge of the terms, particularly exclusion clauses, the question often arises as to whether the document and its contents (were intended to) form the contract and its terms. Although the general principles of contractual liability also apply here, the courts have developed a number of practical 'rules' by which the issuer of the ticket should proceed to prove that the customer is bound by the receipt or ticket.[278] These rules derive from English law and are usually set out as follows:

(a) Did the customer know that the ticket contained writing, and did he or she know that the writing contained the terms of the contract? If so, the customer is bound. If either of these two questions is answered in the negative, the next question is:
(b) Did the issuer of the ticket take reasonable steps to bring the terms to the notice of the customer, for example, by reasonably drawing attention to the terms?

If he or she did so, the writing constitutes the contract or terms of the contract, and the customer is bound; if not, the customer is not bound.

It must be remembered that these so-called rules should be regarded only as guidelines for the courts for applying the general principles of the creation of contracts.[279]

E. Probative Effect of the Date of a Signed Document

173. A document is assumed to have been executed on the date that it bears. If there is evidence to the contrary, a court may find differently.

278. *See*, for example, *Micor Shipping (Pty) Ltd v. Treger Golf & Sports (Pty) Ltd* 1977 2 SA 709 (W); *Bok Clothing Manufacturers (Pty) Ltd v. Lady Land (Pty) Ltd* 1982 2 SA 565 (C); *Durban's Water Wonderland (Pty) Ltd v. Botha* 1999 1 SA 982 (SCA); *Sun Couriers (Pty) Ltd v. Kimberley Diamond Wholesalers* 2001 3 SA 110 (NC); *Cape Group Construction (Pty) Ltd t/a Forbes Waterproofing v. Government of the United Kingdom* 2003 5 SA 180 (SCA).

279. *See* Van Huyssteen, Lubbe & Reinecke, *Contract General Principles* paras 9.209–9.215 (Juta 2016); *Union Spinning Mills (Pty) Ltd v. Paltex Dye House (Pty) Ltd* 2002 4 SA 408 (SCA); *D & H Piping Systems (Pty) Ltd v. Trans Hex Group Ltd* 2006 3 SA 593 (SCA).

F. Registration

174. As has already been indicated in the context of formalities required for the validity or external effect of contracts, certain contracts (commercial and otherwise) must be registered, mostly after their notarial execution. To the examples already given may be added contracts by which spouses change their matrimonial property regime. Such contracts must be notarially executed and registered in a deeds registry.

G. Admissibility and Probative Effect of Copies, Books of Account, and Other Records

175. Copies of original documents are admissible as evidence only in exceptional circumstances, such as the following:

- when the document is in the possession of the opposing party, who has failed to produce it;
- when the document is in possession of a third party who fails to disclose it on grounds of privilege;
- when the document is destroyed or lost; and
- when the production of the original is otherwise impossible or inconvenient;

176. Copies of the books of account of a bank are admissible. Entries in such books are prima facie proof of their contents upon the production of an affidavit in which certain facts are stated. There are specific requirements relating to notice to the opposing party.

H. Evidence by Testimony, Presumptions of Law and Fact, and Inferences

177. Oral evidence, as will be clear, is the most important form of evidence in South African law. This applies also to evidence in civil matters and to the use of documents as evidence. With respect to civil proceedings, it is specifically provided by legislation that judgment may be given upon the evidence of any single competent and credible witness. Testimony must be given under oath or affirmation. Since the system of judicial enquiry generally is by trial in an adversarial system, testimony is subject to cross-examination by the opponent.

178. True presumptions (often called presumptions of law) must be distinguished from inferences (sometimes called presumptions of fact) and prima facie evidence or proof. Presumptions may be irrebuttable, in which case they are not different from a rule of law, or they may be rebuttable. A true presumption does not depend on any inference but must be accepted as correct until disproved by contrary evidence – it compels the provisional assumption of a fact. If, for example, service of a document is required by law to be made by post, a communication sent by registered post is presumed to be an effective service. The use of presumptions relating to the law of contract, even indirectly, is very limited. Thus, for example, there is no presumption of compliance with formalities, legality, possibility of performance, or the existence of an intent when a document has been signed.

179. In light of the importance and pervasiveness of oral evidence in South African law, the drawing of inferences by a court from circumstantial or surrounding evidence is an everyday occurrence. In fact, a central aspect in the creation of a contract, the intention to be legally bound, must usually be ascertained by way of inference. An example of a more weighted inference in the field of contracts is the inference that if a defect in goods is found shortly after its purchase, it is inferred that the defect was present at the time of the sale. A court should always be satisfied that the inference is probable in the circumstances.

Prima facie evidence means that a court may infer, in the absence of evidence from the opponent, that the litigant who bears the burden of proof has probably fulfilled it. Examples of what constitute such proof have been mentioned already.

I. Proving a Tacit Contract or Tacit Term

180. Although, in principle, there is no difference in quality between express and tacit contracts or terms, the latter must, in the nature of things, be proved by inference from indirect or circumstantial evidence. When deciding whether a tacit term or its content has been proved, South African courts have adopted the so-called innocent-bystander test of English law.[280] The matter is not free from controversy; yet it would seem that the courts will be willing to accept a tacit term even when the parties did not actually have the term in mind, but when, in all the circumstances, it may reasonably be assumed or inferred that the parties would have agreed on those terms had their attention been drawn to the circumstances requiring the term.[281] To some extent thus, the test has been objectified, but the term must still be compatible with the parties' expressed intention.[282] The courts will also generally be slow to import a tacit term.[283] Factors that a court will take into account are the business efficacy of the contract without the term and the so-called imputed intention of the parties, in other words, what reasonable parties in the circumstances

280. The case most often referred to in this regard is *Reigate v. Union Manufacturing Co. (Ramsbottom)* 118 LT 479, restated, for example, in *Alfred Mc Alpine & Son (Pty) Ltd v. Transvaal Provincial Administration* 1974 3 SA 506 (A) 532–533.

281. *See*, for example, *Alfred Mc Alpine & Son (Pty) Ltd v. Transvaal Provincial Administration* 1974 3 SA 506 (A); *Van den Berg v. Tenner* 1975 2 SA 268 (A); *Wilkens v. Voges* 1994 3 SA 130 (A) *Botha v. Coopers and Lybrand* 2002 5 SA 347 (SCA); *South African Forestry Co Ltd v. York Timbers Ltd* 2005 3 SA 323 (SCA 339E; *McDonald v. Young* 2012 3 SA 1 (SCA) para. 25; *Airports Company South Africa Ltd v. Airport Bookshops (Pty) Ltd t/a Exclusive Books* 2016 1 SA 473 (GJ) paras 25–33.

282. *See McDonald v. Young* 2012 3 SA 1 (SCA).

283. *See*, for example, *Birkenruth Estates (Pty) Ltd v. Unitrans Motors (Pty) Ltd (formerly Malbak Consumer Products (Pty) Ltd)* 2005 3 SA 54 (W) 64; *City of Cape Town (CMC Administration) v. Bourbon-Leftley and Another NNO* 2006 3 SA 488 (SCA) 494–495; *Scopeful 130 (Pty) Ltd v. Mechani Mag (Pty) Ltd* 2008 3 SA 483 (W); *Nedcor Bank Ltd v. SDR Investment Holdings Co. (Pty) Ltd and Others* 2008 3 SA 544 (SCA).

would have agreed upon. Since this is always a matter of inference, the term alleged must be axiomatic, in the sense that it must be the only reasonably plausible term that can be inferred and not merely one of the number of possible terms. An inference that an entire contract has been concluded tacitly will, by nature of the circumstances, usually be difficult to draw in practice.

J. Admissions

181. Admissions can be either formal admissions or informal admissions. Formal admissions are usually made in the pleadings or at pre-trial conferences and serve to define or limit the issues. The content of these admissions need not be proved. Informal admissions may be adduced as evidence against the maker of the admission to disprove his or her case or to prove his or her opponent's case. An admission may be proved by the evidence of the person to whom it was made. Often, in the course of attempting to settle a matter, parties make admissions 'without prejudice'. Such admissions are generally inadmissible.

K. Expert Evidence

182. In general, the opinion of expert witnesses on the correct or most probable inference to be drawn from certain facts is admissible if the court is satisfied that the witness is sufficiently qualified or experienced to give assistance. It remains for the court to decide on the weight to be attached to such evidence. A litigant in civil proceedings who wishes to call an expert witness must notify his or her opponent accordingly.

L. Direct and Circumstantial Evidence

183. In principle, there is no difference in quality between direct evidence and circumstantial evidence, at least in civil trials. The difference will lie in the weight attached to the kinds of evidence, in light of what evidence is available to a litigant.

M. Other Admissible Evidence

184. Apart from oral testimony or documentary evidence, a litigant may persuade a court to hold an inspection *in loco*. Photographs, audio and visual tapes, film, microfilm, and authenticated computer printouts are, in principle, admissible as evidence. In exceptional circumstances, evidence provided on commission and by affidavit may be adduced instead of oral evidence, such as in the case of expert scientific or medical evidence.

N. Discovery of Documents and Pre-trial Conference

185. 185 In terms of the statutes and rules governing both the High Court and the Magistrates' Court, a party to an action may, by notice, after the close of pleadings but before the trial, require any other party to provide a schedule of and to specify all documents that are or have at any time been in his or her possession or control, and that relate to any matter in question in the trial. No document that has not been disclosed in this manner may be used for any purpose at the trial. Documents that have been disclosed may be inspected.

To curtail proceedings at the trial, it is required in a High Court matter that the party who wishes to set the case for trial should invite the other party to attend a pre-trial conference. The parties may, for example, reach agreement on admissions, the exchange of experts' reports, and the amount of damages. Costs may be awarded against a party who refuses to attend such a conference. In the lower courts, it is the court that calls a conference at the request of a party or *suo motu.*

III. Burden of Proof

186. In principle, and apart from the influence of presumptions, the basic general rule of evidence that 'he who asserts must prove' applies also to the proof of the existence and contents of a contract. Thus, the party who alleges a contract must prove all the facts that founded its existence. Generally this applies also to proof of the contents of the alleged contract, even to the point that the contract assertor must, if necessary, prove the absence of a term on which the other party seeks to rely.[284]

As far as the requirement of legality is concerned, it will normally be assumed to be present, unless the party who wishes to rely on its absence raises the issue and brings just enough evidence to raise doubt about the legality – there is no presumption of legality, nor does the burden of proof shift to the other party: he or she merely has to satisfy the need for rebuttal. In principle, one would expect the same approach to apply to proof of possibility of performance and of contractual capacity, although with respect to the latter and the capacity to act in general, it is often said that there is a presumption in favour of the existence of such a capacity.[285]

187. With respect to proof that liability exists even in the absence of consensus, it should be required in principle that the contract assertor must directly prove facts to support the elements of reliance. Accordingly, he or she must prove that he or she relied reasonably on the existence of consensus (usually by showing that his or her mistake was caused by an unacceptable misrepresentation by the other party), and that the reliance coincided with his or her intention. However, it seems clear, at least when there is prima facie evidence of consensus (particularly when the party sought to be bound has signed a document that includes contractual terms), that the

284. *See Topaz Kitchens (Pty) Ltd v. Naboom Spa (Edms) Bpk* 1976 3 SA 470 (A).

285. In *Theron v. AA Life Assurance Association Ltd* 1995 4 SA 361 (A), the Appeal Court accepted that an insurer who denied the insurance proposer's 'mental capacity to conclude the contract of insurance' bore the 'onus' of proving the lack of such capacity.

contract assertor is required only to bring such evidence, and that the burden then shifts to the contract denier to prove that *his or her* mistake was material and reasonable (*iustus*). This approach is commonly called the *iustus error* approach. Although the issue has not been decided in clear terms, the duty on the contract denier seems to be regarded as a full onus rather than a mere need for rebuttal.[286]

188. A party who asserts that he or she has validly rescinded a contract on the grounds of improperly obtained consensus must prove all the necessary facts.

189. Similarly, a party who claims a remedy for a breach of contract must prove the breach. Whether or not a breach of contract is a new cause of action does not affect this position. When the question of mitigation of damage for a breach of contract arises, the onus to prove that the claimant failed to take reasonable steps to do so rests on the other party.

§3. Liability and Negotiations

190. In principle, in a legal system in which consensus is a central concept in the creation of contractual liability, pre-contractual negotiations by themselves do not bring about any direct contractual liability, unless, of course, the negotiations have reached such a stage that all the requirements for the formation of a contract have been met. Whether this is so is ordinarily a question of fact and can be established by inference from all the surrounding circumstances, including the negotiations and any admissible documents and memoranda drafted in the course thereof. However, when the conduct of a negotiating party has created in the mind of the other party the reasonable expectation that contractual liability has been established, such an expectation may be upheld by the law. Also, in many legal systems, unacceptable conduct or conduct that does not conform to the requirements of good faith during negotiations and that has caused harm may create liability to compensate the harm, to the extent to which the particular legal system may find it to be politic.

I. No General Theory of Pre-contractual Liability

191. So far, no general theory of pre-contractual liability has developed in South African law. Instead, the general principles of a delict have been applied directly or indirectly as guidelines to establish liability in certain instances of pre-contractual conduct, even in the case of liability for so-called restitutional damages. The doctrine of *culpa in contrahendo* has not taken root to provide a wider basis of liability,

286. For a more complete discussion of these matters, *see* Van Huyssteen, Lubbe & Reinecke, *Contract General Principles* para. 2.125 but in particular paras 2.130 and 2.132 (full onus)(Juta 2016); cf. also *George v. Fairmead (Pty) Ltd* 1958 2 SA 465 (A) and *Sonap Petroleum (SA) (Pty) Ltd (formerly known as Sonarep (SA) (Pty) Ltd v. Pappadogianis* 1992 3 SA 234 (A). In *Steyn v. LSA Motors Ltd* 1994 1 SA 49 (A), the question of onus was not considered by the Court – in fact, the pleadings were not analysed at all, since they did not assist in clarifying the issues.

nor has the doctrine of abuse of rights been developed beyond its strict field of application. However, in the context of mistakes, the law has recognized a wider basis than blameworthy conduct for establishing liability, namely the protection of the reasonable expectations of a negotiating party. As has been mentioned above it is possible that the duty to negotiate in good faith may result in the creation of norms of conduct and duties *in contrahendo* in specific circumstances.[287]

In practice, then, one has to consider the question of liability arising from negotiations with reference to the different specific situations in which the question arises.

II. When Consensus and Other Elements for Formation of a Contract Are Not Present and No Contract Results

192. As has been said above, a party will in certain circumstances be held bound to the terms of an ostensible agreement even when there is dissensus because of a material mistake. To put it briefly, such liability will follow when the contract denier has, usually by way of an unacceptable misrepresentation, created an impression in the mind of the contract assertor that he or she agreed to be bound to the terms as they ostensibly exist. His or her mistake in believing that there is no contract or that the terms are different from those upon which the contract assertor relies will then not be *iustus*, and the reliance of the other party will be reasonable.

In practice, it seems that the courts will be satisfied to hold the denier bound when the misrepresentation was wrongful. In this context, the courts have construed a *duty to speak* in circumstances that appear to be beyond the usual limits that apply to other situations. Fault on the part of the misrepresentor need not be present. There is tentative support for the approach that the contract assertor's reliance will be regarded as reasonable, even though it was not induced by a misrepresentation or when the misrepresentation was not wrongful in the strict delictual sense.[288]

193. There has been very little development regarding the elements of pre-contractual liability in the absence of the other requirements for the existence of a contract. Such development as there has been relates to a situation in which a party suffered loss (e.g., wasted expenses) in the belief that a contract existed, but when, because of initial impossibility of performance, it did not. Case law supports the approach that the loss may be recouped from the other party if he or she caused the loss by wrongful and blameworthy conduct. The principles of the law of delict will then be applicable,[289] and the damages will be calculated on the basis of compensation of the negative interest. In the absence of such conduct, the basic rule that the loss remains where it falls should apply. The risk principle, which is also relevant in a situation such as this, has not been specifically recognized or applied.

287. *See* paras 61, 66, 101–102 above and the authorities referred to there.
288. *See* further the discussion below and Van Huyssteen, Lubbe & Reinecke, *Contract General Principles* paras 2.91–2.124 (Juta 2016).
289. *See*, for example, *Coombs v. Muller* 1913 EDL 430.

There can be no objection in principle to the recognition of delictual liability in other situations within the broad context set out above.

194. Certain pre-contractual conduct, although it does not give rise directly to liability, may limit the right to reclaim performance in the case of an illegal agreement. In this sense, the conduct will create and perpetuate liability. In terms of the *par delictum* rule, participation in an illegal agreement precludes the granting of an enrichment action for the return of performance, unless the application of the rule is relaxed by the court in particular circumstances for reasons of policy.[290] Of course, post-contractual conduct must also be considered and will often be of more importance than the pre-contractual conduct.

III. Breakdown of Negotiations

195. In the absence of any agreement that regulates the conducting of further negotiations (e.g., so-called agreements to agree and option contracts), any party is, in principle, free to break off negotiations in any way and for any reason. Such conduct will not attract liability.

It has been pointed out above that, as the law stands, the concepts of good faith and ubuntu may well in future in specific circumstances develop to form the basis of norms and duties with respect to conducting negotiations according to South African law. The doctrine of *culpa in contrahendo* or any derivative of it has not taken root, despite traces of the doctrine in South African common law. There are no direct examples in case law; yet, when the elements of a delict are present, the loss caused may possibly be claimed by way of the extended *actio legis Aquiliae*. Thus, for example, when a negotiating party, knowing that he or she is not going to proceed with negotiations, and that a contract will certainly not result, intentionally leads the other into negotiations and causes him or her to expend money, delictual liability may result.

IV. Liability for Pre-contractual Conduct When a Contract Has Come into Being

196. Pre-contractual delictual conduct that induces a party to enter into a contract, which he or she would otherwise not have concluded, entitles that party to rescind the contract. If he or she nevertheless elects not to rescind the contract, he or she may claim compensation for *damages* according to the delictual measure of the negative interest. This will hold true irrespective of the kind of conduct in question, as long as all the elements of a delict are present.

Thus far, the courts have entertained claims for damages as a result of intentional and negligent misrepresentation and duress. A claim for damages based on undue influence has not yet been brought before the courts, although there is no reason in

290. Cf., for example, the leading case of *Jajbhay v. Cassim* 1939 AD 537.

principle why it should not be entertained. This may well also apply to the more recently recognized ground for rescission, namely 'commercial bribery'.[291]

The elements of fault and wrongfulness are central concepts in the context of liability for pre-contractual conduct. The latter element, insofar as it relates to a breach of a duty or a right, is a particularly useful instrument to limit or expand the grounds for liability in a legal system. Thus, it is of interest to note that the South African courts have only recently been prepared to recognize unequivocally delictual liability to compensate purely economic loss when a contract was concluded as a result of a negligent misstatement made *in contrahendo*. In this regard, the negotiations were an important part of the 'circumstantial matrix' for the requirement of wrongfulness.[292] In regard to a duty to inform, it has now been stated expressly by the Appeal Court that the test for wrongfulness in a pre-contractual setting (when it is alleged that the omission gave rise to a contract) is the same as in a non-contractual (delictual) setting.[293] It is improbable that the courts will readily extend liability to compensate for damages beyond the grounds mentioned.

The exact causal effect of conduct is an important aspect, particularly in relation to the application of the general measure of calculation of damages. In this regard, the distinction between *dolus dans causam contractui* and *dolus incidens in contractum* is significant in practice.

V. Duty to Inform

197. Although until very recently, the question of a duty to disclose information to one's co-contractant during negotiations has been dealt with rather haphazardly in South African case law, the principles of delict, in particular, those relating to the wrongfulness of an omission in the context of misrepresentation, have appeared to serve as the basis for construing such a duty. In many cases (mainly those dealing with insurance), the courts have explicitly applied concepts of delictual liability.

Recently, however, the Supreme Court of Appeal has stated unequivocally that the test for wrongfulness in this context is the same as that in a non-contractual context, and that the policy considerations regarding a failure to inform one's co-contractant have been synthesized into a *general* test for liability, based on the

291. Viz. when, succinctly put, a contracting party, without the knowledge of his or her co-contractant, bribes, by promise of reward, a third party, who is in a position to influence the co-contractant, indeed to exert such influence so as to persuade the co-contractant to conclude a contract with the briber or a related party. *See Extel Industrial (Pty) Ltd v. Crown Mills (Pty) Ltd* 1999 2 SA 719 (SCA).

292. *See Bayer South Africa (Pty) Ltd v. Frost* 1991 4 SA 559 (A); L.F. van Huyssteen, S. van der Merwe & J.H. Herbots, 'Onzorgvuldige en Onjuiste Informatie bij de Contractsluiting in het Zuidafrikaans Recht', *Tijdschrift voor Privaatrecht* 1 (1993): 61.

293. *See ABSA Bank Ltd v. Fouche* 2003 1 SA 176 (SCA), and the discussion below. Cf. *Fourway Haulage SA (Pty) Ltd v. SA National Roads Agency Ltd* 2009 2 SA 150 (SCA).

legal convictions of the community.[294] This recognition of a general test will no doubt lead to a nuanced and sophisticated application suited to the circumstances of each particular case.

Although the concept of good faith has been raised in this connection, its role here seems to be limited to that of a broad underlying value rather than a practically useful principle that is capable of delimitation.[295]

198. In general, an omission to disclose facts will be regarded as wrongful when a party to the negotiations has a duty to prevent a wrong impression from arising or to remove an existing wrong impression. Until recently, the courts seemed loath to construe such a duty, except in limited and specific circumstances. Thus, a duty exists when one party of necessity has to rely on the knowledge of the other, such as an insurer that has to rely on the knowledge of the insurance proposer in regard to the risk, and a purchaser who has to depend on the seller with respect to latent defects. Likewise, a duty may be construed when a fiduciary relationship exists, such as between attorney and client or financial adviser and client. For reasons of policy, specific duties may be imposed, such as the duty of an insolvent to disclose his or her insolvency in particular circumstances.

Now, however, a general duty based on the legal convictions of the community has been recognized by the Supreme Court of Appeal.[296] The duty was circumscribed in general terms to the effect that a contractant need not tell his or her co-contractant all that he or she knows about anything that may be material. He or she is only expected to speak when the information falls within his or her exclusive knowledge – when, in a practical and business sense, he or she is the only source – and the information is such that a right to have it communicated would be mutually recognized by honest people in the circumstances.[297]

199. When, in the process of assessing whether or not a material mistake about the existence of a consensus is reasonable, it appears that the mistake was caused by the contract assertor's failure to remove a wrong impression on the part of the contract denier, a duty to speak may be construed, even when the court would not have construed such a duty in the context of a claim for damages in the same circumstances. Thus, a duty will exist when the contract assertor knew or ought to have known that the other party was in error; or when, before the conclusion of the

294. *See ABSA Bank Ltd v. Fouche* 2003 1 SA 176 (SCA). In *Meintjes NO v. Coetzer* 2010 (5) SA 186 (SCA) the majority of the court saw fit to base its decision, not directly on the fact that there had been fraudulent, and thus wrongful, conduct in terms of the common law, but on the fact that such conduct was contrary to the Constitution and against public policy. Such an approach unnecessarily relies on constitutional principles, despite the existence of tried and tested rules of the common law – cf. the minority judgment of Leach J.

295. Cf. *Mutual & Federal Insurance Co. Ltd v. Oudtshoorn Municipality* 1985 1 SA 419 (A); *Brisley v. Drotsky* 2002 4 SA 1 (HHA). However, in other contexts as has been explained above, there is a trend to regard good faith as a concrete principle on which to base specific rules.

296. *See ABSA Bank Ltd v. Fouche* 2003 1 SA 176 (SCA).

297. In *ABSA Bank Ltd v. Fouche* 2003 1 SA 176 (SCA), it was alleged that the bank should have disclosed the absence of certain security measures at its safety deposit facility, and that if it had, the client would not have concluded a contract hiring a deposit box from the bank. As a result, the client had suffered financial loss as a result of a burglary at the facility.

contract, the contract assertor created an impression that was in direct conflict with what he or she now alleges to be the contract, and he or she had no reason to believe that the other party would have agreed if that party had been aware of the inconsistency.[298]

VI. Rescission and Restitution

200. Certain conduct by one party during negotiations may provide grounds for the other party to avoid (rescind) the contract, with resultant rights and duties to return any performance that has been rendered.

Traditionally, the grounds justifying rescission have been limited to misrepresentation (including misrepresentation that is not accompanied by fault, so-called innocent misrepresentation), duress, and undue influence. Although these grounds, except perhaps innocent misrepresentation and undue influence, may all be classified as delicts, the right to rescind does not appear to depend on the existence of all the elements of a delict, but rather on the presence of improper conduct that amounts to an unacceptable inroad into a contractant's freedom of decision and expression – hence the frequent reference to 'defects of will' or the quality of the conduct in this context.

201. It now seems clear that the courts are willing to allow rescission on the basis of any kind of conduct by which the aggrieved party's consent has been obtained improperly; the courts have acknowledged that the traditional grounds cannot be airtight, and it seems that the recognition of general grounds for rescission on the basis of improperly obtained consensus is in progress and well-advanced.[299] For the time being, the concept of wrongfulness as applied in a pre-contractual setting will probably be employed by the courts as the main element to limit the right to rescind and to provide the content of the notion of improperly obtained consensus. In principle, prejudice or detriment should not be a requirement, although the presence of serious prejudice is a factor relevant to the impropriety of conduct and also to the existence of a causal link. Prejudice is a requirement in some legal systems (sometimes because of a link with the doctrine of *laesio enormis*), but this issue has not yet been addressed directly in South African law.

---

298. *See*, for example, *Du Toit v. Atkinson's Motors Bpk* 1985 2 SA 893 (A); *Spindrifter (Pty) Ltd v. Lester Donovan (Pty) Ltd* 1986 1 SA 303 (A); *Prins v. ABSA Bank Ltd* 1998 3 SA 904 (C); *Bam v. Rafedam Boerdery BK* 2004 1 SA 484 (O).

299. *See* Van Huyssteen, Lubbe & Reinecke, *Contract General Principles* ch. 4 E (Juta 2016) and the cases cited there but see the conservative approach of the Court in *BOE Bank Bpk v. Van Zyl* 2002 5 SA 165 (KPA). The Consumer Protection Act 68 of 2008 empowers a court to declare a consumer contract void and to order restitution where unconscionable or false misleading or deceptive conduct led to its conclusion. Unconscionability is defined very widely to include undue influence, unfair tactics and abuse of circumstances. It is quite possible that the courts might eventually extend the common law grounds for rescission or might even accept a general ground of improperly obtained consensus for other contracts.

202. In contrast to the position in some other legal systems, rescission is construed in South African law as a unilateral act that extinguishes the obligation concerned. The role of the court is merely to confirm the act in cases of dispute. As a consequence of rescission, the parties may claim restitution of what has been performed. Both rescission and restitution are contractual remedies and are therefore not dependent on the elements of delict, particularly fault. Restitution entails a *full* return to the previous position: a party is entitled not only to that which has been performed, but also to a sum of money that may be necessary to bring about full restitution, such as compensation for wasted costs and a depreciation in the value of the performance that is returned.[300]

VII. Damages

203. To establish whether damage has been suffered as a result of pre-contractual conduct and to assess the extent of such loss, the principles of delictual liability are applied. Whether a claimant has indeed suffered damage is established in South African law by the well-known 'difference theory' as it has evolved in some European systems: the claimant's present patrimonial position is compared with the hypothetical position in which he or she would have been, had the conduct complained of not been committed. If, by comparison, he or she is worse off, the difference has to be compensated. This difference is usually typified as the claimant's negative interest as distinguished from his or her positive interest, which is regarded as a more appropriate measure of damages for a breach of contract. Although this distinction is currently used by the courts, there is a tendency to view the distinction not as an immutable principle but rather as a useful method for assessing whether the act complained of has caused loss and, if so, the extent of that loss.

204. If the test of negative interest is applied to a case in which a contract is rescinded, the claimant is usually entitled to his or her direct losses, such as wasted costs (which could well be simply part of restitution). Consequential loss may also be claimed, for example, when an insecticide, which was represented to be safe, causes crop losses.[301]

205. When a contract is not rescinded but damages are claimed nevertheless, the exact factual causal effect of the conduct complained of must be carefully considered. In this context, the distinction between *dolus dans* (when no contract would have been concluded at all) and *dolus incidens* (when a contract would have been concluded, but on different terms) has been consistently applied by the courts in the calculation of damages. The effect of such an application is, for example, that a

300. The relation between the modern remedy of rescission and restitution and *restitutio in integrum* of Roman and Roman-Dutch law is not clear. Also, it is often difficult to distinguish between restitution and damages.

301. Cf. *Kroonstad Westelike Boere-Ko-operatiewe Vereniging Bpk v. Botha* 1964 3 SA 561 (A).

claimant may claim damages even when the value of his or her performance as actually agreed upon (e.g., a purchase price) is less than the value of the performance of the other party (e.g., the market value of property), *provided* that the claimant can prove that the parties would have agreed on an even lower performance (the putative performance) were it not for the misrepresentation – in other words, if the claimant can prove that he or she would have made a better bargain.[302] Sometimes the onus to prove the putative performance will be very difficult to discharge. Therefore, the courts have been willing to accept that the putative price will usually be equal to the market value. It is doubtful that an actual presumption in this respect has evolved – more probably, the courts mean that, in the absence of proof to the contrary, it may be accepted prima facie as probable that the parties as reasonable negotiators would have agreed on the market value as the performance.

This manner of applying the test for damages has been severely criticized as being incorrect and unfair. It is said that if, on the whole, the claimant is not worse off, he or she should not be awarded damages, even if he or she can prove that he or she would have made a better bargain. In the end, the question involves a policy decision, including the extent to which normative considerations should form part of the requirement of causation.

206. It will be clear that in the nature of this test for damages, the claimant cannot ask to be put in the position that he or she would have occupied if the misrepresentation had been true. He or she therefore cannot claim directly the loss of the expected profits.

VIII. Reduction of Performance or 'Restitutionary Damages'

207. When a misrepresentation *in contrahendo* not accompanied by fault induces a person to purchase a thing for more than its value, he or she may claim that the purchase price be reduced to the market value of that thing. The claim must be brought in terms of the *actio quanti minoris* of Roman law, which is still applied in South African law. It must be noted that this claim is only available when the innocent misrepresentation amounts to a *dictum et promissum*. This concept has been judicially defined as 'a material statement made by the seller to the buyer during the negotiations, bearing on the quality of the *res vendita* and going beyond mere praise and commendation'.[303] Since the appropriate remedy is an aedilitian action, it is only available with respect to contracts of sale and of exchange.[304]

Although this development may perhaps be rightly criticized as not being historically correct and an instance of judicial lawmaking, it represents an attempt to create pre-contractual liability based on unacceptable (wrongful) conduct in the circumstances, albeit in a very limited field.

302. *See*, for example, *Ranger v. Wykerd* 1977 2 SA 976 (A).

303. *See Phame (Pty) Ltd v. Paizes* 1973 3 SA 397 (A).

304. *See Janse van Rensburg v. Grieve Trust CC* 2000 1 SA 315 (C), in which the action was extended to a trade-in contract on the basis of public policy and good faith.

Chapter 2. Requirements for Substantive Validity

§1. Capacity of Parties

208. To make an expression of will to which the law will attach consequences, a person must have the necessary capacity to act. The law will usually accept that a person who has adequate mental abilities to make a reasonable decision will have the capacity to act, and it is accepted that persons normally have such abilities.

Against this background, the law sets out to identify those who do not have the capacity to act. In the process, a distinction is made between persons who have no capacity to act at all and those who have limited capacity to act. The latter may have the capacity to carry out particular juristic acts independently but to carry out other acts only with the necessary assistance.

I. Minors

209. As in some other comparable systems, the influence of Roman law and Roman-Dutch law is noticeable with regard to the capacity of minors to carry out juristic acts. South African law distinguishes between infants and minors. Infants are persons who have not completed 7 years. Infants have no capacity to act, and all juristic acts are carried out for them by guardians. Minors are people over the age of 7 and below the age of 18 years.[305] Minors have a limited capacity to act. They may conclude, without assistance, contracts in terms of which they do not undertake any duties but obtain only rights and benefits. Thus, a minor may, without the assistance of his or her guardian, accept an offer of donation.

When a minor, without assistance, concludes an agreement purporting to bind him or her to another, he or she will not be bound in terms of an enforceable obligation, although a natural obligation may arise. The other party, however, will be bound to the minor to the extent that the minor can claim performance, subject, of course, in the case of reciprocal contracts, to performance being made by the minor. An agreement that has been concluded without assistance can be ratified subsequently by the guardian or by the minor himself or herself upon attainment of majority. If the agreement is not ratified, any performance that has been rendered by any party may be reclaimed by an enrichment action.[306] The agreement creating a natural obligation is often, with reference to its practical effect, described as a 'limping contract'. A minor cannot, even with the assistance of his or her guardian, alienate or mortgage his or her immovable property without the consent of a court.

305. Section 17 of the Children's Act 38 of 2005. The section itself came into operation on 1 Jul. 2007 – previously, the age of majority was 21 years, subject to a number of statutory exceptions, one of the most important of which was that a minor of 18 years of age could contract to insure his or her own life without the assistance of his or her guardian (s. 58 of Act 52 of 1998).

306. When a natural obligation has arisen with respect to the minor's promise, his or her right to reclaim on the basis of enrichment may result from the fact that his or her own performance did not effect proper fulfilment.

A minor who fraudulently represents that he or she has reached the age of majority may be contractually bound as if he or she had full capacity to contract, even in the absence of the necessary assistance or subsequent ratification.

Even when a minor has bound himself or herself with the assistance of his or her guardian or when the guardian has acted on the minor's behalf, the minor may, on reaching majority, claim restitution if, at the time of its conclusion, the contract was prejudicial to the minor. Restitution may not be claimed when the agreement was ratified by the claimant himself or herself upon reaching majority, nor when the minor had misrepresented himself or herself as an adult.

II. Aliens

210. The contractual capacity of aliens in terms of the South African rules of conflict of laws depends on the type of contract involved. When immovable property is concerned, the law of the country where the property is situated will determine the capacity of the parties. When a commercial contract is concluded, capacity is determined by the local law, that is the *lex loci contractus*. Regarding non-commercial contracts (donations, antenuptial contracts, and contracts of engagement), it seems as if the law of the domicile of the parties is the governing system. Of course, parties may agree that a certain system of law other than the above shall apply to all aspects of their contract.

Alien enemies cannot sue but may be sued in civil actions.

III. Married Women

211. As a result of the abolition of the marital power of the husband of a married woman by Act 132 of 1993, which amended the Matrimonial Property Act 88 of 1984, a married woman is not restricted in any way regarding the conclusion of contracts.

212. Even if a woman is married in community of property, she and her spouse have the same powers and obligations regarding their joint estate.

213. The special protection of women regarding suretyship contracts in terms of common law has been abolished.

214. The position regarding contracts for household necessities is regulated by common law or the Matrimonial Property Act. Briefly put, a married woman may bind the joint estate, if she is married in community of property, or her husband, if she is married out of community of property.

IV. Insanity

215. An insane person has no capacity to act at all. If it is proved that, at the time of the conclusion of an agreement, a party was mentally deficient to the extent that he or she was incapable of understanding the nature or consequences of the agreement, he or she will be regarded as insane for the purposes of contractual capacity with respect to that agreement. A person who has been declared insane and for whom a curator has been appointed by the court may, of course, at any given time, be perfectly sane. However, a party who alleges that the person who has been declared insane was not insane at the time of the conclusion of a contract must prove it.

216. A party to an agreement may lack the necessary mental ability for reasons other than insanity, such as the influence of alcohol or drugs. The rules applicable to insanity will apply in these cases. A person who is not completely under the influence of alcohol or drugs may nonetheless avoid a contract when his or her state of intoxication has been improperly abused.

217. A person who, for whatever reason, squanders his or her property in an irresponsible and excessive manner may, upon application, be declared as a prodigal and be placed under curatorship by the court. The prodigal has limited capacity to act, and his or her position approximates that of a minor.

V. Juristic Persons

218. An association of persons may, by registration in terms of specific or generally empowering legislation,[307] or otherwise by virtue of its constitution, obtain an existence and capacity separate from that of its constituent parts. The capacity of the agents of such separate entities, called juristic or legal persons, to enter into agreements, and the consequences thereof for third parties, depend on the capacity that the particular juristic person has by law. Thus, for example, a close corporation has, by its nature and by law, full capacity in as much the same way as a natural person, and the statement of its sphere of business in its incorporating document has no limiting effect on its capacity. However, in the case of a limited company, there is a need to restrict its capacity to act. In this regard, the extensive operation of the *ultra vires* doctrine in its classical form has been limited by statute. Even though directors are bound, as against the company and its members, to act within the scope of its stated sphere of business, acts beyond that scope are not invalid.[308]

307. For example, the Companies Act 71 of 2008; the Act on Close Corporations 69 of 1984.
308. Section 20 of the Companies Act, although application may be made to the High Court by certain interested parties to prohibit such acts.

§2. MISTAKES AND DEFECTS OF CONSENT

219. As a result of the strong theoretical development of South African law regarding the basis of contractual liability (resulting in part from the absence of a codified system and the acceptance of both the subjective and objective approaches to the basis of contract),[309] the tendency in modern South African law is to deal with the problem of mistakes (errors) primarily in the context of consensus and dissensus,[310] that is, in relation to the *creation* of a contract, and not first in the context of 'defects of consent' as may result from fraud and duress. Thus, a material mistake is construed as excluding consensus, and no contract will arise at all (reference often being made to a 'void contract'). However, a mistake in motive will not prevent the creation of a contract but will at most lead to voidability of the contract. This location of the problem of a material mistake squarely within the realm of the creation of contractual liability has been a factor in the overt development of a clear concept of the protection of the reasonable expectation of a party who reasonably relied on the existence of consensus. This development has also been prompted by the influence of relevant English law.

220. This approach to the problem of mistakes has tended, with respect to the more traditional instances of defects of will, to emphasize the nature of the conduct that causes such defects. This, in turn, has facilitated the development towards the recognition of general grounds for the avoidance (rescission) of a contract when a party has improperly interfered in the free expression of will of the other party, which resulted in the conclusion of a contract. The recognition of the English notion of undue influence as grounds for rescission may be described as a stepping-stone in this development.

I. Mistakes

221. The essential feature of the modern South African law of mistake is the increased acceptance of, and the distinction made between, the basic notions of a material mistake, which results in disagreement excluding consensus, and a non-material mistake, such as a mistake in motive.[311] A non-material mistake does not affect the existence of a contract, except insofar as the mistake may have been induced by improper conduct (e.g., a misrepresentation), which makes the contract rescindable.

309. It must be remembered that the Roman and Roman-Dutch law on this topic gives little guidance. The earlier theoretical development in South African law was influenced by continental systematists and theoreticians such as Pothier and von Savigny, as well as by English law. In this connection cf. the influence of the English concept of mutual mistake.

310. *See*, for example, *Steyn v. LSA Motors Ltd* 1994 1 SA 49 (A); *Constantia Insurance Co Ltd v. Compusource (Pty) Ltd* 2005 4 SA 345 (SCA).

311. Cf. *Trollip v. Jordaan* 1961 1 SA 238 (A); and *see* G.F. Lubbe & C.M. Murray, *Contract Cases, Materials and Commentary* 142–144 (Juta 1988); Van Huyssteen, Lubbe & Reinecke, *Contract General Principles* paras 2.27–2.48 (Juta 2016); Hutchison & Pretorius (eds) *The Law of Contract in South Africa* ch. 3.2 (OUP 2017).

The concepts of a mistake and dissensus may, of course, eventually be completely divorced, leaving a mistake solely in the domain of a non-material mistake or a mistake in motive, and thus approximating the theory in some continental systems (cf. the distinction between *oneigenlijke* and *eigenlijke dwaling*, or mistake).

A. *Material Mistakes and Errors in Substantia, in Persona, and in Corpore*

222. A mistake will be material (sometimes referred to as 'essential') if it relates to the obligation itself (its actual existence or the intention to be bound), its content, or the persons between whom the obligation is created. Whether a mistake is material in these respects is a question of fact. A material mistake will, of course, only be operative if it affected a party's decision to agree.

223. As a result of certain concepts taken from English law and also in an attempt to identify a material mistake, various classifications of mistakes are used by the courts. These classifications have not always served to enhance clarity about the nature of a material mistake.

The concept of a *unilateral mistake* is an example in point. It is often used to describe a situation in which there is disagreement, that is, when both parties are actually under different impressions of each other's intention, but when, prima facie, it appears as if only one party was mistaken, for example, when the 'mistaken' party signed a contractual document without reading it. The actual need here is to decide whether to uphold a reasonable reliance of consensus and not so much to identify a particular type of material mistake. A 'unilateral mistake' has also been used to describe the material mistake of one party caused by the fraud of the other party to an agreement.[312] The term has even been used to indicate the error in motive or non-material mistake of one party, which does not affect the existence of the contract at all.[313]

The classification of a *mutual mistake* may be indicative of a material mistake, but it is sometimes used with reference only to a disagreement caused by an ambiguity,[314] or as being synonymous with a *common mistake*. However, a common mistake, such as when both parties are labouring under the same wrong impression regarding a fact relating to the object of their agreement (e.g., both think that a house has a view of the mountains), does not lead to a disagreement.[315] It may nonetheless absolve the parties from contractual liability because of the failure of a supposition or assumption on which the parties have based their agreement. This

312. *Botha v. Road Accident Fund* 2017 2 SA 50 (SCA) para 9 – misrepresentation by one party's attorney.

313. *See*, for example, *Trollip v. Jordaan* 1961 1 SA 238 (A); *Van Aartsen v. van Aartsen* 2006 4 SA 131 (T). Nevertheless the courts sometimes persist in the use of the term, cf. *Slip Knot Investments 777 (Pty) Ltd v. Du Toit* 2011 4 SA 72 (SCA);*cf Botha v. Road Accident Fund* 2017 2 SA 50 (SCA) para 8.

314. *See*, for example, *Diamond v. Kernick* 1947 3 SA 69 (A).

315. *See*, for example, *Dickinson Motors (Pty) Ltd v. Oberholzer* 1952 1 SA 443 (A); *Van Reenen Steel (Pty) Ltd v. Smith NO* 2002 4 SA 264 (SCA); *Laco Parts (Pty) Ltd t/a ACA Clutch v. Turners Shipping (Pty) Ltd* 2008 (1) SA 279 (W).

construction of the effect of a common mistake has been said to partially obviate the need for a doctrine of *error in substantia*.

224. There is a large body of judicial and academic opinion in modern South African law that the doctrine of *error in substantia*, which is known to many comparable legal systems, is not part of South African law, or at least does not deserve special recognition as a separate doctrine.[316] Many, if not most, of the examples usually given of *error in substantia* amount to material mistakes, or to common mistakes in the form of suppositions, or give rise to the remedies afforded to victims of misrepresentation, including innocent misrepresentations. In this regard, the development of an extended duty to inform will also offer relief. The instances of errors in substance that cannot be dealt with in terms of this analysis will usually be mistakes in motive, for which current legal policy would seem to accept that the mistaken party must himself or herself bear responsibility.

225. An *error in persona* is likewise not governed by a separate doctrine or classified as a special type of mistake in modern South African law. If an error regarding the identity of the other contracting party is material, as set out above, it will exclude consensus.[317] A mistake relating to the object of performance (*error in corpore*) or a mistake relating to the nature or type of juristic act concerned (*error in negotio*) is dealt with according to the same approach.

B. Mistakes That Will Not Affect the Creation of a Contract

226. As has been indicated above, a non-material error will not affect the creation of a contract. This applies even when the mistake induced the mistaken party to enter into a contract that he or she would otherwise not have concluded at all. A mistake is non-material when it does not relate to the obligation, but relates only to the reasons or motives for making the agreement. A mistake that does relate to the obligation will be inoperative if it did not affect the decision to make the agreement. These rules are best illustrated by examples.

227. A non-material mistake in motive occurs when, for example, a purchaser of land, in terms of a deed of sale, agrees to buy a farm called *Soetwater*, as it is described in the deed of sale. The extent and boundaries of the farm are correctly recorded. If the purchaser mistakenly believes that the land within the boundaries includes a certain orchard, his or her mistake is not material; it is a mistake in motive. If this mistake was induced by a misrepresentation, the purchaser may for

---

316. *See*, for example, *Trollip v. Jordaan* 1961 1 SA 238 (A); *Papadopoulos v. Trans-State Properties & Investments Ltd* 1979 1 SA 682 (W); G.F. Lubbe & C.M. Murray, *Contract Cases, Materials and Commentary* 124–125 (Juta 1988); Van Huyssteen, Lubbe & Reinecke, *Contract General Principles* paras 2.46 -2.48 (Juta 2016).

317. *See Kok v. Osborne* 1993 4 SA 788 (SE); *Venter v. Credit Guarantee Insurance Corporation of Africa Ltd* 1996 3 SA 966 (A). This approach is more in accordance with the views of Pothier (*Traité des Obligations*, s. 19), than with the views of von Savigny (*System des heutigen Römischen Rechts*, vol. 3, 136).

that reason be able to rescind the contract. If the purchaser mistakenly thought that the seller had warranted that the orchard was part of the farm, the mistake is a material mistake concerning the content of the obligation. The purchaser should therefore be entitled to escape liability, provided that his or her mistake was at once reasonable, or *iustus*. The fact that he or she signed the deed of sale would be prima facie evidence that his or her material mistake was not reasonable and that the other party may have relied reasonably on the presence of consensus. To escape liability in these circumstances, the purchaser would have to produce additional evidence that he or she was reasonably mistaken, for example by showing that the other party had caused the mistake by a misrepresentation or in some other unacceptable manner.

When a seller agrees to sell to A, whom he or she mistakenly thinks is B, the seller's mistake will be inoperative if the mistake does not influence his or her decision to contract, because the identity of the purchaser is not of essential importance to the seller.

C. Protection of Reasonable Reliance on Consensus in Cases of Material Mistakes That Lead to Dissensus

228. As has been discussed above, a material mistake, despite resultant dissensus, may nevertheless not be fatal to the existence of contractual liability. This will be the case when a party to an agreement reasonably relies on the impression that a consensus does actually exist between him or her and the other party. For example, when an offeror intends to make an offer only to a certain class of persons, and someone who is not a member of that class 'accepts' the offer with the intention of doing so and in the reasonable belief that the offeror intended that he or she should be able to accept, a court will uphold the reasonable belief and the offeror will be bound.[318]

It appears from case law that the question as to the reasonableness or unreasonableness of a reliance on consensus may arise both when a claim is brought on a contract and when a party seeks to escape liability.[319] When the matter of a reasonable mistake is raised, the category of such mistake is irrelevant,[320] as long as it is material.

229. It is often stated in case law that the appropriate test for the existence of reasonable reliance is whether a reasonable person in the position of the particular party would have been misled, or (often with reference to the English case of *Smith*

---

318. Cf. *Steyn v. LSA Motors Ltd* 1994 1 SA 49 (A).
319. *See*, for example, *Steyn v. LSA Motors Ltd* 1994 1 SA 49 (A), in which the plaintiff attempted to hold the defendant bound but the Court found that his reliance was not reasonable, and *Sonap Petroleum (SA) (Pty) Ltd (formerly known as Sonarep (SA) (Pty) Ltd) v. Pappadogianis* 1992 3 SA 234 (A), in which the plaintiff alleged that no contract existed.
320. *See Steyn v. LSA Motors Ltd* 1994 1 SA 49 (A) 61.

v. Hughes [321]), whether the conduct of the other party was such as to cause the reasonable reliance. In this regard, the courts also often make use of the *iustus error* approach, as it is now integrated with the doctrine of reasonable reliance (sometimes called quasi-mutual assent).[322]

Although this whole question has not yet been fully considered by the courts, it is clear that when reliance or a mistake, as the case may be, was caused by a *wrongful misrepresentation*, even without fault, by the other party (or someone for whose conduct he or she is legally responsible), the reliance could be reasonable or the mistake *iustus*. Such a misrepresentation will be required, particularly in cases in which a person has signed a document in error signifying his or her assent and then subsequently attempts to deny liability on the basis of dissensus.[323] In fact, the burden of proof will rest more heavily on the contract denier in such a case: the contract assertor need only prove the existence of a contract prima facie, whereupon the burden to prove an *iustus error* shifts to the contract denier. This is the context in which the so-called maxim of *caveat subscriptor* is to be applied – it is not a rule of law. There are many examples in case law in which the courts found that a reasonable mistake had been made despite the fact that the contract denier had signed a document.[324]

230. The above question is clearly one of policy as to what is worthy of protection in the eyes of the law. Accordingly, a court may in future well decide that a mistake may be reasonable even in the absence of a misrepresentation, for example, when a mistake did not cause the contract assertor to believe reasonably that the contract denier had assented and when he or she attempts to 'snatch at a bargain'. In such a case, the contract assertor would, of course, not be reasonably relying on the existence of a consensus and should not be able to hold the other party bound. It also appears that the courts, in cases of alleged reasonable mistakes, have

---

321. (1871) LR 6 QB 597.

322. *See* above; Van Huyssteen, Lubbe & Reinecke, *Contract General Principles* ch. 2 F & G (Juta 2016).

the sources already quoted and *Maresky v. Morkel* 1994 1 SA 249 (C); *Dlovo v. Brian Porter Motors Ltd t/a Port Motors Newlands* 1994 2 SA 518 (C); *Lake & Others NNO v. Caithness* 1997 1 SA 667 (E); *Goldberg v. Carstens* 1997 2 SA 854 (C); *Hlobo v. Multilateral Motor Vehicle Accidents Fund* 2001 2 SA 59 (SCA); *Brink v. Humphries & Jewell (Pty) Ltd* 2005 2 SA 419 (SCA); *Hartley v. Pyramid Freight (Pty) Ltd t/a Sun Couriers* 2007 (2) SA 599 (SCA); *Pillay v. Shaik* 2009 (4) SA 74 (SCA); *Absa Bank Ltd v. Trzebiatowsky and Others* 2012 5 SA 134 (ECP); cf. *Slip Knot Investments 777 (Pty) Ltd v. Du Toit* 2011 4 SA 72 (SCA); *Botha v. Road Accident Fund* 2017 2 SA 50 (SCA) paras 10-1; *cf Eskom Holdings Ltd v. Grundy* 2018 4 SA 242 (KZP) para 14. Also see S. van der Merwe & L.F. van Huyssteen, *Reasonable Reliance on Consensus, Iustus Error and the Creation of Contractual Obligations*, S. African L. J. 679 (1994).

323. *See*, for example, *George v. Fairmead (Pty) Ltd* 1958 2 SA 465 (A); *Spindrifter (Pty) Ltd v. Lester Donovan (Pty) Ltd* 1986 1 SA 303 (A); *Blue Chip Consultants (Pty) Ltd v. Shamrock* 2002 3 SA 231 (W) (which illustrates the position particularly well).

324. Apart from the sources already quoted, *see Diners Club SA (Pty) Ltd v. Livingstone* 1995 4 SA 493 (W); *Prins v. ABSA Bank Ltd* 1998 3 SA 904 (C); *Home Fires Transvaal CC v. Van Wyk* 2002 2 SA 375 (W); *Cape Group Construction (Pty) Ltd t/a Forbes Waterproofing v. Government of the United Kingdom* 2003 5 SA 180 (SCA) 184–186; In *Eskom Holdings Ltd v. Grundy* 2018 4 SA 242 (KZP) para 14 the court cautioned that the 'rule' only applied to terms of the contract and not to questions of fact, such as whether an annexure had been attached or not. This simply seems to be an enquiry into the issue of reasonable reliance.

extended the duty to inform, which rests on the other party to the agreement.[325] Mutatis mutandis, the above considerations should apply to an alleged reasonable reliance on a consensus.

231. There are indications that the courts may be willing to go further than the circumstances set out above in the recognition of situations that would render a mistake or a reliance on a consensus reasonable.[326]

II. Improperly Obtained Consensus and Grounds for Rescission of a Contract (Defects of Will or Consent)

232. The grounds for rescission of a contract in South African law are based on conduct that may be typified in general terms as improper interference by a contracting party in the freedom of decision and expression of the other contracting party, and that induced him or her to enter into a contract that he or she would otherwise not have concluded. Previously, in South African law, as was the case in Roman-Dutch law and still is the case in some other civil law systems, a contract could be rescinded or impugned only on the grounds of fraud and duress. Subsequently, partially under the influence of English law and the development in South Africa regarding delictual liability for negligent misstatements, it came to be accepted that a contract could be rescinded on the grounds of a negligent or completely innocent misrepresentation.[327] More or less simultaneously, the concept of undue influence that had developed in English equity law was applied by South African courts and, despite criticism, came to be accepted as a further ground for the rescission of a contract.

A further development in this field is the apparent acceptance by the courts of the fact that conduct that would justify rescission cannot always be neatly classified as one or another of the already crystallized grounds for rescission. Moreover, it is accepted that the facts that justify rescission in a particular instance will not always justify a conclusion of wrongfulness in the strict delictual sense. Rescission must therefore, theoretically at least, depend on the existence of wider, more general grounds or principles. Despite the acknowledgement that this is theoretically and dogmatically sound, it has been specifically held that legal developments in South Africa have not yet reached the stage of recognizing one single overarching ground for rescission based on an improperly obtained consensus, unconscionability or good faith. Despite this limiting approach there are important indications of a wider application of the principle of improperly obtained consensus by the courts. The content and limits of such a general ground have also not yet been determined by the courts. However, it should not be too difficult a task in light of the requirements

325. Cf., for example, *Sonap Petroleum (SA) (Pty) Ltd (formerly known as Sonarep Petroleum (SA) (Pty) Ltd v. Pappadogianis* 1992 3 SA 234 (A); *Maresky v. Morkel* 1994 1 SA 249 (C); *Prins v. ABSA Bank Ltd* 1998 3 SA 904 (C).

326. For a fuller discussion of these issues, *see* Van Huyssteen, Lubbe & Reinecke, *Contract General Principles* para. 2.100 et seq. (Juta 2016).

327. Note that the classification of 'innocent misrepresentation' as opposed to 'fraud' as it appears in English law has undergone some refinement in South African law.

that have already been developed with respect to the specific grounds for rescission. In this regard, the concept of wrongfulness (in a contractual sense) will no doubt be an important guideline, even though rescission alone may not depend on wrongful conduct in the delictual sense.[328]

A piece of legislation that is bound to affect the making and consequences of a large number of contracts, which qualify as 'consumer contracts' or 'transactions', is the Consumer Protection Act 68 of 2008.[329] The influence that it will have on appropriate contracts – in addition to and perhaps even in distinction to existing common law – is yet to be interpreted and decided by the appropriate judiciary authorities. Since the Act applies to transactions 'occurring within the Republic' of South Africa,[330] foreign suppliers of goods and services may well find that South African law, particularly the Consumer Protection Act, governs their contracts with consumers.

The overriding objective of the Act is 'to promote and advance the social and economic welfare of consumers in South Africa',[331] not only referring to consumers in general but also to especially vulnerable consumers in particular. The latter approach is in keeping with the stated purpose of protecting the rights of 'historically disadvantaged persons'.[332] This protection of the Act seeks to achieve, *inter alia*, by providing a legal framework for maintaining a fair and efficient marketplace for consumers, promoting fair business practices, and protecting consumers of goods and services against unconscionable, unfair, unreasonable, improper, and unjust trade practices, and against fraudulent, misleading, deceptive, and unfair conduct.

The Act is not aimed at contracts between persons on a one-on-one basis, but at persons who contract for and who supply, 'in the ordinary course of … business',[333] goods and services, including anything marketed for human consumption and all other tangible objects; certain legal interests in immovable property, gas, water, and electricity; work performed for the benefit of others; the provision of education, information, advice, or consultation (with some exceptions); banking, financial, and underwriting services (with some exceptions); accommodation, entertainment, and access to property in terms of a rental agreement (as described in the Act); access to electronic communication infrastructure; and access to premises, events or facilities, and franchise agreements under certain circumstances.[334]

The most important rights of consumers that stand to be protected by the Act are described as the right to equality, the right to choose, the right to privacy, the right to disclosure and information, the right to fair and responsible marketing, the right to fair and honest dealing, the right to fair, just, and reasonable terms and conditions, and the right to fair value, good quality, and safety.

328. *See* above and Van Huyssteen, Lubbe & Reinecke, *Contract General Principles* ch. 4 E (Juta 2016); *cf.* also Hutchison & Pretorius (eds) *The Law of Contract in South Africa* para. 4.1.3 (OUP 2017).
329. For a detailed discussion of the Act, often with comparative references, *see* the looseleaf work of Naude & Eiselen (eds) *Commentary on the Consumer Protection Act* (Original service 2014 Juta).
330. Section 5.
331. Section 3(1).
332. Preamble to the Act.
333. *See*, for example, s. 1 *s.v.* 'transaction'.
334. *See* s. 1 *s.v.* 'goods' and 'service'.

The Act requires purposive interpretation[335] and will undoubtedly result in careful (re)consideration of earlier court decisions with respect to fairness and good faith in the context of contracts, referred to in this work. All told, the Act attempts to cover the entire process of moving goods and services in the general course of business, from the moment of offering (marketing), the nature and quality of the goods and services concerned, and any contracts concluded with respect to such goods and services, as well as the consequences of those contracts. Contracts that fall within the ambit of the Act will therefore have to be drafted with careful consideration of the provisions of the Act.

A special administrative body, the National Consumer Commission, was created by the Act to enforce the provisions of the Act,[336] and the Act provides for various methods of dispute-resolution.[337]

A. Laesio Enormis

233. The Roman law doctrine of *laesio enormis*, in terms of which a seller was protected from selling a thing for less than half of its value and the purchaser was protected from paying more than double the value, was a part of South African law until it was finally abolished by statute in 1952. Insofar as *laesio enormis* might have served as a basis for the development of a general concept of contractual fairness (sometimes referred to as substantive fairness) or may even have prompted the development of a principle of good faith (the essence of which would be analogous to the idea of equivalence of performances), its abolition is deplorable. Insofar as the doctrine might have served to develop wider grounds for rescission of a contract as a result of unacceptable pre-contractual conduct (as appears to be the case in some continental systems; for example, the development of the concept of qualified lesion in Belgian law), other concepts capable of providing such a basis exist in South African law.

B. Fraud and Negligent Misrepresentation

234. In practice, both fraud (intentional misrepresentation) and negligent misrepresentation during pre-contractual negotiations are regarded as specific delicts (although such an approach is not essential in theory or in practice). As such, a successful claim on the basis of one of these two grounds requires all the elements of a delict to be present. When, however, only rescission and not damages is claimed, the element of prejudice need not be proven.

335. *See* s. 2.
336. *See* s. 85.
337. Chapter 3 of the Act (referral to the Commission, Tribunal or Consumer Court, Ombud, or finally to an ordinary court).

235. To qualify as a misrepresentation leading to rescission or damages, the representation must be *false or at least inaccurate* and must have been made by a contractant or someone for whose acts the contractant can be held liable. A misrepresentation made by an outsider can at most form the basis of a claim against him or her, and not against the other contractant. A misrepresentation may be made by commission (expressly or by conduct)[338] and by omission when there is a duty to speak. A misrepresentation may relate to a fact of the past or present, and may even be in the form of an opinion about the future, when the circumstances are such that the opinion can be regarded as wrongful. In principle, a misrepresentation about the law may also be actionable, provided that the requirements for misrepresentation have been met.

236. The misrepresentation must be *wrongful.* Often, this requirement is expressed in practice with reference to the concept of *materiality.*[339] It appears to be accepted that this element has been complied with when a misrepresentation was made with the intention to mislead the other party and to induce him or her to contract. This approach is completely acceptable in as much as such conduct clearly infringes upon a norm protecting a contractant from being misled, and subjective elements may also serve to determine the wrongfulness of conduct. When the misrepresentation is inadvertent, the requirement of materiality in the sense that the misrepresentation must relate to material facts is of particular significance – that is, the facts must be reasonably likely to induce a person to act upon them and to enter into the contract.[340] This approach makes it relatively easy to deal with the perennial problems of liability for an opinion and puffery. A statement that purports to be based on actual fact and that misleads another and induces him or her to contract will probably be wrongful. However, a statement that, to a reasonable person, would appear to be a mere personal point of view or prediction will not be wrongful. Puffery can be construed in the same way.[341]

237. By definition, fraudulent or negligent misrepresentation must be accompanied by *fault*, in the form of either intent or negligence. In this context, *dolus* usually consists of an intention to mislead, combined with the knowledge that the representation is false. *Dolus* will, however, also be present when the misrepresentor, intending to induce a contract, is reckless as to whether or not the representation is false (so-called *dolus eventualis*). Negligence in the context of misrepresentation exists when the representor should reasonably have realized that

338. *See Government of the Republic of South Africa v. Thabiso Chemicals (Pty) Ltd* 2009 1 SA 163 (SCA) 168.

339. In cases of non-compliance with a duty to inform, the requirement of wrongfulness is directly and explicitly set by the court. Materiality (presumably in the sense as described here) is then a further requirement. *See ABSA Bank Ltd v. Fouche* 2003 1 SA 176 (SCA) and the discussion above of the duty to inform.

340. *See*, for example, *Karroo & Eastern Board of Executors & Trust Co. v. Farr* 1921 AD 413; *Bayer South Africa (Pty) Ltd v. Frost* 1991 4 SA 559 (A); cf. *Presidency Property Investments (Pty) Ltd v. Patel* 2011 5 SA 432 (SCA).

341. Cf. G.F. Lubbe & C.M. Murray, *Contract Cases, Materials and Commentary* 337–339 (Juta 1988) and the cases cited there.

the representation was false and that it could cause harm, and when he or she should have taken reasonable steps to prevent such harm but did not do so. Thus, for example, when a respected and experienced banker, in the course of negotiating a private transaction, expressed an opinion about matters within the field of his or her known expertise, it was held that he or she should reasonably have realized that the party to whom the opinion was expressed would rely on it and that he or she should have taken steps to ensure that the information was correct.[342]

238. Causation is a further element of actionable misrepresentation: the misrepresentation must have caused (induced) the misrepresentee to enter into a contract, which otherwise he or she would not have done at all, or at least not on the terms to which he or she consented. The test for causation in the context of misrepresentation is the test generally applied in the law.[343] In practice, it has become a two-tiered test, involving, in the present context, first, an inquiry as to whether the misrepresentation *in fact* caused the contract (so-called factual causation) and second, an inquiry as to whether the factual consequence is legally close enough to justify liability, in other words, whether it is a *legally effective cause* (so-called legal causation).[344] It is generally maintained that the perpetrator of a fraud cannot allege that the misrepresentee should not have believed and acted upon the deception. However, when the misrepresentation is inadvertent and not intentional, a belief in a misrepresentation that is not material will not be actionable even when the misrepresentee concluded the contract upon that belief.

239. Damage or *prejudice* is generally said to be a requirement for misrepresentation. When damages are claimed, the requirement is obvious. However, it is not clear whether damage or prejudice has to be proven when only rescission is claimed. For reasons of policy, of course, a legal system may wish to limit the right to rescind by requiring proof of damage or prejudice. In South African case law, however, there are indications that such a requirement is not set, particularly when the misrepresentor intended to induce the misrepresentee to enter into the contract. In principle, there would seem to be no reason to set such a requirement for rescission alone, if it is accepted that the right to rescind is based on an improper interference with the rescinding party's free expression of will. On this basis, prejudice will at most indicate the presence of a causal link or be a factor serving to determine the wrongfulness of a misrepresentation.

342. Cf. the facts of *Kern Trust (Edms) Bpk v. Hurter* 1981 3 SA 607 (C). *See also Bayer South Africa (Pty) Ltd v. Frost* 1991 4 SA 559 (A).

343. *See* P.Q.R. Boberg, *The Law of Delict* vol. 1, 380 et seq. (Juta 1984); M.F.B. Reinecke *et al, South African, Insurance Law,* paras 8.125–8.131 (Lexis Nexis 2013); *Minister of Police v. Skosana* 1977 1 SA 31 (A); *International Shipping Co. (Pty) Ltd v. Bentley* 1990 1 SA 680 (A) 700–701; *Smit v. Abrahams* 1994 4 SA 1 (A) 14–15; *Minister of Safety & Security v. Carmichele* 2004 3 SA 305 (SCA) 327–329.

344. *See*, in the context of rescission of a contract, *Extel Industrial (Pty) Ltd v. Crown Mills (Pty) Ltd* 1999 2 SA 719 (SCA) 730; cf. *Fourway Haulage SA (Pty) Ltd v. SA National Roads Agency Ltd* 2009 2 SA 150 (SCA).

C. Innocent Misrepresentation

240. In a number of cases, the courts have allowed a contract to be rescinded when a misrepresentation that induced a contract had been made entirely without fault on the part of the misrepresentor.[345] The grounds of principle on which this relief was based have not been expressed clearly by the courts, and in this respect, criticism has been raised. Considering the essential basis of the remedy of rescission, it would seem that such relief is appropriate when the misrepresentation can be construed as improper in the sense described above.

241. According to the South African Appeal Court, the classical Roman law relating to the aedilitian actions (the *actio rehibitoria* and the *actio quanti minoris*) for latent defects in goods sold has been developed to the extent that an innocent misrepresentation that amounts to a *dictum et promissum* may also lead to redhibition or a reduction in the purchase price.[346] This extension of the field of application of the Roman actions has been criticized as being unjustified and historically incorrect, but it has also been defended as being practical and equitable. In light of the new developments in the field of negligent misstatements *in contrahendo*, the extension will probably not develop further to cover contracts other than sale and exchange.[347]

D. Duress (Violence)

242. In South African law, duress as a so-called defect of consent is treated on the same footing as misrepresentation accompanied by fault, namely, as a delict. Briefly, duress may be described as an act by which a party to contractual negotiations is compelled to assent to a contract by a threat of harm or by the application of physical force that does not physically overpower the party but moves him or her to consent. The act of duress must be wrongful (sometimes described as *contra bonos mores*). Factors such as the seriousness of the threatened harm, its imminence, or the nature of the threatened interest would be relevant in determining wrongfulness. A threat of criminal prosecution is usually not wrongful, but if it is used to obtain more than that to which the threatening party is reasonably entitled, it could be wrongful. It has not been clearly decided by the courts whether fault is an absolute requirement for duress, but, in practice, duress is usually accompanied by fault. The remarks about damage or prejudice made above in relation to misrepresentation would apply mutatis mutandis.

Although the requirements for duress are not commonly described in case law in terms of the elements of a delict, an analysis of the requirements as formulated in

345. *See*, for example, *Viljoen v. Hillier* 1904 TS 312; *Hall v. Milner* 1959 2 SA 304 (O).

346. *See Phame (Pty) Ltd v. Paizes* 1973 3 SA 397 (A), in which a *dictum et promissum* is defined as a material statement made during negotiations by the seller to the buyer with respect to the quality of the *merx* and that goes beyond mere praise and commendation (at 418A).

347. *See Janse van Rensburg v. Grieve Trust CC* 2000 1 SA 315 (C).

the leading case of *Broodryk v. Smuts* [348] supports an interpretation in the terms set out above. However, as indicated above, the stated requirements would dogmatically more correctly and practically more easily be classified as conduct by which consent has been improperly obtained. [349]

243. The concept of duress of goods was applied in some earlier cases as if it were a special ground for reclaiming performance. Nevertheless, it does not express a separate principle. A threat to property could amount to duress in the ordinary sense; similarly could so-called economic duress in certain circumstances amount to improperly obtained consensus.[350]

E. Undue Influence

244. Undue influence has come to be recognized as a separate ground for rescission of a contract in South African law. There have been attempts to relate undue influence to extended Roman and Roman-Dutch concepts of *dolus* and *metus*, or to find its root in the *clausula generalis* or the *exceptio doli generalis*. Nonetheless, undue influence as accepted in South African law is probably based on English law, although, of course, English law on the subject has not as such been incorporated into South African law.

245. To rescind a contract on the basis of undue influence, a contractant must prove that the other party, in persuading him or her to conclude a contract that he or she would not have concluded if he or she had acted with normal freedom of will, abused a position of ascendancy that the other party had obtained over the contractant.[351] In South African law, the relationship between contracting parties does not by itself give rise to a presumption of undue influence, but the nature and closeness of the relationship is certainly an important factor in the process of determining undue influence. Whether fault is a requirement has not been decided expressly, but considering the basis of rescission, it should not be necessary to prove fault when only rescission is claimed. The remarks regarding damage or prejudice made above in connection with the other grounds for rescission apply equally here. When undue influence amounts to a delict, there is no reason in principle why damage that has been suffered should not be compensated. The matter has not come up for decision

348. 1942 TPD 47. *See also Arend & Another v. Astra Furnishers (Pty) Ltd* 1974 1 SA 298 (C); *BOE Bank v. Van Zyl* 2002 5 SA 165 (KPA).

349. *See* specifically Van Huyssteen, Lubbe & Reinecke, *Contract General Principles* para. 4.54 (Juta 2016).

350. *See* specifically Van Huyssteen, Lubbe & Reinecke, *Contract General Principles* paras 4.69–4.70 (Juta 2016); *Medscheme Holdings (Pty) Ltd and Another v. Bhamjee* 2005 5 SA 339 (SCA) 346B-D.

351. *See Preller v. Jordaan* 1956 1 SA 483 (A); *Patel v. Grobbelaar* 1974 1 SA 532 (A); *BOE Bank v. Van Zyl* 2002 5 SA 165 (KPA). (Thus, for example, the influence must have weakened the party's resistance and made his will pliable, and the influence must have been exercised in an unconscionable manner.). In *Gerolomou Constructions (Pty) Ltd v. Van Wyk* 2011 4 SA 500 (GNP) the court emphasized that unconscionability was a core factor to establish undue influence.

in South Africa, but the restriction on a claim for damages brought about by the origin of the English concept of equity should not result in similar restrictions here.

F. A General Ground for Rescission

246. In South African case law and literature,[352] there is support for the notion that the underlying basis of the above grounds for rescission, to wit, the improper conduct by one party to a contract in obtaining the assent of the other party, may serve as a general ground for rescission. It may then not be necessary to bring the facts of an instant case within the ambit of one of the specified grounds. Thus, for instance, in *Plaaslike Boeredienste (Edms) Bpk v. Chemfos Bpk*,[353] the Appeal Court recognized rescission of a contract that had been induced by one contractant who bribed an agent of the other contractant to persuade the latter to conclude the contract. A similar decision by the Supreme Court of Appeal in *Extel Industrial (Pty) Ltd v. Crown Mills (Pty) Ltd*,[354] in which the Court identified the 'elements' of 'commercial bribery', may, however, be interpreted to mean that new, further specific grounds for recission had been created.[355] However, other examples in the decided cases fall in the grey area between duress and undue influence,[356] or relate to the exploitation of a party's state of necessity (such as charging an exorbitant salvage fee[357]) or his or her ignorance, inexperience, or other weaknesses.[358]

However, as mentioned above, a full bench of the High Court, while acknowledging that the existence of a more general ground of an improperly obtained consensus was theoretically not disputable, expressly held that the legal development in South Africa had not yet reached the stage of recognizing one single overarching ground for rescission of a contract based on an improperly obtained consensus or good faith.[359]

The above-mentioned judgment, in the *BOE* case,[360] has obviously not put an end to all further development in this context. In due course, a court will be confronted

352. *See* Van Huyssteen, Lubbe & Reinecke, *Contract General Principles* ch. 4 in general paras 4.6–4.12 and 4.93–4.104 (Juta 2016); Hutchison & Pretorius (eds) *The Law of Contract in South Africa* para. 4.1.3 (OUP 2017).
353. 1986 1 SA 819 (A).
354. 1999 2 SA 719 (SCA).
355. *See* Van Huyssteen, Lubbe & Reinecke, *Contract General Principles* ch. 4 E (Juta 2016).
356. For example, *Savvides v. Savvides* 1986 2 SA 325 (T); *Malilang v. MV Houda Pearl* 1986 2 SA 714 (A); *Van Den Berg & Kie Rekenkundige Beamptes v. Boomprops 1028 BK* 1999 1 SA 780 (T); *Medscheme Holdings (Pty) Ltd and Another v. Bhamjee* 2005 5 SA 339 (SCA) 346B-D.
357. For example, *Blackburn v. Mitchell* (1897) 14 SC 338; *see also Gerolomou Constructions (Pty) Ltd v. Van Wyk* 2011 4 SA 500 (GNP) – threat to withhold money owing to an economically weaker party to obtain a commercial advantage.
358. For example, *LB Konitsky v. L Freeman* (1893) Hertzog 135. *See* the authorities in notes above.
359. *BOE Bank v. Van Zyl* 2002 5 SA 165 (KPA) 182–184. The case was an appeal against a finding by the Court *a quo* that a suretyship contract was rescindable on the basis of duress by the bank. On appeal, the Court considered the grounds of duress, undue influence, and fraud, and found that the facts did not support any of these. It is interesting to note that the Court found that even if there were such a ground as an improperly obtained consensus, the facts would not support a claim for rescission.
360. *BOE Bank v. Van Zyl* 2002 5 SA 165 (KPA) 182–184.

with a matter that clearly cannot be classified as one or another of the specific grounds for rescission, but when, at the same time, it would be manifestly unjust and against the Constitution not to allow rescission of the contract. Thus, the measure for branding conduct as 'improper' will be refined further in due course of time, always taking into account that each case will depend on its own facts. The delictual concept of wrongfulness, possibly coupled with the norm of conscionability,[361] or good faith, should be a useful guideline in the eventual development of a norm of proper conduct specifically appropriate to a contractual setting, and always with reference to Constitutional values.

The development described above corresponds in broad terms with the recognition of the concept of inequality of bargaining power in English law and with similar developments in some codified systems of civil law (cf., for example, the German and Dutch codes), although the theoretical and jurisprudential 'location' of the subject matter may be completely different.

§3. Other Requirements for the Existence of a Contract

I. Causa (Just Cause)

247. Although a just or licit cause (*justa causa*) may have been required in Roman-Dutch law for the creation or validity of a contract, it is clear that in modern South African law, it is not a separate requirement, nor is it in any way to be related to the doctrine of valuable consideration of English law. The doctrine of *pacta sunt servanda* is reflected very strongly in the principles and rules of the South African law of contract, and the intention to create legal relations (*animus contrahendi*), an ensuing agreement, and compliance with the other constitutive elements (in particular legality) suffice to create a binding contract.

248. From the weight attached to the central role of consensus and *pacta sunt servanda*, it follows (at least logically) that the concept of 'just cause', insofar as it may regulate the internal equilibrium of contractual relations, or serve to require an objectively acceptable motive or to provide a *Geschäftsgrundlage* (*basis for a contract*), will not be a part of South African law.[362]

361. Cf. the reference in *Barkhuizen v. Napier* 2007 5 SA 323 (CC) to the abuse of a situation of inequality of bargaining power; cf. also *Uniting Reformed Church, De Doorns v. President of the Republic of South Africa and Others* 2013 5 SA 205 (WCC) where the Court, in the context of legality and public policy, found that inequality of bargaining power was a factor which impacts on the minimum degree of fairness in contract, as required by the Constitutional values of equality and dignity – a freely and voluntarily concluded contract was a vital factor in respect of *pacta sunt servanda* (paras 33, 34).

362. The case of *Siyepu and Others v. Premier, Eastern Cape* 2013 2 SA 425 (ECB) unnecessarily complicates the issue: if the parties did not intend to create an enforceable obligation, as ascertained by objective interpretation if necessary, then *cadit quaestio*. If they did, the question of ultimate enforceability (possibility of performance, certainty and legality) is a further objective enquiry based on the legal convictions of the community.

Thus, a gratuitous contract is an ordinary contract and is dealt with in terms of general principles, and if an agreement is grossly unfair or 'unequal', it still, in principle, creates obligations, although it may be unenforceable for offending the public interest.

A unilateral mistake in a contracting party's motive for entering into a contract will not affect the existence and enforceability of the contract, unless the mistake is material or was caused by a misrepresentation to the extent of making the contract voidable. A mistake in motive that is common to both parties will also have no effect, unless the motive has been made a term of the contract, for example, by way of a supposition, or perhaps, unless the performance is initially impossible.

249. Insofar as 'just cause' may, in a legal system, relate to an objective or external requirement that the reasons or motive for the agreement must not be *contra bonos mores* or against the public interest, it is, in South African law, subsumed in the constitutive requirement of legality.

II. Certainty

250. From the definition and nature of a contract in South African law, it follows that there is no independent requirement that a contract must have an *object* (*objet*) to exist. Clearly, however, there cannot be an (enforceable) agreement, or for that matter obligations, if the parties have not determined the desired consequences of their agreement with sufficient precision. The obligations to be created must therefore be certain.[363]

251. Any further requirements relating to the object, such as that it must be possible, must be licit, and must be *in commercio*, are dealt with in terms of the separate requirements of the possibility of performance and legality.

252. Certainty is usually stated to be a distinct requirement for the creation of a contract. If this requirement is not met, the agreement, it is often said, will be 'void for vagueness'.[364] The whole agreement will be affected unless the uncertain part can be severed.

253. When parties do not formulate the express terms of their agreement exhaustively, the tacit terms and the terms implied by law *(naturalia)* that form part of the agreement are also considered to ascertain whether the agreement is *sufficiently certain for a court to enforce it.* A court will not supplement deficiencies in an agreement, but it will at least favour an interpretation that lends validity.

363. *See*, for example, *Patel v. Adam* 1977 2 SA 653 (A); *Genac Properties Jhb (Pty) Ltd v. NBC Administrators CC (previously NBC Administrators) (Pty) Ltd* 1992 1 SA 566 (A); *De Beer v. Keyser* 2002 1 SA 827 (SCA). *See* Van Huyssteen, Lubbe & Reinecke, *Contract General Principles* ch. 8 (Juta 2016); Hutchison & Pretorius (eds) *The Law of Contract in South Africa* ch. 8.2 (OUP 2017).

364. *See*, for example, *Lambons (Edms) Bpk v. BMW (Suid-Afrika) (Edms) Bpk* 1997 4 SA 141 (SCA); *Rosebank Mall (Pty) Ltd v. Cradock Heights (Pty) Ltd* 2004 2 SA 353 (W).

Parties may of course agree to leave certain aspects of their contract open for later determination in terms of an agreed mechanism, as long as the consequences are certain enough.[365]

254. Parties may agree on an objective standard or formula by means of which the relevant content of the intended obligation may be determined, without recourse to the parties themselves. The test for sufficient certainty here seems to be that the standard set forth in the agreement must itself provide enough certainty, without recourse to a further agreement or the exercising of unilateral, unlimited discretion by one of the parties.[366]

When the 'usual' or 'market price' of a commodity is agreed upon, the price can readily be determined by evidence. Whether or not a 'reasonable price or performance' in cases of sale and lease is certain enough has been called into question by courts and commentators; in relation to contracts for the rendering of a service, however, an agreement to render a reasonable performance has been held to be sufficiently certain. The reason generally advanced for the distinction is that, in the first case, it will not be easy to bring convincing evidence to quantify the performance, whereas in the second case, it will. This reasoning is not wholly convincing, and the matter cannot be regarded as settled.

Parties may also agree that the performance shall be determined by an identifiable third party. The law requires that such a third party must exercise his or her judgment objectively and reasonably. Escalation clauses are generally regarded as effective.

The position regarding contractual discretion given to a contractant is rather uncertain. It appears that discretion relating to basic matters, such as the existence of the contract, will not be effective, whereas limited discretion to vary an aspect of performance (such as the rate of interest) may be acceptable.[367] Such a discretion should, however, be exercised *arbitrio boni viri* and subject to judicial control, allowing the courts to consider the public interest and the interest of the parties involved. It appears probable that a contractual discretion will be acceptable with respect to any kind of contract. To what extent unrestricted discretion in a contract will be effective is uncertain, since the question was left open by the Supreme Court of Appeal. However, it seems to be reasonably clear that the principle of public policy will be applied to decide the question.[368]

---

365. *See*, e.g., *De Beer v. Keyser and Others* 2002 1 SA 827 (SCA).
366. *See* the cases referred to in the notes above, and *Westinghouse Brake & Equipment (Pty) Ltd v. Bilger Engineering (Pty) Ltd* 1986 2 SA 555 (A).
367. *See NBS Boland Bank v. One Berg River Drive CC; Deeb v. ABSA Bank Ltd; Friedman v. Standard Bank of South Africa Ltd* 1999 4 SA 926 (SCA); *Juglal v. Shoprite Checkers (Pty) Ltd t/a OK Franchise Division* 2004 5 SA 248 (SCA); *Harlequin Duck Properties 204 (Pty) Ltd v. Fieldgate t/a Second Hand Rose* 2006 3 SA 456 (C); *Erasmus v. Senwes Ltd* 2006 3 SA 529 (T). The discretion must be circumscribed with reference to objective factors.
368. For a more complete discussion, *see* Van Huyssteen, Lubbe & Reinecke, *Contract General Principles* ch. 8 D (Juta 2016).

III. Initial Possibility of Performance

255. In keeping with the concepts of volition and consensus, which are basic to the South African law of contract, a performance must be objectively possible at the time when the agreement is concluded. If performance is not objectively possible, the position is simply that no contract or obligation will arise,[369] nor will any obligation arise with respect to a counter-performance. When expenses have been incurred in the mistaken belief that performance is possible and that a contract has been created, the loss can probably be recouped by a delictual claim – provided that the loss was caused wrongfully and culpably.[370]

256. Whether or not performance is indeed objectively and not merely subjectively impossible is determined with reference to what is objectively reasonable in the circumstances, taking into consideration, *inter alia*, factors such as economic expediency.[371]

IV. Legality and Enforceability

257. South African law follows what may be called a unitary approach to legality as a requirement for the creation of a contract: the sole question is whether the particular agreement is legal or not; the legality of *causa* and object is not considered separately.

However, with respect to the consequences of an illegal agreement, the difficulty experienced in other legal systems is also experienced in South African law, namely to distinguish the basis on which some agreements will be absolutely void *ab initio*, and others will be merely unenforceable or voidable (cf. the idea of absolute and relative nullity in some civil law systems).

258. An agreement will be illegal when it is contrary to a statute or in conflict with common law in that it conflicts with good morals or the public interest. This may be the case when the *conclusion* of the agreement, or the *performance* to be rendered or the *purpose* for which the agreement was concluded, conflicts with the law. In practice, it is often not possible, or necessary, to distinguish these different types or categories of illegality. Non-compliance with a formality required by law does not in itself amount to illegality.

A distinction in principle between good morals and the public interest is not of much use in ascertaining whether an agreement is illegal, since the first ground can be subsumed under the latter, wider ground. In practice, however, the term 'good morals' is usually applied to agreements relating to matters concerning the 'everyday morals or standards of conduct set by a society, such as the norms governing

369. *See Peters, Flamman & Co. v. Kokstad Municipality* 1919 AD 427; *Rosebank Mall (Pty) Ltd v. Cradock Heights (Pty) Ltd* 2004 2 SA 353 (W).

370. Cf., for example, *Coombs v. Muller* 1913 EDL 430.

371. For a general discussion, *see* Van Huyssteen, Lubbe & Reinecke, *Contract General Principles* ch. 6(Juta 2016); also ch. 6 D with reference to the provisions of the CPA regarding overselling or overbooking by suppliers.

sexual morals and honest and proper conduct'.[372] 'Public interest', however, is generally used in relation to agreements that are detrimental to the State or to the administration of justice, that unreasonably restrict individual freedom in the economic sphere, or that are excessively unreasonable to one of the parties.

259. The courts have not attempted to lay down general guidelines by which to determine illegality, nor to define concepts such as the public interest or public policy. When an agreement appears to be contrary to legislation,[373] the question of its legality and the effect of eventual illegality must be determined in the first place, with reference to the wording of the legislation, by applying the ordinary rules of statutory interpretation.

260. It has been acknowledged that the concepts of good morals and the public interest are not immutable but are subject to change and that therefore – at least when agreements are regarded as valid but unenforceable – the time when a party seeks to enforce such an illegal agreement, rather than the time of its conclusion, may be the appropriate time with reference to which its legality should be determined, depending on the circumstances of the case.[374] It appears that an agreement that affects sectional interests or the individual interests of the other contractant unreasonably may, for that reason, at once be against the public interest and therefore illegal. This is so even though South African law recognizes that it is manifestly in the public interest to enforce contractual claims, and that an agreement will not be illegal or unenforceable *merely* because it is unreasonable *inter partes* or 'unfair'.[375] As discussed earlier in this work, the norms of good faith and ubuntu may play a role in this process of a balancing of interests.

---

372. *See* Van Huyssteen, Lubbe & Reinecke, *Contract General Principles* paras 7.5–7.10 (Juta 2016).

373. Some examples are legislation relating to the sale and distribution of alcohol, drugs, dangerous weapons, and precious stones. The matter of conflict with the Constitution would also be brought to bear in this regard – cf., for example, *Afrox Healthcare Bpk v. Strydom* 2002 6 SA 21 (SCA); *Canon Kwazulu-Natal (Pty) Ltd t/a Canon Office Automation v. Booth* 2005 3 SA 205 (N); *Uniting Reformed Church, De Doorns v. President of the Republic of South Africa and Others* 2013 5 SA 205 (WCC), where the right to property was considered; *Naidoo v. Birchwood Hotel* 2012 6 SA 170 (GSJ) where the right to access to the courts was considered.

374. Cf. *Magna Alloys & Research (SA) (Pty) Ltd v. Ellis* 1984 4 SA 874 (A), in which an unreasonable restraint of trade was held to be unenforceable and not void (*see* further the discussion below in the text); *Administrator, Natal v. Edouard* 1990 3 SA 581 (A); cf. the facts in *Afrox Healthcare Bpk v. Strydom* 2002 6 SA 21 (SCA).

375. Cf., for example, *Ismail v. Ismail* 1983 1 SA 1006 (A); *Magna Alloys & Research (SA) (Pty) Ltd v. Ellis* 1984 4 SA 874 (A); *Basson v. Chilwan* 1993 3 SA 742 (A) 762, 767; *Sasfin (Pty) Ltd v. Beukes* 1989 1 SA 1 (A); the line of decisions in provincial divisions after the *Sasfin* case and *Ex Parte Minister of Justice: In Re Nedbank Ltd v. Abstein Distributors (Pty) Ltd & Donelly v. Barclays National Bank Ltd* 1995 3 SA 1 (A) (cases dealing mostly with the legality of suretyship agreements and agreements to cede); *Brisley v. Drotsky* 2002 4 SA 1 (HHA); *Afrox Healthcare Bpk v. Strydom* 2002 6 SA 21 (SCA). Cf. the weighing of interests (including 'free-market principles') in *Bulk Deals Six CC v. Chairperson, Western Cape Liquor Board* 2002 2 SA 99 (C) 107–108 and, further, the approach in *Bafana Finance Mabopane v. Makwakwa* 2006 4 SA 581 (SCA) to the construction of a clause excluding an application for an administration order; *Potgieter and Another v. Potgieter NO and others* 2012 1 SA 637 (SCA); *Mohamed's Leisure Holdings (Pty) Ltd v. Southern Sun Hotel Interests (Pty) Ltd 2018 2 SA 314 SCA paras 21–30.*

261. Many of the questions referred to the above are specifically apposite to the legality and consequences of an agreement or clause that restrains or limits a contracting party in the free exercise of his or her work or profession or other participation in economic activity (generally called 'agreements in restraint of trade'). In considering whether such an agreement is against the public interest and therefore illegal, the basic approach is that it is in the public interest that agreements should be enforced, unless the party opposing the enforcement can show them to be against the public interest. A clear and deliberate choice has thus been made in favour of the primacy of freedom of contract and the principle of *pacta sunt servanda* over the interest of the public that agreements should not advance or enforce unproductivity or diminished productivity. In this respect, the approach in South African law differs from the approach followed in English law.[376] To what extent the Constitution will influence this position is unclear, since the relation between the weight that is attached to freedom of trade, freedom of contract, and freedom of personal choice, in general, is left undefined. However, in practice, the courts still follow the basic approach set out above, while at the same time acknowledging the requirements of the Constitution.[377]

When considering whether a restraint is against the public interest, a court will have regard to the interests of the public in general, but also to the private interests of the parties. A restraint will be against the private interests of the parties if, for example, it does not protect a legitimate proprietary interest of one of the parties, such as trade secrets, trade connections, or client goodwill, but serves merely to stifle competition. Such a restraint will probably also be against the public interest,[378] but not necessarily so. In certain circumstances, of course, a restraint that is reasonable between the parties may nevertheless be against the public interest and therefore illegal.[379]

A court will consider the above aspects at the time when the enforceability of the restraint is at issue. Clearly then, the parties' own view, expressed in terms of their agreement, about the reasonableness of the restraint or the legitimacy of the interest sought to be protected, as well as the degree of 'bargaining power' that they could bring to bear when concluding the agreement (particularly when a prospective

376. *See*, for example, *Roffey v. Catterall, Edwards & Goudré (Pty) Ltd* 1977 4 SA 494 (N); *Magna Alloys & Research (SA) (Pty) Ltd v. Ellis* 1984 4 SA 874 (A); *Basson v. Chilwan* 1993 3 SA 742 (A) 767; *Dickinson Holdings (Group) (Pty) Ltd and Others v. Du Plessis and Another* 2008 (4) SA 214 (N).

377. *See* specifically s. 22 of the Constitution (basic right to free economic activity). Cf. *Kotze & Genis (Edms) Bpk v. Potgieter* 1995 3 SA 783 (C); *Knox D'Arcy v. Shaw* 1996 2 SA 651 (W); *Turner Morris (Pty) Ltd v. Riddell* 1996 4 SA 397 (E); *Coetzee v. Comitis* 2001 1 SA 1254 (C); but cf. the contrary comment in *Fidelity Guards Holdings (Pty) Ltd t/a Fidelity Guards v. Pearmain* 2001 2 SA 853 (SE). *See also* the discussion of the scope of s. 22 of the Constitution in *Affordable Medicines Trust v. Minister of Health* 2006 3 SA 247 (CC) 274–276; *Reddy v. Siemens Telecommunications (Pty) Ltd* 2007 2 SA 486 (SCA) 495 et seq. In *Mozart Ice Cream Franchises (Pty) Ltd v. Davidoff* 2009 3 SA 78 (C), the Court reiterated that the Constitution required that cases of restraint of trade essentially concern a balance between the bargain as phrased in the contract and the demands of public policy; so that, even if a protectable interest is prejudiced, it must still be weighed against other interests.

378. *See*, for example, *Canon Kwazulu-Natal (Pty) Ltd t/a Canon Office Automation v. Booth* 2005 3 SA 205 (N) 208–209; *Hirt & Carter (Pty) Ltd v. Mansfield and another* [2007] 4 All SA 1358 (SCA).

379. Cf. *Mozart Ice Cream Franchises (Pty) Ltd v. Davidoff* 2009 3 SA 78 (C) 85 I–J, 86 A–B.

employee agrees to be restrained), would merely be factors for the court to consider in the process of balancing the various interests involved.

262. A matter that is now increasingly being considered by the courts in the context of legality is the enforceability of an agreement that is alleged to be unreasonably prejudicial to a party, and that does not on the face of it appear to be a restraint of trade. This development has probably resulted partly from the demise of the *exceptio doli generalis* at the hands of the Appellate Division and from the dearth of other clearly defined concepts for dealing with the matter, such as good faith and the notion of equivalence of performances. Another reason is the increased awareness of the public and the courts that, in general, freedom of contract cannot have absolute and unfettered application, and that other values (as entrenched in the Constitution) must also find application.

In the leading case of *Sasfin (Pty) Ltd v. Beukes,* [380] the Appellate Division found that the effect of certain terms of a cession agreement was to place one party (a medical specialist) almost entirely within the economic power of the other (a financial enterprise), while far exceeding the reasonable protection of the latter's own interests.[381] This, the Court found, was 'unconscionable and incompatible with the public interest, and therefore contrary to public policy'. In coming to this conclusion, the Court weighed the value of the sanctity of the contract against the idea of 'simple justice between man and man'. The latter criterion is not of much practical use, as it contains no indication of the relationship between unreasonableness *inter partes* and the public interest. An analysis of the *Sasfin* case and the line of cases that followed in its wake, however, appears to indicate that when a contract restricts a debtor's capacity to participate freely in economic or professional activity, while unreasonably protecting the interests of the creditor (e.g., the security of his or her investment), it may be contrary to the public interest.[382] In some of these cases, the Court nevertheless did not expressly consider the public interest with reference to these aspects but seemed to concentrate more on the disproportionate protection of the interests of one party to the exploitation and detriment of the other.

In recent decisions, the Supreme Court of Appeal has accepted the existence of the so-called *Sasfin* principle in a wider context – namely, that a contract or term

380. 1989 1 SA 1 (A).

381. 'He [Beukes] would ... virtually be relegated to the position of a slave, working for the benefit of Sasfin' – (at 13H). The purpose of the agreement 'was not merely to provide security for Beukes' indebtedness to Sasfin – it sought to ensure maximum protection of Sasfin's rights while at the same time subjecting Beukes to the most stringent burdens and restrictions' (at 10A–B).

382. *See*, for example, *Baart v. Malan* 1990 2 SA 862 (E); *Donelly v. Barclays National Bank Ltd* 1990 1 SA 375 (W), in which a so-called certificate of balance clause in an agreement of suretyship was found not to be objectionable and *Interland Durban (Pty) Ltd v. Walters* 1993 1 SA 223 (C), in which a clause in practically identical terms in a cession for security was found to be illegal because of different circumstances; *First National Bank of South Africa Ltd v. Sphinx Fashions CC* 1993 2 SA 721 (W), in which a clause in a suretyship agreement, providing that payments made by the surety need not be applied to the debt but may be held free of interest as a cash security by the creditor, was found to be illegal; *Standard Bank of S A Ltd v. Wilkinson* 1993 3 SA 822 (C) 828–830; *Ex Parte Minister of Justice: In Re Nedbank Ltd v. Abstein Distributors (Pty) Ltd & Donnelly v. Barclays National Bank Ltd* 1995 3 SA 1 (A), in which the Appeal Court held that a clause that provided that a certificate of balance issued by a creditor was conclusive proof of indebtedness was against good morals and void.

(even though the term is objectively not objectionable) or its enforcement as such may be unreasonable or unfair to such an extent that it is against the public interest (public policy) and accordingly unenforceable.[383] Again, the warning is sounded that the public interest in general requires freedom of contract that may only be restricted in clear cases when the harm to the public would be incontestable.[384] In this context, good faith, as an underlying basis for the development of legal rules, will certainly be applied in the process of concretizing the concept of the public interest.[385]

§4. Consequences of Absence of Constitutive Elements of a Contract and Consequences of Consent Improperly Obtained

263. South African law has a rather fragmented approach to the consequences that attach when factors relating to the existence or continued existence of a contract are absent. There are various reasons for this position. Thus, for instance, the central role of consensus with respect to the creation of a contract and the emphasis

383. *See Brisley v. Drotsky* 2002 4 SA 1 (HHA); *Afrox Healthcare Bpk v. Strydom* 2002 6 SA 21 (HHA). In both of these cases, the Court held that the relevant clauses (a non-variation clause and an exclusion clause) were in fact not against the public interest. *See also Napier v. Barkhuizen* 2006 4 1 (SCA); *Barkhuizen v. Napier* 2007 5 SA 323 (CC) (regarding a time-bar clause in an insurance contract); *Citibank NA v. Thandroyen Fruit Wholesalers CC* 2007 6 SA 110 (SCA) (debtor-creditor relationship); *Bredenkamp v. Standard Bank of South Africa Ltd* 2010 4 SA 468 (SCA) (contract entitling banker to cancel without any cause); *Naidoo v. Birchwood Hotel* 2012 6 SA 170 (GSJ) where the enforcement of an exemption clause was held to be unjust and unfair in the circumstances; *Uniting Reformed Church, De Doorns v. President of the Republic of South Africa and Others* 2013 5 SA 205 (WCC); *Combined Developers v. Arun Holdings and Others* 2015 3 SA 215 (WCC) where the enforcement of an acceleration clause (in itself not objectionable) was held to be contrary to public policy in the circumstances. *Cf Paulsen and Another v. Slip Knot Investments 777 (Pty) Ltd* 2015 3 SA 479 (CC) paras 71, 72 (*in duplum* rule); *W v. H* 2017 1 SA 196 (WCC) (unilateral waiver of right to claim maintenance unenforceable); *Bondev Midrand (Pty) Ltd v. Madzhie and Others* 2017 4 SA 166 (GP) (repurchase clause grossly unfair and infringing the right to housing); *Beadica 231 CC and Others v. Trustees, Oregon Unit Trust and Others* 2018 1 SA 549 (WCC) (enforcing of cancellation and eviction clauses in lease disproportionate and against public policy in the particular circumstances); *Four Wheel Drive Accessory Distribution CC v. Rattan NO* 2018 3 SA 204 (KZD) (terms in standard contract too small to read and unenforceable against public policy).

384. Factors that may be relevant are the inequality of bargaining power, the nature and purpose of the contract, and the extent of the contractual duties undertaken. These factors are to be weighed in light of the constitutional values of dignity, freedom, and equality and other constitutional rights. *See*, e.g., *Uniting Reformed Church, De Doorns v. President of the Republic of South Africa and Others* 2013 5 SA 205 (WCC) where the plaintiff agreed to transfer its immovable property at the expiry of a long-term lease to the defendant for no compensation. The Court found that inequality of bargaining power was a factor which impacts on the minimum degree of fairness in contract, as required by the Constitutional values of equality and dignity – a freely and voluntarily concluded contract was a vital factor in upholding *pacta sunt servanda* (paras 33, 34). In analysing the facts the Court established whether the bargaining position of the plaintiff was in fact weaker than that of defendant, and whether the effect was against public policy or public interest (the Constitutional prohibition against the arbitrary deprivation of property was also a factor). The offending clause in the contract of lease was found to be void and unenforceable.

385. *See* the discussion above on the role of good faith and also see Van Huyssteen, Lubbe & Reinecke, *Contract General Principles*, paras 7.75–7.82(Juta 2016).

on defects of will lead to distinctions between validity, nullity, voidability, and unenforceability. Then again, in the absence of contractual liability, discrete and specific remedies based on unjustified enrichment (there being as yet no general enrichment action) are distinctly applied, whereas contractual remedies of rescission and restitution are available when a contract has indeed come about, but the consensus has been obtained improperly.

I. Absence of Obligations, or So-Called Nullity

264. When no actual consensus exists between prospective contractants or when one of them did not reasonably rely on the existence of actual consensus, there can be no contract. Consequently, no rights or duties in relation to performance will arise. It is often said that such a contract is 'null and void', although, strictly speaking, such terminology is incorrect in light of the preferred definition of a contract.

265. When the constitutive elements of certainty and the initial possibility of performance are lacking, there is no contract at all, and no obligations arise.

266. Obviously, in the above circumstances, no action for damages for non-performance of contractual duties can exist.

II. Nullity or Unenforceability in Cases of Illegality

267. When an agreement is illegal, the position is different, not only regarding the consequences of illegality, but also with respect to the remedy available to reclaim performance. As has been indicated above, an agreement that is illegal may be either void (in which case, the maxim *ex turpi vel iniusta causa non oritur actio* would find unqualified and literal application, in the sense that no obligation and hence no action arises) or merely unenforceable at the time when it is sought to be enforced. In this latter case, a natural obligation may have arisen. In South African law, as in many other legal systems, the basis for the distinction is not clear – keeping in mind, of course, that in many cases of statutory illegality, the statute itself determines the consequences of non-compliance.

In practice, the courts have apparently come to accept that, in the typical examples of certain wagers and gambling agreements, unreasonable restraints of trade, and other agreements that unreasonably protect the interests of one contracting party to the prejudice of the other, such agreements are not void but unenforceable.[386] It is significant that in past cases such as these, the private interests of the parties (and not so much the general social interests) were paramount or were at

386. Cf., for example, in connection with these three categories, *Gibson v. Van der Walt* 1952 1 SA 262 (A); *Magna Alloys & Research (SA) (Pty) Ltd v. Ellis* 1984 4 SA 874 (A); *Sasfin (Pty) Ltd v. Beukes* 1989 1 SA 1 (A). *See also FirstRand Bank Ltd v. National Lotteries Board* 2008 4 SA 548 (SCA) in connection with an investment scheme offered by a banking institution.

least important factors in the determination of the public interest and policy. Accordingly, it may be said that the *nature of the protected interest* is at least partly the basis for the distinction and that, in the end, the public interest or policy should dictate what the consequences of illegality will be.

On this basis, an agreement will be void if, in the particular circumstances, the social interests are regarded as paramount; whereas it will be only unenforceable or voidable at the choice of one of the parties if the private interests should prevail. Such a flexible approach is necessitated, *inter alia,* by the fact that the concepts of the public interest and good morals are changeable and can only practically be adjudicated upon at the time when an allegedly illegal agreement is sought to be enforced.[387] The position at the time of conclusion of the agreement is not decisive – a court may also have regard to the future when determining the public interest. A court has the discretion to enforce an agreement only partially, insofar as it may be in the public interest to do so. Thus, for example, a court may decide that a restraint that, by agreement, was intended to apply for ten years shall be enforced for only five years.

III. Claim for Return When No Legal Obligations Arise

A. *Nature of the Claim*

268. When no obligations arise because of the *lack of a basis for a contract*, or *vagueness*, or *initial impossibility of performance*, any 'performance' consisting of the payment of money or delivery of property may be reclaimed by means of the action of the owner, if ownership has not passed, or on the basis of unjustified enrichment by way of the *condictio indebiti.* The requirements for the latter special enrichment action must be complied with, the most important being that the performance must have been made in error, traditionally an error of fact, but latterly including an excusable error of law. Recovery on the basis of a *factum* can probably not be claimed by means of this *condictio.*

269. When an agreement is void or unenforceable because of *illegality*, the return of performance may be claimed by a specific enrichment action, the *condictio ob turpem vel iniustam causam.*[388] Because of the nature of this action, the right to reclaim is limited and, in principle, return will not be granted if the claimant himself or herself was *in delicto* when performing. This is commonly known as the '*par delictum* rule'.[389] The meaning of the concept of *delictum* and the scope of application of the rule is (still) subject to some uncertainty, particularly since it has

387. *See* S. van der Merwe & L.F. van Huyssteen, 'The Force of Agreements: Valid, Void, Voidable, Unenforceable?', *Tydskrif vir Hedendaagse Romeins-Hollandse Reg* (1995): 549; Van Huyssteen, Lubbe & Reinecke, *Contract General Principles*, paras 7.28–7.35 (Juta 2016).

388. A recent example of a case in which a performance made in terms of an agreement that the Supreme Court of Appeal deemed invalid as being contrary to public policy is *ST v. CT* 2018 (5) SA 479 (SCA). In this case, however, the court wrongly identified the enrichment action in question as the *condictio indebiti*.

389. *In pari delicto potior est conditio defendentis (possidentis).*

become accepted that it should not be applied without exception or strictly and inflexibly in all cases.[390] It has been argued that return should be refused when the agreement was immoral, but should be granted when it was illegal but not immoral (dishonourable). Another argument is that the courts should refuse or grant return of performance depending on the varying degrees of turpitude demonstrated by the respective parties. The party who acted with less turpitude should then either get back his or her performance or retain the other's performance, as the case may be. In the final analysis, however, it appears that the proper basis for relaxing the rule and granting a claim for return even when the claimant participated in an illegal agreement is public policy.[391] Factors that have been taken into account by the courts in this regard are whether a fair result will be achieved between the parties by refusing or granting return, whether one of the parties had kept to the terms of the agreement, and the moral turpitude of the parties.[392]

B. Consequences with Respect to Third Parties and Between Parties Themselves

270. When property has been transferred in terms of an invalid agreement and ownership has not passed, the property may be reclaimed in the hands of any possessor by the action of the owner of property, the *rei vindicatio.* Most often, however, ownership will have passed, since the abstract system of transferring ownership applies in South African law, and a valid underlying *causa* is not necessary for a real right to be transferred. Accordingly, an enrichment action must be used. Enrichment actions are personal actions that lie only against the enriched party. If ownership has been transferred further to a third party, the reclaiming party may, in principle, claim only the value of the property from the enriched party.

390. Cf., for example, the leading case of *Jajbhay v. Cassim* 1939 AD 537, in which the Court found that the rule could be relaxed on the grounds of 'simple justice between man and man'. *See* the criticism by, for example, J.C. de Wet & A.H. van Wyk, *Die Suid-Afrikaanse Kontraktereg en Handelsreg*, vol. 1 (Durban: Butterworths, 1992), 91–92.

391. *See Kylie v. CCMA* 2010 (4) SA 383 (LAC): '[37] Not only does the par delictum rule reflect a manifestation of public policy to guide the courts in the interpretation, application and development of the law, but, contrary to the approach adopted by the court a quo, the determination as to whether the par delictum rule is inflexibly enforced in all circumstances depends upon public policy, ultimately sourced in the Constitution.' Cf. also *Barkhuizen v. Napier* 2007 (5) SA 323 (CC) 333.

392. Cf., for example, *Jajbhay v. Cassim* 1939 AD 537; *Visser v. Rousseau* 1990 1 SA 139 (A); Van Huyssteen, Lubbe & Reinecke, *Contract General Principles* ch. 7 C (c)(Juta 2016) and the other sources referred to there. *See also Afrisure CC v. Watson* 2009 2 SA 127 (SCA), in which it was held that no definite rules or even guidelines should be laid down to decide this question, and that return could be granted even though the plaintiff had acted illegally, but not dishonourably. However, when a strict application of the rule would defeat the purposes of a statute (in the instant case, to protect members of a medical scheme) public policy required its relaxation.

IV. Severability

271. Absence of the constitutive elements of a contract usually affects the whole agreement. When the agreement or performance is divisible, severance of only the affected part may be allowed, so that the remainder that is not affected may be a contract and as such fully enforceable. Thus, for example, when a part of an agreement lacks the required certainty, the other part may be a contract. The same would apply to a partially illegal agreement, provided that severance, on grounds of policy, might not be allowed, even though the illegal part of the agreement is severable. In general, the test for severability is based on the nature of the performance agreed upon or the intention of the parties that the agreement or the performance is severable.[393]

V. Rescission and Restitution in the Case of an Improperly Obtained Consensus

272. When a contractant's consent to a contract is obtained improperly, a contract arises, but it may be *rescinded* at the choice of the consenting party – or, as it is often put, the contract is not void but voidable. Although there is some support for the view that the remedy of rescission is not available in cases in which a contractant would have contracted in any event, but on different terms, it can be argued that, as a matter of principle, rescission should be possible in all cases in which a consensus is obtained improperly. The presence of fault on the part of the party against whom rescission is invoked is not a requirement. A right of rescission gives the aggrieved party an option to rescind or to abide by the contract.[394] Rescission is a unilateral legal act and needs no confirmation by a court (except, of course, when the existence of a right to rescind is disputed). The right to rescind lapses within a reasonable time after the commission of the act complains of or after the rescinding party becomes aware of the act.

273. When a contract is rescinded, the contractual remedy of *restitution* or return to the previous position (*restitutio in integrum*) also becomes available to the aggrieved party. In spite of its Latin name, the modern remedy is most probably not the exact counterpart of the Roman or Roman-Dutch remedy. Although the situation is not certain, it seems that restitution is not regarded as an automatic consequence of rescission, but as the subject of a separate claim.[395] On this basis, rescission will extinguish the obligations as from the moment of rescission (*e nunc*), while restitution, when granted, will then operate retrospectively *(e tunc)* by restoring the parties to their previous positions. The position of third parties with respect to rights received or benefits accrued before rescission will not be affected,

393. For a discussion of this topic, *see* Van Huyssteen, Lubbe & Reinecke, *Contract General Principles* paras 7. 36–7.37(Juta 2016).

394. *See*, for example, *Extel Industrial (Pty) Ltd v. Crown Mills (Pty) Ltd* 1999 2 SA 719 (SCA). *See also* the provisions of the Consumer Protection Act 68 of 2008.

395. Cf. the dictum in *Johnson v. Jainodien* 1982 4 SA 599 (C) 605F.

nor will continuing obligations in terms of which rights and duties arose before rescission be affected (e.g., obligations arising from an indeterminate lease on a monthly basis or a contract of insurance).

The granting of a claim for restitution is subject, in principle, to the ability of the claimant to return to the other party what he or she has received.[396] The qualification does not appear to be absolute: the underlying equities of granting or refusing return of performance have been considered by the courts, although no finite ruling has been made.[397] The purpose of restitution is to return the claimant, as far as is practicable, *fully* to his or her previous position, not only by return of his or her performance, but also by payment of a sum of money (e.g., when a purchaser had disbursed monies to maintain the thing that was bought). The line between restitution and damages is not always easy to draw. It may well be of practical importance to make such a distinction, since damages may only be claimed when fault is present.

VI. Damages and Reduction of Purchase Price

274. A claim for damages in delict is available when the innocent party's consent to a contract was obtained wrongfully and with fault, and when he or she has suffered loss as a result. As has been explained above, the innocent party is entitled to be compensated for his or her negative interest, calculated in terms of the so-called difference theory. This holds true in the case of either intent or negligence and whether or not the contract is rescinded. When the contract is rescinded, the distinction between restitution and damages as such is sometimes difficult to draw. When the contract is not rescinded, but the aggrieved party elects to abide to it, the specific causal effect of the conduct complained of must be considered when the amount of damages is calculated.

275. When a misrepresentation that induces a contract of sale is made innocently (in other words, it is not accompanied by fault) and amounts to a *dictum et promissum*, a reduction of the purchase price to the market value of the thing sold may be claimed by means of an *actio quanti minoris*. This amount is sometimes called 'restitutionary damages'.

396. *See*, for example, *Feinstein v. Niggli* 1981 2 SA 684 (A).

397. *See* Van Huyssteen, Lubbe & Reinecke, *Contract General Principles*, para. 4.109–4.122 (Juta 2016); cf. *Bouygues Offshore v. Owner of the MT Tigr* 1995 4 SA 49 (C) 57; *Extel Industrial (Pty) Ltd v. Crown Mills (Pty) Ltd* 1999 2 SA 719 (SCA) 730–733; *Mkhwanazi v. Quarterback Investment (Pty) Ltd and Another* 2013 2 SA 549 (GSJ); *Botha and Another v. Rich NO and Others* 2014 4 SA 124 (CC) paras 45, 50–51 where in the context of cancellation for breach of contract the duty to return performance was not enforced even where the party was able to do so, in circumstances where enforcement would amount to an injustice and unfair burden which was against the principle of good faith.

Chapter 3. The Contents of a Contract

§1. The Different Clauses

I. Ascertainment and Classification of Terms

276. Essentially, and in the first place, the content of the obligation or obligations created by a contract, as contained in the terms of the contract, is ascertained with reference to the intention of the parties. These terms, determined by the parties, are usually classified as either *express* or *tacit terms.* Sometimes tacit terms are called 'implied terms', but this nomenclature causes confusion with terms implied by law and is best avoided in this context.[398] As far as their nature and effect are concerned, there is no difference between express and tacit terms. To ascertain the presence and content of unexpressed tacit terms, the so-called innocent-bystander (or officious-bystander) test of English law is usually applied by South African courts.[399] Ultimately, the test refers to what may reasonably be inferred as falling within the scope of the parties' expressed intention, even though they may not have had the particular term in mind.[400] Whether a representation made during contractual negotiations is part of the ensuing contract is a question of fact, to be adjudicated according to the general principles relating to the creation of a contract. This question is of particular importance with respect to insurance contracts.

277. As in other systems of law, South African law recognizes that certain terms may be implied in a contract by law, as a matter of course and without reference to the intention of the parties. These terms are most often called *implied terms,*[401] although they have sometimes been referred to as 'residual terms'. In South African law, implied terms are usually *naturalia,* which are attached to a contract once it can be classified as a nominate contract belonging to a particular class, according to the *essentialia* of such a type of contract. The implied terms attached to many contracts in South African law are derived from Roman law, the prime example being

398. Cf. *Bredenkamp v. Standard Bank of South Africa Ltd* 2010 4 SA 468 (SCA), 473D-E, where Harms DP stated that '[a]n implied term is one implied by law into all contracts of a particular nature (a *naturale*). This means that it is a rule of law that can be varied or made inapplicable by agreement. A tacit term is one that has to be implied with reference to the presumed intention of the parties to a particular contract'. *Grainco (Pty) Ltd v. Van der Merwe and Others* 2016 4 SA 303 (SCA) paras 26–27.

399. *See*, for example, *Maphango v. Aengus Lifestyle Properties (Pty) Ltd* 2011 5 SA 19 (SCA), paras 13–21.

400. *See*, for example, *Stalwo (Pty) Ltd v. Wary Holdings (Pty) Ltd* 2008 1 SA 654 (SCA); *Plaaskem (Pty) Ltd v. Nippon Africa Chemicals (Pty) Ltd* 2014 5 SA 287 (SCA). For a more complete discussion of the proof of tacit terms, *see* the discussion on evidential requirements above.

401. *See*, for example, *South African Forestry Co. Ltd v. York Timbers Ltd* 2005 3 SA 323 (SCA) 339; *Bredenkamp v. Standard Bank of South Africa Ltd* 2010 4 SA 468 (SCA), 473D-E, where Harms DP stated that '[a]n implied term is one implied by law into all contracts of a particular nature (a *naturale*). This means that it is a rule of law that can be varied or made inapplicable by agreement. A tacit term is one that has to be implied with reference to the presumed intention of the parties to a particular contract'. *Grainco (Pty) Ltd v. Van der Merwe and Others* 2016 4 SA 303 (SCA) paras 26–27.

the terms implied in the contract of sale.[402] Whether terms that form part of a contract through trade usage can properly be called implied terms is uncertain.[403] When dealing with the question of whether a trade usage has become a term in a contract, the courts tend to base their decisions on the test for determining a tacit consensual term.[404] However, since modern South African law appears to make no distinction in principle between trade usage and custom, one would expect that, like custom, a trade usage should be treated as a term implied by law. Whatever the correct construction may be, terms emanating from such sources are recognized, and they can even adapt *naturalia*. Existing *naturalia* may notionally be extended or curtailed, or new ones may develop.[405] The extent to which equity, good faith, or the public interest (including, of course, constitutional values) can serve as a direct basis for such developments in South African common law is unclear – for the moment, the courts will probably simply extend existing *naturalia* by interpretation according to the historical method.[406]

278. In principle, parties are free to amend or exclude implied terms by agreement,[407] subject to restrictions imposed by public policy and the requirement of legality.

279. Broad classifications of terms as 'material', 'essential', 'vital', 'major', 'important', 'minor', or 'trivial' are, in general, of no special consequence as far as the nature of such terms are concerned. However, when the appropriate remedy for a breach of contract is considered, these classifications are applied to determine whether a party may cancel a contract. Although, by themselves, the classifications do not provide the test for cancellation, they are guidelines to determine whether the breach is of such a serious nature that it cannot reasonably be expected of the aggrieved party to be satisfied with a claim for damages alone. This test has been given more specific content with respect to the various forms of breach of contract recognized in South African law.

280. In South African law, 'conditions' and 'warranties' are special contractual terms with particular content and specific consequences.

402. Although some are derived from English law, such as the term implied in contracts for the sale of a business stipulating that the seller is prohibited from canvassing the business's customers: *see*, for a detailed discussion, *GrainCo (Pty) Ltd v. Van der Merwe and Others* 2014 5 SA 444 (WCC); *Grainco (Pty) Ltd v. Van der Merwe and Others* 2016 4 SA 303 (SCA) paras 26–27.
403. For a discussion of 'trade usage' as a tacit term, *see* G. B. Bradfield, *Christie's Law of Contract in South Africa*, 190 –196 (Lexis Nexis 2016).
404. *See*, for example, *Absa Bank Ltd v. Blumberg & Wilkinson* 1995 4 SA 403 (W) 409.
405. *South African Forestry Co Ltd v. York Timbers Ltd* 2005 3 SA 323 (SCA) para. 28; *Replication Technology Group and Others v. Gallo Africa Ltd* 2009 5 SA 531 (GSJ) at 546B. *See*, for example, *GrainCo (Pty) Ltd v. Van der Merwe and Others* 2014 5 SA 444 (WCC); *Grainco (Pty) Ltd v. Van der Merwe and Others* 2016 4 SA 303 (SCA) paras 26–27.
406. Cf., for example, *Phame (Pty) Ltd v. Paizes* 1973 3 SA 397 (A); *A Becker & Co. (Pty) Ltd v. Becker* 1981 3 SA 406 (A); *Videtsky v. Liberty Life Insurance Association of Africa Ltd* 1990 1 SA 286 (W); *Schoeman v. Constantia Insurance Co. Ltd* 2003 6 SA 313 (SCA) 321–323. In this regard, also see *Bredenkamp v. Standard Bank of South Africa Ltd* 2010 4 SA 468 (SCA).
407. *Bredenkamp v. Standard Bank of South Africa Ltd* 2010 4 SA 468 (SCA) at 473D-E; cf. *GrainCo (Pty) Ltd v. Van der Merwe and Others* 2014 5 SA 444 (WCC).

II. Exemption and Limitation Clauses

281. In principle, terms excluding or limiting the liability of a party for misrepresentation or for breach of contract, or diminishing liability imposed by *naturalia* of a specific contract, are regarded as operative and enforceable in South African law.[408] In practice, such clauses often fall away together with the contract in which they are contained. This may be because of a lack of a consensus or an unreasonable reliance on the consensus, as when, for example, a duty to draw the other party's attention to the clause has not been fulfilled, resulting in justifiable ignorance. Also, a party's consent to an exemption or limitation clause may have been improperly obtained, and he or she may choose to invoke the normal remedies. In certain circumstances, the clause may confer discretion on a party whether or not to perform, and no obligation will arise because of a lack of certainty.

282. Often, when exemption and similar clauses are not enforced, it is on the grounds that they are against the public interest.[409] Other examples of exemption clauses that have not been enforced are clauses exempting a contractant from liability for fraud and clauses excluding liability for intentional breach of contract. Widely drafted exemption clauses that would have the effect of excluding liability for gross negligence or serious breach of contract have been held to be effective,[410] but the decisions, of course, would have depended on the public interest in the particular cases. Whether liability for a breach amounting to total non-performance can properly be excluded has not been decided.

In the determination of what the public interest is, regard will be given to the interests of the involved parties insofar as they are included in the concept of the public interest. Thus, exemption clauses that result in an unacceptable degree of unfairness towards a contractant and that transgress the relevant norms of society (as also reflected in the Constitution) will be struck down, or will at least not be enforced.[411]

408. *See Afrox Healthcare Bpk v. Strydom* 2002 6 SA 21 (HHA) 34.

409. *See*, for example, *Freddy Hirsch Group (Pty) Ltd v. Chickenland (Pty) Ltd* 2011 4 SA 276 (SCA), 386–387. Cf. *Afrox Healthcare Bpk v. Strydom* 2002 6 SA 21 (HHA), in which the Supreme Court of Appeal had to consider the validity of a clause in a private hospital admission contract excluding the hospital's liability for damage resulting from any cause, except intentional conduct. Also see *Naidoo v. Birchwood Hotel* 2012 6 SA 170 (GSJ), where the court refused to enforce a clause that exempted a hotel from liability for injury or death on the premises, whether caused by negligence or wrongful acts of hotel employees.

410. *See*, for example, *Anani Training Enterprise (Pty) Ltd and Another v. Transnet Ltd and Others* [2018] ZANCHC 62 paras 23–27. The doctrine of fundamental breach, as it was applied in English law at some stage with respect to the interpretation of exemption clauses, has now authoritatively been held by the Appeal Court not to be part of South African law – *see Elgin Brown & Hamer (Pty) Ltd v. Industrial Machinery Suppliers (Pty) Ltd* 1993 3 SA 424 (A).

411. Cf. *Afrox Healthcare Bpk v. Strydom* 2002 6 SA 21 (HHA), in which the Court considered the relative bargaining positions of the contractants, the scope of the exclusion clause, and the applicability of the constitutional right to healthcare. *See also Freddy Hirsch Group (Pty) Ltd v. Chickenland (Pty) Ltd* 2011 4 SA 276 (SCA) where the court described the exclusion as 'so gratuitously harsh and oppressive that public policy could not tolerate it' (para. 23). Similarly, in *Naidoo v. Birchwood Hotel* 2012 6 SA 170 (GSJ), the court refused to enforce an exemption clause because to do so would have been 'unfair and unjust' in the circumstances (para. 54).

283. In principle, exclusion clauses are interpreted no differently from other clauses, but when an exemption clause is widely drafted, restrictive interpretation, mostly by an application of the *contra proferentem* rule, is an important and commonly used tool to limit the exclusion of liability.[412] Thus, the wording of a clause may be wide enough to cover two possible grounds for liability, one involving more extensive liability than the other, such as strict liability as compared with liability for negligence. The clause may then be interpreted to exclude strict liability only. Also, an additional phrase, which may appear to limit the extent of an indemnity but which does not render the exclusion of liability totally ineffective, will be interpreted as a proviso or qualification and will be given effect.

284. In some cases, the legislature has directly prohibited the inclusion of exemption or limitation clauses in particular contracts. The most common examples are contained in the Alienation of Land Act 68 of 1981, the National Credit Act 34 of 2005, and the Consumer Protection Act 68 of 2008.[413]

III. Penalty Clauses

285. In South Africa, the legal position regarding penalty clauses is now regulated by the Conventional Penalties Act 15 of 1962, subject to the qualification that if the provisions of this Act should conflict with those of the National Credit Act 34 of 2005, the provisions of the latter Act will prevail.[414] The distinction, taken from English law, between a penalty and a pre-estimate of damages was abolished by the Conventional Penalties Act, which covers all such terms that are contingent upon a breach of contract and are intended to prevent a breach of contract. A forfeiture of the right to restitution upon cancellation and the imposition of a duty to perform future obligations despite cancellation are also deemed to be penalties.[415]

286. The courts tend to interpret the Conventional Penalties Act strictly in relation to its ambit of application. This is true particularly with regard to the concept of 'penalty', so that, for example, an acceleration clause per se will not be affected by the Act, nor will a cancellation clause requiring restitution. The position is less clear with respect to the question of whether the clause at issue relates sufficiently directly to a breach of contract, although it would appear that a typical *roukoop*

412. *See*, for example, *Durban's Water Wonderland (Pty) Ltd v. Botha* 1999 1 SA 982 (SCA); *Afrox Healthcare Bpk v. Strydom* 2002 6 SA 21 (HHA); *Van der Westhuizen v. Arnold* 2002 6 SA 453 (SCA); *Johannesburg Country Club v. Stott* 2004 5 SA 511 (SCA); *Mutual & Federal Insurance Co. Ltd v. Da Costa* 2008 3 SA 439 (SCA); *Mercurius Motors v. Lopez* 2008 3 SA 572 (SCA); *Swinburne v. Newbee Investments* 2010 5 SA 296 (KZD), 307ff; *City of Cape Town v. Rhoode* [2018] ZAWCHC 49, at paras 85–98; *M J Repapis Enterprises CC t/a Inyama Rama Butchery v. Red Alert (Pty) Ltd* [2018] ZAECGHC 42.

413. *See*, for example, s. 51, which prohibits terms waiving or depriving consumer rights in terms of the Act.

414. The National Credit Act 34 of 2005, First Schedule.

415. *See*, for example, *Royal Anthem Investments 129 (Pty) Ltd v. Lau and Another* 2014 3 SA 626 (SCA); *cf. Botha and Another v. Rich NO and Others* 2014 4 SA 124 (CC).

clause (a clause that allows a party to withdraw from the contract upon payment of money) does not fall within the ambit of the Act.

287. When a claim for the enforcement of a penalty clause resulting from a breach of contract is brought before a court, the court may (upon application or *mero motu*) reduce the penalty insofar as it is out of proportion to the prejudice suffered by the claimant as a result of the particular breach of contract. In determining the prejudice, the court must also consider non-proprietary interests, such as convenience and reputation. In general, damage to such interests may not be compensated in an ordinary claim for damages. The penalty debtor must, at least prima facie, prove that the penalty is out of proportion to the prejudice suffered by the plaintiff.

288. A claim in terms of a penalty clause is an alternative to an ordinary claim for damages, and a party may only claim damages, rather than the penalty, when the contract so provides.

IV. Arbitration Clauses

289. Terms in a contract providing for the submission to arbitration of future disputes arising from the contract are valid and enforceable,[416] provided that they do not purport to oust the jurisdiction of the courts totally. In such cases, they would be against the public interest and therefore illegal. The courts will always have the inherent jurisdiction and residual power to set an arbitration award aside. An arbitration contract may also be entered into with respect to an existing dispute. In general, arbitration clauses are to be interpreted so as 'to give effect to their essential purpose, which is to resolve legal disputes arising from commercial relationships before privately agreed tribunals, instead of through the courts'.[417]

290. The law of arbitration in South Africa is basically civil law, supplemented by legislation in terms of the Arbitration Act 42 of 1965.[418] The Act does not exclude South African common law, but mainly provides for the facilitation of proceedings and the efficient enforcement of awards made by arbitrators. An arbitration agreement, under the Act, must be in writing, whereas a common law agreement of arbitration may be an oral one. The Act does not apply to common

416. An arbitration clause may even validly require the parties to submit to arbitration a dispute as to the validity of the entire contract, but this depends on the intention of the parties: *see North East Finance (Pty) Ltd v. Standard Bank of South Africa Ltd* 2013 5 SA 1 (SCA), particularly at 7C ff.

417. *Riversdale Mining Ltd v. Du Plessis and Another* [2017] ZASCA 7, para. 28. Also see *North East Finance (Pty) Ltd v. Standard Bank of South Africa Ltd* 2013 (5) SA 1 (SCA); [2013] 3 All SA 291 (SCA), para. 25.

418. For a full discussion of the law of arbitration in general, *see*, *The Law of South Africa* vol. 1, paras 542 et seq. (W.A. Joubert ed., 2d ed., Butterworths 2003). There are also a number of private arbitration organizations with their own rules supplementing the legislation and providing logistical support.

law agreements. In terms of the International Arbitration Act 15 of 2017 the Model Law on International Commercial Arbitration is incorporated into South African law.

291. An arbitration clause must be distinguished from a valuation clause when no dispute exists, and a third person is appointed to fix the value of a thing without the parties having to resort to evidence in regard to the value.

§2. INTERPRETATION

292. South African law, in common with other civil law systems, acknowledges the existence of certain nominate contracts, such as sale and lease. Whether a contract is a particular nominate contract will depend on whether the terms of the contract accord with the essential terms (*essentialia*) laid down by common law for the particular class of nominate contract. Classification may require interpretation by a court, which will consider the true intention of the parties, rather than the (simulated)[419] form in which they may have cast the agreement. When there is doubt, the court may refer to the terms of the contract and classify it in accordance with what the preponderance of the terms indicate.[420] Once it has been determined which nominate contract the parties have concluded, if any, the law will attach the implied terms (*naturalia*) relevant to such a contract. In principle, of course, the parties may vary these terms by agreement.[421]

293. Strictly speaking, the process of interpretation or construction of contracts, in practice, in South Africa, does not cover the question of the determination of the existence and content of tacit or unexpressed terms.[422] That is dealt with by reference to the expressed intention of the parties and other external objective factors, as explained above.

294. When, however, the language or symbols used by the parties to express their agreement are ambiguous or vague, the meaning of those express terms has to be determined by interpretation. From this it follows that, in principle, in South African law, the purpose (or 'golden rule') of interpretation is to ascertain the common

---

419. *See Commissioner for the South African Revenue Service v. NWK Ltd* 2011 2 SA 67 (SCA), para. 55: the court should also examine the 'commercial sense' and the 'real substance and purpose' of the transaction; *Bosch and Another v. Commissioner, South African Revenue Service* 2013 5 130 (WCC).

420. The question often arises in connection with contracts of sale and exchange, in the context of credit sales. *See*, for example, *Wastie v. Security Motors (Pty) Ltd* 1972 2 SA 129 (C). *See also Automotive Tooling Systems (Pty) Ltd v. Wilkens and others* 2007 (2) SA 271 (SCA) (contract with an independent contractor – letting and hiring of work).

421. Cf. *GrainCo (Pty) Ltd v. Van der Merwe and Others* 2014 5 SA 444 (WCC).

422. A case which illustrates how the court deals with determination of a tacit term, on the one hand, and interpretation of the contract as a whole, on the other, is *Sentinel Mining Industry Retirement Fund v. Waz Props* 2013 3 SA 132 (SCA). In some cases, parties seek to circumvent the application of the parol evidence rule by alleging the existence of a tacit term: *see* Hutchison & Pretorius (eds) *The Law of Contract in South Africa* ch 11, 11.5.2 (OUP 2017).

intention of the parties as expressed by their words or conduct – what did they intend their contract to mean?[423] However, it will already have become clear that the intention of the parties is not the exclusive cornerstone of contractual liability – in cases of dissensus, the reasonable reliance of a party on a consensus may be the objective basis of a contract. Also, in matters of interpretation as such, South African law often has regard to objective factors without any pretence at finding the intention of the parties.[424] However, at the present stage of development, a norm such as good faith (or equity) has no direct interpretative function[425] – if the terms of the contract are clear, the ordinary meaning of the words used will prevail and, in principle, will be enforceable as such, no matter whether a hard or one-sided bargain may have been struck. However, when the terms are expressed ambiguously, the courts will lean toward an interpretation that will prevent one party from having an unreasonable advantage over the other.[426] In a similar vein, exemption and penalty clauses are often interpreted restrictively.

295. To assist in this process, a number of guidelines or 'rules' (also now called 'interpretational factors') were traditionally applied by the courts. These guidelines were largely a synthesis of the rules, proposed by the institutional writers on the civil *jus commune* and rules of interpretation applied in English law. They were classified as primary, secondary, and tertiary rules, corresponding to the stages in the process of interpretation.

Insofar as evidence to support interpretation is meant to explain and clarify the intention of the parties as expressed by their words or conduct, the parol evidence rule, which prohibits extrinsic evidence that tends to contradict the terms of a written agreement, will not apply. The courts may accept extrinsic evidence about surrounding circumstances and background.[427]

423. The interpretative process is an exercise to ascertain the meaning of the words used or conduct displayed by the parties; *see*, e.g., Van Huyssteen, Lubbe & Reinecke, *Contract General Principles* para. 9.220 (Juta 2016); cf. *Natal Joint Municipal Pension Fund v. Endumeni Munipality* 2012 4 SA 593 (SCA) para. 18 (more objective); *North East Finance (Pty) Ltd v. Standard Bank of South Africa Ltd* 2013 5 SA 1 (SCA) paras 24–25 (more subjective); *Novartis SA (Pty) Ltd and Another v. Maphill Trading (Pty) Ltd* 2016 1 SA 518 (SCA) para. 27: *'I do not understand these judgments to mean that interpretation is a process that takes into account only the objective meaning of the words (if that is ascertainable) and does not have regard to the contract as a whole or the circumstances in which it was entered into. This court has consistently held, for many decades, that the interpretative process is one of ascertaining the intention of the parties – what they meant to achieve. And in doing that, the court must consider all the circumstances surrounding the contract to determine what their intention was in concluding it.'*

424. Cf. *Natal Joint Municipal Pension Fund v. Endumeni Munipality* 2012 4 SA 593 (SCA) para. 18, where the court said that '[t]he process is objective, not subjective'.

425. *See* C. Lewis, *The Demise of the Exceptio Doli: Is There Another Route to Contractual Equity?* S. African L. J. 26 (1990).

426. *See Rand Rietfontein Estates Ltd v. Cohn* 1937 AD 317. Cf. *Van der Westhuizen v. Arnold* 2002 6 SA 453 (SCA) 469.

427. The SCA has rejected the – always problematic – distinction drawn between evidence of 'background circumstances', which was admissible, and evidence of 'surrounding circumstances', which was not: *see*, for example, *Bothma-Batho Transport (Edms) Bpk v. S Bothma & Seun Transport (Edms) Bpk* 2014 2 SA 494 (SCA) at 499G-H; *Novartis SA (Pty) Ltd and Another v. Maphill Trading (Pty) Ltd* 2016 1 SA 518 (SCA) para. 27.

296. According to the traditional approach, the first step in interpretation was to give the words used their ordinary meaning,[428] in the context (sometimes described as the 'factual matrix') of the whole contract[429] (including its nature and purpose)[430] and in such a manner that it did not detract from the actual intention of the parties. When the words used could still bear more than one meaning, the secondary rules were applied. At this stage, background and surrounding circumstances, and more objective factors, could be considered.[431] Thus, for example, the nature and genesis of the contract could be regarded, or previous negotiations between the parties, their subsequent conduct, or the rule that a contract should be interpreted to be valid rather than invalid. If ambiguity still remained, the tertiary rules that the least possible burden should be placed on the debtor, and that the ambiguous term must be construed against the party by or for whom the term was formulated, came into operation.[432] The new approach of the Supreme Court of Appeal is to regard interpretation of contracts as 'essentially one unitary exercise'.[433] According to a recent judgment:

> [w]hilst the starting point remains the words of the document, which are the only relevant medium through which the parties have expressed their contractual intentions, the process of interpretation does not stop at a perceived literal meaning of those words, but considers them in the light of all relevant and admissible context, including the circumstances in which the document came into being.[434]

---

428. *Rand Rietfontein Estates Ltd v. Cohn* 1937 AD 317 at 325; *Coopers & Lybrand v. Bryant* 1995 3 SA 761 (A), 767E; *Brink v. Premier, Free State, and Another* 2009 4 SA 420 (SCA), 424D-E. Also see *Bruwer v. Nova Risk Partners Ltd* 2011 1 SA 234 (GSJ): '[E]very word should, if possible, be given effect.'
429. Including the headings of the contract, except in so far as they contradict the body of the contract: *see Sentinel Mining Industry Retirement Fund v. Waz Props* 2013 3 SA 132 (SCA); *Novartis SA (Pty) Ltd and Another v. Maphill Trading (Pty) Ltd* 2016 1 SA 518 (SCA) para. 27; *G4S Cash Solutions (SA) (Pty) Ltd v. Zandspruit Cash & Carrry (Pty) Ltd and Another* 2017 2 SA 24 (SCA) para. 12.
430. For a recent example, *see North East Finance (Pty) Ltd v. Standard Bank of South Africa Ltd* 2013 5 SA 1 (SCA); *Unica Iron and Steel (Pty) Ltd v. Mirchandani* 2016 2 SA 307 (SCA) para. 21.
431. *See Coopers & Lybrand v. Bryant* 1995 3 SA 761 (A); *Van der Westhuizen v. Arnold* 2002 6 SA 453 (SCA). However, in *KPMG Chartered Accountants v. Securefin Ltd* 2009 4 SA 399 (SCA), the Court suggested that the concepts of background and surrounding circumstances led to confusion and the acceptance of inadmissible evidence – context was the proper test to use. This approach was confirmed conclusively in *Bothma-Batho Transport (Edms) Bpk v. S Bothma & Seun Transport (Edms) Bpk* 2014 2 SA 494 (SCA); *Unica Iron and Steel (Pty) Ltd v. Mirchandani* 2016 2 SA 307 (SCA) para. 21 (subsequent conduct).
432. The classic case was *Coopers & Lybrand v. Bryant* 1995 3 SA 761 (A). This has now been superseded by cases such as *Natal Joint Municipal Pension Fund v. Endumeni Municipality* 2012 4 SA 593 (SCA) and *Bothma-Batho Transport (Edms) Bpk v. S Bothma & Seun Transport (Edms) Bpk* 2014 2 SA 494 (SCA);
433. *Bothma-Batho Transport (Edms) Bpk v. S Bothma & Seun Transport (Edms) Bpk* 2014 2 SA 494 (SCA) para. 12.
434. *Bothma-Batho Transport (Edms) Bpk v. S Bothma & Seun Transport (Edms) Bpk* 2014 2 SA 494 (SCA); *cf GPC Developments CC v. Uys* [2017] 4 All SA 14 (WCC) 36. Also see *Airports Company South Africa v. Big Five Duty Free (Pty) Ltd and Others* [2018] ZACC 33; 2019 (2) BCLR 165 (CC).

Moreover, according to the Supreme Court of Appeal, '[i]t is not sufficient to merely regurgitate the relevant principles and to cite the leading authorities without actually applying them. It must be evident from the interpretive process itself that the principles have been applied.'[435]

§3. CONDITIONAL CONTRACTS

297. A condition as a special term in a contract qualifies the continued existence and operation of contractual obligations subject to the occurrence or not, of an uncertain future event.[436] The event to which the condition relates must be objectively uncertain and must relate to the future.

I. Conditions and Other Terms

298. The characteristics just mentioned distinguish a condition from other terms.[437] When a qualification relates to a past or present event, or to a fact about which the parties are uncertain, the term may be a supposition. When a certain moment or event of the future is contemplated as a qualification, even though it is uncertain when it will occur, the parties have agreed on a time clause.[438] Time clauses, by their nature, have different consequences from those of conditions.

II. Classification of Conditions

299. The most important classes of condition are suspensive and resolutive conditions. A *suspensive* condition postpones the full operation of the obligation that it qualifies,[439] whereas a *resolutive* condition qualifies the continued existence and operation of the obligation.

300. Conditions may be framed *positively* or *negatively*, and may be classified as potestative, casual, or mixed. A condition is *potestative* when its fulfilment depends on the will and act of one contractant.[440] There is no duty on the part of the contractant on whose discretion the fulfilment of the condition depends to act to that effect. When, however, the fulfilment of the 'condition' depends only on the will of

435. *Auction Alliance (Pty) Ltd v. Wade Park (Pty) Ltd* [2018] ZASCA 28; 2018 (4) SA 358 (SCA) para. 19.

436. *See* Van Huyssteen, Lubbe & Reinecke, *Contract General Principles* para. 9.146 (Juta 2016) and the authorities referred to there in n. 257; *Southern Era Resources Ltd v. Farndell NO* 2010 4 SA 200 (SCA), 206–207.

437. *See Scott and Another v. Poupard and Another* 1971 2 SA 373 (A), 378H: '[A] contractual obligation can be enforced, but no action will lie to compel the performance of a condition.' Also see *Southern Era Resources Ltd v. Farndell NO* 2010 4 SA 200 (SCA).

438. Cf. *Dormell Properties 282 CC v. Renasa Insurance Co Ltd and Others NNO* 2011 1 SA 70 (SCA).

439. *Southern Era Resources Ltd v. Farndell NO* 2010 4 SA 200 (SCA), 206G.

440. *Southern Era Resources Ltd v. Farndell NO* 2010 4 SA 200 (SCA), 207C-D.

the promisor (a so-called purely potestative condition), no conditional obligation will arise, since such an arrangement is contrary to the nature of an obligation and unenforceable. A condition is *casual* if it relates to an event that is outside the power of both parties, for example, 'if it rains'. A condition is *mixed* when its fulfilment depends partly on the act of the creditor and partly on an event that is outside the power of both parties, for example, 'if you should marry my sister'.

III. Impossible and Illegal Conditions

301. In accordance with general principles and because of the lack of certainty, impossible conditions, which can never be fulfilled, will have no effect, and no obligation will arise at all. When, however, such a condition is framed negatively and can never be unfulfilled, an unconditional obligation will arise.

302. An illegal condition will itself be of no effect, but whether it will affect the whole agreement will depend on whether the obligation that it qualifies is severable from the rest of the terms.

IV. Effect of a Condition

A. Pendente Conditione

303. When considering the legal position pending the occurrence or not of an uncertain future event, a distinction must be made between suspensive and resolutive conditions.

1. Suspensive Condition

304. Despite the uncertainty that endures with respect to a suspensive condition, it is generally recognized that obligations have been created, that the nature of the contract is not affected, and that conditional rights exist, which form an asset in the estate of the creditor. The obligations may thus be ceded and may form the basis of a suretyship contract. The rights may be protected against infringement by an interdict or declaratory order, and neither party may resile from the contract. Obviously, the obligation that is suspended by the condition cannot be enforced until fulfilment and cannot be validly performed.

305. When, however, parties add a suspensive condition to an intended contract of sale, the position, according to the courts, is that no contract of sale as such arises pending fulfilment but that there is 'a very real and definite contractual relationship'.[441] A sale, then, only comes about when the condition is fulfilled. Despite the acknowledged criticism against this anomaly, the courts still refuse to regularize the position for practical reasons, mainly the protection of vested rights.

306. The effect of a suspensive time clause is, by nature, different from that of a suspensive condition. If the time clause is included *pro debitore*, the enforceability is suspended, but the obligation may be performed at any time. If it is included *pro creditore*, the performability is suspended, but performance may be enforced at any time.

2. Resolutive Condition

307. Pending the fulfilment or failure of a resolutive condition, obligations that have full operation arise immediately. Their continued existence is uncertain.

3. Fictional Fulfilment of a Condition

308. When a contractant deliberately acts to prevent fulfilment (or non-fulfilment) of a condition contrary to the intention of the parties, the condition will by law be regarded as fulfilled.[442] The full scope and meaning of the rule, as well as its basis, is uncertain. Good faith or reasonableness has been advanced as a possible basis, with the result that fault will then probably not be a requirement for the operation of the doctrine.[443]

B. Eveniente Conditione

309. When a *suspensive* condition is fulfilled, the obligation simply becomes unconditional – a new obligation is not created, except in the case of a sale. When a *resolutive* condition is fulfilled, the obligations are terminated, usually with retroactive effect. The consequences of a continuing obligation that has already arisen will not be affected, for example, the liability for rent in terms of a lease.

441. *See Corondimas v. Badat* 1946 AD 548 558. *See also* the decisions listed in Van Huyssteen, Lubbe & Reinecke, *Contract General Principles* para. 9.169, at n. 285 (Juta 2016).

442. *See*, for example, *Scott v. Poupard* 1971 2 SA 373 (A); *Lekup Prop Co No 4 (Pty) Ltd v. Wright* 2012 5 SA 246 (SCA).

443. For a discussionm *see* Van Huyssteen, Lubbe & Reinecke, *Contract General Principles* paras 9.160–9.165 (Juta 2016).

C. Deficiente Conditione

310. When a *suspensive* condition fails, the obligation comes to an end, as any counter-obligation. When such a condition has been inserted solely for the benefit of one party, that party may waive the benefit and so prevent the other from relying on non-fulfilment. If a *resolutive* condition fails, the obligations continue to operate without the uncertainty of being terminated.

Chapter 4. Privity of Contract

§1. Privity of Contract

I. Third Parties and a Contract

311. The doctrine of privity of contract is an important, albeit obvious, principle in South African law. Briefly stated, the doctrine entails that only the contracting parties themselves acquire rights or incur duties in terms of the obligation or obligations created by the contract and that third persons are not directly affected; the rights derived from the obligation are personal and relative. The importance of the doctrine in practice probably lies in its negative application – in other words, that a particular litigant has no contractual cause of action against another litigant when the latter is an outsider to the contract.[444] Parties to the contract may, however, be replaced by third persons as new parties, so that the rights and duties, or only the rights or only the duties of a party are transferred to the new party by assignment, cession, or delegation. The rules relating to such transfers are discussed below.

312. The doctrine is not absolute in application. The universal successor (e.g., an heir) of a party succeeds, *inter alia,* to any contractual rights or duties of his or her predecessor and is bound to discharge all duties, except if they are of a highly personal nature. Also, a particular lucrative successor to property (e.g., a legatee) may be bound to grant a real right in the property that his or her predecessor undertook to grant. More importantly, in the field of contract law, a person who acquires an asset *ex titulo oneroso* with knowledge that his or her predecessor had granted to another a right to the asset may be bound in terms of the doctrine of notice to give effect to that right. Thus, in the case of a 'double' sale, the second purchaser may have to transfer the thing sold to the first purchaser in spite of having received ownership, if he or she bought the thing with knowledge of the first sale.[445]

313. There are no real exceptions to the doctrine of privity of contract in South African law, and there are no direct actions (such as exist in some other systems of law) by a contracting party against a third person or by a third person against a contracting party.

314. Two concepts that may at first appear to be exceptions to the doctrine of privity of contract are the contract in favour of third parties (*stipulatio alteri*) and

444. *See*, for example, *Cullinan v. Noordkaaplandse Aartappelkernmoerkwekers Koöperasie Bpk* 1972 1 SA 761 (A); *Barclays National Bank Ltd v. H J de Vos Boerdery Ondernemings (Edms) Bpk* 1980 4 SA 475 (A); *Minister of Public Works & Land Affairs v. Group Five Building Ltd* 1999 4 SA 12 (SCA).

445. Or perhaps it suffices if he or she foresaw the possibility that there was a prior sale: *see Meridian Bay Restaurant (Pty) Ltd and Others v. Mitchell NO* 2011 4 SA 1 (SCA), paras 17–18.

representation or agency. Of particular interest with respect to agency are the position of a sub-agent vis-a-vis the principal and the doctrine of the undisclosed principal. The first aspect is discussed below in this chapter, and the doctrine of the undisclosed principal is discussed in the chapter on agency in Part II of this work.

315. There was previously some uncertainty in South African law regarding the question of privity of contract between a principal and a sub-agent appointed by an empowered agent, especially with respect to a duty to account to the principal. It was finally decided by the Appeal Court that the mere fact that the sub-agent may bind the principal to an outsider does not create privity of contract between the sub-agent and the principal – that would depend on the terms of the main and secondary mandates and whether a tacit contract of mandate exists between the principal and sub-agent.[446]

316. An apparent exception is to be found in the so-called Himalaya-clause in a bill of lading, by which certain limitation clauses in favour of one party, the carrier, are extended to stevedores, who are apparently not parties to the contract. Such a clause will only be valid in South African law if it is either a *stipulatio alteri* or if the carrier acted as the authorized agent (express, tacit, or by ratification) for the stevedores.[447]

317. Of course, the existence of a contract may affect the rights of an outsider to the contract in other, more indirect ways. Delict is an important basis for liability in the absence of privity of contract. An outsider who induces a debtor to breach his or her contract with a creditor may be liable in delict to the creditor for damages. The existence of a contract may be an important factor in the establishment of a duty of care owed by one contractant to an outsider, which, if breached, may result in delictual liability.[448] Debtor and creditor liens and other liens arising from a contractual relation between parties may affect the rights of third parties. A lessor, for example, has a tacit hypothec over the property of the sub-lessee of his or her tenant for rental arrears to the extent that the sub-lessee is in arrears to the sub-lessor; the hypothec also extends in certain circumstances to property of third parties that is on the leased premises.

II. Contract for the Benefit of a Third Party

318. The notion that two parties may contract so that one of them (the *promittens*) will perform something for the benefit of a third person has long been accepted by the institutional writers of South African common law and by the courts.[449] There

446. *See Watson v. Sachs* 1994 3 SA 655 (A).
447. *See Santam Insurance Co. Ltd v. SA Stevedores Ltd* 1989 1 SA 182 (D), with reference to *Scruttons Ltd v. Midland Silicones Ltd* [1962] 1 All ER 1 (HL).
448. *See*, for example, *Compass Motors Industries (Pty) Ltd v. Callguard (Pty) Ltd* 1990 2 SA 520 (W).
449. Particularly Grotius and Voet; for example, *McCullogh v. Fernwood Estate Ltd* 1920 AD 204; *Hofer v. Kevitt NO* 1998 1 SA 382 (SCA). At an earlier stage, the view that the English doctrine

is, however, a fundamental debate regarding the construction of the contract for the benefit of a third party, probably as a result of the influence of the English doctrine of consideration.

319. The *stipulatio alteri* must be clearly distinguished from the option contract, agency,[450] the *adiectus solutionis causa* (whereby a debtor may perform to somebody other than the creditor), and an ordinary tripartite contract, for example, when an estate agent inserts a clause about commission into a contract of sale between two other parties.

320. The practical uses of the contract for the benefit of third parties are manifold. It is of particular importance in the creation of an *inter vivos* trust and is widely used in the form of a pre-incorporation contract to create a benefit for an association that is yet to be formed or incorporated.[451] The *stipulatio alteri* is a popular method of arranging for the payment of pensions and insurance monies to beneficiaries who are not party to the contract.[452]

321. According to the current view as expounded by the courts, the essential feature of a contract in favour of a third party is that it is a 'contract between two persons that is designed to enable a third person to come in as a party to a contract with one of the other two'.[453] The crucial point is that the right of the beneficiary is vested only upon acceptance by him or her.

A. *Requirements for Validity*

322. The *stipulatio alteri*, being a contract, must comply with all the requirements for the creation of a contract and may be express or tacit. In the course of the development of this type of contract, the exact nature of the requisite intention of the parties, the *stipulans* and the *promittens*, has not always been clear. At the least, it may be described as an intention to confer on the third party certain benefits and to empower the third party to adopt those benefits (or perhaps the rights in terms of

---

of consideration was part of South African law created, to some extent, a hindrance to the acceptance and development of the contract in favour of third parties.

450. In some of the older cases, the courts tended to explain the contract for the benefit of a third party in terms of agency.

451. Section 35 of the Companies Act 61 of 1973 has created a statutory alternative method of creating a benefit for a company to be formed.

452. So-called 'beneficiary clauses' in life insurance contracts have been held to be *stipulationes alteri*: *see*, for example, *Borman en De Vos, NNO en 'n° Ander v. Potgietersrusse Tabakkorporasie BPK en 'n° Ander* 1976 (3) SA 488 (A) at 506H; *Naidoo v. Discovery Ltd and Others* [2018] ZASCA 88 at para. 8.

453. *Crookes v. Watson* 1956 1 SA 277 (A) 291. *See also Joel Melamed & Hurwitz v. Cleveland Estates (Pty) Ltd, Joel Melamed & Hurwitz v. Vorner Investments (Pty) Ltd* 1984 3 SA 155 (A); *Total SA (Pty) Ltd v. Bekker NO* 1992 1 SA 617 (A).

the contract or even the contract itself).[454] An intention to enrich the third party is not necessary. By its nature, an intention to create a *stipulatio alteri* will not be easily inferred – it is sometimes stated that a positive intention must be present. To comply with the requirement of certainty, the beneficiary must be described so as to be identifiable, but the beneficiary need not be in existence when the contract is concluded.

B. Position Prior to Acceptance by a Third Party

323. Prior to acceptance by the beneficiary, the obligation between the *stipulans* and the *promittens* entails mainly that the *promittens* may do nothing to prevent, or interfere with, the fulfilment of the obligation. Depending on the terms of the contract, he or she may also have a duty to take steps to enable the beneficiary to accept.

324. The position of the beneficiary during this phase, in terms of the construction favoured by the courts, can be likened to the position of the holder of a right qualified by a suspensive condition. His or her position is insecure and depends on the continued existence of the contract in his or her favour. He or she is, however, protected indirectly. Thus, for example, the *promittens* cannot unilaterally renege on his or her duties in terms of the contract – that would require release by the *stipulans;* an executor in the beneficiary's estate may accept; and even before acceptance by the beneficiary, a life policy that contains a *stipulatio alteri* is not treated as part of the estate of the insured.

C. Position after Acceptance by a Third Party

325. Although the position as to what exactly the third party must accept is not quite clear, the courts mostly seem to construe the acceptance of the benefit as the acceptance of an offer. Thus, the general rules pertaining to offer and acceptance are applied to ascertain whether acceptance has taken place. Accordingly, notification of acceptance to the *promittens* will ordinarily be required.

326. It is only upon acceptance that an obligation between the *promittens* and the third party is created.[455] A common construction is that acceptance completes or stabilizes the right of the beneficiary that stems from the original contract between the *stipulans* and the *promittens*. The construction that a second contract arises between the third party and the *promittens* seems to enjoy less support.[456]

---

454. *See Pieterse v. Shrosbee N.O.; Shrosbee N.O. v. Love* 2005 1 SA 309 (SCA) 313H. For a discussion of the debate on the various constructions, *see* Van Huyssteen, Lubbe & Reinecke, *Contract General Principles* paras 9.92–9.107 (Juta 2016) and the authorities cited there.

455. The only exception is the so-called Perezian exception, whereby acceptance of the benefits of a family settlement enures to the benefit of all the other beneficiaries.

456. *See Wessels NO v. De Jager NO* [2000] 4 All SA 440 (SCA) and further Van Huyssteen, Lubbe & Reinecke, *Contract General Principles* para. 9.104 (Juta 2016).

327. Should the third party not accept, the contract fails and simply falls away.

§2. Transfer of Contractual Rights and Duties

328. In principle, South African law recognizes the transfer of contractual rights or duties without formalities, by a mere agreement between the creditor and a new creditor in the case of a transfer of rights, or between the debtor and a new debtor, with the assent of the creditor, in the case of a transfer of duties.

329. In general, no restrictions are placed on the freedom to transfer, except to protect the interests of the original co-contractant. In this respect, the interests of third parties or the public are probably not protected sufficiently. This raises serious practical problems, particularly with respect to the transfer of rights in terms of a contract of sale on instalments.

330. It must be noted that a transfer agreement is not a contract, but a real agreement, and it is to be distinguished in principle from the *causa* or reason for the transfer, which may well be a contract, such as a sale or donation. In practice, however, the transfer agreement and the causal contract are often combined in one legal act. The *causa* may, of course, also be a juristic act other than a contract, such as payment or securing of a debt.

331. The effect of transfer is to replace the creditor or debtor with a new creditor or debtor as the case may be, so that the new party steps into the shoes of the previous party.

I. Transfer of Rights: Cession

332. The juristic act by which a personal[457] incorporeal right emanating from an obligation is transferred by a creditor to another, who thereby becomes the creditor in his or her place, is a real agreement (called cession) between the transferor (cedent) and the transferee (cessionary).[458] The transfer agreement is, in principle, an act of transfer,[459] which, being a matter of fact, must be proven on a balance of probabilities, in light of all admissible evidence.[460] The debtor need not be a party

457. Although the courts are moving towards accepting that real rights, such as ownership, can also be ceded: *see Caledon & Suid-Westelike Distrikte Eksekuteurs-Kamers Bpk v. Wentzel en Andere* 1972 1 SA 270 (A) (obiter); *Page Automation (Pty) Ltd v. Profusa Properties CC t/a Homenet OR Tambo and Others* 2013 4 SA 37 (GSJ) at 44A-C.

458. Cession, which keeps the obligation intact, must be distinguished from other means to secure a substitution of creditors, such as a novation (which entails a tripartite agreement with *animus novandi*) or subrogation.

459. *See Johnson v. Incorporated General Insurances Ltd* 1983 1 SA 318 (A); *Standard General Insurance Co. Ltd v. SA Brake CC* 1995 3 SA 806 (A).

460. *See*, for example, *PG Bison Ltd v. The Master* 2000 1 SA 859 (SCA).

to the agreement, nor need he or she be aware of the cession. The debtor's interests are, however, protected in various ways.[461]

A. Requirements for Effective Cession and Formalities

333. As will have appeared from the above, the requirements for an effective cession are simple: First, there must be a right inhering in the cedent.[462] After much uncertainty, it now seems that the courts prefer the view that a *spes actionis* as such cannot be ceded,[463] although an anticipatory cession is probably in order.[464] Second, there must be an agreement between the cedent and the cessionary to give and accept transfer of a right capable of cession. In general, an agreement to prohibit or limit the right to cede is enforceable. Third, the cession should not be illegal. Fourth, the cession should not prejudice the debtor. Finally, such formalities as may be prescribed by law, or by the parties themselves, must be complied with.

334. While a cession does not generally need to be in writing in order to be valid, in certain circumstances, a cession must comply with formalities. The agreement to transfer rights that is embodied in a negotiable instrument must be accompanied by delivery of the instrument. The cession of a right to mortgage is totally ineffective unless the cession is duly registered in terms of the Deeds Registries Act 47 of 1937. Whether, in the case of ordinary written contracts, when the right of action exists independently of the document reflecting the contract,[465] the document itself must be delivered to the cessionary to make the cession valid or fully effective was, for a long while, a matter fraught with controversy. The Appeal Court[466] has subsequently authoritatively confirmed that cession is, in principle, a transfer agreement for which mere consensus is an adequate basis. Consequently, it has been held that delivery of the document is not a requirement for validity, nor is compliance with the so-called all-effort rule. The duty on the seller of shares to deliver the share certificates to the buyer together with a blank signed transfer form arises from the underlying causal contract of sale.[467] However, it was pointed out by the Court in

461. For example, his or her position may not be made more burdensome, such as splitting one cause of action between two creditors – *see Van der Merwe v. Nedcor Bank Bpk* 2003 1 SA 169 (SCA).
462. *Carlswald & another v. Brews* 2017 (5) SA 498 (SCA) . In addition, the relationship between the creditor and debtor should not be such that there exists a *delectus personae*; in other words, where the right in question relates to a performance that only this particular debtor can render. In such circumstances, the right may not be ceded: *Propell Specialised Finance (Pty) Ltd v. Attorneys Insurance Indemnity Fund NPC* [2019] 1 All SA 79 (SCA).
463. *See First National Bank of SA Ltd v. Lynn* 1996 2 SA 339 (A).
464. *See Smit v. Carniasaad* 1998 4 SA 877 (SCA), and the discussion of these issues in Van Huyssteen, Lubbe & Reinecke, *Contract General Principles* paras 12.24–12.28 (Juta 2016).
465. As opposed to rights that are embodied in a document, such as a negotiable instrument.
466. *Botha v. Fick* 1995 2 SA 750 (A).
467. Since the adoption of the STRATE system for registration of shares in listed companies and the resultant dematerialization of shares, the existing form of cession will become obsolete. For a discussion of some of the problems in this regard, *see* Van Huyssteen, Lubbe & Reinecke, *Contract General Principles* para. 12.20 (Juta 2016).

the *Botha* case that in situations where a claimant is competing for recognition as a cessionary, the delivery of the document may well be a decisive evidential factor.[468]

B. Consequences of Cession

335. The legal consequence of a cession to alienate a right (often called an out-and-out cession, as opposed to a cession *in securitatem debiti*) is that a complete transfer of the right in question is effected – the cessionary steps into the shoes of the cedent as the creditor, and the ceded right becomes an asset in his or her estate.

336. Since publicity and notice to the debtor are not required by South African law for the effectiveness of a cession, the debtor is protected in the sense that, if he or she performs to the cedent in good faith and (generally) without knowledge of the cession, he or she will have fulfilled his or her duties in terms of the obligation. This principle does not apply with respect to a negotiable instrument, for which payment must be made to the holder. If notice of the cession has been given to the debtor, the rule will not apply. The rule finds an extended application in favour of the debtor in cases of compromise, release, set-off, and extension of time. The most plausible theoretical basis for this rule, and one that has received some support from the courts, is that of estoppel by representation or perhaps a wider form of protection of a reasonable reliance, or fulfilment of a reasonable expectation on the part of the debtor.

337. The cessionary does not receive better rights than the cedent had (*nemo plus iuris ad alium transferre potest, quam ipse haberet*).[469] Therefore, in principle, the cessionary's position against the debtor can never be stronger than that of the cedent before him or her. Accordingly, the debtor may raise against the cessionary all the defences in rem that he or she might have raised against the cedent, including the right to withhold his or her performance in the case of a reciprocal contract (the *exceptio non adimpleti contractus*). The most important exception to this rule is that the transferee of rights embodied in a negotiable instrument may, in certain circumstances, receive rights free from defects in the title of the transferor.

338. The controversy in South African law regarding the consequences of a cession *in securitatem debiti* and its legal nature now appears to be settled. Two constructions have been advanced in this connection: the view that the cession *in securitatem debiti* is a pledge of an incorporeal right to the cessionary, and the opposing view that it is a complete transfer for security, a *fiducia cum creditore contracta,* which may be subject to conditional recession. Despite a number of decisions and *obiter dicta* by the Appeal Court to the contrary, and despite cogent theoretical and practical objections, it appears as if the pledge construction is the most favoured. This was explicitly affirmed in a number of judgments of the Appeal

468. At 778.
469. *Carlswald & another v. Brews* 2017 (5) SA 498 (SCA).

Court as the proper construction to be placed on a cession for the purpose of providing security.[470] The cedent is regarded as retaining the ownership of the ceded right, while the cessionary pledgee has a security interest – a real right of pledge – in the ceded right. The ceded right thus remains an asset in the estate of the cedent and is not affected by the insolvency of the cessionary.[471] The cedent may, however, not exercise any rights as a creditor of the debtor, since the cessionary is entitled to realize the pledged right by claiming from the debtor upon default by the cedent. The cessionary, as holder of a real right, is fully protected in the event of insolvency of the cedent. The cessionary may, unless the parties intend otherwise, further dispose of his or her interest in performance by the debtor.

Apart from the above method of transferring rights as security, the so-called security transfer is often used in practice. In this case, the contract that accompanies the cession usually provides that the cessionary becomes the creditor, the cedent retaining no rights against the debtor but a right to claim recession of the right upon fulfilment of the secured debt.[472]

Questions have been raised as to whether these two methods of cession to secure a debt can, by law, exist side-by-side. The answer seems to be that it depends ultimately on the intention of the parties.[473]

C. Consequences of Out-and-Out Cession for Third Parties Other than the Debtor

339. As has been pointed out above, the so-called document rule may sometimes (particularly when the right being ceded is so closely identified with the document that embodies it that it can, notionally, neither be separated from the document nor be enforced without it) affect the consequences of a cession of the same right by a cedent to various cessionaries; in the sense that the cessionary to whom the document that evidences the right has been delivered may be regarded as the true cessionary.[474] In principle, a double cession will be invalid – once the right has been properly ceded, there is nothing left to cede for the second time. It is not clear to what extent the evidentiary advantage of possession of the document will by itself undermine this principle, or whether possession of the document may serve as the basis for protecting a reasonable impression in the minds of affected parties. The

---

470. *See Leyds v. Noord-Westelike Koöperatiewe Landboumaatskappy Bpk* 1985 2 SA 769 (A); *Bank of Lisbon & South Africa Ltd v. The Master* 1987 1 SA 276 (A); *Millman v. Twiggs* 1995 3 SA 674 (A); *First National Bank of South Africa Ltd v. Lynn* 1996 2 SA 339 (A); *Louis Pasteur Hospital Holdings (Pty) Ltd v. Bonitas Medical Fund* [2018] ZASCA 82 para. 32.

. However, many problems relating to this construction are still not resolved – *see* Van Huyssteen, Lubbe & Reinecke, *Contract General Principles* paras 12.62–12.79 (Juta 2016).

471. For a recent example, *see Nedbank Ltd v. Cooper NO and Others* 2013 4 SA 353 (FB).

472. For a discussion of the security transfer, *see* Van Huyssteen, Lubbe & Reinecke, *Contract General Principles* para. 12.68 et seq. (Juta 2016).

473. *See* Van Huyssteen, Lubbe & Reinecke, *Contract General Principles* para. 12.66 (Juta 2016).

474. *See*, for example, *Trust Bank of Africa Ltd v. Standard Bank of South Africa Ltd* 1968 3 SA 166 (A); *Standard Bank of South Africa Ltd v. Ocean Commodities Inc.* 1983 1 SA 276 (A); *Botha v. Fick* 1995 2 SA 750 (A).

courts have yet to formulate a standpoint as to the extent to which rights of third parties ought to be protected in the case of cession, or the most appropriate method by which to do so.

340. The fact that the ceded right becomes an asset in the estate of the cessionary means that it is subject to attachment by creditors of the cessionary and that, upon his or her insolvency, the performance of the debtor enures for the benefit of the creditors of an insolvent cessionary.

II. Transfer of Duties: Delegation and Assignment

341. The traditionally accepted method of transferring duties or debts in South African law is by way of a novatory agreement, in the form of *delegation,* between the creditor and debtor and the new debtor.[475] This entails an *animus novandi* and results in the discharge of the original obligation between the creditor and debtor and its replacement by a new obligation between the original creditor and the new debtor in place of the old one. A creditor may agree in advance that his or her debtor may delegate his or her duties to another. All the requirements for a novation have to be complied with, most importantly that the obligation that is intended to be novated must exist and be valid.

342. Of late, it seems that the courts may be willing to give effect to a more direct way of transferring duties by way of *assignment.*[476] Assignment is similar to cession, except that the agreement of the creditor is required, albeit in advance. It effects a direct transfer of duties, and the assignee steps into the shoes of the assignor as the new debtor. No formalities are required, and, in principle, any duty can be assigned, except probably (despite the consent of the creditor) a duty of a highly personal nature.

§3. SUBCONTRACTING

343. The notion of subcontracting is well-known in South African law: a debtor (such as an independent contractor for the rendering of services or the doing of work) often enters into a separate contract with another to fulfil the debtor's duties to his or her creditor; or a creditor (like a lessee of immovable property) by contract affords another the benefits of the creditor's own contractual rights. The agreement between the original party (often called the 'main contractor') and the other party (often called the 'subcontractor') is an independent contract and does not create a direct link or privity between the co-contractant of the main contractor and the subcontractor. This remains the position even when the main contract provides that the

475. *See Froman v. Robertson* 1971 1 SA 115 (A).

476. *See Botha v. Van Niekerk* 1983 3 SA 513 (W); *Mignoel Properties (Pty) Ltd v. Kneebone* 1989 4 SA 1042 (A); Van Huyssteen, Lubbe & Reinecke, *Contract General Principles* paras 13.38–13.44 (Juta 2016).

co-contractant (such as the building owner (*conductor*) in terms of a building contract) may directly pay the subcontractor and recoup the amount from the main contractor. The same would apply when, for example, the owner nominates a subcontractor and controls the price and other terms of the subcontract.

In principle, the right to subcontract is not limited by law, but it is often refused or restricted by agreement between the parties, and this is usually entrenched by a non-variation clause in the contract.

I. Liability of the Main Contractor for the Conduct of a Subcontractor

344. In principle, the main contractor remains liable to the creditor for the full and specific performance of his or her duties in terms of the contract, and the fact that he or she has subcontracted with respect to all or certain of his or her duties does not affect this position. Usually, in terms of the applicable standard contract, the subcontractor undertakes towards the main contractor the same duties as the main contractor undertakes towards the creditor in the main contract.

345. The principles of vicarious liability do not apply in the case of independent contractors. Thus, the main contractor will not be liable for delicts committed by any of his or her subcontractors in the way that an employer would be liable for acts by his or her employees committed in the course and scope of their duties. In terms of the general principles of delict, a main contractor might be liable to his or her co-contractant or to a member of the public for a delict committed by a subcontractor when all the requirements for Aquilian liability are present. In particular, the existence of a duty to take steps to prevent harm (the element of wrongfulness) will have to be construed with reference to the facts.[477]

II. Relationship Between a Co-contractant and Subcontractor

346. As a result of the absence of privity of contract between a subcontractor and the co-contractant in terms of the main contract, neither can sue the other in terms of the contract. South African law does not recognize direct contractual actions between litigants in the absence of privity of contract. A subcontractor has no lien against the co-contractant of the main contractor for payment of the contract price agreed upon between the subcontractor and the main contractor.[478] In certain limited circumstances, a subcontractor may have a claim against the co-contractant, based on unjust enrichment and brought in terms of the *condictio indebiti.*

347. When the subcontractor commits a breach of contract, for example, by negligently failing to apply the required standard of skill and expertise, and thereby causes the co-contractant financial loss, the latter is, in principle, entitled to a claim

477. Cf. *Langley Fox Building Partnership (Pty) Ltd v. De Valence* 1991 1 SA 1 (A).

478. However, as indicated above, in certain circumstances, a lessor has a tacit hypothec over the property of the sub-lessee.

in delict from the subcontractor, provided that all the requirements for such an action are present. The limitations set by the courts in cases of concurrence between delictual and contractual actions would not be relevant in this case, nor would the reasons of policy advanced by the courts for such a limitation apply.[479] Proof of the element of wrongfulness would, in practice, be the most problematic aspect of such a claim and would depend mainly on the existence of facts that would create a duty to guard against harm. The fact that the co-contractant institutes a claim for mere financial loss would not affect the possible success of the claim.

§4. Effect of Insolvency on a Contract

348. In South African law, the Insolvency Act 24 of 1936 (as amended) provides a method of dealing with the sequestration of the estate of an insolvent natural person so as to protect his or her creditors. The liquidation of an insolvent juristic person is dealt with in terms of the Companies Act 61 of 1973.

349. Briefly stated, the general effect of sequestration is that the estate of the insolvent person is vested in a trustee; civil proceedings are stayed; and a *concursus creditorum* results.

350. An insolvent person under sequestration may conclude contracts in his or her own name. However, in the case of contracts that have or that will probably have a prejudicial effect on the estate, the written consent of the trustee is required. When the insolvent person, without such consent, purports to alienate for valuable consideration property that he or she acquired after the sequestration of his or her estate, the alienation will be valid if the acquirer proves that he or she was not aware and had no reason to suspect that the estate of the insolvent person was under sequestration.

351. In general terms, the sequestration of an insolvent person's estate does not terminate uncompleted contracts entered into before the sequestration. The trustee has the choice to be bound or not to be bound to such contracts. If it is in the interests of the estate to abide by a contract and the trustee elects to adhere to it, the trustee must fulfil the duties of the insolvent person in terms of the contract, and the trustee can be sued by the creditor for the usual relief.[480] When the trustee elects to abandon the contract, the creditor has a concurrent claim for any damage that he or she may have suffered as a result. When a debtor purports to fulfil to the insolvent person an obligation in terms of a contract, the debt will not be discharged, and the debtor will have to perform to the trustee as well, unless he or she can show that he

479. *See Lillicrap, Wassenaar & Partners v. Pilkington Brothers (SA) (Pty) Ltd* 1985 1 SA 475 (A) and the discussion in G.F. Lubbe & C.M. Murray, *Contract Cases Materials and Commentary* 10 et seq. (Juta 1988).

480. *See*, in the context of lease, *Ellerine Brothers (Pty) Ltd v. McCarthy Ltd* 2014 4 SA 22 (SCA).

or she acted in good faith and without knowledge of the insolvency. A right to cancel the contract on the basis of the insolvent party's breach will only survive the concursus if such right had been accrued and completed prior to concursus.[481]

352. The Insolvency Act contains special provisions for dealing with the following: the uncompleted acquisition of immovable property in the case of the insolvency of the purchaser[482] (section 35); the position in which movable property was purchased by the insolvent person prior to sequestration and not paid for (section 36); and the position regarding leases (section 37), contracts of service (section 38), and credit agreements (section 84).

353. Although the Insolvency Act provides for the setting aside by the trustee (or a creditor in the name of the trustee) of dispositions without value, voidable preferences, undue preferences, and collusive dealings, the *actio Pauliana* is still recognized as a remedy to attack alienations or any contract *in fraudem creditorum.* Rescission may be obtained by an individual creditor in this way, even when the insolvent estate has not been formally sequestrated in terms of the Insolvency Act. The requirements for the remedy are the following:[483] there must be an 'intention to defraud' on the part of the debtor, in the sense that the object of the transaction is to give one creditor an unfair advantage in insolvency over the other creditors; the debtor's assets must be diminished by the transaction (a distinction being made between alienations *ex titulo lucrativo* and *ex titulo oneroso*); and the person who receives from the debtor must not receive his or her own property.

481. *See Roering and Others NNO v. Nedbank Ltd* 2013 3 SA 160 (GSJ).
482. In the case of an uncompleted sale of immovable property, when the estate of the seller is sequestrated, the property remains in his or her estate, and the buyer merely has a concurrent claim, subject to a measure of protection provided by the Alienation of Land Act 68 of 1981.
483. It is interesting to note that the requirements for the Paulian action as set out by the French writer Pothier are accepted in South African practice as being the Roman-Dutch law on this point – cf. *Hockey v. Rixom & Smith* 1939 SR 107.

Chapter 5. The End of a Contract

§1. Performance and Breach

I. Performance

354. An obligation is extinguished when it is fulfilled in that the envisaged performance is properly made. Ordinarily, performance requires the participation of the performer and the creditor and as such is a bilateral juristic act. The parties generally conclude a 'debt-extinguishing agreement', which may be express or tacit.[484] Performance is a unilateral juristic act only when the cooperation of the creditor is not required, such as in the case of *obligationes non faciendi* and certain *obligationes faciendi.* Furthermore, the performer must intend to effect a discharge, and the creditor must regard the obligation as being extinguished. This subjective aspect of performance is apparent in many of the rules regarding performance, such as the allocation or appropriation of payment to one of various debts owed by the debtor to the creditor and payment 'in full and final settlement' of an amount less than the amount actually due.

A. *Who May Perform?*

355. A third party may, without the consent of the debtor or the creditor, discharge the obligation of the debtor by performance, provided that he makes such performance in the name of the debtor.[485] When, however, the performance is dependent on the personal attributes of the debtor, the creditor may refuse to accept performance by a third party. Discharge of the debtor will result only when the third party has a specific intention to that effect, and it does not occur when the third party intends, for example, merely to perform to the creditor so as to obtain transfer of his or her claim against the debtor or to fulfil his or her duty as surety. In the latter case, the obligation is not extinguished, and the surety can make use of the benefit of cession of actions. When a co-debtor who is bound jointly and severally with others fully performs to the creditor, the obligation is discharged. Any right of recourse that he or she may have against the other debtors depends on the relationship between all the debtors. This principle also applies to the right of recourse that the third party who performs the debtor's duties may have against the debtor, such as an action based on mandate or *negotiorum gestio.*

484. *B & H Engineering v. First National Bank of SA* 1995 2 SA 279 (A); Absa Bank Ltd v. Lombard Insurance Co Ltd 2012 6 SA 569 (SCA) at 579. Such an agreement will be invalid if it is *contra bonos mores* e.g., where both parties are aware that the debt is being discharged with stolen money. If the recipient is *bona fide* unaware that the money was stolen, however, the agreement will be valid, and the debt will be discharged: *Absa Bank Ltd v. Lombard Insurance Co Ltd* 2012 6 SA 569 (SCA) at 579D-E.

485. *Absa Bank Ltd v. Lombard Insurance Co Ltd* 2012 6 SA 569 (SCA) at 579.

B. To Whom Must Performance Be Made?

356. Performance must be made to the creditor or to his or her agent and may be made to a person designated by the creditor. In the latter case, performance will also extinguish the debt.[486] A debtor may have the right, usually in terms of a contract, to perform to a third party (an *adiectus solutionis causa*, such as when an employer has the right to pay a subcontractor directly).

357. In principle, when the circumstances set out above are not present, payment to a creditor of the original creditor does not release the debtor, even when the original creditor benefits from the payment. There are a number of special exceptions to this position: so as to release his or her goods from the lessor's tacit hypothec, when a sub-lessee pays to the lessor rent owed by the lessee, he or she discharges his or her liability to the lessee in the same amount; in terms of section 11 of the Alienation of Land Act 68 of 1981, a purchaser of land on instalments may, in certain circumstances, reduce his or her liability to the seller by payment to the seller's creditors; an employer who pays the creditor of his or her employee in terms of a garnishee order (an order obtained by a creditor directing the employer to make deductions from the employee's wages for payment to that creditor) will reduce his or her liability to pay wages *pro tanto*.

C. What Must Be Performed?

358. In principle, specific performance exactly according to the terms of the contract must be rendered. A creditor may refuse to accept a different performance (including damages as a surrogate of performance) or piecemeal performance. In certain circumstances, a creditor may reject an incomplete or defective performance. In principle, a creditor is entitled to specific performance and only in exceptional circumstances, and when it is required by public policy to reach a just result, will a court not grant an order for specific performance. A court will not grant an order amounting to an amendment of the contractual duties of the debtor, except when the agreed upon performance is illegal for being against the public interest, in which case the court may order the debtor to perform to the extent to which it is legal. When the court does grant such an order, it should not be interpreted as if the court has written a new contract for the parties – the court merely refuses to enforce a contract to the extent that it conflicts with the norms of society. To this extent, individual freedom to bind another by contract is subject to the interests of the broader society.

359. The creditor may agree to accept a different performance (*datio in solutum*). In such a case, the obligation of the debtor is only conditionally fulfilled. The

486. *See Viljoen v. Trakman* 1994 3 SA 116 (A); *Standard Bank of SA Ltd v. Harris NNO (JA du Toit Inc. Intervening)* 2003 2 SA 23 (SCA); *De Villiers NNO v. BOE Bank Ltd* 2004 3 SA 1 (SCA). Payment to a so-called stakeholder will not extinguish the debt.

original obligation is not novated, and if the substituted performance is defective, the creditor may enforce the original obligation, or he or she may proceed with respect to the substitute.

360. In the case of an *alternative* obligation, the debtor may have been given the power to select which alternative to perform. If it is a *facultative* obligation, the debtor has the power to render a different specified performance. If the obligation is *generic*, the debtor must select the required performance unless someone else has been nominated by the parties to do so.

D. Special Rules as to Payment of Money Debts

361. In principle, an obligation to pay money must be discharged by the delivery of legal tender – that is, banknotes or coins (the latter to a limited extent) in the currency unit of South Africa, namely the Rand (ZAR). Unless the parties have agreed otherwise,[487] a creditor may refuse to accept payment in any other currency. When the amount due is expressed in a foreign currency but is payable in South Africa, the debtor may pay the equivalent in ZAR at the exchange rate as at the time when payment is due. A South African court has the power on appropriate cases to pass judgment for an amount that is expressed in a foreign currency.[488]

362. It appears that South African courts will not adjust the amount payable so as to take account of a change in the value of the currency – the so-called principle of nominalism is applied.[489] The parties themselves must make a contractual provision for such an eventuality, which is often done by relating the amount payable to the consumer price index.

363. Since a cheque is not legal tender, a creditor is, in principle, entitled to refuse to accept it in payment of a monetary obligation. Exercising this power depends on the intention of the parties, the impression created by the creditor in the mind of the debtor considered in light of their previous course of dealing, and the reason why the cheque is refused. Acceptance of a cheque discharges the debt only conditionally upon the cheque being honoured. If it is dishonoured, the creditor may sue on the basis of the original obligation or the obligation created by the cheque and may be entitled to a provisional sentence. If the debtor chooses to pay by cheque, and the creditor accepts this, the risk that the cheque may be lost or stolen

487. For example, they have agreed that payment may be made by cheque or by electronic transfer.
488. Although this conclusion was previously contradicted by a provincial court (*see Voest Alpine Intertrading Gesellschaft MBH v. Burwill & Co. SA (Pty) Ltd* 1985 2 SA 149 (W)), the Appeal Court has now settled the matter – *see Standard Chartered Bank of Canada v. Nedperm Bank Ltd* 1994 4 SA 747 (A) 774.
489. Cf. *SA Eagle Insurance Co. Ltd v. Hartley* 1990 4 SA 833 (A).

before it has been honoured lies with the debtor.[490] In practice, a variety of acceptable alternative methods of payment have evolved, such as payment by credit card or Electronic Funds Transfer (EFT). Other specialized methods of payment, mostly in terms of the particular type of contract, are bank guarantees in sales of land, letters of credit in international transactions, and payment certificates with respect to engineering and building contracts.

364. When a debtor gives a cheque for an amount less than that due and stipulates that it is 'in full and final settlement', the courts tend to distinguish between offers made with the intention to fulfil the obligation and offers made with the intention to effect a compromise. In the first case, it appears that liability is admitted, and acceptance and presentation of the cheque will not preclude the creditor from claiming the balance. In the second case, acceptance of the cheque amounts to acceptance of the offer to compromise, and this would preclude a claim for the balance, even when the acceptance was stated to be without prejudice to the right to claim the balance, that is, when the attempt at compromise has been rejected. This approach of the courts has been strongly criticized as being conceptually dubious and impracticable. Presently, however, the courts will apply the general principles regarding the creation of contracts to the creation of compromises.[491]

365. When, in the case of various debts to the same creditor, a debtor does not allocate his or her payment to a particular debt, and the creditor does not advance an acceptable proposal, the payment will be allocated in a particular order by operation of law. Liability for interest is extinguished first, then capital, and so on.

366. When the creditor does not cooperate in accepting payment, he or she may be guilty of breach of contract in his or her capacity as creditor. The debtor may then, in appropriate circumstances, cancel the contract, which would release him or her from the duty to pay. With respect to other cases, there is uncertainty as to whether the institution of consignation, that is, payment to the court with notice to the creditor, still exists in South African law and whether consignation would extinguish the debt. There is no general statutory regulation on this matter.

E. Payment with Subrogation

367. In South African law, 'subrogation' in a complete sense (i.e., the substitution of one party for another as creditor with transfer of rights and duties) takes

490. *See*, for example, *Mannesmann Demag (Pty) Ltd v. Romatex Ltd and Another* 1988 4 SA 383 (D). But if the *creditor* chooses a method of payment (such as payment by cheque) and the debtor carries out his wishes, the creditor will bear 'any risk inherent in the stipulated method': *Stabilpave (Pty) Ltd v. South African Revenue Service* 2014 1 SA 350 (SCA).

491. *See* Van Huyssteen, Lubbe & Reinecke, *Contract General Principles* paras 13.9–13.16 (Juta 2016) and the cases cited there; *See* now *Be Bop a Lula Manufacturing & Printing CC v. Kingtex Marketing (Pty) Ltd* 2008 (3) SA 327 (SCA); but the offer must be clear and unambiguous and will be strictly interpreted; *see Hubbard v. Mostert* 2010 2 SA 391 (WCC).

place in general by way of cession or assignment. In principle, payment to a creditor does not entitle the person paying to step into the shoes of the creditor as cessionary and to exercise his or her rights against a debtor. In practice, substitution often occurs in terms of a contract that provides for the transfer of rights in certain circumstances, such as payment of a debt to the creditor by a third party. A very common example of this is the discounting of instalment-sale contracts by the seller to a financial enterprise, whereby the seller cedes his or her right against the purchaser to the financial enterprise against payment or credit received from the financial enterprise.

368. In the law of insurance, the concept of subrogation has taken on a special meaning and has become a separate doctrine. It was received into South African law from English law as being fully compatible with local principles.[492] Briefly stated, once the insured has been fully indemnified, the insurer, in terms of the contract of insurance (e.g., expressly, tacitly, or often by operation of common law by way of an implied term), becomes entitled to reimbursement out of the proceeds of any right that the insured may have against third parties as a result of his or her loss. This means that the insured may not prejudice the insurer's right, for example, by releasing the third party from liability, and the insurer is entitled to bring an action in the name of the insured against the third party as *dominus litis*. As such, subrogation does not effect a transfer of rights by the insured to the insurer, nor does it in any other way affect third parties. Subrogation operates only upon the indemnification of the insured. At this stage, it is not clear whether the doctrine will be accepted as applicable with respect to other contracts of indemnity.

369. In certain cases, a complete substitution or subrogation may result by operation of the rules of the common law. A surety who has paid the principal debt is entitled to a cession of action from the creditor, including all relevant securities. The cession need not take place simultaneously with payment, but may also be given at a later stage. The surety may refuse to pay unless cession is given.

370. South African law provides many examples of protecting the interests of a person who pays the creditor of another. This is attained by way of a right of retention or lien, rather than by way of obligatory cession or subrogation in the limited sense discussed above. In certain circumstances, for example, a mandatary has a right of retention so as to compel the grantor of the mandate to indemnify him or her against expenses. Similarly, in appropriate circumstances, a depositary has a lien against the depositor.

492. For a detailed discussion of the doctrine *see*, *The Law of South Africa* vol. 12, 1st re-issue, paras 373 et seq. (W.A. Joubert ed., Butterworths 2002).

II. Breach

A. Nature of a Breach

371. In practical terms, breach of contract occurs in South African law when the conduct of a party to the contract results in failure to attain the purpose for which the contract was concluded. However, this description does not indicate the juridical nature of a breach of contract, nor does it address the requirements for liability for breach, in particular whether fault is necessary. These matters are controversial, and the courts have not expressed any clear view on them. The reason is probably that conduct which may amount to breach of contract is usually dealt with in terms of the commonly recognized forms of breach of contract, which have crystallized in practice without specific analysis on a theoretical basis. In this respect, it may be said that the South African law of breach of contract is casuistic.

372. Various explanations have been advanced so as to find a unitary concept that can accommodate the different recognized forms of breach and can at once serve as a basis for future developments. Thus, a breach has been said to be a form of a delict, or at least a wrongful act that infringes upon a personal right, or a wrongful act that infringes upon an obligation as a *vinculum iuris*. None of these explanations is completely satisfactory. In particular, it appears that the courts do not favour the construction that a breach of contract is a delict in full technical sense.[493] All in all, it seems most appropriate to describe a breach as wrongful conduct (which would encompass commissions and omissions) in that it is contrary to the norms that protect the contractual interests of one contractant against infringement by the other contractant. The creditor has an interest in the timeous and proper fulfilment by the debtor of his or her duties, as well as a reasonable expectation that such performance will indeed take place in due course.[494] The creditor has a concomitant duty to cooperate towards performance by the debtor.

B. Forms of Breach and Requirements

373. The forms of breach of contract, by a debtor or by a creditor (in his or her capacity as creditor), are delay, positive malperformance, prevention of performance, and repudiation.[495] The qualification of a breach as 'fundamental' is not

493. Cf. *Protea International (Pty) Ltd v. Peat Marwick Mitchell & Co.* 1990 2 SA 566 (A); *Administrator, Natal v. Edouard* 1990 3 SA 581 (A).In *Scoin Trading (Pty) Ltd v. Bernstein NO* 2011 2 SA118 (SCA) the court, in dealing with a case of delay by the debtor, held in general that breach was not a delict (paras 17–20).

494. Cf. Van Huyssteen, Lubbe & Reinecke, *Contract General Principles* paras 10.1–10.16 (Juta 2016).

495. A variety of classifications and sequence of treatment of the subject is to be found in the textbooks, a general distinction being the one between malperformance in the wider sense (further distinguished into 'negative' malperformance, that is, delay, and 'positive' malperformance) and anticipatory breach of contract. Cf., for example, Van Huyssteen, Lubbe & Reinecke, *Contract General*

often used in South African law to denote a form of breach. However, it is of importance insofar as, generally, only a fundamental breach will justify cancellation of a contract by the party who is not in breach, except, of course, if the contract provides otherwise.

1. Delay by a Debtor: *Mora Debitoris*

374. Late or non-timeous performance by a debtor will be regarded as breach of contract (*mora debitoris*) when the following requirements are present:[496]

1. The debt must be due and enforceable.
2. The delay must be wrongful (in the contractual sense as described above). Usually, this will be the case when the debtor knows exactly when he or she must perform, either in terms of the contract (a stipulation that performance must be made immediately on conclusion of the contract being sufficient) or in terms of a demand to perform by a certain date (provided that the demand allows the debtor a reasonable time). When no date for performance has been fixed in this manner, the creditor may, of course, always claim specific performance from the debtor in terms of the contract. He or she can, however, not claim damages or cancel the contract, since no breach has been committed. In certain circumstances, such as when the debtor knows that the creditor requires performance urgently and when it is impracticable to send a demand, an excessively long delay may possibly be regarded as wrongful and thus as a breach, even when no date has been fixed. The latter approach is not strictly in accordance with Roman-Dutch law and would seem to draw more on the concept of default as it is known in English common law. Yet, it may be regarded as being in accordance with an acceptable jurisprudential analysis of the matter, and the Appeal Court may eventually decide that it is good law.[497]
3. In spite of previous uncertainty as to whether fault was a requirement for delay, the Supreme Court of Appeal has now unequivocally held that it is not, and that the basis for delictual and contractual damages is completely different.[498]

Principles paras 10.33–10.39 (Juta 2016); J.C. de Wet & A.H. van Wyk, *Die Suid-Afrikaanse Kontraktereg en Handelsreg*, vol. 1 (Durban: Butterworths, 1992), 157 et seq.; R.H. Christie, *The Law of Contract in South Africa* 515 et seq. (Butterworths 2011).

496. The leading case on this topic is *Nel v. Cloete* 1972 2 SA 150 (A). *See also MV Snow Crystal Transnet Ltd t/a National Ports Authority v. Owner of MV Snow Crystal* 2008 4 SA 111 (SCA); *Dormell Properties v. Renasa Insurance NNO* 2011 1 SA 70 (SCA).

497. In terms of s. 19(2) of the Consumer protection Act 68 of 2008 it is an implied term in every consumer transaction that a supplier must deliver on the agreed date and time, if any, or otherwise within a reasonable time.

498. *See Scoin Trading (Pty) Ltd v. Bernstein NO* 2011 2 SA118 (SCA) paras 15–20. The court approved of the judgment in *Legogote Development Co. (Pty) Ltd v. Delta Trust & Finance Co.* 1970 1 SA 584 (T). Also see *Mokala Beleggings v. Minister of Rural Development and Land Reform* 2012 4 SA 22 (SCA) para. 8.

375. When, as a result of the delay, performance is no longer possible, *mora debitoris* is excluded. However, another form of breach, prevention of performance, may occur. Performance by the debtor after he or she has fallen *in mora* cannot cure the breach, and if performance becomes impossible while the debtor is *in mora*, he or she will not be excused.

2. *Mora Creditoris*

376. *Mora creditoris* is the form of breach most often committed by a creditor in his or her capacity as creditor. It is based on delay by the creditor in cooperating with the debtor with respect to performance by the latter. The rules relating to *mora debitoris* apply here mutatis mutandis.

3. Positive Malperformance by a Debtor

377. Breach of contract in the form of positive malperformance by a debtor[499] occurs, first, when the debtor renders performance that does not comply with the terms of the contract. In this regard, a tacit term that work will be done by applying reasonable skill and knowledge is often the basis of an alleged breach. Second, such a breach occurs when the debtor does something which he or she undertook not to do. Positive malperformance can take place irrespective of whether an important (principal) or minor duty has been breached. Usually, the debtor need not be given the opportunity to rectify a defect in his or her performance.

378. Whether fault is a requirement for this form of breach was a controversial question and had not received specific attention in case law. This was not surprising, since fault will almost always be present, at least in the form of negligence.[500] Among the writers who did address the question, opinion was divided. On the basis of the finding in *Scoin Trading (Pty) Ltd v. Bernstein NO* 2011 2 SA118 (SCA), it can now be said that fault is not a requirement.[501]

4. Prevention of Performance by a Debtor

379. A debtor who, by his or her conduct after the conclusion of the contract, renders performance impossible, commits a breach of contract. Impossibility not

499. *See*, for example, *Spies v. Lombard* 1950 3 SA 469 (A); *Ver Elst v. Sabena Belgian World Airlines* 1983 3 SA 637 (A); *Thompson v. Scholtz* 1999 1 SA 232 (SCA); *South African Forestry Co. Ltd v. York Timbers Ltd* 2005 3 SA 323 (SCA) 341.

500. This would be the case where a contract of mandate is breached due to the nature of mandate and the terms implied by law (naturalia).

501. 2011 2 SA 118 (SCA) paras 17–19 where the court opined that it is 'erroneous … that a breach of contract is only established if the debtor acted "wrongfully" or "culpably"'.

only denotes physical, absolute impossibility, but it is also considered to be present when performance is for all practical and reasonable purposes impossible in the eyes of the law.

380. It is generally accepted that the party alleging prevention of performance need not prove fault, but that the party in breach may advance reasons for being excused from the consequences of his or her conduct.

5. Repudiation by a Debtor

381. The concept of repudiation as an anticipatory breach of contract was taken into South African law from English law and has long been recognized as an independent form of breach. Repudiation as breach of contract consists in conduct from which it is reasonable to conclude that the other party will not fulfil his or her duties in terms of the contract.[502] The test for this conclusion is objective.[503] Accordingly, the subjective state of mind of the debtor is irrelevant: 'repudiation is … not a matter of intention, it is a matter of perception'.[504] Thus, for example, repudiation can take place when a contractant tenders defective performance in the bona fide belief that it is complete and proper performance, when a contractant in good faith misinterpreted the terms of the contract and acted accordingly, or when he or she attempts to resile from the contract without valid grounds. Mere delay in performing will usually not amount to repudiation. Repudiation of a minor part of the debtor's duties may amount to a breach, but the creditor may not be allowed to cancel the contract, for lack of seriousness of the breach.

382. There has been some uncertainty as to whether an act of repudiation immediately amounts to an actionable breach or whether it must first be accepted as such by the other party. The Appeal Court in the *Tuckers Land* case[505] construed an existing duty on contractants not to repudiate, based on the requirements of good faith; and in the *Datacolor* case,[506] repudiation in itself was held to be wrongful conduct amounting to breach of contract. Consequently, acceptance is not necessary to constitute a breach by way of repudiation. Rather, the aggrieved party can elect to ignore the repudiation and expect the repudiating party to perform, or he or she may

502. *See Tuckers Land & Development Corporation (Pty) Ltd v. Hovis* 1980 1 SA 645 (A); *Metalmil (Pty) Ltd v. AECI Explosives & Chemicals Ltd* 1994 3 SA 673 (A); *Datacolor International (Pty) Ltd v. Intamarket (Pty) Ltd* 2001 2 SA 284 (SCA); *Bierman v. Mutual & Federal Versekerings-maatskappy Bpk* 2004 1 SA 205 (O).

503. *B Braun Medical (Pty) Ltd v. Ambasaam CC* 2015 3 SA 22 (SCA) paras 8–10; *Datacolor International (Pty) Ltd v. Intamarket (Pty) Ltd* 2001 2 SA 284 (SCA) para. 16.

504. *Datacolor International (Pty) Ltd v. Intamarket (Pty) Ltd* 2001 2 SA 284 (SCA) para. 16.

505. *Tuckers Land & Development Corporation (Pty) Ltd v. Hovis* 1980 1 SA 645 (A).

506. *Datacolor International (Pty) Ltd v. Intamarket (Pty) Ltd* 2001 2 SA 284 (SCA).

react to the repudiation and cancel the contract.[507] Any continued usage of the term 'acceptance' in this connection should be interpreted in terms of the decision to cancel. Once repudiation has occurred, the aggrieved party should be entitled to claim damages as a result of the breach.

383. The courts have not positively required fault as an element of repudiation, and there appears to be no reason to do so.[508] By the nature of repudiation, the wrongful conduct can hardly be excused, since it depends on an objective impression created in the mind of the other party.

C. Fault as a General Requirement

384. Since breach of contract is generally not regarded as a delict, it follows that fault (intent or negligence) cannot, on the basis of delictual liability, be set as a general requirement for liability for a breach. This has now been confirmed in *Scoin Trading (Pty) Ltd v. Bernstein NO.* [509] However, the question still remains whether fault should nevertheless be insisted upon as a method of limiting liability for (particularly) damages for the positive interest. However, it can be argued with some degree of conviction that the element of wrongfulness in the contractual sense, as it has been applied in South African law in regard to the specific forms of breach, provides adequate limitation of liability, bearing in mind that there is room for finding justification for conduct that would otherwise have amounted to breach of contract. It should also be borne in mind that the remedy of cancellation is only available in exceptional circumstances. Acceptance of this construction would, in effect, place South African law more in line with English common law than with civil law on this point.

385. Obviously, contractual duties may be formulated in such a way that they can only be breached intentionally or negligently (such as when reasonable care in the execution of contractual duties is either expressly or tacitly required), or parties may exclude the possibility of justification (or absence of fault as an excuse) by the inclusion of a warranty.

D. Consequences of Breach of Contract in General

386. In principle, a contractant may always enforce the contract specifically (*in forma specifica*), whether a breach has been committed or not, since the claim is based simply on the contents of the contract itself. Damages and cancellation of the

507. In *Sandown Travel (Pty) Ltd v. Cricket South Africa* 2013 2 SA 502 (GSJ) it was held that the 'repentance principle' applied in our law: where the aggrieved party elects to abide by the agreement the repudiating party may repent the repudiation and make performance when it is due. If, however, the repudiating party persists in the repudiation, the aggrieved party may change his/her mind and elect to cancel instead.
508. *See also* now *Scoin Trading (Pty) Ltd v. Bernstein NO* 2011 2 SA118 (SCA) referred to above.
509. *Ibid.*

contract may, however, only be claimed if the contract has been breached, the claim being based on that fact. Breach of contract is then best construed as a new and independent obligationary fact. A breach per se does not result in termination of the contract. The contract may be cancelled by a contractant only when the breach is serious enough, or, as it is often put, when it is 'fundamental' or goes to the 'root of the contract', or in terms of a cancellation clause in the contract. Cancellation need not be confirmed by a court order.

§2. Impossibility of Performance, Frustration, and Hardship

I. Irresistible Force

387. The concept of irresistible force (*vis maior* or force majeure), as affecting the operation of a contract, has been developed in South African law not so much in the context of an excuse for breach of contract that would exclude fault, but rather in the context of supervening objective impossibility of performance, which would extinguish the obligation and release the debtor from performance. It has certainly not developed as a doctrine of general application in the law of contract.

II. Supervening Impossibility of Performance

388. The consequences of a change in circumstances after the conclusion of the contract, to the extent that performance has become objectively impossible, are dealt with in terms of the concept of supervening impossibility of performance.[510] Supervening impossibility must be distinguished from initial impossibility of performance, which is usually treated systematically with the requirements for the validity of a contract, as in this monograph. If performance is initially objectively impossible, no obligations arise in principle. Many of the considerations and rules that apply with respect to initial impossibility also apply to supervening impossibility. The latter concept also must be distinguished from prevention of performance by one of the contractants, which could amount to breach of contract, unless it is excusable. The latter case may amount to supervening impossibility. When the impossibility constitutes a breach, the contract exists but may be cancelled by the aggrieved party.

389. When, after conclusion of the contract, performance has become objectively and unavoidably impossible, the obligation is, in principle, extinguished, and rights and duties with respect to performance of the obligation fall away, even if the impossibility relates to the performance of only one of the parties. Exceptions to the rule are dealt with below. It is clearly equitable in general that not only the debtor

510. Generally on the topic, *see* W.A. Ramsden, *Supervening Impossibility of Performance in the South African Law of Contract* (Juta 1985); *see also Peters, Flamman & Co. v. Kokstad Municipality* 1919 AD 427, in which the English law approach was rejected; *Bob's Shoe Centre v. Heneways Freight Services (Pty) Ltd* 1995 2 SA 421 (A).

should bear the risk of such an occurrence by being held to performance, but also that the advantages and disadvantages of impossibility should affect both parties. In South African law, this conclusion is not based on the fiction of an implied term to that effect.

III. Objective or Practical Impossibility

390. In South African law, it is generally accepted that the obligation will only be extinguished if the performance has indeed become objectively impossible.[511] Mere subjective or relative impossibility or hardship does not affect the contract and will not release the debtor, nor will a frustration of the purpose or object for which the contract was concluded.[512] In the final analysis, the test for objective impossibility of performance is whether, in all the circumstances of the case, performance is reasonably no longer possible, even if it may physically still be possible. The relative cost of performance measured against the probable prejudice to the other party is an important factor in the process of determining such impossibility. Traditionally, impossibility has been linked to the concepts of *vis maior* and *casus fortuitus*. These relate to events, emanating from nature or humans, which are irresistible, unavoidable, and outside the control of the ordinary person, and may be unforeseen or unforeseeable.[513] Whether an event that was foreseeable but unavoidable in the circumstances will be regarded as creating objective impossibility is doubtful at this stage of the development of South African law.

IV. Consequences of Supervening Impossibility

391. Except for instances in which the risk of impossibility is for the account of one or other of the parties by agreement or by operation of law, the effect of impossibility is that the obligation is extinguished. In principle, when the obligation is reciprocal, the counter-obligation is also extinguished, except when the parties have agreed differently or the law rules otherwise. Obviously, no action for damages for breach of contract will apply, nor can a forfeiture clause relating to breach of contract be enforced. Performance in terms of a contract affected by supervening impossibility may be reclaimed by an enrichment action, but the position relating to the adjustment of preparatory expenses is not at all clear in the absence of a term to that effect.

392. Partial impossibility extinguishes a divisible obligation *pro tanto*, with a pro rata reduction in the performance of the other party. Whether the creditor can elect to treat the whole obligation as extinguished is not clear.

---

511. Thus, for example, the performance of a debtor's obligation is not rendered impossible by his or her death, unless the performance was of a personal nature: *see Scoin Trading (Pty) Ltd v. Bernstein NO* 2011 2 SA 118 (SCA), 123–124. Also see *Quinella Trading v. Minister of Rural Development* 2010 4 SA 308 (LCC).
512. *See*, for example, *Rosebank Mall (Pty) Ltd Cradock Heights (Pty) Ltd* 2004 2 SA 353 (W).
513. *See*, for example, *South African Forestry Co. Ltd v. York Timbers Ltd* 2005 3 SA 323 (SCA).

393. Temporary impossibility affecting an indivisible obligation only suspends the obligation for all parties until such time as the impossibility no longer exists.

394. Supervening impossibility of performance cannot occur with respect to a generic obligation, and the obligation is not affected by impossibility – a *genus* is indestructible *(genus non perit)*. An alternative obligation is extinguished only if all the alternatives become impossible to perform.

V. Different Allocation of Risk for Supervening Impossibility by Contract and Operation of Law

A. Contractual Allocation of Risk

395. In South African law, too, it is common and acceptable for parties to contract expressly regarding the effect of changed circumstances on the future operation of the contract and the incidence of the risks thereanent, thus going beyond the constraints of common law rules regarding supervening objective impossibility of performance.

396. Terms such as the above may also be tacit terms and will often (but not necessarily) be inferred as such when a change in the circumstances was foreseen or was reasonably foreseeable. Regard must also be given to the nature of the contract, the relationship of the parties, and the nature of the supervening impossibility.[514] It must, however, be stressed that the ordinary rules and limitations regarding an inference of tacit terms apply here with equal force.

397. If an express or tacit common supposition regarding the basis of the contract fails, the effect will be that the contract itself fails. This approximates the effect of the English doctrine of frustration or of the German concept of *Geschäftsgrundlage.* There is some support for the notion that the doctrine of frustration is generally recognized in South African law[515] (cf. the reference to the *clausula rebus sic stantibus* (a clause that things remain the same)), but it seems reasonably clear that the courts will only regard a contract as having failed for lack of a basis if a supposition to that effect is part of the contract. The extent to which other notions such as good faith may be employed in this regard is discussed below.

514. Cf., for example, *Bischofberger v. Van Eyk* 1981 2 SA 607 (W); *Orda AG v. Nuclear Fuels Corporation of South Africa (Pty) Ltd* 1994 4 SA 26 (W) 82–85.

515. Cf. *Bayley v. Harwood* 1954 3 SA 498 (A) and the interpretation placed on the judgment of Greenberg JA by some writers, for example, A.J. Kerr, *The Principles of the Law of Contract* 407–410, at 549–552 (Butterworths 2002).

B. Allocation of Risk by Operation of Law

398. The most important instance of an allocation of risk for supervening impossibility that departs from the rule is the risk rule in regard to contracts of sale. It is implied by law that once the sale is *perfecta*, the purchaser bears the risk for an accidental destruction of or calamity affecting the thing sold, even if delivery to the purchaser has not yet taken place. The purchaser thus remains liable for payment of the full purchase price, even if the seller can no longer deliver the thing at all or can only deliver it in a damaged state. The parties may vary these consequences by agreement.

399. As has been indicated above, if performance becomes impossible while the debtor is *in mora*, the obligation will not be extinguished, and he or she will remain bound.

VI. Changed Circumstances and Good Faith

400. As will be apparent from the above, South African common law will, in future, probably not make provision for the effect of changed circumstances by manipulating or extending the existing rules and concepts relating to terms agreed upon by the parties or on the basis upon which they contracted, nor does the concept of objective impossibility readily lend itself to plausible expansion to the necessary extent. A refinement of the requirements of 'unconscionable conduct' and 'some great inequity' resulting from it, as they were formulated with respect to the applicability of the *exceptio doli generalis*, might have led to the development of a doctrine of changed circumstances, especially since the *exceptio*, before its demise, was most successfully applied in that context. As explained earlier, the Appeal Court was, however, not prepared to recognize the *exceptio doli generalis* as part of modern South African law.[516]

401. It is possible to come to a fair answer to the question of who should bear the risk for changed circumstances by applying an economic analysis to the problem. The concept of the 'superior risk bearer' may, for example, indicate that a seller who is also a dealer in a product sold should usually bear the risk for circumstances that may make delivery by him or her subjectively impossible, since he or she could more easily diversify his or her own buy-in. This kind of approach has not been applied as such in South African law, although the analysis would be relevant to determining what a particular party may objectively reasonably expect in the circumstances. This, in turn, is relevant with respect to the norm of good faith that may come to be used in future to create a rule of law to determine who should bear the risk. It is also possible that the concept of the public interest may be developed to incorporate such a rule. When a court is then requested to give effect to a contract as it was agreed upon, it may refuse to do so and may then indeed give regard to

516. This has been recently confirmed by the Supreme Court of Appeal: *see Bredenkamp v. Standard Bank of South Africa Ltd* 2010 4 SA 468 (SCA), paras 32–35.

factors such as those mentioned above, as well as more external factors, such as the social circumstances against which the agreement between the parties must be considered.[517]

§3. Discharge and Termination by Agreement

I. Release

402. In South African law, a debtor may be freed from a contractual duty, or the parties may release one another from their respective duties in terms of a bilateral contract, by way of an agreement of release, occasionally also called a waiver or a cancellation agreement. Release has, on occasion, been typified as a contract of donation, but this is, strictly speaking, not correct, since a contract creates obligations and does not extinguish them. Of course, donation may be the reason for a consequent agreement of release. In principle, and for reasons of policy, a creditor cannot unilaterally abandon a right and so divest himself or herself of any concomitant obligation. The view has been held judicially that when a term in a contract, such as a condition, can be said to be for the exclusive benefit of one party, that party may unilaterally waive, abandon, or renounce the right. However, a court will assume that prima facie the right was intended to be for the benefit of all parties. Release must be distinguished from the election by a party to make use of one of two or more inconsistent remedies, such as the choice to regard a contract as cancelled because of repudiation by the debtor, rather than to ignore the repudiation and to require performance as agreed upon. This election of one possible choice is sometimes described as a waiver of the other possibility. Release must also be distinguished from unilateral conduct by a party that reasonably leads the other party to believe that the first party did not intend to enforce the terms of their contract strictly. This situation must be dealt with in terms of the doctrine of estoppel by representation.

The exact meaning of the concept of a waiver, especially with respect to the question whether the act of waiving is unilateral or bilateral, has not been finally decided in South African law. The context in which the expression is used in a contract must therefore be considered carefully to determine the meaning that the parties intended it to have.[518]

403. To be valid, an agreement of release must comply with all the requirements for a legally relevant agreement. This entails, *inter alia*, that the party who divests

517. *See*, for example, G.F. Lubbe & C.M. Murray, *Contract Cases Materials and Commentary* 773–774 (Juta 1988); Van Huyssteen, Lubbe & Reinecke, *Contract General Principles* paras 13.66–13.67 (Juta 2016); L.F. van Huyssteen & S. van der Merwe, *Good Faith in Contract: Proper Behaviour amidst Changing Circumstances*, Stellenbosch L. Rev. 244 (1990). *See also* the discussions of the role of good faith above; and the provisions of the Consumer Protection Act 68 of 2008, which may well require some reconsideration of the position presently taken by the courts.

518. For a brief discussion of the differences of opinion with respect to the meaning of the word 'waiver', *see* Van Huyssteen, Lubbe & Reinecke, *Contract General Principles* para. 5.15, and paras 13.24–13.30 (Juta 2016).

himself or herself of a right must have full knowledge of that right; otherwise, a meeting of the minds can hardly take place. Whether this requirement, which has often been acknowledged by the courts, is merely a consequence of the nature of release or whether it is a special requirement for validity is unclear. The practical significance of the requirement is, however, beyond dispute. Further, the right that is the subject of release must exist. Generally, no formalities are required. A release may also be agreed upon tacitly by the parties. In this context, it is often difficult to distinguish between release and the operation of estoppel. Delay in the exercising of a right does not necessarily indicate a tacit release, nor does it necessarily amount to a representation that is adequate to ground an estoppel – the English law doctrine of laches is not part of South African law. Delay would, of course, be a weighty factor from which an intention to release may be inferred, and it could, in certain circumstances, amount to a representation that would lead a reasonable person to believe that the other party intended to waive his or her rights, thereby estopping him or her from relying on them.

404. The effect of a release depends on the intention of the parties. The release may be total or partial and will extinguish any executory obligations *pro tanto*. When an obligation has been performed, restitution of what has been received must be made fully or in part, as the case may be.

II. Novation

405. Parties to a contract may extinguish the existing obligations by creating, by way of an agreement, a new obligationary relationship in place of the old one. This is called novation. The novation may be agreed upon with respect to the content of the obligation between the same parties, for example, when the duty to repay a loan is replaced by the duty to transfer land to the creditor. This is the usual meaning of novation in South African law. Novation may also take place with respect to the substitution of a debtor by a new debtor, in terms of an agreement between all three parties. This kind of novatory agreement is usually called delegation and has been discussed in the previous chapter in the context of the transfer of rights and duties. It must be remembered that the transfer of duties may now in South African law also take place by assignment – the original debtor may transfer his or her duties to another with the assent of the creditor.[519] Substitution of creditors rarely takes place by novation – the method of cession is simpler and more flexible.

406. For a novation to be valid, all the general requirements for a legally effective agreement must be present. In particular, an *animus novandi* – an intention to replace an existing obligation with another – must be clearly apparent.[520] The courts

519. These methods approximate the concepts of *expromissio* and *adpromissio* as used in some European systems of law.

520. *See Tauber v. Von Abo* 1984 4 SA 482 (E); *Pfeiffer v. First National Bank of SA Ltd* 1998 3 SA 1018 (SCA).

will not easily infer a tacit novation: indeed, there is a presumption against novation.[521] The requisite intention will not be inferred simply when a negotiable instrument is given and taken; such conduct will rather be regarded as a reinforcement of the original obligation, which by itself creates further interdependent obligations with respect to the same duties.[522] From this, it follows that a novation can only be effective when the obligation that is intended to be replaced is valid and exists. Any such obligation, including a natural or conditional obligation, may be the subject of novation. It is not necessary that the content of the original obligation be changed or that a new element be introduced in the new obligation; the parties may, for example, simply renew the existing obligation in the same terms to stop the continuance of prescription. Proof of a new element will, however, go a long way towards proving the *animus novandi.*

407. As is intended by the parties, the original obligation is discharged by novation. Pledges and securities are released and sureties are discharged. Interest on the novated obligation ceases to accumulate.[523] A novation may be conditional, with the result that the original obligation is replaced only upon fulfilment of the condition,[524] or the original obligation revives, depending on whether the condition is suspensive or resolutive. When the substitution is unqualified, but the new obligation fails because it is itself subject to a condition, the original obligation is not revived, except when the parties have agreed otherwise. When the new obligation is cancelled for breach, the same applies, but when the new obligation is rescinded due to improperly obtained consensus, the old obligation is revived.[525]

521. *See* Malan et al *Malan on Bills of Exchange, Cheques and Promissory Notes in South African Law* 4 edn. at 198; *Rodel Financial Service (Pty) Ltd v. Naidoo and Another* 2013 4 SA 151 (KZP) 155–156; *National Health Laboratory Service v. Lloyd-Jansen van Vuuren* 2015 5 SA 426 (SCA) para. 15.
522. *See Adams v. SA Motor Industry Employers Association* 1981 3 SA 1189 (A); *Kotzé v. Suid-Westelike Transvaalse Landbou Korporasie* 2005 2 SA 295 (SCA). The same applies to acknowledgements of debt: *Rodel Financial Service (Pty) Ltd v. Naidoo and Another* 2013 4 SA 151 (KZP) 156G. *See* in regard to payment certificates *Martin Harris & Seuns OVS (Edms) Bpk v. Qwa Qwa Regeringsdiens* 2000 3 SA 339 (SCA).
523. *See Swadif (Pty) Ltd v. Dyke* 1978 1 SA 928 (A).
524. Pending fulfilment, the creditor may not enforce the original obligation.
525. *See Crause v. Ocean Bentonite Co. (Edms) Bpk* 1979 1 SA 1076 (O).

Chapter 6. Remedies

§1. General

408. It is usual in treatises on the South African law of contract to discuss remedies for breach of contract as a separate topic. This is appropriate, since breach of contract is construed as a new obligationary fact, distinct from the contract and the obligations created by it, which have subsequently been breached. Breach of contract, although generally not regarded as a delict as such, and not generally requiring proof of fault, is nevertheless wrongful conduct: breach is contrary to the norms that protect the contractual interests of one contractant against infringement by the other. For this reason, breach of contract gives rise to the duty to compensate patrimonial loss by the payment of damages and, in appropriate circumstances, to the right to unilaterally and extra-judicially cancel (resile from) the consequences of the contract. However, these remedies are not regarded as the principal relief for breach: contrary to the position in English common law, specific enforcement of the contract is regarded as the 'first remedy' available as a right to a victim of a breach. Although commonly said to be a remedy, the claim for enforcement of performance in terms of the contract actually depends on the contract and its terms, and not on the fact of the breach. The courts will refuse an order for specific performance only in exceptional circumstances, obviously including cases in which performance is objectively impossible. Although a contractant may not resort to self-help to enforce a contract, the law grants a party to a reciprocal contract[526] the right to withhold his or her own performance (akin in its practical consequences to the holding of a security) when the other party claims performance but has himself or herself not performed fully. This right is often described as the *exceptio non adimpleti contractus*, and it will be upheld unless a court in its discretion orders that a reduced performance be rendered against incomplete or defective performance by the claimant.

409. A contractant may apply to a court for an interdict prohibiting an impending breach of contract. A court order confirming cancellation is inconsistent with a claim for specific performance and may in principle not be requested in the alternative – by their nature, the two remedies are mutually exclusive. In practice, however, an aggrieved party may use a so-called double-barrelled procedure, in terms of which the plaintiff requests the court to order specific performance by a certain date, failing which cancellation is asked for as the alternative. The cancellation is then not based on the breach as such, but on the judgment debtor's failure to comply with the court order.[527] A litigant must sue in a single claim for all the relief that he or she claims to be entitled to with respect to one cause of action and cannot institute different claims at different stages; this is the so-called once-and-for-all rule.[528]

526. But see *Miloc Financial Solutions (Pty) Ltd v. Logistic Technologies (Pty) Ltd* 2008 4 SA 325 (SCA) in connection with the requirement of reciprocity.
527. *See Custom Credit Corp (Pty) Ltd v. Shembe* 1972 3 SA 462 (A).
528. *See Custom Credit Corp (Pty) Ltd v. Shembe* 1972 3 SA 462 (A).

§2. Defence of Non-performance by the Other Party

I. Exceptio Non Adimpleti Contractus (Right to Withhold)

410. Following a protracted development in the South African common law, based, *inter alia*, on aspects of English law, it was finally recognized in modern South African law that, in principle, a party to a reciprocal contract[529] may temporarily[530] withhold his or her own performance until such time as the other party (who must perform first or simultaneously) has performed fully or at least tenders full performance. This right to withhold (often called the *exceptio non adimpleti contractus*) is a consequence of the principle of reciprocity, and it has been likened in its practical consequences to the institution of pledge and the right to withhold retention monies.[531] In the absence of an allegation by the plaintiff that he or she has rendered performance or tenders performance, the *exceptio* can operate as a true procedural exception, namely that the claim is bad in law and discloses no cause of action. If the necessary allegation has been made by the plaintiff, the defendant may, of course, still raise the facts as a substantive defence.

411. The right to withhold performance is independent of any other remedy that a creditor may have, such as the right to reject the other contractant's defective performance and claim proper performance, the right to cancel the contract (in which case the defective performance must be returned or, when return is not possible, an amount based on enrichment will be payable), and the right to claim damages.

412. The right to withhold is temporary, pending performance by the plaintiff, but it has also been described as absolute, in the sense that it may be exercised by the defendant, notwithstanding that the malperformance by the plaintiff is minor, and that substantial performance has been rendered.[532] More recently, however, the

529. Obligations are reciprocal when one obligation is undertaken in exchange for performance of the other. Reciprocity depends on the intention of the parties. Most modern contracts, such as sale, lease, the various other forms of *locatio conductio*, and most contracts of insurance are reciprocal. On the question of reciprocity of obligations in this context, *see* e.g., *TH Restaurants (Pty) Ltd v. Rana Pazza (Pty) Ltd* 2012 5 SA 378 (WCC); *Cradle City (Pty) Ltd v. Lindley Farm 528 (Pty) Ltd* 2018 (3) SA 65 (SCA).

530. Unless defective performance of an *obligatio faciendi* cannot be remedied; in such a case, it is a 'complete defence': *see Smith v. Van den Heever and Others* 2011 3 SA 140 (SCA), 144C.

531. *See* the leading case of *BK Tooling (Edms) Bpk v. Scope Precision Engineering (Edms) Bpk* 1979 1 SA 391 (A) in which the Appeal Court conducted a thorough historical and comparative analysis of the matter. Also see *Motor Racing Enterprises (Pty) Ltd (in liquidation) v. NPS (Electronics) Ltd* 1996 4 SA 950 (SCA); *Grand Mines (Pty) Ltd v. Giddey NO* 1999 1SA 960 (SCA) and *Smith v. Van den Heever and Others* 2011 3 SA 140 (SCA).

532. Although the doctrine of substantial performance has been advanced as being more equitable, it was specifically rejected in this context by the Appeal Court in *BK Tooling (Edms) Bpk v. Scope Precision Engineering (Edms) Bpk* 1979 1 SA 391 (A). The right of a contractant to receive full and complete performance was considered to be inalienable. However, when the defect is trivial and when the notion of *de minimis non curat lex* applies, performance may not be withheld: *see Smith v. Van den Heever and Others* 2011 3 SA 140 (SCA), 144D. It may also not be withheld if withholding the performance would be disproportionate to the breach: *Botha and Another v. Rich NO and Others* 2014 4 SA 124 (CC).

Constitutional Court has held that the principle of reciprocity should be relaxed where it would be unfair to apply it.[533] In other words, the innocent party can be barred from relying on the exceptio non adimpleti contractus if the consequences of withholding performance would be disproportionate to the other party's breach.[534] In principle, the right to withhold applies equally, whether or not the plaintiff's defective performance is being retained by the defendant.

413. When a contractant retains the other contractant's defective performance and withholds his or her own performance, a court, for reasons of fairness, has the discretion to award a reduced counter-performance (in practice, most often a reduced contract price) to the other contractant who has not performed fully. Such an order will be made only upon proof by the plaintiff of specific circumstances:[535]

1. It must be shown that the court indeed has discretion – that is, when the defendant has utilized the incomplete performance to his or her advantage (mere retention not being utilization).
2. Special circumstances must exist that make it equitable for the court to exercise discretion in the plaintiff's favour, such as a bona fide belief that proper performance has been made, the willingness to complete performance, the degree of shortfall of performance, and whether the plaintiff has been given the opportunity to make good on the performance. It must be stressed that these are merely factors to be considered and that the presence or absence of one or more of them is not decisive. A reduced amount may, for example, still be awarded to a contractor who knows, and makes the allegation in his or her claim, that he or she has not performed fully.
3. The plaintiff must prove what the diminished counter-performance to which he or she claims to be entitled should be. This is normally done by proving the cost of bringing the defective or incomplete performance up to the required standard. This claim has been typified by the Appeal Court as a 'contractual' claim and is not based on enrichment, as was long thought to be the case.[536] Although the position is not entirely clear, it seems that the plaintiff does not have a true, independent claim for a reduced performance; insofar as a contractual claim for full performance is ousted by the other contractant's right to withhold, he or she is entitled to request the court in its discretion to award him or her a lesser amount based on equitable considerations.

414. The above approach leads to a deadlock when the defendant withholds his or her own performance, neither utilizing the plaintiff's performance nor cancelling

533. *Botha and Another v. Rich NO and Others* 2014 4 SA 124 (CC), paras 36–49.
534. *Ibid.*
535. *See Smith v. Van den Heever and Others* 2011 3 SA 140 (SCA), para. 18.
536. *See*, for example, *Hauman v. Nortje* 1914 AD 293 and the term quantum meruit, which was used to describe the claim for a reduced performance.

the contract. The Appeal Court has suggested that in such a case, the requirement of utilization may be discarded or qualified, or an enrichment claim may nevertheless be awarded.[537]

The approach set out above also cannot be applied in all respects when the defective performance of the plaintiff cannot actually be rectified after the event, such as in the case of a continuing contractual duty to give occupation of property to the purchaser before transfer. An award of a reduced contract price to the plaintiff is regarded by the courts as unsuitable; instead, an amount based on fairness is awarded, even if it is not possible to calculate the amount with any accuracy. Although the claim here can clearly not be typified as contractual, like the claim for a reduced contract price, there seems to be little practical difference between the end results in both cases, since, in calculating the fair amount, a court also makes reference to the contract amount as a starting point.[538]

II. Lien and Compensation

415. There is no attempt in South African law to compare the institutions of lien and compensation (set-off) to the defence of the *exceptio non adimpleti contractus*, and these concepts are usually not discussed in the same context. The right to withhold is expressly construed as a consequence of the principle of reciprocity, and the references to the institution of pledge made by the Appeal Court in the *BK Tooling* case[539] are made by way of analogy with respect to the function of the right to withhold and the fact that substantial performance should in principle not oust the *exceptio*. Any comparison that there might be between the *exceptio* and lien and set-off would relate only to aspects of the commercial and practical functioning of the various institutions.

A. *Lien*

416. A lien, or right of retention, may be described as a right, conferred by law on a person who is in possession of the property of another on which he or she has expended money or value, to retain possession of the property until he or she has been duly compensated.[540] Two kinds of lien are distinguished in South African law, namely salvage and improvement liens, and debtor and creditor liens. The first kind of lien provides security for an enrichment claim, and the second kind provides security for a claim for the contract price. By virtue of the lien, the possessor will

537. *See BK Tooling (Edms) Bpk v. Scope Precision Engineering (Edms) Bpk* 1979 1 SA 391 (A) 436 et seq.
538. *See Thompson v. Scholtz* 1999 1 SA 232 (SCA).
539. *BK Tooling (Edms) Bpk v. Scope Precision Engineering (Edms) Bpk* 1979 1 SA 391 (A).
540. *See*, for example, F. du Bois (gen. ed.), *Wille's Principles of South African Law* 661–665 (Juta 2007).

be ordered by a court to restore the property to the owner or to the other contractant, subject to the possessor being paid the amount due or being given liquid security for the amount. The lien provides certain preferences upon the insolvency of the owner or other party.

B. Compensation (Set-Off)

417. When two persons are mutually indebted to one another, their separate obligations may be extinguished wholly or in part by the operation of set-off as if they have been discharged by performance.[541]

418. The requirements for set-off can be briefly stated as follows: the debts must exist between the two persons in their personal capacities;[542] the subject matter of the obligations must be of the same kind; set-off must not be contrary to public policy; the opposing debts must be fully due and enforceable, so that a debt subject to a suspensive condition cannot be set-off against a debt that is fully due; both debts must be liquidated, that is, capable of easy proof;[543] and in litigation between the parties, set-off must be pleaded and proved.

419. Whether set-off operates automatically by operation of law once the requirements are present or whether one of the parties must first invoke the operation of set-off by unilateral declaration, and the significance of the requirement that it must be pleaded in any litigation, are matters of great uncertainty in South African law. The weight of authority in the courts appear to be in favour of *ipso jure* operation of set-off, while at the same time requiring that it should be pleaded and allowing a party to deny the occurrence of set-off and to perform his or her own obligation and enforce the obligation of the other by way of action – both aspects that undermine automatic operation.[544]

541. *See Schierhout v. Union Government (Minister of Justice)* 1926 AD 286.

542. *See*, for example, *Road Accident Fund v. Myhill NO* 2013 5 SA 426 (SCA). A cessionary of one of the claims is in the same position as the original creditor: *see*, for example, *Standard Bank of South Africa Ltd v. Renico Construction (Pty) Ltd* 2015 2 SA 29 (GJ).

543. This question entails an exercise of the court's discretion: *Fatti's Engineering Co (Pty) Ltd v. Vendick Spares (Pty) Ltd* 1962 1 SA 736 (T); cf. the misgivings expressed in *Standard Bank of South Africa Ltd v. Renico Construction (Pty) Ltd* 2015 2 SA 29 (GJ) para. 15 et seq. A debtor who has an unliquidated claim against his or her creditor may institute a counter-claim against the creditor, and the claim will be adjudicated simultaneously with the claim in convention. By judgment, the counter-claim becomes liquidated and will be set-off against the claim in convention.

544. *See* Van Huyssteen, Lubbe & Reinecke, *Contract General Principles* para. 13.80 (Juta 2016), for the view that invocation by a contractant is preferable.

§3. Specific Performance and Enforcement of Judgment Debts

I. Claim for Specific Performance

420. In South African law, as in other civil law systems, and subject to the consequences of the principle of reciprocity and to the limitations that may be imposed by good faith and public policy, a contractant is entitled, in principle, to an order for specific performance that the other party performs exactly and to the letter that which he or she has undertaken.[545] It is accepted, however, that the courts have the discretion not to grant such an order, so as to avoid conflict with public policy and an unjust result.[546] The English law influence on this branch of South African law has been specifically rejected, and it has been held that the fact that a claim for damages would adequately compensate the plaintiff (e.g., when delivery of shares freely obtainable on the stock exchange is claimed) will not move to a court to exercise its discretion not to grant an order for enforced performance.[547] Also, the fact that it may be difficult for the court to supervise the execution of an order for specific performance will not influence its discretion (e.g., when a builder has undertaken to do alterations to a house). An order will not be granted when the performance is impossible[548] or when the debtor is insolvent.

A court may refuse to grant an order on the basis of public policy and equity when the disadvantages for the defendant of ordering specific performance outweigh the advantages for the plaintiff excessively.[549] It is not clear to what extent factors such as loss to the defendant that should and could have been mitigated by the plaintiff if he or she were granted a claim for damages only deserve consideration in this respect. Nor is it clear what weight must be attached to the reason for the breach (to provide for so-called hardship breach). Furthermore, the fact that it is often more economical and thus in the public interest to order damages rather than specific performance may sometimes outweigh the public interest in the fulfilment and enforcement of promises.[550]

421. Orders for specific performance with respect to contracts of employment are largely dealt with in terms of labour law and the concept of unfair dismissal. As far as the general principles of contract are concerned, it appears as if an employee has a right to an order for specific performance, always subject to the discretion of the court not to grant it.[551] When an employer seeks such an order, the aspect of

545. *See*, however, the limitation on this right imposed by s. 46 of the Magistrates' Court Act 32 of 1944 and the discussion below.
546. *See Haynes v. King William's Town Municipality* 1951 2 SA 371 (A); *Isep Structural Engineering & Plating (Pty) Ltd v. Inland Exploration Co. (Pty) Ltd* 1981 4 SA 1 (A); *Benson v. SA Mutual Life Assurance Society* 1986 1 SA 776 (A).
547. *See Benson v. SA Mutual Life Assurance Society* 1986 1 SA 776 (A).
548. *See Pretoria East Builders CC v. Basson* 2004 6 SA 15 (SCA).
549. Cf. the facts of *Haynes v. King William's Town Municipality* 1951 2 SA 371 (A); *Isep Structural Engineering & Plating (Pty) Ltd v. Inland Exploration Co. (Pty) Ltd* 1981 4 SA 1 (A).
550. For a discussion of these and other issues, *see* G.F. Lubbe & C.M. Murray, *Contract Cases Materials and Commentary* 541 et seq. (Juta 1988) and the sources cited there.
551. *See*, for example, *National Union of Textile Workers v. Stag Packings (Pty) Ltd* 1982 4 SA 151 (T); *Rossouw v. SA Mediese Navorsingsraad* 1990 3 SA 297 (C).

impingement upon the personal freedom of the employee will be relevant to the court's exercising its discretion not to grant the order.

422. The view has been advanced that an order for specific performance may also take the form of an order for the payment of a sum of money in lieu of, or as a surrogate for, performance – in other words, payment of the monetary value of specific performance may be claimed as an alternative to actual specific performance. If such a claim were to be regarded as separate and distinct from an ordinary claim for compensation of loss, as has indeed been argued, a contractant may become entitled to more than he or she would be able to claim according to the ordinary principles applicable to the granting and calculation of damages.[552] Although the courts have not given a clear decision on the matter, the weight of authority seems to favour the construction that such a claim is a claim for damages in the usual sense.[553] On general principle, it would appear unreasonable and against public policy to allow a plaintiff a claim for damages as a surrogate for performance – the parties did not agree to such payment instead of performance, and the principles of the law of damages are directed at the fair compensation of loss and not at penalizing a contractant for breaching the contract.[554]

423. A plaintiff who claims specific performance may also claim damages in addition. Thus, for example, in the case of delay of payment of a money debt, he or she may claim interest *a tempora morae*.[555] Or, he or she may claim specific performance and damages in the alternative. Somewhat counter to the general principles set out above and probably as a result of influence by English law, it is provided in the Magistrates' Court Act that no claim for specific performance, other than a claim for the payment of money, the delivery of property, or the rendering of an account, may be entertained by a Magistrates' Court without an alternative of payment of damages.[556] This restriction on the right to claim specific performance does not apply to claims instituted in the High Court.

424. The practical consequences of the limitation imposed by legislation governing the lower courts is that the judgment debtor in those courts has a choice whether to comply with an order for specific performance *ad factum praestandum* or to pay damages.

---

552. Cf. the facts of *Isep Structural Engineering & Plating (Pty) Ltd v. Inland Exploration Co. (Pty) Ltd* 1981 4 SA 1 (A).
553. *See Isep Structural Engineering & Plating (Pty) Ltd v. Inland Exploration Co. (Pty) Ltd* 1981 4 SA 1 (A). In *Basson and Others v. Hanna* 2017 (3) SA 22 (SCA), the court distinguished the case from *Isep*'s facts and purportedly granted a claim for damages in lieu of specific performance. It did not explain, however, how the damages in question differed from normal contractual damages.
554. *See* the arguments advanced by Van Huyssteen, Lubbe & Reinecke, *Contract General Principles* paras 11.11–11.15 (Juta 2016).
555. *See*, for example, *Scoin Trading v. Bernstein* 2011 2 SA 118 (SCA).
556. Section 46 of the Magistrates' Court Act 32 of 1944; *see also* s. 16 of the Small Claims Courts Act 61 of 1984.

II. Enforcement of Judgment Debts

425. An order of a court to pay a money debt is not usually accompanied by any special orders as to enforcement. The usual mechanisms for enforcement that are provided for in civil procedure may take effect upon non-payment by the judgment debtor. These include the following: an enquiry into the financial position of the debtor and an order to pay the debt in instalments; garnishee orders; emoluments attachment orders; and a warrant of execution against the property of a debtor issued at the instance of the judgment creditor, which may result in the attachment and judicial sale in execution of the property, so that the proceeds of the sale may be applied to the satisfaction of the judgment debt. Civil imprisonment as a direct method of enforcement has been abolished, and the provisions of the Magistrates' Court Act allowing imprisonment for contempt of court by failing to satisfy a judgment debt has been declared unconstitutional by the Constitutional Court.[557]

426. In appropriate cases, the court may order enforcement directly by the agencies and officers of the State. Thus, the sheriff of the High Court may be empowered to attach a thing for delivery to the creditor or may attach and transfer immovable property to the creditor, or the registrar of deeds may be ordered to make the necessary entries in the deeds register without the usual transfer documents signed by the debtor. The court may even order a third party who is in possession of the object of the order to deliver it directly to the judgment creditor. A South African court probably does not have the power to order punitive damages for default in complying with a court order, such as the system of *astreinte* in Belgian law. When a debtor acts contrary to an obligation to refrain from acting, an order to force him or her to undo the act may be obtained.

In principle, a final foreign judgment can be enforced in South African court. An order for punitive damages will not be enforced if it can, on the facts of the case, be regarded as being against public policy. In this regard, it must be borne in mind that, as a general rule, only patrimonial loss may be claimed for breach of contract.

427. A debtor may also be interdicted from acting contrary to an *obligatio non faciendi*[558] or may be prevented by interdict from frustrating a probable future order of specific performance by disabling himself or herself from performing.

557. *See Coetzee v. Government of the Republic of South Africa* 1995 4 SA 631 (CC).

558. For a discussion of the particular problems relating to the granting of an interdict in the case of a restraint of trade in an employment contract, *see* G.F. Lubbe & C.M. Murray, *Contract Cases Materials and Commentary* 544–545 (Juta 1988).

§4. TERMINATION

I. Right to Cancel

428. The common law of South Africa does not generally recognize cancellation as a remedy for breach of contract in the absence of a contractual right to cancel. Moreover, cancellation is directly opposed to the result that the parties wished to attain when concluding the contract. Consequently, the power or right to cancel is regarded as an extraordinary remedy. Under the influence of English law and for reasons of policy and expediency, it is now accepted as trite that a party may cancel the contract, or put more correctly, may resile from its consequences when the other party has committed a serious breach of contract.[559] This right is not limited to reciprocal contracts and only arises when the breach was serious or fundamental. There is, however, no general requirement that cancellation be fair or reasonable.[560] It appears, however, that a court may refuse to allow cancellation where such cancellation – when considered together with its consequences – would amount to a remedy disproportionate to the breach in question.[561] Cancellation gives rise to a reciprocal duty to return what has been received in terms of the contract. It may therefore be said that, in principle, the contractant who wishes to cancel must be able to restore. In this sense, the duty to return is part and parcel of the right to cancel, but it is probably not correct to regard it as a 'condition precedent' to cancellation, provided that an inability to restore must be inexcusable.[562] When it would be inequitable to require return (e.g., when the inability to restore is not a result of the fault of the particular contractant), a court will nevertheless confirm the validity of the cancellation.

429. The question of whether a breach is fundamental or sufficiently serious to justify cancellation does not depend on the type of term breached, such as a 'condition' or a 'warranty'. It can also not properly be regarded as a matter for the court's discretion,[563] since cancellation may take place extra-judicially by a unilateral act by the aggrieved party. In general, one may say that the right to cancel arises when it cannot reasonably be expected of the aggrieved party to be satisfied with damages. When a party resiles from a contract in terms of an express or tacit cancellation clause in the contract (often called a *lex commissoria*), the breach need not

559. *See*, for example, *Stewart Wrightson (Pty) Ltd v. Thorpe* 1977 2 SA 943 (A); *BK Tooling (Edms) Bpk v. Scope Precision Engineering (Edms) Bpk* 1979 1 SA 391 (A); *Goldberg v. Buytendag Boerdery Beleggings (Edms) Bpk* 1980 4 SA 775 (A); *Masetlha v. President of the Republic of South Africa and Another* 2008 1 SA 566 (CC).

560. *Maphango v. Aengus Lifestyle Properties (Pty) Ltd* 2011 5 SA 19 (SCA), paras 22–25. Cf. the majority judgment in *Maphango v. Aengus Lifestyle Properties (Pty) Ltd* 2012 3 SA 531 (CC), which suggests (*obiter*) that termination of a lease of housing by notice might, in certain circumstances, amount to an 'unfair practice' in terms of the Rental Housing Act 50 of 1999.

561. *Botha and Another v. Rich NO and Others* 2014 4 SA 124 (CC) paras 50–51.

562. Cf. *Uni-Erections v. Continental Engineering Co. Ltd* 1981 1 SA 240 (W).

563. For a contrary view cf. *Spies v. Lombard* 1950 3 SA 469 (A).

necessarily be fundamental,[564] except if the parties agreed otherwise. If the cancellation clause (together with its consequences) would amount to a penalty disproportionate to the breach, it may be deemed to be unenforceable on the grounds that it is unconstitutional.[565] In order to decide whether enforcement of a cancellation clause would be so unreasonable or unfair as to be contrary to public policy, the court must consider 'the objective terms of the agreement, in the light of the relative situation of the parties'.[566] It has recently been emphasized by the Supreme Court of Appeal, with reference to a cancellation clause, that '[t]he fact that a term in a contract is unfair or may operate harshly does not by itself lead to the conclusion that it offends the values of the Constitution or is against public policy.'[567]

430. The general criteria set out above are often expressed more specifically in relation to the various forms of breach. In the case of *wrongful delay by a debtor* (*mora debitoris*), the creditor may cancel the contract when 'time is of the essence'.[568] In other cases, it is regarded as reasonable to restrict the creditor to the other available remedies. Time will be 'of the essence' when, in the circumstances, it is unreasonable to expect the creditor to accept performance and claim damages. Examples are a situation in which the nature of the contract is speculative and when the required performance is perishable, has a short period of marketability, or is subject to frequent and large price fluctuations. These circumstances may provide grounds for inferring a tacit cancellation clause in the contract, but that need not necessarily be the case and would depend on whether the requirements for inferring a tacit term have been met. Following English law, South African law allows the creditor to acquire a right to resile unilaterally by giving the debtor a notice of rescission – that is, by advising the debtor that he or she reserves the right to cancel, should the debtor fail to perform by a certain date. The debtor must be allowed a reasonable time to perform. A conditional notice of cancellation may be incorporated in the notice of rescission. When a debtor is not yet *in mora,* the creditor may place him or her *in mora* by a demand fixing a date for performance. In the same

564. *See Oatorian Properties (Pty) Ltd v. Maroun* 1973 3 SA 779 (A).

565. *See Botha and Another v. Rich NO and Others* 2014 4 SA 124 (CC) para. 50. In weighing up the disproportionality, the court did not consider the cancellation and forfeiture clauses separately, stating that '[t]he fairness of awarding cancellation is self-evidently linked to the consequences of doing so'. In *A B and Another v. Pridwin Preparatory School and Others* [2018] ZASCA 150, the court considered whether it would be unconstitutional for the school to enforce a cancellation clause in a contract with the parents of a pupil, on the basis that the interests of the child and the child's right to education would thus have been infringed. The court held that, while the school had a constitutional duty to consider the best interests of its pupils in enforcing the clause, this did not import an obligation upon the school to act reasonably or to give the parents a hearing. Moreover, the court held that the school had to act in the best interests of all of its pupils, and not merely those directly affected by the cancellation.

566. *Mohamed's Leisure Holdings (Pty) Ltd v. Southern Sun Hotel Interests (Pty) Ltd* 2018 (2) SA 314 (SCA) para. 21.

567. *Mohamed's Leisure Holdings (Pty) Ltd v. Southern Sun Hotel Interests (Pty) Ltd* 2018 (2) SA 314 (SCA) para. 30.

568. *See Nel v. Cloete* 1972 2 SA 150 (A). The concept of time being 'of the essence' was originally imported into South African law from English law. *See also Ver Elst v. Sabena Belgian World Airlines* 1983 3 SA 637 (A).

notice, the creditor may include a notice of rescission to acquire the right to cancel if the debtor fails to perform. This combined notice need only set one reasonable period for performance.

431. In the case of *positive malperformance* by a debtor, the test for cancellation is often expressed in the same terms as the general criterion, namely whether the breach is 'serious' enough. In practice, the degree of malperformance is often considered an important factor in this connection: there must have been a 'substantial' failure to perform.

432. When a debtor *repudiates* the obligation in terms of the contract, the creditor may only elect to cancel if the anticipated malperformance would justify cancellation. Repudiation of a minor part of the obligation would not justify cancellation, but insofar as repudiation most often amounts to complete or substantial repudiation, it will usually be correct to say that a creditor may cancel the contract upon repudiation if he or she so elects.

II. Exercising and Lapse of a Right to Cancel

433. As has been said above, cancellation takes place by a unilateral act by the aggrieved party. An order of a court as a result of litigation, or an application for a declaratory order of cancellation, merely serves to confirm or deny the right to cancel and whether it was properly exercised in the circumstances. Of course, when there was no right to cancel, the party who has purported to do so will himself or herself have committed a breach of contract, usually in the form of repudiation. Unless the parties have agreed otherwise or have agreed to special procedures or requirements for cancellation,[569] the decision to cancel must be communicated to the other party. Although some decided cases have seemed to require it, it is not clear whether the other party should have actual knowledge of the decision to cancel or whether reasonable steps taken by the cancelling party to bring his or her intention to the notice of the other party will suffice.[570] Since the right to cancel is not construed as an offer to bring the contract to an end, nor as a contractual condition, and since legal certainty and fairness will be served adequately by requiring reasonable steps to be taken, the latter approach seems preferable. The notice to cancel must be unambiguous, and it need not contain an offer of restitution nor, in general, a statement of the grounds for cancellation.

569. If they have agreed on a special procedure for cancellation, the cancelling party must strictly comply with such procedure: *Hano Trading CC v. JR 209 Investments (Pty) Ltd and Another* 2013 1 SA 161 (SCA). It is often agreed that a party must be given the opportunity to rectify his or her breach by notice of demand before the contract may be cancelled for non-compliance. Special statutory requirements may also be applicable, such as those in terms of s. 19 of the Alienation of Land Act 68 of 1981.

570. *See Stewart Wrightson (Pty) Ltd v. Thorpe* 1977 2 SA 943 (A); cf. *Swart v. Vosloo* 1965 1 SA 100 (A).

434. In principle, the party who has a right to cancel may elect not to exercise it, but rather to render performance himself or herself (when required) and to claim specific performance and damages. In South African law, no general principle has been developed and applied specifically to restrict the freedom to elect this option. It has been suggested, in the context of repudiation, that policy considerations may be applied to serve this purpose (the English law criterion of 'legitimate interest' in performing has been advanced in this connection), but the question may perhaps best be resolved by the application of existing rules, although the latter may operate less restrictively than may be desirable. Thus, even though specific performance may, in principle, be claimed, an aggrieved party may, in some instances, practically be forced to cancel the contract when the court refuses to grant the order because it would operate unduly harshly towards the defendant. Also, when the aggrieved party wishes to claim damages, his or her so-called duty to mitigate his or her loss may have the effect of compelling him or her to cancel the contract.

In general, the right to cancel the contract lapses when the party who is entitled to cancel fails to advise the other party, within a reasonable time after becoming aware of the breach of contract, that he or she intends to cancel.[571] Whether the omission should be construed as justifying an inference that the party has elected not to cancel or as a tacit waiver is not clear – in practical terms, it would not make a difference.[572] When a party with full knowledge of the facts giving rise to the right to cancel (not necessarily appreciating that he or she has the right) elects to uphold the contract, the right to resile is lost, unless the other party persists in its repudiation despite having been given the opportunity to remedy the breach. In such circumstances, the aggrieved party may change its election and cancel the contract and claim damages.[573]

435. The election of this option can be made expressly or tacitly, for example, when a contractant uses a defective performance while knowing that he or she is entitled to cancel the contract.

436. A right to resile on account of repudiation will lapse when the contractant in breach subsequently offers to perform fully before the other party has elected to resile.[574] When the right to resile is derived from a cancellation clause in a contract of sale, it is not possible to prevent cancellation by an offer to perform. The same applies when a right to cancel results from *mora debitoris*.[575] It is uncertain what

571. *See Mahabeer v. Sharma* 1985 3 SA 729 (A). Note, however, that it depends on all the circumstances of the case: *Paradyskloof Golf Estate v. Stellenbosch Municipality* 2011 2 SA 525 (SCA): '[f]ailure to exercise a right to cancel a contract … within a reasonable time does not necessarily result in the loss of the right'.

572. The Appeal Court has equated election and waiver as types of the same concept – *see*, for example, *Thomas v. Henry* 1985 3 SA 889 (A).

573. *Primat Construction CC v. Nelson Mandela Bay Metropolitan Municipality* 2017 (5) SA 420 (SCA), para. 25.

574. But see *Primat Construction CC v. Nelson Mandela Bay Metropolitan Municipality* 2017 (5) SA 420 (SCA), para. 25.

575. Cf. *Boland Bank Ltd v. Pienaar* 1988 3 SA 618 (A).

the position is in other instances of breach when a right to resile exists, but it is submitted that prevention of cancellation by an offer to perform should in general not be possible.

437. Apart from special statutory provisions (the most relevant being those in terms of labour legislation and the National Credit Act[576]), cancellation of contracts in South African law is governed by the general rules of common law, and not by rules specifically pertaining to classes of contracts.[577] The practical need for such specific rules, so as to expedite cancellation and to protect the interests of the aggrieved party, would not arise in South African law to the same extent as in some other systems, since cancellation does not require an order of a court to be valid. Of course, the parties themselves may agree on special procedures and requirements. A *lex commissoria* that requires a contractant to give the other party an opportunity to rectify his or her fundamental breach will not limit the contractant's right to elect to cancel the contract immediately upon repudiation by the other party.[578]

III. Consequences of Cancellation

438. Cancellation extinguishes the obligations that have been created in terms of the contract and that have not yet been performed,[579] except those that have already become due and enforceable before cancellation, and that are severable from the executory portion of the contract.[580] The duty to perform is extinguished along with the obligation, and the obligation cannot be enforced.[581] In the place of the duty to perform, a reciprocal duty arises to return whatever has been received by way of performance from the other party. The breach also creates an obligation in terms of which the contractant in breach has the duty to compensate for loss caused by the breach. The extent of the loss is usually calculated with reference to the other party's positive interest.

439. It follows that, in principle, cancellation is not regarded as operating retrospectively, in the sense of wiping out the contractual relationship and ridding the cancelling party of all its consequences. Nor is it the purpose of cancellation to restore the contractants fully to their position before conclusion of the contract. One

576. Sections 121–123 of Act 34 of 2005.

577. An exception might be found in the case of a contract of sale (and possibly exchange) when cancellation for latent defects takes place by way of the special action called the *actio redhibitoria*. For further details, *see* the discussion of sale below.

578. *See*, for example, *Metalmil (Pty) Ltd v. AECI Explosives & Chemicals Ltd* 1994 3 SA 673 (A).

579. The reason is that obligations are already extinguished by performance.

580. *See Walker's Fruit Farms Ltd v. Sumner* 1930 TPD 394; *Crest Enterprises (Pty) Ltd v. Rycklof Beleggings (Edms) Bpk* 1972 2 SA 863 (A); *Nash v. Golden Dumps (Pty) Ltd* 1985 3 SA 1 (A); *Shelagatha Properties Investments CC v. Kellywood Homes (Pty) Ltd* 1995 3 SA 179 (A).

581. *See Thomas Construction (Pty) Ltd (in liquidation) v. Grafton Furniture Manufacturers (Pty) Ltd* 1988 2 SA 546 (A).

may say that cancellation operates *e nunc* (from the moment of effective cancellation). Cancellation becomes effective when the other contractant becomes aware of the decision to cancel or (possibly) when he or she should have become aware of the decision.[582]

440. As has been said above, some obligations survive the cancellation of the contract and remain fully enforceable. Thus, even when a continuing obligation such as a lease or an employment contract has been cancelled, the rights that have already become due and enforceable and are severable from the executory part remain extant. Also, as a consequence of the purpose of cancellation, arbitration clauses, penalty clauses, and forfeiture clauses are not affected by cancellation.

441. Cancellation gives rise to a reciprocal duty to return to the other party whatever has been received in terms of the contract between the parties, unless the duty is excluded by agreement (e.g., by a forfeiture clause).[583] The courts have not expressly based this duty on a new, secondary obligation that arises by operation of law. What does seem to be clear is that the claim for such a return or restitution is construed in South African law as a distinct contractual claim and not as an enrichment action.[584] A party claiming return must himself or herself tender return or allege reasons that would excuse him or her from doing so.[585] The presence or absence of fault on the part of the contractant who claims restitution is regarded as an important factor in determining whether inability to restore in part or completely is excusable. There are indications that the courts might be willing to extend the grounds for excusability beyond actual fault. Some examples will illustrate the application of these criteria: when the performance received has been destroyed because of an inherent defect, cancellation will be allowed; when the performance has been used or applied as intended and cannot by its nature be returned, cancellation may take place, subject to payment of an amount equal to the enrichment of the cancelling party;[586] a contractant who has used a defective performance to produce a product of greater value should be allowed to cancel and ordered to return the product, if it is reasonable and equitable in the circumstances, considering the

582. For a discussion of the uncertainty surrounding this question, *see* Van Huyssteen, Lubbe & Reinecke, *Contract General Principles* para. 11.83 (Juta 2016); and *see Swart v. Vosloo* 1965 1 SA 100 (A).

583. *See*, for example, *Royal Anthem Investments 129 (Pty) Ltd v. Lau and Another* 2014 3 SA 626 (SCA) para. 15; *Botha and Another v. Rich NO and Others* 2014 4 SA 124 (CC).

584. *See*, for example, *Baker v. Probert* 1985 3 SA 429 (A); *Kudu Granite Operations (Pty) Ltd v. Caterna Ltd* 2003 5 SA 193 (SCA); *Laco Parts (Pty) Ltd t/a ACA Clutch v. Turners Shipping (Pty) Ltd* 2008 (1) SA 279 (W). There is, however, support for the contrary view – *see* Van Huyssteen, Lubbe & Reinecke, *Contract General Principles* para. 11.117, at n. 217(Juta 2016).

585. Most of the cases dealing with this aspect are instances in which the cancelling party was excused from returning the performance. In principle, the same criteria should apply when the cancelling party claims return. It is not certain whether the fact that he or she acted intentionally or negligently would weigh the scales against him or her.

586. It has become a standard practice to allow an employee who has been justifiably dismissed to claim a salary for the period for which he or she has performed before cancellation – *see*, for example, *Spencer v. Gostelow* 1920 AD 617. *See also BK Tooling (Edms) Bpk v. Scope Precision Engineering (Edms) Bpk* 1979 1 SA 391 (A).

respective values of the defective performance and the new product;[587] and when restitution is partly impossible through the fault of the cancelling party, he or she may cancel, subject to payment of a sum of money to make up the shortfall, but if, through his or her fault, he or she has alienated the entire performance, he or she cannot cancel. Finally, it has been held that as the rule requiring restitution is based on equity, it may be relaxed where equity and justice so require.[588]

§5. RESTITUTION

442. This topic has been discussed above in the context of rescission for improperly obtained consensus and cancellation on the grounds of breach of contract. In modern South African law, it seems reasonably clear that restitution is regarded as a consequence of breaking off contractual relations as a result of unacceptable behaviour by the other party before or after conclusion of the contract, rather than as a substantive remedy closely tied to and based on the reason for the breaking off, as, for example, with respect to the action for *restitutio in integrum propter dolum* of Roman law. Such an approach has important consequences regarding the requirements for rescission and cancellation, the effect thereof, and the nature of the claim for restitution, as has already been discussed in more detail.

§6. DAMAGES

I. General Requirements for a Claim for Damages

443. An obvious prerequisite for a claim for damages in the present context is that breach of contract must have occurred. Breach of contract in general and its various forms have been discussed above, but certain aspects deserve to be repeated here.

444. With respect to *delay of performance (mora)*, it must be noted that, in general, apart from certain special circumstances perhaps, no breach of contract will have occurred unless a time for performance has been fixed, either in the contract or by a notice of demand fixing such a time.[589] In the case of a reciprocal contract, the demand must include a tender of performance. The demand must set a specific time for performance that is reasonable in the circumstances. This will be determined with reference to relevant circumstances of which the parties were aware at the time of conclusion of the contract or of which they could reasonably have been

587. *See*, to the contrary, *SA Oil & Fat Industries Ltd v. Park Rynie Whaling Co. Ltd* 1916 AD 400.

588. *See MacKay v. Fey NO and Another* 2006 3 SA 182 (SCA), para. 10; *Prefix Properties (Pty) Ltd v. Golden Empire Trading 49 CC* 2011 2 SA 334 (KZP).

589. On the distinction between *mora ex re* and *mora ex persona*, *see Scoin Trading v. Bernstein* 2011 2 SA 118 (SCA), 120–121; *Mokala Beleggings v. Minister of Rural Development and Land Reform* 2012 4 SA 22 (SCA) 25–28.

aware at that time.[590] The demand need not be in writing or by way of summons, but for purposes of proof, it is usual to send a registered letter.[591] When a debtor is *in mora* with respect to the payment of a sum of money, the general or usual damages to be awarded to the creditor will be loss of interest on the money as from the date of breach.[592] However, the ordinary principles of the law relating to damages apply, and other damages may be claimed as well. The rate of interest is governed by the Prescribed Rate of Interest Act 55 of 1975, in terms of which *mora* interest rates are fixed from time to time, unless the parties have agreed on an applicable rate, in which case the National Credit Act 34 of 2005 may apply. In the absence of a contrary agreement by the parties, a debtor who is in mora in relation to a debt to pay interest is liable for mora interest on the unpaid interest.[593]

445. With respect to *repudiation*, it must be noted that, since repudiation is regarded as a breach without more, damages may, in principle, be claimed immediately, even before the date for eventual performance. If the aggrieved party does not cancel the contract, it may not be easy in practice to prove that any damage results from the repudiation itself until such time as the anticipated form of breach actually takes place.

446. The other requirements for a claim for damages that will be considered below are that damage, as well as a causal link between the breach and the damage, must be proved.

447. The Apportionment of Damages Act 34 of 1956, in terms of which the contributory negligence of a plaintiff is taken into account in the calculation of damages, does not apply to claims for damages for breach of contract, since contributory negligence is not a defence in the context of contracts.[594] However, when the plaintiff has by his or her own negligence caused damage to accumulate, he or she will not be granted the full extent of his or her actual loss – he or she has a 'duty' to take reasonable steps to mitigate his or her loss, or, to put it more correctly, a loss, not caused by the breach but by his or her own conduct, cannot be claimed.

590. *See*, for example, *Nel v. Cloete* 1972 2 SA 150 (A). In this case, the court refused to take into account that the deed of transfer that was needed by the debtor to effect transfer was lost, since that fact was not known or reasonably foreseeable – hence, the period of two months allowed in the demand was reasonable and catered to all reasonable causes of delay. As a general rule of thumb, it can be said that a time of some three weeks will be regarded as reasonable in cases of a claim for delivery of a movable or the repayment of an ordinary loan. The extent to which the time that has elapsed before the demand is made should be considered is not quite clear, but it would seem to be a factor carrying some weight.

591. Also see *Mokala Beleggings v. Minister of Rural Development and Land Reform* 2012 4 SA 22 (SCA) 26–27.

592. *See*, for example, *Scoin Trading v. Bernstein* 2011 2 SA 118 (SCA), 121C. Also see *Mokala Beleggings v. Minister of Rural Development and Land Reform* 2012 4 SA 22 (SCA).

593. *See Davehill (Pty) Ltd v. Community Development Board* 1988 1 SA 290 (A); *Land and Agricultural Development Bank of SA v. Ryton Estates (Pty) Ltd and Others* 2013 6 SA 319 (SCA).

594. *See Thoroughbred Breeders' Association v. Price Waterhouse* 2001 4 SA 551 (SCA).

448. Damages may be claimed in conjunction with specific performance or with cancellation and restitution. It can also be claimed alone. As has been explained above, a claim for damages in an amount equal to the monetary value of specific performance is regarded as an ordinary claim for damages, subject to the usual rules and limitations; it is not regarded as a form of specific performance (or damages as a surrogate for performance).

II. Damage

449. It is currently accepted by the South African courts, at least in theory, that the test for determining whether a victim of a breach of contract has suffered damage or loss, which entitles him or her to an award of damages, is whether the actual value of his or her total patrimony, as assessed after the breach, is less than the hypothetical value that it would have had if the contract had been properly carried out.[595] This is the so-called differential (or difference) theory of damages, and the interest of the aggrieved party in the performance of the contract is described as his or her positive interest. Thus, the positive interest is generally accepted as the appropriate and correct measure of calculation of damages for breach of contract. The positive interest is usually contrasted with the negative interest: an aggrieved party is entitled to be put in the patrimonial position in which he or she would have been if the act complained of had not been committed. Negative interest is regarded as the proper measure for damages in delict. It is also employed to measure damages claimed when consensus has been improperly obtained, whether the contract is rescinded or not.

The above distinction is not always adhered to, and the argument has been advanced that the law would be better served by the 'interests' approach of Anglo-American law, at least with respect to 'expectation' and 'reliance' interests.[596] Be that as it may, it appears that, in practice, the courts follow a more concrete approach to the matter: damage occurs when, as a consequence of breach, a particular asset (patrimonial rights and expectancies) is destroyed or reduced in value, or a particular liability (not only existing, but also future liability) is incurred or increased.[597] It is thus apparent that nominal damages, when only a breach but no actual damage can be proved, will not be granted, even when the breach was intentional and malicious.

595. *See Isep Structural Engineering & Plating (Pty) Ltd v. Inland Exploration Co. (Pty) Ltd* 1981 4 SA 1 (A).

596. *See Mainline Carriers (Pty) Ltd v. Jaad Investments CC* 1998 2 SA 468 (C) for an analysis of the different approaches. In *Emadyl Industries CC t/a Raydon Industries (Pty) Ltd v. Formex Engineering* 2012 4 SA 29 (ECP), the court held that a party can formulate a claim for contractual damages based on its negative interest provided that the amount claimed does not exceed the party's positive interest.

597. *See* Van Huyssteen, Lubbe & Reinecke, *Contract General Principles* para. 11.132 (Juta 2016).

A. Non-pecuniary Loss

450. Partly as a result of adherence to the differential theory of damages, South African law has a strongly materialistic approach to the awarding of damages for breach of contract. In principle, and (it seems) with a single exception, damages will be awarded only upon proof of patrimonial damage, as described above. As a general rule, therefore, non-patrimonial loss cannot be recovered in an action based on breach of contract.[598] The only recognized exception to the rule is a sui generis action available to a client of a bank whose creditworthiness has been affected by the bank's breach of contract in refusing to honour a cheque drawn on it, even when the plaintiff has failed to establish patrimonial loss.[599] Some earlier cases, the findings of which have been supported by academic commentators, can be interpreted as accepting that a claim for inconvenience caused by a breach can be brought.[600] This possible development has, however, now been curtailed in light of the recent approach of the Court of Appeal.

451. Nevertheless, the question whether or not to allow a claim for non-patrimonial loss is recognized to be ultimately one of policy – the problem being where to draw the line and whether an aggrieved party has adequate other remedies in law, particularly an action in a delict.[601] In this respect, one may well say that South African law is excessively restrictive, since for policy reasons, the Appeal Court seems loath to allow a litigant free choice between a contractual and a delictual action, even when the facts would support either basis. The Court seems inclined to restrict the litigant to a contractual action for damages.[602] This approach has been cogently criticized as being out of line with recent developments in the law of delict and contract. Reference is made in particular to the broadening of the concept of wrongfulness: the recognition of claims in a delict for purely financial loss and the recognition that the intention of the contracting parties should not be regarded as the complete determinant of their legal relations. A more recent development, namely the recognition that the contractual relationship forms part of the matrix for the assessment of wrongfulness, would also support a reconsideration of the majority decision in *Lillicrap, Wassenaar & Partners v. Pilkington Brothers (SA) (Pty) Ltd.*[603]

598. *See Administrator, Natal v. Edouard* 1990 3 SA 581 (A).
599. *See*, for example, *Klopper v. Volkskas Bpk* 1963 1 SA 930 (T).
600. Cf. *Jockie v. Meyer* 1945 AD 354, and the commentary by R.H. Christie, *The Law of Contract in South Africa* 546–547 (Butterworths 2006).
601. *See*, for example, Van Huyssteen, Lubbe & Reinecke, *Contract General Principles* para. 11.136 (Juta 2016); G.F. Lubbe & C.M. Murray, *Contract Cases Materials and Commentary* 602 et seq. (Juta 1988) with reference, for example, to the English case of *Jarvis v. Swan Tours Ltd* [1973] 1 All ER 71. *See also* R.H. Christie, *The Law of Contract in South Africa* 546–547 (Butterworths 2006), who suggests that a breach of contract amounting to discrimination on the grounds of race will clearly constitute an *inuiria* for which delictual damages may be claimed.
602. *See Lillicrap, Wassenaar & Partners v. Pilkington Brothers (SA) (Pty) Ltd* 1985 1 SA 475 (A).
603. *Lillicrap, Wassenaar & Partners v. Pilkington Brothers (SA) (Pty) Ltd* 1985 1 SA 475 (A). *See Bayer South Africa (Pty) Ltd v. Frost* 1991 4 SA 559 (A); L.F. van Huyssteen, S. van der Merwe

452. Non-patrimonial loss may be recovered as part of a conventional penalty. In assessing whether the penalty is out of proportion to the damage in terms of the Conventional Penalties Act 15 of 1962, a court must consider, *inter alia*, any rightful interest (such as convenience, reputation, and sentimental *interesse*) affected by the breach.[604] No doubt, basic rights as protected by the Constitution should also be considered.

B. Damnum Emergens and Lucrum Cessans

453. The victim of a breach of contract is entitled to be compensated for his or her actual loss, such as wasted expenses (*damnum emergens*), and lost opportunities, such as expected profits that do not materialize (*lucrum cessans*).[605] Such an award is fully in conformity with a proper application of the positive *interesse* measure of damages.[606] Although it is sometimes difficult to prove the extent of an expected advantage, the courts seem willing to assume (at least prima facie) that the contract would have enabled the party to break even.[607] The 'interests' approach of Anglo-American law referred to above may well have provided a simpler solution to the matter.

454. It is obvious that a court will not grant a cumulative claim for *damnum emergens* and *lucrum cessans* if the plaintiff would be over-compensated in terms of the comparison required by the differential approach. Nor (it seems) will the courts allow a claimant to be in a better position, as a result of a claim for wasted expenditure only, than the position in which he or she would have been if the contract had been performed properly. It also seems to be accepted, at least as a general rule, that any advantages occasioned by the breach should be taken into account when awarding damages.[608] It is not clear whether these limitations are the result of an application of the requirement of causation or of more general normative considerations. With respect to an award of *lucrum cessans*, it is clear that the award will be limited by the requirement of causality, and, in terms of the current approach of the courts, a claim for loss of profit will be regarded as a special loss that has to be specially proved. This aspect is discussed below.

& J.H. Herbots, 'Onzorgvuldige en Onjuiste Informatie bij de Contractsluiting in het Zuidafrikaansch Recht', *Tijdschrift voor Privaatrecht* 1 (1993): 61. *See also Holtzhausen v. ABSA Bank Ltd* 2008 (5) SA 630 (SCA).

604. *See Van Staden v. Central South African Lands & Mines* 1969 4 SA 349 (W).

605. *See*, for example, *Guggenheim v. Rosenbaum* (2) 1961 4 SA 21 (W); *Shatz Investments (Pty) Ltd v. Kalovyrnas* 1976 2 SA 545 (A); *Whitfield v. Phillips* 1957 3 SA 318 (A).

606. For a contrary view, *see Probert v. Baker* 1983 3 SA 229 (D), in which the Court allowed the plaintiff her negative interest upon cancellation of the contract. For criticism of this view *see*, for example, G.F. Lubbe & C.M. Murray, *Contract Cases Materials and Commentary* 602 et seq. (Juta 1988).

607. *See*, for example, *Trichardt v. Van der Linde* 1916 TPD 148.

608. *See Hunter v. Shapiro* 1955 3 SA 28 (D); *Everett v. Marian Heights (Pty) Ltd* 1970 1 SA 198 (C); *Sandown Park (Pty) Ltd v. Hunter Your Wine & Spirit Merchant (Pty) Ltd* 1985 1 SA 248 (W).

C. *'Certain' Damage*

455. A claimant for an award of damages must prove his or her damage according to the above criteria on a balance of probability. The exact amount need not be proven with precision – some flexibility is allowed. The court will grant damages on the basis of the best available evidence that has been put before it, even if this involves some speculation.[609] Future loss raises problems with respect to causation (particularly concerning the aspect of remoteness), as well as the difficult question of the valuation of an expectancy, more particularly, the determination of the probability that the expectancy will materialize. If the degree of probability is high, the court will usually grant the full value of the expected benefits. When the probability is small, but it is still probable to some degree that the expectancy will materialize, the court will adjust the value with reference to the degree of uncertainty. In this regard, the court will sometimes be satisfied with a rough estimate.[610] The expenses incurred to obtain the future benefit may be used as a prima facie guideline to base the valuation.[611]

D. *Specific Measures of Damages*

456. With respect to particular types of recurring claims for damages, the courts have developed specific methods or measures for quantifying damage and determining the damages to be awarded. Thus, for example, loss of interest is regarded as the primary measure for general damage resulting from a delay in payment of a sum of money. Upon proof of a breach, the relevant date when payment was due, and the applicable rate of interest, the court will usually accept (prima facie at least) that damage has resulted. Other examples are the application of the so-called market value rule and the repair-cost rule.

It must be stressed that these methods or 'rules' are merely regarded as applications of the general principles relating to damages, and they do not preclude a litigant from using other and more appropriate methods of quantifying his or her damage in the particular circumstances of the case. However, the need for such other methods must be proven by the claimant wishing to employ them.

III. Causal Relation

457. The courts have not specifically attempted to distinguish causation as an element of a claim for damages for breach of contract from the theoretical analysis of causation in other parts of the law. It is trite that the breach must, as a fact, have

609. *See Esso Standard SA (Pty) Ltd v. Katz* 1981 1 SA 964 (A).
610. Cf. *Shatz Investments (Pty) Ltd v. Kalovyrnas* 1976 2 SA 545 (A).
611. *See*, for example, *Goedhals v. Graaff-Reinet Municipality* 1955 3 SA 482 (C).

caused the loss: would the loss have occurred but for the breach? This test for factual causation, the *conditio sine qua non* test, has often been applied (albeit not necessarily always by name) by the courts[612] and has been put forward by commentators.[613]

458. It is further generally accepted that the contractant who breaches the contract should not by law be responsible for all the factual consequences of his or her misconduct and that his or her liability for damages must be limited to those consequences that are not too remote in the eyes of the law. This is the second element of the accepted test for causation, namely 'legal' causation.

459. In this respect, South African courts, under the influence of the writings of the French jurist *Pothier* and English law,[614] have developed the concepts of 'general' (or 'intrinsic') and 'special' (or 'extrinsic') damages.[615] *General damage* is said to flow naturally from a breach. It is construed as damage that the parties are by law deemed, at the time of conclusion of the contract, to have foreseen would probably result from a possible future breach. Such general damage is usually recoverable merely upon proof of a breach and a quantum of damages.[616]

All other damage is regarded as *special damage*. Special losses are usually too remote to be recoverable, unless the claimant can prove that, in the special circumstances surrounding the conclusion of the contract, the parties 'actually or presumptively contemplated that they would probably result from its breach'.[617] If the contractant in breach knew or should reasonably have known of the special circumstances, he or she would, the argument goes, either actually have considered the kind of loss resulting from his or her breach as probable or, as a reasonable person, he or she would have foreseen it.[618] This method of determining special damage is often referred to as the 'contemplation principle'. However, it is further required that the special circumstances must have been so obtrusive and the probability of loss must have been contemplated (presumably, actually or presumptively) to such an extent that it may be inferred that the parties actually or tacitly assumed liability

612. Cf. the facts of, for example, *Sommer v. Wilding* 1984 3 SA 647 (A); *Mouton v. Die Mynwerkersunie* 1977 1 SA 119 (A). In *Vision Projects (Pty) Ltd v. Cooper Bell & Richards Inc.* 1998 4 SA 1182 (SCA) 1191, the test for factual causation was specifically identified.
613. *See*, for example, J.C. de Wet & A.H. van Wyk, *Die Suid-Afrikaanse Kontraktereg & Handelsreg*, vol. 1 (Durban: Butterworths, 1992), 225–226.
614. In particular, the decision in *Hadley v. Baxendale* (1854) 9 Ex 341 (1854) 150 ER 145. English law on this point has been said by the Appeal Court to be the same in substance as Roman-Dutch law.
615. *See*, for example, *Victoria Falls & Tvl Power Co. Ltd v. Consolidated Langlaagte Mines* 1915 AD 1; *Lavery & Co. Ltd v. Jungheinrich* 1931 AD 156; *Shatz Investments (Pty) Ltd v. Kalovyrnas* 1976 2 SA 545 (A); *Holmdene Brickworks (Pty) Ltd v. Roberts Construction Co. Ltd* 1977 3 SA 670 (A).
616. For example, loss of interest as a result of delay in the repayment of a money debt, but not loss of profit from the loss of a lucrative business opportunity in which the money owed would have been invested. For further examples from case law, *see* Van Huyssteen, Lubbe & Reinecke, *Contract General Principles* paras 11.164–11.170 (Juta 2016). The degree of probability necessary to prove the damage amounts to a realistic possibility thereof – *see Thoroughbred Breeders' Association v. Price Waterhouse* 2001 4 SA 551 (SCA).
617. *See* the *Holmdene Brickworks (Pty) Ltd v. Roberts Construction Co. Ltd* 1977 3 SA 670 (A) 687.
618. Cf., for example, the *Lavery & Co. Ltd v. Jungheinrich* 1931 AD 156, at 169; *Everett v. Marian Heights (Pty) Ltd* 1970 1 SA 198 (C).

for such damage in the event of a breach. This further limitation is often referred to as the 'convention principle',[619] and it is required of the claimant to allege and prove such an 'agreement'.

460. The above rules do not provide a proper general basis for limiting liability, and if it is intended to apply a normative approach in the guise of a fictitious agreement or by way of the importation of an *ex lege* term or even by the inference of a tacit term, such a purpose is better achieved by the direct application of suitable norms. Despite widespread academic criticism of the continued adherence to the convention principle,[620] despite the fact that the courts have often ignored the convention principle,[621] and despite doubt expressed by the Appeal Court itself,[622] the convention principle still governs a claim for special damages.

461. From a theoretical as well as a practical point of view, it would be desirable to discard the convention principle, so that a uniform norm by which to deal with the question of causation and remoteness of damage may be developed. Although it is by no means the only appropriate approach (an 'interests' approach with close reference to an economic analysis may well be more realistic, or the direct or probable consequences tests may be considered to be more suitable[623]), the South African law of contract seems poised to settle for the test of reasonable foreseeability[624] as the norm for determining legal causation[625] or adequate cause. The concepts of general and special damages are indeed expressions of this test and are sometimes applied as such (albeit not expressly so), but they tend to obscure the real issue. If the foreseeability measure were to be accepted completely, it would be appropriate to determine the issue of foreseeability at the time of the breach, rather than at the time of the conclusion of the contract.

619. The most important cases propounding this principle are *Lavery & Co. Ltd v. Jungheinrich* 1931 AD 156 and *Shatz Investments (Pty) Ltd v. Kalovyrnas* 1976 2 SA 545 (A), in which it is said, respectively, that the contract must have been entered into on the basis of, or in view of, the special circumstances (172 et seq.), and that the contractant in breach must have 'virtually or tacitly' assumed liability for the special loss (555).

620. *See*, for example, Van Huyssteen, Lubbe & Reinecke, *Contract General Principles* paras 11.176–11.183 (Juta 2016); G.F. Lubbe & C.M. Murray, *Contract Cases Materials and Commentary* 626–628 (Juta 1988); R.F. Christie, *The Law of Contract in South Africa* 640–641 (Butterworths 2001).

621. *See*, for example, *Whitfield v. Phillips* 1957 3 SA 318 (A); *Bellairs v. Hodnett* 1978 1 SA 1109 (A).

622. *See Shatz Investments (Pty) Ltd v. Kalovyrnas* 1976 2 SA 545 (A) 554; *see also Thoroughbred Breeders' Association v. Price Waterhouse* 2001 4 SA 551 (SCA).

623. Cf. *Da Silva v. Coutinho* 1971 3 SA 123 (A) 147.

624. It has even been said that the test of reasonable foreseeability holds sway in the law of contract – *see Alston v. Marine & Trade Insurance Co. Ltd* 1964 4 SA 112 (W) 113. In light of the approach of the Appeal Court, this statement is too optimistic. However, this test is now accepted as the standard test for legal causation in the law of delict.

625. It is suggested by academic writers that legal causation in its wide sense may be an even more appropriate test that would also encompass other factors, such as legal policy and fairness. *See* Van Huyssteen, Lubbe & Reinecke, *Contract General Principles* para. 11.183 (Juta 2016); cf. R.F. Christie, *The Law of Contract in South Africa* 640 (Butterworths 2001). This approach would probably be in accordance with the duty of the courts to develop common law in accordance with the Constitution.

IV. Mitigation of Damages

462. The aim of an award of damages for breach of contract is to fairly compensate the victim for his or her loss caused by the breach. It is therefore obvious that a claimant for damages will not be permitted to recover any loss that he or she allowed to accumulate as a result of his or her own failure to take reasonable steps to prevent its occurrence. Although mitigation of damages is often stated to be a 'duty', the claimant does not have to prove that he or she has indeed mitigated his or her loss; the onus being on the defendant to show that the claimant has not taken reasonable steps to prevent the loss.[626] The claimant has to take only reasonable steps to limit his or her loss, and, *inter alia*, does not have to do anything that would harm his or her dignity or reputation. Any costs incurred in taking such reasonable steps may be recovered.

All in all, it would be more in accordance with principle to deal with mitigation in the context of the normative considerations that form part of the concept of legal causation.[627]

V. Moment for Calculation of Damages

463. As a general rule, the moment of the breach is regarded in South African law as the appropriate moment for the calculation of damages.[628] In most cases, this moment would in fact coincide with the time for performance, except in cases of anticipatory breach, namely repudiation and prevention of performance. In the latter cases, damages are calculated with reference to the time when performance was due,[629] and if no such time was fixed, the time when the claimant quantifies his or her loss is usually taken to be the relevant time.[630] In cases in which the cost of repair is taken to be the appropriate measure of damages (e.g., with respect to building contracts), it may be unfair to insist that the moment of the breach or the time for performance should necessarily be the time for assessment of damages. The proper time for assessment may be considered to be the time when it was reasonable for the aggrieved party to have begun repairs.[631]

Future consequences must be determined by way of prognosis. Consequences that have already occurred since the time of the breach must, at the time of the claim, simply be taken into account as facts bearing on the consequences of the breach.

626. *See*, for example, *Da Silva v. Coutinho* 1971 3 SA 123 (A); *Holmdene Brickworks (Pty) Ltd v. Roberts Construction Co. Ltd* 1977 3 SA 670 (A); *De Pinto v. Rensea Investments (Pty) Ltd* 1977 2 SA 1000 (A) [as corrected by 1977 4 SA 529 (A)].

627. Cf. *Jayber (Pty) Ltd v. Miller* 1980 4 SA 280 (W).

628. *See*, for example, *Sandown Park (Pty) Ltd v. Hunter Your Wine & Spirit Merchant (Pty) Ltd* 1985 1 SA 248 (W); *Voest Alpine Intertrading Gesellschaft GmbH v. Burwill & Co. SA (Pty) Ltd* 1985 2 SA 149 (W); *Elgin Brown & Hamer (Pty) Ltd v. Dampskibsselskabet Torm Ltd* 1988 4 SA 671 (N). Cf. *Rens v. Coltman* 1996 1 SA 452 (A).

629. *See Novick v. Benjamin* 1972 2 SA 842 (A).

630. *See Culverwell v. Brown* 1990 1 SA 7 (A).

631. *See Rens v. Coltman* 1996 1 SA 452 (A).

VI. Methods of Assessing Damages in Certain Kinds of Cases

464. Reference has already been made to the practice that, for certain kinds of cases, preferred measures of damages have been developed by the courts. In general, these measures must be applied in a claim for damages, except if it is proven that such a method of calculation is impossible, impracticable, or inappropriate in the circumstances (e.g., because it will result in under-compensation).[632] In this respect, the so-called market price rule, the repair-cost measure, and *mora interest* are most relevant.

465. To assess the difference in value between the actual and hypothetical financial positions of the claimant in the case of a breach with respect to a marketable commodity, the market price or value is used as a measure of calculation. Although this measure is applicable to a wide variety of situations, it is mostly applied as the measure for general damages in cases of breach of contracts of sale by non-performance or malperformance. When the seller fails to perform, the difference between the purchase price and the market price or value at the proper time and place for delivery is usually awarded.[633] When a defective performance is delivered – usually by the seller – the buyer who upholds the contract is awarded the difference between the market value of the thing in the condition agreed upon and the value of the thing in its actual state.[634] The market value is a question of fact and may be proven also by expert evidence. The auction price for a thing may be prima facie evidence of the value. Similarly, when defective performance is at issue, the purchase price may be prima facie evidence of the value of the thing in its proper state. The time and place for determining the market value will vary from case to case, but, in practice, damage is often determined by comparing the value at the time and place set for performance and the value at the time and place when and where performance is actually made.[635]

466. The reasonable cost of remedying or completing a defective or incomplete performance is often applied as a suitable measure of damages in the case of an *obligatio faciendi.*[636] The repair-cost measure may be applied as an alternative to the market value measure if it was reasonable to have the repairs done, even when the cost exceeds the difference in market value.[637]

467. The question of damages in the form of interest on money debts that are paid late has been discussed previously.

---

632. Cf. *Katzenellenbogen Ltd v. Mullin* 1977 4 SA 855 (A); *Novick v. Benjamin* 1972 2 SA 842 (A); *Swart v. Van der Vyver* 1970 1 SA 633 (A).
633. Cf. *Novick v. Benjamin* 1972 2 SA 842 (A) 860.
634. *See Katzenellenbogen Ltd v. Mullin* 1977 4 SA 855 (A) 877, at 880.
635. For a detailed discussion, *see* Van Huyssteen, Lubbe & Reinecke, *Contract General Principles* para. 11.193 et seq. (Juta 2016). *See also*, *The Law of South Africa* vol. 7, para. 52 (W.A. Joubert ed., 2d ed., Butterworths 2005).
636. Cf., for example, *Isep Structural Engineering & Plating (Pty) Ltd v. Inland Exploration Co. (Pty) Ltd* 1981 4 SA 1 (A); *Rens v. Coltman* 1996 1 SA 452 (A).
637. *See Schmidt Plant Hire (Pty) Ltd v. Pedrelli* 1990 1 SA 398 (D).

VII. Exemption Clauses and Penalty Clauses

468. The law relating to clauses exempting a contractant from the consequences of his or her breach of contract or limiting his or her liability (including liability to pay damages) with respect thereto, has been discussed above. Terms in a contract that provide for the payment of a sum of money in case of breach of the contract have also been discussed above.

§7. Prescription and Expiry Periods

469. In South African law, it is generally accepted that it is in the interest of legal certainty and public policy to limit the time within which a creditor may enforce a duty to perform that is owed to him or her in terms of an obligation.[638] It is said that when the time limit has expired, the duty to perform (debt)[639] has prescribed. However, the interests of the particular creditor and the protection of the individual debtor are also considered; thus, for example, prescription does not run against a creditor who is incapable of enforcing his or her right,[640] and a court may not apply prescription *mero motu* if it has not been pleaded. The law is not clear on the question of when and to what extent private interests take precedence over the public interest in this respect. There are decisions that hold that an anticipatory waiver of the right to rely on prescription, or a waiver of such a right during the running of prescription, is effective and not invalid on the grounds of public policy.[641] Contrary views have, however, also been expressed by the courts.[642] The Constitutional Court has stated on more than one occasion that extinctive prescription is a constitutional matter, as it limits section 34 of the Constitution, which reads: 'Anyone has the right to have any dispute resolved by the application of law decided in a fair public hearing before a court or, where appropriate, another independent impartial tribunal or forum.'[643]

---

638. *See* in general on the topic M.M. Loubser, *Extinctive Prescription* (Juta 1996). *See also*, for example, the leading case of *Murray & Roberts Construction (Cape) (Pty) Ltd v. Upington Municipality* 1984 1 SA 571 (A); Van Huyssteen, Lubbe & Reinecke, *Contract General Principles* para. 13.86 et seq. (Juta 2016). *See also Uitenhage Municipality v. Molloy* 1998 2 SA 735 (SCA); *De Jager v. ABSA Bank Bpk* 2001 3 SA 537 (SCA); *Trinity Asset Management (Pty) Ltd v. Grindstone Investments 132 (Pty) Ltd* 2018 (1) SA 94 (CC).

639. The duty to perform in response to an owner's claim for repossession under *rei vindicatio* is not subject to extinctive prescription: *ABSA Bank Ltd v. Keet* 2015 4 SA 474 (SCA).

640. *See*, for example, *Van Zyl v. Hoogenhout* 2005 2 SA 93 (SCA).

641. *See*, for example, *Nedfin Bank Bpk v. Meisenheimer* 1989 4 SA 701 (T), in which the Court based its argument on freedom of contract. Also see *Friedrich Kling GmbH v. Continental Jewellery Manufacturers* 1995 4 SA 966 (C).

642. *See Rylands v. Edros* 1997 2 SA 690 (C); *ABSA Bank Bpk h/a Bankfin v. Louw* 1997 3 SA 1085 (C).

643. *Trinity Asset Management (Pty) Ltd v. Grindstone Investments 132 (Pty) Ltd* 2018 (1) SA 94 (CC); *Makate v. Vodacom Ltd* 2016 (4) SA 121 (CC).

470. Extinctive prescription is, in general, governed by the provisions of Chapter III of the Prescription Act 68 of 1969.[644] The Act is based on the principle of strong prescription, so that a debt is *extinguished* upon the completion of the relevant period of prescription.[645] A subsidiary debt (such as liability for interest) will be extinguished along with the prescribed principal debt.[646] A debt arising from a reciprocal contract does not prescribe before its counter-performance.[647] Despite extinction, payment of a prescribed debt is deemed by law to be effective and cannot be recovered by an enrichment action.[648] This does not affect the basic approach that prescription is a matter of substantive law, rather than procedure.[649]

471. The Prescription Act lays down various periods of prescription, which are applicable to different kinds of debt. The periods mostly applicable to debts arising out of contracts are fifteen years with respect to certain contracts with the State; and three years with respect to ordinary contractual debts,[650] including claims for the return or reduction of the purchase price in the case of a latent defect in a thing sold.[651]

I. Interruption of Prescription

472. The continued functioning or running of the relevant period of prescription will be interrupted by certain occurrences, with the general effect that the period of prescription that has already elapsed will be ignored, and a new period will be calculated afresh as of the time of the interruption. These occurrences and their more specific requirements and consequences are set out in the Prescription Act.[652] In the first place, prescription is interrupted by an acknowledgement of liability by the debtor. To be effective, the acknowledgement must be addressed to the creditor or his agent,[653] and it must contain an admission that the debt exists and that the debtor

644. A variety of other statutes, which may take precedence over this Act (*see* s. 17 of the Act), and international conventions also govern matters of limitation of actions such as the Warsaw Convention, as ratified in South Africa and the Hague Rules. On the question when prescription starts to run, *see* s. 12 of the Act and *see*, e.g., *Drennan Maud & Partners v. Pennington Town Board* 1998 3 SA 200 (SCA); *Truter v. Deysel* 2006 4 SA 168 (SCA); *Minister of Finance v. Gore* 2007 1 SA 111 (SCA); *Claasen v. Bester* 2012 2 SA 404 (SCA).

645. *See* s. 10(1) of the Prescription Act and, for example, *Oertel v. Direkteur van Plaaslike Bestuur* 1983 1 SA 354 (A); *Desai v. Desai* 1996 3 SA 141 (A); *De Jager v. ABSA Bank Bpk* 2001 3 SA 537 (SCA).

646. Section 10(2).

647. Section 13(2).

648. Section 10(3).

649. Cf. *Protea International (Pty) Ltd v. Peat Marwick Mitchell & Co.* 1990 2 SA 566 (A).

650. Section 11. The other periods of prescription are thirty years with respect to mortgage bonds, judgment debts, taxation debts, and other taxes and certain debts payable to the State arising from mineral rights; and six years with respect to bills of exchange and notarial contracts.

651. The shorter periods that applied in Roman and Roman-Dutch law with respect to the *actio redhibitoria* and the *actio quanti minoris* no longer apply in South African law.

652. Sections 14 and 15.

653. *Miracle Mile Investments 67 (Pty) Ltd and Another v. Standard Bank of SA Ltd* 2016 2 SA 153 (GJ) para. 33.

is liable for it.[654] Second, prescription can be interrupted by service on the debtor of any process[655] by which the creditor claims payment of the debt. The service must be such as to effectively start legal proceedings.[656] The test whether a particular process interrupts prescription is objective.[657] To prevent abuse, the Act provides that the interruption shall lapse when the creditor does not prosecute his or her claim to a final judgment, except, of course, when the debtor acknowledges liability.[658]

II. Suspension or Delay of Prescription

473. When there are certain impediments that make it impossible or difficult for the creditor to enforce his or her rights, and such an impediment is still effective a year or less before the period of prescription would normally have expired, the running of prescription is delayed. The completion of prescription is then postponed for one year as of the day when the impediment ceases to exist.[659] The impediments are listed in the Act and include the minority of the creditor;[660] superior force; the absence of the debtor from the country; a partnership between the creditor and debtor (with respect to partnership debts); and where an executor has not yet been appointed for a debtor or creditor who has died.

III. Invalidity or Rescission of a Contract

474. There is no special arrangement in South African law regarding the prescription of claims for an order declaring a contract void or for an order confirming an effective rescission of a contract.

IV. Delict

475. The normal period of prescription for a delictual claim is three years.

654. Repeated partial payments in accordance with a continuous obligation constitute repeated acknowledgements of liability, and therefore repeated interruptions of prescription: *see Roestorf v. Johannesburg Municipal Pension Fund* 2012 6 SA 184 (SCA), 190–191.
655. 'Process' includes 'any document by which legal proceedings are commenced', such as a summons or notice of motion – s. 15(6). A letter of demand will not be sufficient. *See Betterbridge (Pty) Ltd v. Masilo and Others NNO* 2015 2 SA 396 (GP).
656. *See Evins v. Shield Insurance Co. Ltd* 1980 2 SA 814 (A); *Standard Bank of South Africa Ltd v. Oneanate Investments (Pty) Ltd (in liquidation)* 1998 1 SA 811 (SCA). It has also been found that the process in question should have initiated 'an action, judgment in which finally disposes of some elements of the claim': *Cape Town Municipality and Another v. Allianz Insurance Co Ltd* 1990 1 SA 311 (C). Cf. *Peter Taylor & Associates v. Bell Estates (Pty) Ltd and Another* 2014 2 SA 312 (SCA), regarding the question whether an application for joinder constitutes a 'process whereby the creditor claims payment of the debt'.
657. *Standard Bank of South Africa Ltd v. Oneanate Investments (Pty) Ltd (in liquidation)* 1995 4 SA 510 (C) at 553; *Solenta Aviation (Pty) Ltd v. Aviation @ Work (Pty) Ltd* 2014 2 SA 106 (SCA).
658. Section 15(2); *Melamed v. BP Southern Africa (Pty) Ltd* 2000 2 SA 614 (W).
659. Section 13 of the Prescription Act.
660. *See*, for example, *Malcom v. Premier, Western Cape Government* 2014 3 SA 177 (SCA).

V. Conflict of Laws

476. Since prescription extinguishes the prescribed debt and is regarded as a matter of substantive law, the proper law of the contract or *lex causae* will be applied in cases of a conflict of laws. When a mere expiry period is at issue, the matter will usually be regarded as procedural, and the *lex fori* will be applied by the court.[661] In making the distinction, 'the claimant must show [that] the remedy he seeks in the domestic Court will "harmonise with the right according to its nature and extent as fixed by the foreign law"'.[662]

VI. Invocation of Prescription

477. Even though, in principle, prescription extinguishes a debt, it must nevertheless be invoked by the debtor to give effect to it, and the court may not of its own accord take cognizance of it.[663] Since prescription is regarded as a matter of substantive law, it must be pleaded by means of special plea in trial proceedings or in the opposing affidavit in motion proceedings.

VII. Computation of Periods of Prescription

478. In terms of the Prescription Act, the period of prescription commences 'as soon as' the debt is due,[664] that is, from the day the debt becomes due. A debt is due when the debtor must perform immediately and when the creditor has the right to institute action immediately for recovery of the performance.[665] The exigibility of the debt must be determined for each particular case and will depend on factors such as the terms of the contract and the nature of the obligation.[666] The Act further provides that certain circumstances will also postpone the commencement of the

661. *See*, for example, *Kuhne & Nagel AG Zurich v. APA Distributors (Pty) Ltd* 1981 3 SA 536 (W); *Laconian Maritime Enterprises Ltd v. Agromar Lineas Ltd* 1986 3 SA 509 (D).
662. *See Minister of Transport, Transkei v. Abdul* 1995 1 SA 366 (N) 369, quoting Parker LCJ 35 in *Phrantzes v. Argenti* [1960] 2 QB 19 ([1960] 1 ALL ER 778).
663. *See De Jager v. ABSA Bank Bpk* 2001 3 SA 537 (SCA).
664. Section 12. Note, however, that according to s. 12(3), '[a] debt shall not be deemed to be due until the creditor has knowledge of the identity of the debtor and of the facts from which the debt arises: Provided that a creditor shall be deemed to have such knowledge if he could have acquired it by exercising reasonable care'. The SCA has held that this is aimed at preventing negligent, and not innocent, inaction and that, in deciding whether the creditor's inaction was reasonable, the court should consider the creditor's particular circumstances: *see Macleod v. Kweyiya* 2013 6 SA 1 (SCA). In this case, therefore, the court appeared to eschew a purely objective assessment of the standard of care required of the creditor.
665. *See Truter v. Deysel* 2006 4 SA 168 (SCA); *Deloitte Haskins & Sells Consultants (Pty) Ltd v. Bowthorpe Hellerman Deutsch (Pty) Ltd* 1991 1 SA 525 (A); *Martin Harris & Seuns OVS (Edms) Bpk v. Qwa Qwa Regeringsdiens* 2000 3 SA 339 (SCA); *Farocean Marine (Pty) Ltd v. Minister of Trade and Industry* 2007 (2) SA 334 (SCA); *Trinity Asset Management (Pty) Ltd v. Grindstone Investments 132 (Pty) Ltd* 2018 (1) SA 94 (CC); *Frieslaar NO and Others v. Ackerman and Another* [2018] ZASCA 3.
666. *Trinity Asset Management (Pty) Ltd v. Grindstone Investments 132 (Pty) Ltd* 2018 (1) SA 94 (CC).

period.[667] As a general rule, a creditor may not delay the running of prescription by his own act or omission,[668] such as by withholding a demand for payment. This does not apply, however, where such a demand is the condition precedent for the debt's becoming due.[669]

479. The period of prescription is computed according to the ordinary civil method: the calendar day is the unit and the first day is the day upon which the debt is due, the last day being excluded.

VIII. Expiry Periods

480. In general, the main distinction in South African law between periods of prescription and expiry periods is that, with respect to the latter, the debt is not extinguished, and the remedy is simply barred. Two of the most unfair statutory expiry measures have been declared unconstitutional on the grounds of unreasonably infringing upon the constitutional right of access to the courts.[670] The Police Service Act 68 of 1995 probably adequately balances the competing interests involved to the extent that the limitations are reasonable and justifiable in a democratic society.[671] Expiry periods are usually regarded as matters of procedure and not of substantive law.[672]

IX. Estoppel by Representation: Loss of Ability to Claim as a Result of Representation

481. When, for example, a creditor remains inactive in exercising a contractual right, he or she may, by law, be prevented from doing so subsequently, if the debtor reasonably believes that the creditor has waived his or her right or has tacitly agreed not to enforce it in future without prior notice. In South African law, the doctrine of estoppel by representation will be applied to situations such as the above. This doctrine serves approximately the same purpose as the doctrine of *rechtsverwerking* and

667. Section 12(2) and (3): if the debtor wilfully prevents the creditor from becoming aware of the existence of the debt, prescription will only commence when he or she becomes aware; a debt will not be deemed to be due until the creditor has knowledge of the identity of the debtor and of the facts from which it arises.

668. *Trinity Asset Management (Pty) Ltd v. Grindstone Investments 132 (Pty) Ltd* 2018 (1) SA 94 (CC), para. 41.

669. *Standard Bank of South Africa Ltd v. Miracle Mile Investments 67 (Pty) Ltd and Another* [2016] 3 All SA 487 (SCA); 2017 (1) SA 185 (SCA).

670. Section 113(1) of the Defence Act 44 of 1957 (*Mohlomi v. Minister of Defence* 1997 1 SA 124 (CC)) and s. 2(1)(a) of the Limitation of Legal Proceedings (Provincial and Local Authorities) Act 94 of 1970 (*Moise v. Greater Germiston Transitional Local Council; Minister of Justice & Constitutional Development intervening (Women's Legal Centre as Amicus Curiae)* 2001 4 SA 491 (CC).

671. In terms of s. 36 of the Constitution. Cf. *Peens v. Minister of Safety & Security* 2000 4 SA 727 (T).

672. Cf. *Minister of Transport, Transkei v. Abdul* 1995 1 SA 366 (N); *Kuhne & Nagel AG Zurich v. A P A Distributors (Pty) Ltd* 181 3 SA 536 (W).

of doctrines based on the Roman maxim of *venire contra factum proprium*. As has already been mentioned in the context of liability in cases of mistake going against the previous impression and dissensus, the doctrine of estoppel by representation was introduced into South African law under the influence of English law. In the process, the English doctrine has not been received as such, but it has developed into a uniquely distinct and native doctrine.[673] In general, the doctrine may be described as follows: When one person makes an unacceptable misrepresentation to another, who reasonably acts upon it, the latter may insist that his or her position be maintained if probable prejudice would otherwise result.

482. The basis of estoppel in South African law is (as can be expected, given its lineage) a matter of controversy. Among the various possible bases that have been advanced, the most prominent are fault and the *exceptio doli generalis*. Both of these are seriously inadequate for such a purpose. However, it is clear from the application of the doctrine by the courts that it is employed as a tool of equity to mitigate the harsh consequences of the operation of the ordinary rules of law by protecting the reasonable impression of the estoppel assertor in circumstances in which unfair prejudice would otherwise result. In South African law, too, estoppel may only be raised as a defence and may not be used directly as a cause of action.[674] This rule is wholly compatible with the purpose and function of the doctrine and should not be explained on the basis that estoppel is a rule of evidence – it is a matter of substantive law.

483. The requirements for a successful estoppel are not uniform and vary according to the nature of the misrepresentation and the policy considerations applicable to certain rights that may be affected by estoppel.

At the very least, there must have been a *misrepresentation* of such a nature that a reasonable person would be misled by it. When the misrepresentation was made with the intention to induce the other to act upon it (and if it was, to boot, clear and unequivocal, or direct), no accompanying *dolus* or *negligence* on the part of the misrepresentor seems to be required. If the misrepresentation occurred by conduct or silence when there was a duty to speak, negligence seems to be required in addition. Requirements such as that 'the misrepresentation must relate to a fact' should be interpreted to refer to the required nature or quality of the misrepresentation. In cases in which an estoppel is raised by a possessor of a thing against the *rei vindicatio* of an owner, the courts usually require proof that the owner was at least negligent in making the misrepresentation. It appears that ownership, which is considered in principle as a basically inviolable right in South African law, should, as a matter of policy, only be undermined when the owner was blameworthy in the

673. *See* on the topic in general J.C. Sonnekus, *The Law of Estoppel in South Africa* (Butterworths 2000); J.C. de Wet, *'Estoppel by Representation' in die Suid-Afrikaanse Reg* (Leiden: Sijthoff's, 1939). *See also* S. van der Merwe & L.F. van Huyssteen, 'A Perspective on the Elements of Estoppel by Representation', *Tydskrif vir die Suid-Afrikaanse Reg* (1988): 571; L.F. van Huyssteen & S.W.J. van der Merwe, 'Estoppel by Representation: The Ambiguity of an 'Unambiguous Representation', *Tydskrif vir die Suid-Afrikaanse Reg* (1900): 86.

674. *See*, for example, *Mann v. Sydney Hunt Motors (Pty) Ltd* 1958 2 SA 102 (GW). Estoppel may, of course, be raised by way of replication.

eyes of the law.[675] Some exceptions are allowed by the courts, particularly when the representor acted with such directed intent (though not *dolo*) and with sufficient freedom of will so as not to warrant further protection by the law.

The misrepresentee must have acted reasonably in believing the misrepresentation and acting upon it.[676] His or her act must have been *caused* by the misrepresentation. The courts have often stated that the representation must have been the 'proximate cause' of the act of the misrepresentee. Strictly, this would mean that when the estoppel denier put a third party in a position to mislead the estoppel assertor, the requirement of causation could not be met. However, in many cases, the courts have upheld a plea of estoppel in such circumstances, without expressing themselves on the exact test for causation.[677] If one further considers some cases in which it was expressly accepted that, as long as the misrepresentation was a sufficiently inducing cause, the estoppel could be granted, it may be submitted that the requirement of causation will be satisfied, if there was a factual causal link and if the misrepresentation was adequately connected to the act of the misrepresentee (the generally accepted elements of factual and legal causation).

A further essential requirement for the operation of estoppel is probable *prejudice* to the misrepresentee, should the estoppel not be allowed. Again, the content of the requirement is not clear and could be related to what is considered to be the basis and other requirements for estoppel. If estoppel is considered to be based on fault, it would follow that prejudice means actual patrimonial loss, which has to be proved with the same degree of certainty as damage. However, since it is now increasingly accepted that fault is not the basis of the doctrine, and bearing in mind its function, it may be submitted that the estoppel assertor must prove only that some loss or prejudice of a patrimonial nature would probably result.[678] It is not required that the amount of the loss be quantified in monetary terms, but mere sentimental or other non-patrimonial prejudice (such as the loss of a business reputation) will not be sufficient.

Finally, as a matter of policy, an estoppel will not be upheld by the courts if the result would be against the public interest – when, for example, a statutory prohibition would be rendered ineffective,[679] or when it would amount to giving effect to an *ultra vires* act.[680]

484. The doctrine of estoppel by representation finds application in many fields of law. For example, it is applied in cases in which an owner institutes a *rei vindicatio* but has placed his or her property in the possession of a third party in such

675. *See*, for example, the leading case of *Johaadien v. Stanley Porter (Paarl) (Pty) Ltd* 1970 1 SA 394 (A). However, the Court pointed out that there might be exceptional circumstances in which fault would not be required.

676. Cf., for example, *Absa Bank Ltd v. Arif and Another* 2014 2 SA 466 (SCA) at para. 34 *(obiter)*.

677. *See*, for example, *Quenty's Motors (Pty) Ltd v. Standard Credit Corporation Ltd* 1994 3 SA 188 (A).

678. *See*, for example, *Peri-Urban Areas Health Board v. Breet* 1958 3 SA 783 (T); *Resisto Dairy (Pty) Ltd v. Auto Protection Insurance Co. Ltd* 1963 1 SA 632 (A); *Autolec Ltd v. Du Plessis* 1965 2 SA 243 (O). *See also* S. van der Merwe & L.F. van Huyssteen, 'A Perspective on the Elements of Estoppel by Representation', *Tydskrif vir die Suid-Afrikaanse Reg* (1988): 568.

679. *See*, for example, *Trust Bank van Afrika Bpk v. Eksteen* 1964 3 SA 402 (A).

680. *See*, for example, *Strydom v. Die Land & Landboubank van Suid-Afrika* 1972 1 SA 801 (A).

a way as to lead a purchaser to think that the third party is the owner or has the authority to dispose of the property; in cases in which an owner has misrepresented to a prospective purchaser that he or she no longer has any interest in the property; in cases in which a landlord, in terms of the lease, attempts to evict a tenant for late payment of rent but has accepted late payment often in the past; in cases in which an insurance company has represented that it would accept a late claim but later attempts to deny the claim in terms of the policy; in cases in which a firm has allowed an employee to issue cheques but then attempts to deny the employee's authority to do so; in cases in which a 'consultant' has been represented by his or her employer to have a certain expertise and area of operation, and the employer later attempts to show that the consultant acted beyond the scope of his or her employment; in cases in which a property developer has by acquiescence represented that a local authority may in due course acquire a water reticulation free of charge and later attempts to deny the undertaking; and, finally, in cases in which a person signs a bogus credit agreement, which is discounted by the 'seller' to a finance house, and the 'buyer' then attempts to deny liability on the contract as against the cessionary. It is obvious that the doctrine of estoppel by representation serves as a very important and all-pervasive tool of equity to ameliorate the consequences of a strict application of the law.

485. Although the rules of the doctrine of estoppel are regarded as part of substantive law, the effect of an estoppel is not permanent, nor does it operate on a wider level between representor and representee. Thus, for example, the majority opinion seems to be that a possessor in whose favour an estoppel operates does not become the owner – his or her position is regarded as if he or she were the owner vis-à-vis the true owner only. Consequently, a further acquirer will not be protected as against the owner.

It may, of course, happen that the doctrine is so regularly applied to a particular type of case that it provides the impetus and basis for the development of a permanent rule of substantive law, while estoppel itself then loses importance in that field of application and eventually falls into disuse. A case in point is the role of estoppel in the development of reasonable reliance as an alternative basis of a contract. Estoppel itself might even create a permanent legal position directly, for instance, by becoming an acknowledged and full-fledged method of acquiring ownership. Estoppel would then be a cause of action and not merely a defence.

Part II. Specific Contracts

Chapter 1. Agency

486. The term 'agency', although widely used in law and commerce in South Africa, must be employed with caution and discrimination.

'Agency' may denote the concept of *representation* by which one person (an agent or representative), acting in terms of an authority, concludes a juristic act in such a way (usually by acting overtly on behalf of another)[681] that the consequences of the act ensue for another person (the principal). The agent is then not personally bound or entitled. The act that the agent concludes for the principal may include entering into a contract, discharging obligations, or waiving certain rights.

'Agency' is, however, often used to denote – not the concept of representation as such – but the concept of *authorization* by agreement, such as by a 'contract of agency' or as part of another contract, such as a contract of employment or mandate.

The term 'agency' is also used to refer specifically to a contract of *mandate*, in terms of which the mandatary undertakes to do a task for the mandator; in addition, the mandatary may or may not be a properly authorized agent or representative in the sense described above, depending on whether the elements of representation are present or absent.[682]

487. The following kinds of function or position, often described as 'agent' or 'agency', illustrate the distinctions made above:

- An employee may be an authorized agent (representative) of his or her employer, depending on whether the employer has authorized the employee, and authorization can often be inferred from the surrounding facts, such as the scope and nature of the employment (an executive secretary or commercial agent).

681. But see *Van der Merwe v. Nedcor Bank Bpk* 2003 1 SA 167 (SCA) 174 I–J, in which it was held that a contract concluded by the representative of another with himself or herself will not necessarily be void.

682. *See* in general Van Huyssteen, Lubbe & Reinecke, *Contract General Principles* paras 9.27–9.73 (Juta 2016); J.C. de Wet & A.H. van Wyk, *Die Suid-Afrikaanse Kontraktereg en Handelsreg*, vol. 1 (Durban: Butterworths, 1992), 96–128; *The Law of South Africa* vol. 1, paras 175 et seq. (W.A. Joubert ed., 2d ed. Butterworths 2003); *Wille's Principles of South African Law* 983–1003 (F. du Bois ed., Juta 2007); A.J. Kerr, *The Law of Agency* (Butterworths 2006).

- The board of directors of a company is authorized to act as an agent (representative) by the articles of the company, and other functionaries are usually authorized in terms of their employment contracts.
- A member of a close corporation is by law an authorized agent (representative) of the corporation (section 54 of Act 69 of 1984).
- An insurance agent is usually a canvassing (sometimes also collecting) agent employed by the insurer without any authority to act on its behalf (keeping in mind that authority to represent the insurer or insurance proposer may exist, depending on the facts).[683]
- An estate agent is usually only a mandatary,[684] with the duty to find a purchaser or seller for the immovable property of the mandator against payment of a commission – the agent rarely has the authority to conclude a contract on behalf of the mandator.[685]
- Brokers are usually only intermediaries who negotiate contracts but normally do not conclude them as agents (representatives).
- Factors are usually not agents (representatives) but conclude contracts in their own names when selling goods entrusted to them by their principals.

488. In principle, authorized agents may enter into any kind of contract on behalf of their principals. In some cases, formalities are required, such as that the agent must have written authority from the principal.[686]

489. Contracts of mandate are often used to vest a representative with authority. In South African law, it is no longer an essential element of a mandate that the services be rendered gratuitously by the mandatary, as was the position in Roman-Dutch law. A problem that often arises with respect to contracts of mandate is whether an express or tacit agreement to pay a 'reasonable' amount is sufficiently certain to be enforceable. It has been found by the courts to be acceptable.[687] The basic test appears to be whether a sufficiently clear meaning can be given to 'reasonable amount' in light of the contract as a whole, objectively interpreted in its factual context. The courts will not change an agreed amount on the basis that it is unreasonable.[688]

490. Where the agent's authority derives from authorization by the principal,[689] the authorization need not, in general, comply with any formalities.[690] In principle,

683. *See* in detail M.F.B. Reinecke et al., *General Principles of Insurance Law* 461 et seq. (Butterworths 2002); P. Havenga *The Law of Insurance Intermediaries* (Juta 2001).
684. *See*, for example, *Muller v. Pam Snyman Eiendomskonsultante (Pty) Ltd* 2001 1 SA 313 (C).
685. Cf. *Sedibe v. United Building Society* 1993 3 SA 671 (T).
686. *See*, for example, s. 2(1) of the Alienation of Land Act 68 of 1981 and s. 5 of the General Law Amendment Act 50 of 1956 with respect to executory donations.
687. *See Chamotte (Pty) Ltd v. Carl Coetzee (Pty) Ltd* 1973 1 SA 644 (A).
688. Except, perhaps, where it can be regarded as against the public interest or against good faith.
689. Authority may of course derive from operation of law (e.g., a guardian who acts on behalf of his or her ward), from ostensible authority (*see* below), or from ratification.
690. In some cases, written authorization (sometimes attested to by witnesses) is required by law – for example, with respect to the conclusion of contracts of sale of land, the registration of any deed in a deeds office, or instituting or defending an action in the High Court.

authorization is a *unilateral juristic act*, and authority may be given orally or in writing, expressly or tacitly, and may be embodied in a contract. The authority given may be general or specific, with reference to a particular juristic act only. The latter kind of authority will often, tacitly, or by implication as a trade usage, extend to acts that are, in a business sense, necessary for the efficient execution of the agent's instructions. To facilitate proof of authority, it has become a standard practice in some areas of commerce, particularly in dealings with banks, to record the authorization and authority in a written document, called a power of attorney.[691] Provided that the act in question falls within the scope of a power of attorney, and the wording of the document is unambiguous, the agent will be regarded as having been validly authorized to carry out the act in question.[692]

491. A minor with limited contractual capacity may act as an agent on behalf of a principal, as long as the minor is able to express a legally recognized will. Insofar as the minor may be personally liable, his or her liability is limited to his or her enrichment in terms of the general rules applicable to minors.

§1. Duties of an Agent

492. An authorized agent, whether authorized unilaterally or by contract with the principal, has certain duties arising from the fact that he or she is a representative. These duties may be supplemented or varied by contract. The agent must exercise his or her authority and follow his or her instructions personally[693] and in accordance with their terms and limits. He or she must act with a reasonable degree of care and skill, and with (utmost) good faith[694] in the interests of his or her principal, and must account to the principal for all that he or she has done as the principal's agent.

493. An agent whose own interests conflict with those of his or her principal will not be acting in good faith and may not acquire any benefits for himself or herself arising from such conflict. When an agent causes damage to his or her principal by not acting as required, he or she will be liable to compensate for the loss, either on the basis of a delict or, when applicable, on the basis of breach of contract.

691. General powers of attorney may be registered in the deeds office in terms of the Deeds Registries Act 47 of 1937.
692. *De Villiers v. Elspiek Boerdery (Pty) Ltd and Another* [2017] ZASCA 4.
693. He or she may not 'without the consent of the principal' delegate his or her authority or employ a sub-agent.
694. The implications of the demise of the requirement of *uberrima fides* for agency, as was found by the Appeal Court with respect to insurance contracts, has not been considered – *see Mutual & Federal Insurance Co. Ltd v. Oudtshoorn Municipality* 1985 1 SA 419 (A).

§2. Duties of a Principal

494. It is a consequence of representation that the principal is bound to the third party by his or her agent's acts on his or her behalf. If the principal does not fulfil his or her duties towards the third party, he or she will be liable vis-à-vis that party. This duty of the principal is not seen in South African law as a duty to the agent.

495. The duties owed by the principal to the agent are to compensate the agent for all expenses reasonably incurred in carrying out his or her duties, to indemnify the agent for all loss duly incurred by him or her while acting as such,[695] and to remunerate him or her for services where so agreed, provided that the duties have been substantially performed.

§3. Consequences of Direct Representation

496. As has already been indicated in different contexts above, when an agent acts with authority on behalf of a principal, the principal and not the agent is bound and entitled with respect to that act. Likewise, the third party is bound to the principal and not to the agent. This occurs because the principal clothes the agent with authority to act and because the agent and third party intend the consequences of their acts to be as described and agreed upon. When considering, for example, whether consensus was reached or whether the contract may be rescinded on the grounds of improperly obtained consensus, the relevant intentions and conduct are those of the agent and the third party.

§4. Apparent or Ostensible Authority

497. When a person (P) acts in such a way that he or she creates the reasonable impression in the mind of another (T) that a third person (A) (who has ostensibly acted on P's behalf) is authorized to do so, and T acts on this belief to his or her detriment, P will be bound to T as if he or she had actually clothed A with authority.[696] This kind of authority is usually called 'ostensible authority'.

It is not entirely clear whether fault, at least in the form of a *negligent* representation of authority, is required in all cases for liability based on ostensible authority to arise. However, the qualification (often stated by the Appeal Court) that the representation must be of such a nature that it could reasonably have been expected to

695. But cf. s. 113 of the Consumer Protection Act 68 of 2008, which states that a principal is jointly and severally liable for any acts or omissions made by the agent in the course of carrying out his or her duties. This excludes any criminal liability.

696. *See* the minority judgment in *Makate v. Vodacom Ltd* 2016 4 SA 121 (CC) at para. 154 et seq. Cf., regarding consumer contracts, s. 41 of the Consumer Protection Act 68 of 2005, which prohibits a person acting on behalf of a supplier of any goods or services from making any false, misleading, or deceptive representations, which would include falsely stating or implying, or failing to correct an apparent misapprehension on the part of a consumer to that effect, that an agent has the necessary authority to negotiate the terms of, or conclude, an agreement.

mislead – considered from the points of view of the representor and the representee – leads to the conclusion that negligence is indeed a requirement, at least when the representation was by conduct or in the course of dealing.[697] A typical example of the operation of the doctrine of ostensible authority occurs where a principal, without notice to his or her former co-contractants, withdraws the authority of a long-standing agent and the 'agent' nevertheless purports to enter into contracts 'on behalf of' his or her erstwhile principal. The latter will then be bound as if his or her former agent had indeed been authorized.

Until recently, it was generally accepted that the doctrine of ostensible authority was merely an application of the broader doctrine of estoppel by representation.[698] In *Makate v. Vodacom Ltd.*,[699] a majority of the Constitutional Court has now decided that this is incorrect, and that it is a form of actual authority. It is uncertain what effect this decision will have on the settled law regarding the requirements for proof of ostensible authority.[700]

§5. Relationship Between an Agent and a Third Person

498. Where an authorized agent acts for a principal within the scope of his or her authority, the agent will not be bound to the third party as explained above, but the principal will. However, where a person professes to act as an agent but has no authority to do so and where no ostensible authority can be construed, the agent will, in principle, not be bound to the third party and neither will the 'principal'.

499. An important exception to this rule is where the principal, after the act has purportedly been concluded on his or her behalf, accepts or ratifies the act. The legal effect of *ratification* is that the unauthorized act is assumed to have been duly authorized at the time of its execution.[701] There can be no valid ratification if the principal was not in existence at the time of the transaction.[702]

697. Cf. *Johaadien v. Stanley Porter (Paarl) (Pty) Ltd* 1970 1 SA 394 (A); *Connock's (SA) Motor Co. Ltd v. Sentraal Westelike Ko-operatiewe Maatskappy Bpk* 1964 2 SA 47 (T); *Union National South British Insurance Co. Ltd v. Padayachee* 1985 1 SA 551 (A). *See also* the discussion of estoppel above.

698. *See* generally P.J. Rabie & J.C. Sonnekus, *The Law of Estoppel in South Africa* 156 et seq. (Butterworths 2000); *Strachan v. Blackbeard & Son* 1910 AD 282; *Monzali v. Smith* 1929 AD 382; *NBS Bank Ltd v. Cape Produce Co. (Pty) Ltd* 2002 1 SA 396 (SCA) 411 H; *Northern Metropolitan Local Council v. Company Unique Finance (Pty) Ltd* 2012 5 SA 323 (SCA). Note that a party who is aware that a transaction is illegal and is also 'aware or should reasonably be aware that the principal of the agent with whom it is contracting would not countenance the conclusion of such a transaction' may not rely on the ostensible authority of the agent: *Absa Bank Ltd v. Arif and Another* 2014 2 SA 466 (SCA) para. 34 *obiter*.

699. 2016 4 SA 121 (CC).

700. Cf. the comments of Wallis AJ in a strong minority judgment at paras 109–110. Cf. also M. Wallis *Commercial Certainty and Constitutionalism: Are they compatible?*, S. African L. J. 545 (2016).

701. *See*, for example, *Mort NO v. Henry Shields-Chiat* 2001 1 SA 464 (C).

702. An important statutory exception to this rule is to be found in s. 35 of the Companies Act 61 of 1973, in terms of which pre-incorporation contracts, entered into on behalf of a company still to be formed, may be ratified by the company after its incorporation.

500. Where a person who purports to act as an agent has no authority or exceeds his or her authority, he or she will not be personally bound to execute the duties concerned or to fulfil any contract that he or she may have intended to conclude as an agent.[703] He or she may, however, be liable to the third party for damages on the grounds of breach of what the court has called an 'implied warranty of authority'.[704] The measure of damages, it has been held, is the positive interest – the amount of loss sustained by the third person as a result of the 'principal' not executing his or her duties in terms of the intended obligation. However, it seems as if this warranty is actually based on a representation, in which case the true basis of liability of the 'agent' is a delict, and the appropriate measure of damages is the negative interest. In a given case, it may, of course, be properly inferred that the 'agent' has tacitly warranted his or her authority, and the contractual measure of damages would then be appropriate. This ambiguity has led the Appeal Court to express reservations about the warranty construction, but the matter has not been finally settled.[705] An 'agent' may, of course, expressly or tacitly warrant that the person on whose behalf he or she has purportedly acted will ratify the act, in which case the agent will be bound on the basis of breach of warranty if ratification does not take place.

§6. Relationship Between the Agent and the Principal

501. The duties and rights of the agent and principal have been discussed above. Although the fact of authority is a matter between agent and principal, it directly affects third parties, as explained above.

§7. Termination of an Agent's Authority and the Contract Between the Agent and the Principal

502. Because of its source and the very nature of the act of authorization, authority that derives from an act by a principal may, as a rule, be terminated or revoked by the principal unilaterally, without liability accruing to him or her.[706] Even where the authorization is embodied in a contract, such a revocation will be effective, but it may be contrary to the terms of the contract and may then amount to breach of contract. Authorization and the contract in which it may be embodied are distinct juristic acts.[707]

---

703. Some older decisions are contrary to this self-evident rule, but have not been followed since. There is also no authority in South African law for the rule that an agent acting for a foreign principal will be bound personally.
704. *See Blower v. Van Noorden* 1909 TS 890; *Road Accident Fund v. Shabangu* [2004] 2 All SA 356 (SCA).
705. *See Claude Neon Lights (SA) Ltd v. Daniel* 1976 4 SA 403 (A).
706. Estoppel by representation may result in liability to the third person – *see* above. *See also* the discussion below with respect to so-called irrevocable authority.
707. Cf. *The Firs Investment Ltd v. Levy Bros Estates (Pty) Ltd* 1984 2 SA 881 (A); *Eileen Louvet Real Estate (Pty) Ltd v. AFC Property Development Co. (Pty) Ltd* 1989 3 SA 26 (A).

503. If the principal wishes to terminate a contract containing the authorization, the ordinary rules relating to termination of contracts apply. However, an *executory* contract of mandate may be terminated unilaterally by either party, unless the parties have agreed otherwise. This rule is contrary to the general principles of contract and should at least be limited to executory gratuitous contracts of mandate.[708]

504. Authority also comes to an end in a number of other ways. It lapses automatically upon the death or insolvency of the principal, or when he or she loses his or her capacity to act. It terminates automatically upon the death or insanity of the agent. It may lapse by the effluxion of time. It also lapses when the authorized act has been concluded. Where it derives from statute, it lapses in terms of the statute, and where it derives from the constitution of an association, it lapses when the constitution is changed accordingly. Where it is based on contract, it lapses when the contract comes to an end.

505. As has been stated above, authority may, in principle, be revoked at any time, since it is granted unilaterally and is primarily for the benefit of the principal. This would remain the position despite an undertaking not to revoke; revocation would then only result in liability for contractual damages, but it would still be an effective retraction of the authority to bind the principal. However, there is a series of older decisions in which it was held that when an 'irrevocable' authority was granted and when the authority was 'coupled with an interest' or when it was 'part of a security', it could indeed not be retracted.[709] This approach, which was adopted under the influence of English law, is essentially contrary to Roman-Dutch law and contrary to the nature of representation. In light of more modern decisions contrary to this approach[710] and the criticism against it, it is doubtful whether the Appeal Court will sanction its further application. The agent's interest is protected well enough by the availability of a claim for damages.

506. On termination of his or her authority, the agent must return any power of attorney held by him or her.

§8. Indirect Representation and the Doctrine of the Undisclosed Principal

507. Distinct from true or direct representation, where a legal bond is created directly between a third person and a principal by an authorized agent acting on behalf of the principal is the phenomenon of indirect representation. Here, a person mandates another to act in the mandator's interest by concluding in his or her own name a juristic act with a third party and subsequently to transfer or cede the rights

708. Cf. *Eileen Louvet Real Estate (Pty) Ltd v. AFC Property Development Co. (Pty) Ltd* 1989 3 SA 881 (A).
709. *See*, for example, *Natal Bank Ltd v. Natorp & Registrar of Deeds* 1908 TS 1016.
710. *See*, for example, *Kotsopoulos v. Bilardi* 1970 2 SA 391 (C).

so obtained to the mandator. The mandatary is bound to the third party, and the relationship between them should take its normal course.

508. However, where a mandatary acts within the scope of his or her instructions, a full substitution of parties may take place by virtue of the *doctrine of the undisclosed principal.*[711] This doctrine was introduced from English law into South African law in 1869[712] and is still consistently applied by the courts, despite the general acknowledgment (even in its country of origin) that the doctrine is unsound, anomalous, and inconsistent with the general principles of the law of contract. The courts do, at least, voice the proviso that the ambit of the doctrine should be limited in the interest of justice.

509. The doctrine of the undisclosed principal, as it operates in South Africa, may be briefly described as follows. Where a mandatary acts within the scope of his or her instructions from his or her mandator (principal)[713] in his or her own name[714] and concludes a juristic act (e.g., a contract) with another (third) party,[715] the following situation arises: the obligation or obligations, and rights and duties in terms thereof exist, as is to be expected, between the mandatary and the third party directly. However, the undisclosed principal may come forward (without having received cession or transfer) and claim that he or she is the 'real' creditor or debtor.[716] In this case, he or she is in law actually treated as a cessionary: when the third party becomes aware of the existence of the undisclosed principal, he or she may choose to hold the principal and not the mandatary bound as debtor or creditor.

§9. Broking

510. Generally, in South Africa, a broker does not conclude juristic acts for his or her client, either as an authorized agent or as a mandatary who acts in his or her own name in the interest of the client, with a duty to eventually cede to the client any rights accruing to him or her as broker. A broker is usually a mere intermediary who negotiates an agreement with a third party on the instruction of a client – he or

711. *See* in general J.C. de Wet & A.H. van Wyk, *Die Suid-Afrikaanse Kontraktereg en Handelsreg*, vol. 1 (Durban: Butterworths, 1992), 123–128; Van Huyssteen, Lubbe & Reinecke, *Contract General Principles* paras 9.70–9.73 (Juta 2016); *Wille's Principles of South African Law* 999–1000 (F. du Bois ed., Juta 2007); A.J. Kerr, *The Law of Agency* 210–213 (Butterworths 2006); J.C. van der Horst, *Die leerstuk van die 'undisclosed principal'* (Annale van die Universiteit Stellenbosch 1971 vol. 33 series B no. 2); *Cullinan v. Noordkaaplandse Aartappelkernmoerkwekers Koöperasie Bpk* 1972 1 SA 761 (A); *Karstein v. Moribe* 1982 2 SA 282 (T).
712. *See Lippert & Co. v. Desbats* 1869 *Buch* 189.
713. The existence of a relationship of mandate at the time of the act is a prerequisite – the term 'authority' in this context must not be taken to refer to true authorization, which would make the mandatary a representative.
714. This situation should not be confused with the situation in which an authorized agent acts on behalf of his or her principal but without identifying the principal.
715. It is not required that the third party should be aware of the relationship between the mandator and mandatary.
716. It has been suggested that the undisclosed principal may not step in where the third party would not have concluded the contract if he or she had known about the hidden principal.

she is a mandatary with a limited mandate. The eventual obligation that may arise is then the result of agreement directly between the client and the third party. However – usually expressly, but sometimes tacitly, or even by ostensible authority, or by trade usage – some kinds of brokers, such as insurance brokers, may be authorized to conclude contracts as representatives on behalf of clients.

Chapter 2. Bailment

§1. Contract of Bailment (Deposit) and Rights and Duties of Parties

511. Bailment, or 'deposit', as it is more generally called, is commonly defined in South African law as a contract in terms of which a person delivers a thing to another for safekeeping, and in terms of which the same thing must be returned upon demand.[717] Although it is not at all clear whether a deposit is a real contract or a consensual contract[718] and whether delivery to the depositary is a necessary prerequisite for the existence of the contract,[719] it may be suggested that it is (or at least should be) regarded as an ordinary consensual contract.[720] This approach is in accordance with the generally accepted view that an agreement with the intention to be bound to a lawful obligation is, without more, an adequate cause for contractual liability. It must also be remembered that a court will not necessarily specifically order a recalcitrant depositor 'who refuses to deliver to the depositary' to do so; damages may well be awarded instead. A further moot point, whether a contract of deposit can exist when the deposit is not gratuitous, seems to have been settled: the general view is that a deposit for reward[721] does not alter the nature of the contract. However, the standard of care required of the depositary will be higher when the deposit is for reward. It appears that immovable property may be the object of deposit in South African law, although the legal position is not clear, and, in practice, such a deposit will seldom occur. Delivery in terms of a deposit will not affect transfer of ownership.[722]

512. Briefly, the duties of the depositary[723] are to keep and take due care of the property and to restore it on demand or when otherwise agreed upon, in an uninjured state and with any fruits or profits. The depositary may not use the property. As far as risk is concerned, the depositary is not liable for loss resulting from *vis maior* or *casus fortuitus*. When the deposit is gratuitous, the depositary must exercise the same care as he or she would with respect to his or her own property and is thus only liable for loss or damage caused by his or her own intentional or grossly

717. *See*, for example, *Wille's Principles of South African Law* 962 et seq. (F. du Bois ed., Juta 2007); *The Law of South Africa* vol. 8, para. 174 (W.A. Joubert ed., 2d ed., Butterworths 2005). *See*, for example, *Minister of Posts and Telegraphs v. Daddy Bros and Johnstone (Pty) Ltd* 1965 3 SA 394 (E); *Gabriel and Another v. Enchanted Bed and Breakfast CC* 2002 6 SA 597 (C).
718. *See* D. Kleyn, 'The Reality of Real Contracts', *Tydskrif vir Hedendaagse Romeins-Hollandse Reg* (1995): 16 for a discussion of the various views.
719. *See Randfontein Transitional Local Council v. ABSA Bank Ltd* 2000 2 SA 1040 (W) 1048 H: 'A deposit slip ordinarily is prima facie proof that money was deposited with the bank ... Upon the deposit being completed, ownership of, and therefore the risk in, the money passes to the bank.' Also see the comments at 1054 G and 1055 D of the same judgment.
720. Cf. D.J. Joubert, *General Principles of the Law of Contract* 33, at n. 61 (Juta 1987).
721. Often termed 'bailment'.
722. But cf. *Randfontein Transitional Local Council v. ABSA Bank Ltd* 2000 2 SA 1040 (W) 1048. The word 'deposit' is used in various ways in South African law. Care should thus be taken not to confuse a contract of deposit with a loan, pledge, or an advance payment.
723. *See*, *The Law of South Africa* vol. 8, paras 177 et seq. (W.A. Joubert ed., 2d ed., Butterworths 2005).

negligent action or omission. However, when the deposit is for reward, the depositary is liable for any degree of negligence.[724] If the property is not duly returned, a court will infer fault on the part of the depositary, unless he or she proves otherwise.[725] The duty to take care of the property may be limited by an agreement, such as by way of an 'owner's risk' clause, which can exclude a claim based on negligence.[726] However, the burden to prove the terms of the contract, including the absence of a limitation of liability, still rests on the depositor.[727]

These duties are reinforced by the Consumer Protection Act.[728] According to section 65(2), a supplier who has possession of any property owned or ordinarily possessed by a consumer must not treat the property as his or her own. In addition, the supplier 'must exercise the degree of care, diligence, and skill that can reasonably be expected of a person responsible for managing any property belonging to another person'. Finally, the supplier is liable for any loss arising from a failure to comply with these provisions.

513. Unless otherwise agreed, the depositor has the following duties:[729]

- he or she must remove the property on expiry of the deposit;
- he or she must compensate the depositary for loss caused by a defect in the property of which he or she was or should have been aware;
- he or she must compensate the depositary for necessary expenses incurred – the depositary has a right of retention until he or she has been reimbursed; and
- he or she must perform any other duties undertaken in the contract.

§2. *NEGOTIORUM GESTIO*

514. Some instances of what in certain legal systems may be called 'bailment of necessity' (e.g., storing goods salvaged from a fire on another's premises) are dealt with in South African law in terms of the legal institution of *negotiorum gestio.*[730]

---

724. *See*, for example, *Randfontein Transitional Local Council v. ABSA Bank Ltd* 2000 2 SA 1040 (W) 1059; *Padiachy v. Motor Mecca JHB CC* 2002 4 SA 351 (W); *Mercurius Motors v. Lopez* 2008 3 SA 572 (SCA).
725. *See*, for example, *Stocks & Stocks (Pty) Ltd v. T J Daly & Sons (Pty) Ltd* 1979 3 SA 754 (A).
726. *See*, for example, *Mensky v. ABSA Bank Ltd t/a Trust Bank* [1997] 4 All SA 280 (W) and *Randfontein Transitional Local Council v. ABSA Bank Ltd* 2000 2 SA 1040 (W) 1058 H, in which it was stated that this is not one of the *naturalia* of the contract of deposit.
727. *See*, for example, *Randfontein Transitional Local Council v. ABSA Bank Ltd* 2000 2 SA 1040 (W) 1058: A party 'who pleads a contract of deposit or carriage bears the *onus* of proving that such contract did not contain an owner's risk clause'.
728. Act 68 of 2008.
729. *See The Law of South Africa* vol. 8, paras 182 et seq. (W.A. Joubert ed., 2d ed., Butterworths 2005); *Wille's Principles of South African Law* 966 (F. du Bois ed., Juta 2007).
730. *See* ch. 13 below.

§3. Special Liability of Hoteliers

515. The Roman edict *de nautis, cauponibus et stabulariis*[731] is in force in modern South African law and has specifically been held by the Appeal Court not to be obsolete.[732] Hoteliers and stable keepers are thus liable, *ex lege*, for the return of deposited goods in an undamaged state.[733] This liability obviously only arises when there is a valid contract between the depositor and the depositary. In the case of innkeepers, it is not necessary that the goods should have been specially entrusted for safekeeping. The liability is strict (i.e., it is not necessary to prove fault) and will be implied unless the parties have specifically excluded or limited it by contract, or when there are special circumstances, such as superior force.

731. *Digesta* 4.9.1.
732. *See Davis v. Lockstone* 1921 AD 153. For more recent applications of the edict, *see Gabriel and Another v. Enchanted Bed and Breakfast CC* 2002 6 SA 597 (C); *Roy v. Basson NO* 2007 5 SA 84 (C).
733. Until fairly recently, there was uncertainty as to whether this liability also extended to public carriers (*see*, for example, *United Building Society v. D I Stone (Pty) Ltd and Another* 1988 4 SA 795 (E) 799). This appears to have been settled by the case of *Anderson Shipping (Pty) Ltd v. Polysius (Pty) Ltd* 1995 3 SA 42 (A), in which it was held that the praetor's edict does not apply to public carriers by land.

Chapter 3. Gaming and Wagering

516. In South African law, some agreements of chance, or aleatory agreements,[734] are legal and enforceable as contracts. These include insurance contracts,[735] wagers that depend on the outcome of a game of skill in which at least one of the parties has an independent interest,[736] and those sanctioned by legislation.[737] At the other end of the spectrum, certain other aleatory agreements are illegal and thus completely void and unenforceable, either because they are prohibited by statute[738] or because they are regarded as immoral in terms of common law.[739] Still others, such as wagers with respect to games that are not prohibited but that do not fall into the categories mentioned above, are classified as illegal for being against the public interest, but they are not void – they are merely unenforceable[740] and thus occupy a middle ground between the extremes of validity and enforceability on one hand, and voidness and unenforceability on the other hand. These distinctions are sometimes arbitrary and subject to change in accordance with the changing interests and mores of society.[741] In particular, the basis of the distinction relating to the consequences of illegality is unclear.[742]

---

734. For a definition, *see*, for example, M.F.B. Reinecke et al., *General Principles of Insurance Law* para. 153 (Butterworths 2002), D.J. Joubert, *General Principles of the Law of Contract* 139–140 (Juta 1987), or Van Huyssteen, Lubbe & Reinecke, *Contract General Principles* para. 7.56 (Juta 2016).
735. On insurance, generally, *see*, for example, M.F.B. Reinecke et al., *General Principles of Insurance Law* (Butterworths 2002).
736. *See* D.H. Hutchison et al., *The Law of Contract in South Africa* 194 (Oxford U. Press S. Afr. 2012); Van Huyssteen, Lubbe & Reinecke, *Contract General Principles* para. 7.56 n. 153 (Juta 2016). For a discussion of this category, *see*, for example, *Rademeyer v. Evenwel* 1971 3 SA 339 (T).
737. *See* s. 8 of the National Gambling Act 7 of 2004; Van Huyssteen, Lubbe & Reinecke, *Contract General Principles* 7.59 (Juta 2016). The activities thus sanctioned are informal betting, betting on horse races, participating in the national lottery, and gambling at licensed casinos. Gambling online is illegal, unless the online casino is licensed in terms of South African law: *see* s.11 and *Casino Enterprises (Pty) Ltd v. Gauteng Gambling Board* 2011 6 SA 614 (SCA), where it was also held that persons physically present in South Africa are regarded as gambling within South Africa when they frequent an online casino of which the server is located outside South Africa. For an example of a prohibited lottery, *see FirstRand Bank Ltd v. National Lotteries Board* 2008 4 SA 548 (SCA). On the gambling legislation in general, *see The Law of South Africa* vol. 10, paras 216 et seq. (W.A. Joubert ed., Butterworths 2005).
738. *See* the National Gambling Act 7 of 2004.
739. *See* Van Huyssteen, Lubbe & Reinecke, *Contract General Principles* para. 7.60 (Juta 2016).
740. *See*, for example, Van Huyssteen, Lubbe & Reinecke, *Contract General Principles* paras 7.30 and 7.63 (Juta 2016); *Gibson v. Van der Walt* 1952 1 SA 262 (A); *Rademeyer v. Evenwel* 1971 3 SA 339 (T).
741. Cf. the *Lotteries and Gambling Board Main Report on Gambling in the Republic of South Africa* (RP 85/1995) and the subsequent passing of the National Gambling Act 33 of 1996, the Lotteries Act 57 of 1997 and the more recent National Gambling Act 7 of 2004. Also *see*, *The Law of South Africa* vol. 10 (W.A. Joubert ed., Butterworths 2005); Van Huyssteen, Lubbe & Reinecke, *Contract General Principles* paras 7.32–7.33 (Juta 2016); G.F. Lubbe, 'Bona Fides, Billikheid en die Openbare Belang in die Suid-Afrikaanse Kontraktereg', *Stellenbosch Law Review* (1990): 7; *Coetzee v. Comitis* 2001 1 SA 1254 (C) especially 1270 F–H (para. 31).
742. Cf. S. van der Merwe & L.F. van Huyssteen, 'The Force of Agreements: Valid, Void, Voidable, Unenforceable?', *Tydskrif vir Hedendaagse Romeins-Hollandse Reg* (1995): 549.

§1. WAGERS AND BETS

517. In essence, a wager or bet is an agreement in terms of which two parties[743] agree that, depending on the outcome of an uncertain future event, one will win over the other, who shall then pay or hand over a stake to the winner, in circumstances in which neither has any interest in the transaction except the money or stake that he or she stands to win or lose.[744]

518. The consequences of a wager or bet depend on the circumstances referred to in paragraph 517. There is not much more to be said here about wagers that are enforceable and those that are void. However, the position regarding wagers that are regarded as being against the public interest but not as improper or immoral, or that are not declared void by legislation, is rather more complicated – such agreements are usually classified as 'illegal' *(ongeoorloofd)* but are merely unenforceable and not void.[745] Thus, no direct enforcement of a debt arising from such an agreement is allowed, nor is indirect enforcement generally allowed:[746] a claim for enforcement framed in a delict is unenforceable; a subsequent promise to pay, or a claim based on novation of the debt or on a cheque issued in payment, is similarly unenforceable.[747]

Since South African law is not clear on whether a natural obligation is created by a wager agreement, there is some uncertainty about whether a wagering debt can be set-off.[748] For the same reason, it is unclear whether a performance made in terms of a wager can be reclaimed, albeit subject to the *par delictum* rule.

By way of exception, a wager agreement may form the basis of an enforceable claim in certain circumstances.[749] Thus, an action by a winner of a wager against a stakeholder for a payout is enforceable. So is a contract of mandate with respect to a wager, and a loan to enable the borrower to participate in a wager is recoverable.

743. A pool or totalizator scheme seems to be regarded rather as a lottery than as a wager – *Christie v. Mudaliar* 1962 2 SA 40 (N).

744. *See*, for example, Van Huyssteen, Lubbe & Reinecke, *Contract General Principles* (Juta 2016) who state, atpara. 7.57, that a wager comes into being when 'the parties by their very agreement create an uncertainty that would otherwise not have carried for them the potential of loss'. *See* s. 4 of the National Gambling Act 7 of 2004 for a statutory definition of a wager.

745. *See*, for example, Van Huyssteen, Lubbe & Reinecke, *Contract General Principles* para. 7.58 (Juta 2016); *Gibson v. Van der Walt* 1952 1 SA 262 (A). This common law rule is confirmed by statute: s.16(e) of the National Gambling Act 7 of 2004.

746. *See Gibson v. Van der Walt* 1952 1 SA 262 (A); *Christie v. Mudaliar* 1962 2 SA 40 (N).

747. *See*, for example, *Rademeyer v. Evenwel* 1971 3 SA 339 (T).

748. *See* Van Huyssteen, Lubbe & Reinecke, *Contract General Principles* para. 7.58, at n. 151 (Juta 2016) and the cases referred to there. Cf. J.C. de Wet & A.H. van Wyk, *Die Suid-Afrikaanse Kontraktereg en Handelsreg* (Durban: Butterworths, 1992), 277.

749. *See* Van Huyssteen, Lubbe & Reinecke, *Contract General Principles* para. 7.59 (Juta 2016); s. 16(b) of the National Gambling Act 7 of 2004.

§2. Insurance Contracts

519. Since insurance agreements and wagers share an important basic element, namely that performance is related to an uncertain future event, and since insurance agreements are in practice sometimes barely discernable from wagers, it is important to distinguish the elements of a valid insurance contract, lest it also suffers the fate of voidness or unenforceability. As case law stands, it appears that the critical distinguishing element is that of interest: the insured has an insurable interest, or, in the case of non-indemnity insurance, such as in some life insurance contracts, at least a legitimate or genuine interest in the uncertain event.[750]

520. An agreement, then, albeit aleatory, can be a valid and enforceable insurance contract if it provides for the following rights and duties:[751] payment of a premium in money; performance by the insurer, usually in the form of payment of a sum of money, in exchange for the premium; an uncertain event, the outcome of which determines the performance of the insurer; and an insurable interest in the uncertain event on the part of the party who agrees to pay the premium.

750. *See* M.F.B. Reinecke et al., *General Principles of Insurance Law* paras 97, 49 and 51 et seq. (Butterworths 2002). Cases dealing with the requirement of an insurable interest include *Refrigerated Trucking (Pty) Ltd v. Zive NO (Aegis Insurance Company Ltd, Third Party)* 1996 2 SA 361 (T), *Manderson t/a Hillcrest Electrical v. Standard General Insurance Company Ltd* 1996 3 SA 434 (D); *Lorcom Thirteen (Pty) Ltd v. Zurich Insurance Company South Africa Ltd* 2013 5 SA (WCC).

751. *See*, for example, *Law of South Africa* vol. 12, 1st re-issue, paras 147 et seq. (W.A. Joubert ed., Butterworths 2002).

Chapter 4. Sale of Goods

521. In South African law, a contract relating to the alienation of goods will be a contract of sale[752] only if it contains certain essential and distinctive terms.[753] The contract must contain an undertaking by one party to sell a thing to the other party, who undertakes to pay a sum of money in exchange. These terms distinguish a contract of sale from other contracts, for example, from a contract of exchange or barter, in which the counter-performance consists of goods (or mainly of goods) and not only of money, and when there is no intention to alienate in the sense of passing complete and final legal control (often called 'the intention to sell and to buy').[754] Determining whether a contract is a sale or not is of particular importance because, once a contract has been classified as a sale, certain far-reaching rights and duties ensure to the parties by operation of the common law,[755] unless they have agreed otherwise.[756]

Unless it amounts to a credit agreement, a contract of sale concluded by a consumer with a supplier in the ordinary course of business will fall within the ambit of the Consumer Protection Act.[757]

The Act grants consumers the rights that effectively impose various pre-contractual duties on suppliers. Thus, for example, a supplier has a duty not to discriminate against any person or category of persons when marketing goods or services or when dealing with consumers in any way.[758] Suppliers also have a duty

752. *See* in general J.C. de Wet & A.H. van Wyk, *Die Suid-Afrikaanse Kontraktereg en Handelsreg*, vol. 1 (Durban: Butterworths, 1992), Ch. 10; K. Lehmann & G. Bradfield, *Principles of the Law of Sale and Lease* (Juta 2010); *Wille's Principles of South African Law* ch. 27 (F. du Bois ed., Juta 2007); G.R.J. Hackwill, *Mackeurtan's Sale of Goods in South Africa* (Juta 1984); G. Glover, *Kerr's The Law of Sale and Lease* (LexisNexis 2014); R. Zimmermann & D. Visser, *Southern Cross: Civil Law and Common Law in South Africa* 361 et seq. (Juta 1996).

753. A court will give effect to the true intention of the parties and not to simulated transactions: *see*, for example, *Commissioner for Inland Revenue Services v. Woulidge* [1997] 4 All SA 519 (C); *Nedcor Bank Ltd v. ABSA Bank Ltd* 1998 2 SA 830 (W); *Commissioner for Inland Revenue v. Conhage (Pty) Ltd (formerly Tycon (Pty) Ltd)* 1999 4 SA 1149 (SCA); *Maize Board v. Jackson* 2005 6 SA 592 (SCA); *Van Aardt v. Van Aardt* 2007 1 SA 53 (E). On this topic generally, *see* N.L. Joubert *Asset-Based Financing, Contracts of Purchase and Sale, and Simulated Transactions*, S. African L. J. 707 (1992); A. Hutchison & D. Hutchison, *Simulated Transactions and the Fraus Legis Doctrine* S. African L. J. 69 (2014).

754. The distinction is of practical importance in the motor trade with respect to so-called trade-in contracts. *See*, for example, *Wastie v. Security Motors (Pty) Ltd* 1972 2 SA 129 (C); *Janse van Rensburg v. Grieve Trust CC* 2000 1 SA 279 (SCA).

755. For example, the warranty against latent defects, the warranty against eviction, and the rules relating to the risk for accidental damage or loss of the thing.

756. The courts have tended to deny that a contract amounts to a sale, even if it contains the *essentialia* of a sale, if it contains certain 'uncharacteristic' terms: *see*, for example, *Commissioner for Inland Revenue v. Wandrag Asbestos (Pty) Ltd* 1995 2 SA 197 (A). This approach has been criticized by, for example, G.F. Lubbe, *Law of Purchase and Sale*, Annual Survey S. African L. 181, at 182 (1995) and *Law of Purchase and Sale*, Annual Survey S. African L. 208, at 212 et seq. (1998). The better view is that a contract will be a sale provided that it contains the essential terms, and any additional terms are merely incidental. More recent cases seem to indicate that the courts are now moving in the right direction: *see*, for example, *Commissioner for Inland Revenue v. Conhage (Pty) Ltd (formerly Tycon (Pty) Ltd)* 1999 4 SA 1149 (SCA).

757. Act 68 of 2008.

758. Section 8.

not to invade a consumer's right to privacy for the purpose of direct marketing.[759] When marketing goods, sellers may not advertise goods at a specified price in such a way that a consumer could be misled as to the availability of those goods from that supplier at the advertised price.[760] Suppliers must provide consumers with certain information; for example, sellers may not display goods for sale without also displaying the price,[761] and they must clearly indicate whether they are selling reconditioned or rebuilt goods or 'grey products'.[762] When a seller displays or sells any goods from open stock, a consumer has the right to select or reject any particular item from that stock.[763] In the process of marketing or concluding a contract, the supplier may not engage in unconscionable conduct.[764]

The contents, performance, and enforcement of consumer contracts are also extensively regulated by the Consumer Protection Act. For example, goods may not be sold at a price that is unfair, unreasonable, or unjust, or include any terms that are unfair, unreasonable, or unjust.[765] Certain particular terms are prohibited. Examples of such prohibited terms include the following:[766] those that have the general aim or result of defeating the ends of the Act, misleading the consumer, or 'subject[ing] the consumer to fraudulent conduct'; those that purport to deprive a consumer of his or her statutory rights or evade a supplier's duties under the Act; those that purport to evade the provisions of the Act; those that are intended to 'limit or exempt a supplier of goods or services from liability for any loss directly or indirectly attributable to the gross negligence of the supplier or any person acting for or controlled by the supplier'; those in terms of which the consumer falsely acknowledges that neither the supplier nor its representative made any representations or warranties in relation to the agreement; those in terms of which a consumer authorizes a supplier's representative to enter premises so as to take possession of goods received under the agreement; those in terms of which a consumer agrees to deposit any of his or her identity documents or bank card with the seller or his or her representative.

Contracts of sale not regulated by the Consumer Protection Act or the National Credit Act are governed by the common law.[767] The common law thus covers contracts of sale concluded by parties who do not ordinarily conclude such agreements in the course of business, contracts in which the supplier is the State, or the consumer is a juristic person with assets or an annual turnover above a certain threshold, and certain other exempt contracts.[768, 769]

759. Section 11(1).
760. Section 30.
761. Section 23. In this regard, *see also* H. Du Plessis, Display *of Goods for Sale, Advertisements and the Consumer Protection Act* S. African L. J. 150 (2015).
762. Section 25.
763. Section 18(2).
764. Section 40. Also see s. 41, which deals with various kinds of misrepresentation.
765. Section 48.
766. Section 51.
767. Act 35 of 2005.
768. Section 5 of the Consumer Protection Act 68 of 2008.
769. *Ibid.*

522. In principle, no formalities are required for a contract of sale to be validly concluded. The most important exceptions relate to the sale of immovable property[770] and the sale of goods on credit.[771] According to the Consumer Protection Act,[772] a supplier must provide a consumer with a written record of any transaction.[773] Moreover, the relevant Minister may prescribe that certain contracts be rendered in writing.[774] The Act further stipulates that when an agreement is expressed in writing, it must be in plain and understandable language;[775] it must set out in detail all the financial obligations of the consumer;[776] and a free copy thereof must be provided to the consumer.[777]

523. Apart from the special terms or consequences arising *ex lege*, the contract of sale is an ordinary reciprocal contract, which creates only personal rights and duties for the parties but no real rights.

524. The contract of sale is a *causa* for transfer of the thing sold, and, as such, it must be distinguished from the actual transfer of the thing,[778] which takes place by way of a separate act of delivery accompanied by an intention to transfer the thing.[779]

525. South African law makes no special distinction between a sale and an agreement to sell when the goods are to pass to the buyer only in the future.[780] If

770. *See* the Alienation of Land Act 68 of 1981. In terms of this Act, the material terms of a contract for the alienation of immovable property must be in writing: for recent judicial pronouncements on this matter, *see*, for example, *Fraser v. Viljoen* 2008 4 SA 106 (SCA); *Just Names Properties 11 CC v. Fourie* 2008 1 SA 343 (SCA); *JR 209 Investments (Pty) Ltd v. Pine Villa Country Estate (Pty) Ltd; Pine Villa Country Estate (Pty) Ltd v. JR 209 Investments (Pty) Ltd* 2009 4 302 (SCA). Also see the Housing Consumers Protection Measures Act 95 of 1998, insofar as the latter relates to contracts of sale.

771. *See* the National Credit Act 34 of 2005. In this regard, *see* J.M. Otto, *The National Credit Act Explained* (Butterworths 2006).

772. Act 68 of 2008.

773. Section 26.

774. Section 50.

775. Section 22.

776. Section 50.

777. Section 50.

778. *See*, for example, *Legator McKenna Inc and Another v. Shea and Others* 2010 1 SA 35 (SCA); *Air-Kel (Edms) Bpk h/a Merkel Motors v. Bodenstein* 1980 3 SA 917 (A); *Macard Stein and Co. v. Port Marine Contractors (Pty) Ltd* 1995 3 SA 663 (A) 667 B. The same distinction applies to the sale of incorporeal property: *see Botha v. Fick* 1995 2 SA 750 (A) 762 C–D; *Etkind v. Hicor Trading Ltd and Another* 1999 1 SA 111 (W) 124 D; *Page Automation (Pty) Ltd v. Profusa Properties CC t/a Homenet OR Tambo and Others* 2013 4 SA 37 (GSJ).

779. For a very brief discussion of the methods of delivery, *see* below. *See* further C.G. van der Merwe, *Sakereg* (Durban: Butterworths, 1989); *Wille's Principles of South African Law* 525 et seq. (F. du Bois ed., Juta 2007).

780. Such as where the goods are not yet in existence, for example, a future crop: *see Nieuwoudt and Another NNO v. Vrystaat Mielies (Edms) Bpk* 2004 3 SA 486 (SCA).

the parties intend to contract *de futuro,* they may enter into a contract of sale subject to a suspensive condition or a time clause (a so-called sale *in diem*), or they may conclude some form of *pactum de contrahendo*, such as an option contract or a contract of pre-emption.

§1. Delivery

526. The content of the seller's duty to deliver the thing sold depends on the terms of the contract. If the parties have not agreed on a time and place for delivery, the seller must deliver within a reasonable time,[781] generally at the place where the thing was when the sale was concluded. If the thing is not yet specified, delivery must take place at the seller's place of business or abode. The seller must deliver the thing with all its accessories and appurtenances and must, at his or her own expense, take all steps to prepare the thing for delivery and to effect delivery. Since a sale is a reciprocal contract, the seller's duty to deliver is concurrent with the purchaser's duty to pay or tender the price at the time and place of delivery, unless agreed otherwise. Thus, the seller in a cash sale may withhold delivery (by way of the *exceptio non adimpleti contractus*) until the price is paid or tendered.[782]

527. The seller must deliver the thing to the purchaser in such a way that the latter is physically capable of dealing with the property without disturbance (he or she must have detention (*detentio*) of the property) while intending to deal with it as the owner (*animus possidendi*). While the seller is required to provide the purchaser with *vacua possessio*,[783] he or she is, in principle, not required to pass ownership – the contract will therefore still be valid when the seller sells property belonging to a third party.[784]

528. In general, delivery may be effected by any act of the seller by which the buyer is placed in physical detention of the goods or is enabled to take detention, coupled with the requisite mental element,[785] namely an agreement between the parties that the buyer may deal with and retain the property as his or her own. Parties

781. What is reasonable would depend on the circumstances – in many cases, immediate delivery or delivery on demand would be reasonable, but in others, the seller should be afforded more time.

782. *See Lendalease Finance (Pty) Ltd v. Corporacion de Mercadeo Agricola* 1976 4 SA 464 (A). Similarly, it has been held that a purchaser can withhold payment of occupational interest when the seller has not given *vacua possessio* as agreed: *see Scholtz v. Thompson* 1996 2 SA 409 (C) 416. When, in terms of the contract, the seller must deliver first, he or she may not withhold delivery even if he or she reasonably believes that the buyer will not be able to pay – he or she may, however, require security for payment.

783. Unless the parties agree otherwise: *see*, for example, *Sheriff for the District of Wynberg v. Jakoet* 1997 3 SA 425 (C) 430 E–F.

784. Cf. *Pretoria East Builders CC v. Basson* 2004 6 SA 15 (SCA): a purchaser cannot obtain specific performance to enforce transfer when the seller is not the owner.

785. *AXZS Industries v. AF Dreyer (Pty) Ltd* 2004 4 SA 186 (W).

may agree to any effective method of delivery. Quite apart from special methods agreed upon by the parties, the following methods of delivery are recognized by South African law:[786]

1. Physical delivery: The seller is not required physically to take movables to the purchaser but should make it possible for the purchaser to remove or appropriate them immediately. The mental element of delivery must, of course, also be present.
2. When the purchaser already has custody of the thing sold, delivery would require that the purchaser, in addition, must have the necessary animus of acquiring the thing. Following the civilian tradition, the term *traditio brevi manu* is often used to refer to this form of delivery. South African law also recognizes a form of *traditio brevi manu* whereby the agent of a seller continues to hold the thing as the agent for the purchaser, thus requiring a tripartite agreement. Delivery in this manner is often called 'attornment', as in English law.
3. When a seller who is in possession of the thing retains custody for the purchaser (e.g., as the purchaser's agent), delivery to the purchaser takes place by the mere agreement that the latter shall henceforth be in possession as the owner. This form of delivery is called *constitutum possessorium.*
4. Delivery of movables that by their nature, size, or weight can be moved only with difficulty may take place by agreement and the act of pointing out: *traditio longa manu.*
5. When a thing can be controlled by way of another thing (e.g., a key to a warehouse where the thing is stored or a bill of lading with respect to the goods listed in it), delivery may take place by agreement and the handing over of the control mechanism.

529. When the seller does not deliver timeously, the buyer may claim specific performance of the contract. Whether he or she may claim damages or resile from the contract depends on whether the seller has, by his or her delay, committed a breach of contract (*mora debitoris*) and on whether he or she has the right to cancel. In this regard, it must be remembered that South African law recognizes that, when 'time is of the essence', an aggrieved party may unilaterally cancel the contract by giving notice to the other party, even when there is no contractual right to rescind. When the seller delivers a thing that does not comply with the terms of the contract, the buyer's remedies may vary from a claim for specific performance to cancellation and, in any event, damages. He or she may also withhold payment of the price or any unpaid part of it by relying on the *exceptio non adimpleti contractus.*[787]

Rules imposed by the Consumer Protection Act regarding performance of consumer contracts include, for instance, the requirements that any person who delivers goods must provide clear proof of his or her identity,[788] that the supplier may

786. For further details, *see* C.G. van der Merwe, *Sakereg* (Durban: Butterworths, 1989); *Wille's Principles of South African Law* 525 et seq. (F. du Bois ed., Juta 2007).

787. *See* the cases referred to in para. 527, n. 11 above.

788. Section 28.

not require the consumer to accept delivery at an unreasonable time,[789] and that the consumer must be given the opportunity to examine the goods upon delivery.[790] The consumer is also granted a cooling-off period: when a contract results from direct marketing, the consumer has five days in which he or she may unilaterally rescind the contract.[791] In such a case, the consumer must return the goods in question. He or she may also return the goods if he or she was not given an opportunity to examine them before delivery.[792]

§2. Transfer of Ownership and Risk

I. Ownership

530. As has been indicated above,[793] the mere conclusion of a contract of sale does not affect the transfer of ownership of the thing sold. Delivery is therefore an additional and separate requirement in this regard,[794] without which ownership cannot be transferred. The seller is not obliged to pass ownership if he or she is not the owner (in fact, he or she cannot transfer a right that he or she does not have: *nemo plus iuris transferre potest quod ipse haberet*);[795] he or she merely has to deliver the goods, as described above, and divest himself or herself of all rights that he or she has in the thing. The seller warrants against eviction[796] and does not warrant title.[797] Of course, if he or she is the owner, then the seller must transfer ownership, except if ownership is reserved for him or her by an agreement.

531. In the case of a *cash sale*, whereby the price is to be paid simultaneously with delivery,[798] it is usually accepted that the parties intend that ownership will

789. Section 19(3).
790. Section 19(5).
791. Section 16(3).
792. Section 20(2).
793. *See* para. 525.
794. *See also Legator McKenna Inc and Another v. Shea and Others* 2010 1 SA 35 (SCA); *Lendalease Finance (Pty) Ltd v. Corporacion De Mercadeo Agricola* 1976 4 SA 464 (A); *Commissioner of Customs & Excise v. Randles, Brothers & Hudson Ltd* 1941 AD 369.
795. *See*, for example, *Knox NO v. Mofokeng and Others* 2013 4 SA 46 (GSJ).
796. That is, permanent deprivation of possession. *See*, for example, *Vrystaat Motors v. Henry Blignaut (Edms) Bpk* 1996 2 SA 448 (A) 459 A–B. This warranty is a term implied by law: *see*, for example, the obiter dictum in *Göbel Franchises CC v. Kadwa* 2007 5 SA 456 (C). Should eviction indeed take place, the seller must repay the purchase price: *see*, for example, *Vrystaat Motors v. Henry Blignaut (Edms) Bpk* 1996 2 SA 448 (A). But cf. the decision in *Plit v. Imperial Bank Ltd* 2007 1 SA 315 (SCA) and the critical analysis of this decision by T. Naudé, *The Law of Purchase and Sale*, Annual Survey S. African L. 1039, at 1041–1042 (2007). Also see *Cordiant Trading CC v. Daimler Chrysler Financial Services (Pty) Ltd* 2005 4 SA 389 (D).
797. On the case of a so-called double sale, *see Meridian Bay Restaurant (Pty) Ltd and Others v. Mitchell NO* 2011 4 SA 1 (SCA).
798. Where there is no express agreement on whether the sale is for cash or credit, it is rebuttably presumed that the sale is for cash. When a conditional credit sale is concluded but the condition is not fulfilled, the sale is regarded as a cash sale. When a cheque is accepted by the seller as payment, the sale is for cash, irrespective of where the cheque is payable, except when the cheque is post-dated.

only pass when the price has been paid in full, even if delivery takes place earlier.[799] This rather anachronistic rule (the so-called cash-price rule) has been severely criticized by the Appeal Court (since as long ago as 1921) as being at variance with every modern mercantile system of law.

532. When the seller has warranted ownership but cannot transfer it, he or she breaches the warranty and may be liable for damages. When the buyer reasonably believes that the seller has agreed to warrant ownership but is mistaken, he or she may hold the seller bound on the basis of his or her reasonable reliance that the consensus included a warranty. When the seller has induced the buyer to purchase by misrepresenting (by commission, or by silence when there is a duty to speak) that he or she is the owner, he or she may be liable for damages for misrepresentation.[800] In terms of general principles, the contract may be cancelled or rescinded.

533. Parties intending to enter into a contract of sale may agree that ownership of the thing is reserved subject to the fulfilment of a certain requirement, such as the payment of the full contract price and of finance and other charges in the case of instalment sales. Despite the fact that such a reservation usually entails a sale subject to a suspensive condition, the normal consequences of a suspensive condition, namely that a contract (*in casu* sale) arises and that only (some of) its consequences (*in casu* the passing of ownership) are made subject to the fulfilment of the condition, do not apply in the case of a sale. In a long series of decisions since the previous century, the courts have, despite admitting the incongruity of their approach, held that, in such a case, no sale arises – the whole agreement being suspended – until the condition is fulfilled.[801] However, the interim relationship between the parties is described as 'a very real and definite contractual relationship'.[802] The most important practical effect of this position is that, when ownership is reserved, the special rules as to the passing of the risk in sales do not apply at all.

534. If the passing of ownership has been reserved and the buyer sells the thing, he or she will be committing a criminal offence. Such a reservation of ownership will be effective even against third parties to whom the buyer had sold the thing. The owner may thus, in principle, vindicate his or her property, except when he or she is estopped from doing so by his or her own representation that the buyer was the owner or had the *jus disponendi.*

799. *See*, for example, *Lendalease Finance (Pty) Ltd v. Corporacion de Mercadeo Agricola* 1976 4 SA 464 (A) 490 A; *De Wet v. Santam Bpk* 1996 2 SA 629 (A); and *Sefalana Employee Benefits Organisation v. Haslam* 2000 2 SA 414 (SCA).

800. The rules regarding misrepresentation are reiterated by the Consumer Protection Act: *see* s. 41.

801. *See*, for example, *Tuckers Land & Development Corporation (Pty) Ltd v. Strydom* 1984 1 SA 1 (A).

802. *See Corondimas v. Badat* 1946 AD 548 558.

535. A sale on approval, however, is generally treated as a sale subject to a suspensive condition, that is, there is a contract of sale, but the operation of the consequences thereof, including delivery (by *traditio brevi manu*), is suspended until the buyer indicates his or her approval.[803]

II. Option to Repurchase

536. In South African law, the option to repurchase, a type of *pactum de retrovendendo*, is a contract between the seller and the purchaser in terms of which the seller has the right to repurchase the thing from the buyer within a certain time, or within a reasonable time, at a fixed price or, if a price has not been fixed, probably (by way of a tacit agreement) for the same price as the original purchase price. Such an agreement is not regarded as a condition to a sale, but as a distinct option contract, giving rise to personal rights. The purchaser is thus bound to sell if the seller exercises his or her right to repurchase, and the purchaser will breach the contract if he or she sells to another.

537. With respect to matters such as liability for damage to the thing or accessions or improvements to it, South African law still seems to be influenced to a great extent by the writings of Pothier on contracts of sale. However, on the basis of a tacit agreement, it will probably be held by the courts that accessions that form part of the thing at the time when the seller exercises his or her option accrue to him or her. When the purchaser has made improvements and does not remove them, the repurchasing seller must compensate the buyer for his or her enrichment.

538. The option to repurchase must be distinguished from the *ius retractus*, which gives the seller a preference to repurchase, should the purchaser later wish to sell the thing. Such a right is regarded as a right of pre-emption, which differs in material respects from the option.

III. Passing of Risk

539. The rule in the South African law of sale is that once the sale is complete or *perfecta* (in the technical sense, as set out below), the risk with respect to the thing sold, as far as accidental destruction, damage, deterioration, or other detrimental occurrences are concerned, passes to the buyer, notwithstanding that neither delivery nor transfer of ownership to him or her has taken place.[804] The maxim *res perit domino*, therefore, does not apply in South African law.[805] It follows that the

803. *See* G.R.J. Hackwill, *Mackeurtan's Sale of Goods in South Africa* 39–40 (Juta 1984).
804. *See Southern Era Resources v. Farndell NO* 2010 4 SA 200 (SCA), para. 8.
805. Cf. *Pahad v. Director of Food Supplies & Distribution* 1949 3 SA 695 (A).

purchaser remains liable for the price even when the thing is destroyed and the seller has, by the operation of the rule, been released from the duty to deliver.[806]

540. South African law is, in this respect, also at variance with the United Nations Convention on Contracts for the International Sale of Goods, which provides as a general rule that the risk passes to the purchaser when he or she takes delivery of the goods.

541. Equally, any benefits accruing to the thing, such as fruits and rental, go to the purchaser.

542. The sale is complete (*perfecta*) for the purposes of the passing of the risk when the following requirements have been met:

1. The purchase price must be determined or determinable by simple calculation.[807] When a certain mass is sold at a price per unit (*ad mensuram*; for example, a heap of ore at ZAR 2,000 per ton) or when a third party must fix the price, the risk will not pass until the mass has been weighed or the price has been fixed. There is an authority with the view that, in a sale *ad mensuram*, the risk of deterioration or damage does pass to the purchaser, but not the risk of destruction.
2. The goods must be determined. When unascertained goods have been sold, such as in the case of an alternative sale or a generic sale, the goods must have been appropriated to the contract or individualized before the risk will pass. Generally, it seems that the purchaser may unilaterally appropriate the goods, although there is support in favour of bilateral appropriation.
3. The sale must not be subject to a suspensive condition.[808] Pending the fulfilment of the condition, the risk remains with the seller.

543. It is therefore clear that the passing of the risk from the seller to the purchaser is contingent upon special requirements and is not merely dependent on the fact that a valid contract of sale has been concluded, nor is it tied to delivery or passing of ownership.

544. The parties may, at their will, vary the general-risk rule by an express or tacit agreement.[809] When goods are to be delivered over a distance, it may well be inferred that the parties have tacitly agreed that the risk will only pass upon delivery; this may be so particularly in cases of cost, insurance, and freight (CIF), free

---

806. This consequence militates against the general principle that when performance becomes impossible, the duty to render counter-performance also falls away.
807. *See Tebe Trading (Pty) Ltd v. Mediterranean Shipping Co. (Pty) Ltd* 2006 4 SA 495 (N).
808. *See Southern Era Resources v. Farndell NO* 2010 4 SA 200 (SCA).
809. Note that a reservation of ownership has the effect that the risk remains with the seller, but that the reason for this consequence is related to the particular approach in South African law that no sale as such has arisen – it is not related to the passing of ownership.

on board (FOB), or free on rail (FOR) contracts.[810] It cannot, however, be inferred merely from the fact that the seller undertakes to deliver over a distance.

545. When the seller has breached the contract by delaying delivery (and is therefore *in mora*), the risk remains with him or her even when the sale is complete. This is a special consequence of this form of breach of contract.

§3. The Seller's Liability for Eviction and Latent Defects

I. Sale by a Non-owner and Warranty Against Eviction

546. As has been indicated above, the seller in South African law need not warrant the title: a perfectly valid contract of sale can be concluded even when the seller is not the owner.[811] However, to protect the purchaser, and as an automatic incident of sale and by operation of common law, the seller is obliged to deliver the thing in such a manner that vacant possession is given, and he or she warrants against subsequent eviction – that is, he or she warrants that no one with a better title (including himself or herself) will deprive the purchaser of possession and the undisturbed use and enjoyment of the thing sold.[812]

547. It is therefore apparent that the warranty against eviction covers not only actual lawful dispossession, but also all proper acts having the effect of depriving the purchaser of quiet and undisturbed possession or enjoyment of the thing, in whole or in part.[813] The warranty clearly does not cover unlawful acts of interference, but only impairments based upon a better title than that which the purchaser acquires from the seller.

548. To enable the seller to fulfil his or her warranty, the purchaser must notify the seller of a threatened eviction, so that the seller may intervene as a co-defendant or take over the defence in the name of the purchaser.[814] Should the seller fail to do so, the purchaser must nevertheless conduct a strong defence (*virilis defensio*). When no such steps are taken, the seller may nevertheless be liable in terms of the warranty, but then the purchaser must prove the seller's defective title. When the

810. *See*, for example, *Chong Sun Wood Products Pte Ltd v. K & T Trading Ltd and Another* 2001 2 SA 651 (D).
811. These are not the only ex lege terms imported into contracts of sale in terms of the common law. Another example would be the term imported into contracts for the sale of a business prohibiting the seller from canvassing the existing customers of the business being sold. For a comprehensive and critical analysis of the law in this regard, *see GrainCo (Pty) Ltd v. Van der Merwe and Others* 2014 5 SA 444 (WCC).
812. In terms s. 44 of the Consumer Protection Act, consumer contracts of sale contain an implied term to the effect that the seller either has a right, or has been authorized by the owner, to sell the goods in question.
813. For examples of acts of eviction, *see* G.R.J. Hackwill, *Mackeurtan's Sale of Goods in South Africa* 165–166 (Juta 1984).
814. Cf. *Katzeff v. City Car Sales (Pty) Ltd* 1998 2 SA 644 (C).

purchaser has been successfully evicted, the ordinary remedies for breach of contract apply in favour of the purchaser: cancellation, restitution of the price,[815] and, when applicable, damages including legal costs.[816]

549. The warranty may be excluded by an agreement.[817] However, when the seller knew that his or her title was defective, his or her fraud will render the exclusion clause of no effect (the seller may in any event be liable for misrepresentation), but when the seller was ignorant, the purchaser cannot claim damages, although he or she may still claim return of the price, despite the exemption of liability. When the purchaser knew of the seller's defective title or when he or she assumed the risk regarding title, he or she has no claims against the seller.

II. The Seller's Liability for Defects and Warranty Against Latent Defects

550. In South African law, the purchaser's remedies against the seller for defects in the thing sold may conveniently be classified as the ordinary remedies usually available to a contractant in terms of general principle, as well as the special remedies that apply in cases of sale only when certain circumstances are present.

551. When a seller is aware of defects in the thing (of which the purchaser is unaware) and, in full awareness that he or she is acting wrongfully, remains silent, thereby inducing the purchaser to buy, he or she commits a fraudulent misrepresentation.[818] In principle, the defrauded purchaser may rescind the contract, if he or she chooses, and, in certain circumstances, the seller may be liable for restitution and for damages calculated with reference to the purchaser's negative interest, which may include consequential loss. The same remedies are available for other instances of fraudulent as well as negligent misrepresentation inducing a contract of sale.[819] When a seller, through an innocent misrepresentation, induces the purchaser to buy, the purchaser may be entitled to withdraw from the contract and claim restitution,

815. *See*, for example, *Vrystaat Motors v. Henry Blignaut (Edms) Bpk* 1996 2 SA 448 (A).

816. On the remedies available in such circumstances, *see Katzeff v. City Car Sales (Pty) Ltd* 1998 2 SA 644 (C); G.F. Lubbe, *Purchase and Sale*, Annual Survey S. African L. 208, at 222 et seq. (1998); A.J. Kerr, *The Warranty against Eviction in Contracts of Sale*, S. African L. J. 455 (1999).

817. *See*, for example, *Göbel Franchises CC v. Kadwa* 2007 5 SA 456 (C) (*obiter*) but cf. *Vrystaat Motors v. Henry Blignaut (Edms) Bpk* 1996 2 SA 448 (A) and *Alpha Trust (Edms) Bpk v. Van der Watt* 1975 3 SA 734 (A). On the need to approach such exclusion clauses with care, *see Van der Westhuizen v. Arnold* 2002 6 SA 453 (SCA) 469 D–G (para. 40). The seller may not exclude his or her liability to repay the purchase price in the case of eviction but may exclude his or her liability for further loss occasioned by the eviction – *see Vrystaat Motors v. Henry Blignaut (Edms) Bpk* 1996 2 SA 448 (A) and *Alpha Trust (Edms) Bpk v. Van der Watt* 1975 3 SA 734 (A) but cf. the decision in *Plit v. Imperial Bank Ltd* 2007 1 SA 315 (SCA) and T. Naudé, *The Law of Purchase and Sale*, Annual Survey S. African L. 1039, at 1041–1042 (2007).

818. On the seller's duty to disclose information regarding defects, *see Banda and Another v. Van der Spuy and Another* 2013 4 SA 77 (SCA); *Waller v. Pienaar* 2004 6 SA 303 (C); *Ellis and Another v. Cilliers NO and Others* 2016 1 SA 293 (WCC).

819. In future, liability for negligent misrepresentation will probably become an increasingly important method of protecting a purchaser against defects in the thing sold – cf. *Bayer South Africa (Pty) Ltd v. Frost* 1991 4 SA 559 (A).

or claim a reduction in the agreed purchase price.[820] These remedies apart, a mistake by the purchaser relating to the quality or substance of the goods may allow him or her to escape liability for the price when the mistake results in the absence of consensus.

When a seller has expressly or tacitly[821] by contract warranted the quality of the goods or the absence of defects and then delivers defective goods, he or she may be liable for breach of contract, the remedies being cancellation, restitution, and damages calculated according to the positive interest, which may include consequential loss and loss of profit. It is sometimes said that the purchaser who claims these remedies (particularly damages) is claiming by way of the *actio empti*. In modern South African law, however, no special significance is attached to such a technical action[822] – depending on the circumstances, a purchaser is simply claiming on the grounds of either misrepresentation or breach of contract.

552. In the absence of the above-mentioned bases of liability, a seller is nevertheless liable to a limited extent for certain latent defects in the thing sold, even if he or she was unaware of those defects.[823] This liability arises by operation of law,[824] by way of the reception, and the expansion of the ambit of certain edicts that applied in Roman law and that allowed a purchaser an *actio quanti minoris* or an *actio redhibitoria*. Such liability is often said to arise from an 'implied warranty against latent defects'.

The thing sold will be regarded as *defective* for these purposes if it is of abnormal quality or has an abnormal attribute that has the effect of destroying or substantially reducing its usefulness for the purpose for which it was sold or for which it is commonly used.[825] An objective test is applied, with reference to the nature of the goods, for example, whether they are new or used. The defect must have existed at the time of the sale.

820. *See*, for example, *Phame (Pty) Ltd v. Paizes* 1973 3 SA 397 (A); *Janse van Rensburg v. Grieve Trust CC* 2000 1 SA 315 (C).
821. A tacit warranty may well be inferred when the seller is an expert in relation to the goods. Such a warranty would be contractual and must be distinguished from the special case of the liability of the manufacturer-seller or the expert seller for consequential loss, which will be discussed below. In terms of s. 56 of the Consumer Protection Act, consumer contracts of sale contain an implied warranty of quality of the goods in question.
822. This is particularly true since the prescription periods for the action on the sale and the special actions to be discussed below have been made the same.
823. *See Consol Ltd t/a Consol Glass v. Twee Jonge Gezellen (Pty) Ltd* 2005 6 SA 1 (SCA). In *Van Nieuwkerk v. McCrae* 2007 5 SA 21 (W), it was held that contracts of sale of residential property contain an *ex lege* term to the effect that the seller warrants that any building on the property was constructed in compliance with the requirements of s. 7(1)(a) of the National Building Regulations and Building Standards Act 103 of 1977. Cf. the comments of T. Naudé, *The Law of Purchase and Sale*, Annual Survey S. African L. 1047 (2007). In *Odendaal v. Ferraris* 2009 4 SA 313 (SCA) para. 27, the Court held that this was 'apparently no more than a reiteration of the rule that the seller of a *merx* warrants that it is free of latent defects'.
824. *See Consol Ltd t/a Consol Glass v. Twee Jonge Gezellen (Pty) Ltd* 2005 6 SA 1 (SCA).
825. *See*, for example, *Odendaal v. Ferraris* 2009 4 SA 313 (SCA), in which it was held that even the absence of statutory approval may constitute a latent defect. Also see *Ellis and Another v. Cilliers NO and Others* 2016 1 SA 293 (WCC).

The defect will be *latent* if it would not be apparent to the purchaser upon a reasonable inspection in this circumstances. Expert examination is not required, but when it does take place and the expert remains ignorant of the defect, the same standard as to what is reasonable will be applied as when no expert is used.[826]

When the purchaser is aware of the defect or when knowledge can be imputed to him or her, the purchaser has no special remedy.

553. The remedies of the purchaser are limited to restitution by way of an *actio redhibitoria* or a reduction of the purchase price by way of an *actio quanti minoris*, but the purchaser cannot claim damages. In the first case, the purchaser may claim return of the purchase price with interest and costs of upkeep of the thing, and he or she must return the thing and all its fruits. Restitution may only be claimed when the purchaser would not have bought the thing if he or she had known of the defect, or when the defect is so serious that the thing is rendered useless.[827] By an *actio quanti minoris*, the purchaser may claim a reduction of the price to the amount of the difference between the value of the thing and the purchase price.

554. Although not directly pertaining to latent defects, the Appeal Court has, by extensive interpretation of the field of application of the two *actiones* mentioned above, created liability for restitution or reduction of the purchase price on the part of the seller in the case of an incorrect *dictum et promissum*, upon the faith of which the buyer entered into the contract or agreed to the purchase price. A *dictum et promissum* is defined as a material statement made by the seller to the buyer during the negotiations that bears on the quality of the *res vendita* and goes beyond mere praise and commendation. In effect, the Appeal Court has created *ex lege* liability for what is sometimes called 'restitutionary damages' (a price reduction) in the case of an innocent misrepresentation, provided, of course, that the representation complies with the requirements for a *dictum et promissum*. This liability does not replace liability for breach of a contractual warranty or other similar term but is additional to it, nor should it be equated with any similar common law liability.

It may not be easy to distinguish a statement giving rise to liability from a simple commendation; the question will have to be determined according to the circumstances of every case. The Appeal Court, in the leading case of *Phame (Pty) Ltd v. Paizes*,[828] and other courts have given examples of some relevant considerations: whether the statement was in answer to a question from the buyer; its materiality to the known purpose for which the buyer wanted to buy; whether the statement was one of opinion; whether it would be obvious even to gullible persons that the statement was simply a commendation; and whether the statement was made deliberately to induce the purchaser to buy.

826. Cf. in general *Holmdene Brickworks (Pty) Ltd v. Roberts Construction Co. Ltd* 1977 3 SA 670 (A).
827. *See*, for example, *Vousvoukis v. Queen Ace CC t/a Ace Motors* 2016 3 SA 188 (ECG).
828. 1973 3 SA 397 (A). In this case the seller gave wrong information upon a question by the buyer as to the amount of the annual property rates payable on an investment property registered to the seller company. The buyer was interested in buying the full shareholding of the company. It was held that the statement influenced the price for the shares as agreed to, since the amount of the rates affected the return on the purchase price. As to the meaning of quality, *see Gannet Manufacturing Co. Ltd v. Postaflex Ltd* 1981 3 SA 216 (C).

555. In terms of South African common law and under the influence also of Pothier, South African courts recognize a further special incidence of liability on the part of a seller: when a seller is also the manufacturer of the goods sold or when he or she is a merchant and publicly professes to have expert knowledge or skill in relation to the goods sold,[829] he or she may be liable for damages (including consequential loss)[830] resulting from a latent defect in the thing, even if he or she was unaware of the defect. This liability arises by operation of law, but the exact theoretical basis for it is still uncertain: it could be based either on misrepresentation or on an *ex lege* warranty of fitness, or even on the risk principle. The method of calculation of damages may depend on which construction is finally recognized.[831]

556. In principle, any liability for latent defects, including liability arising by operation of law, may be excluded by agreement (often called a *voetstoots* clause).[832] The exemption will, however, not operate to protect the seller when he or she was actually aware of the defect and deliberately failed to disclose it[833] – such a failure would be fraudulent, and it would be against public policy to recognize an exemption from liability for fraud. In terms of legislation covering the sale of goods on credit, an exemption from or restriction of liability for latent defects arising by operation of law may not form part of a contract.[834]

557. The principle of privity of contract applies unabated in this context. The seller will only be liable to his or her co-contractant, the purchaser, and the liability does not attach to the thing sold. It follows that South African common law does not recognize any direct action against any previous seller or manufacturer.

558. Regarding liability of the seller, manufacturer, or distributor in favour of a consumer for defects in the thing sold, see the discussion of product liability below.[835]

---

829. *See*, for example, *Kroonstad Westelike Boere Ko-operatiewe Vereniging Bpk v. Botha* 1964 3 SA 561 (A). Thus, when the seller is a manufacturer, it will incur liability even if it does not profess to have expert knowledge or skill in relation to the goods sold: this was confirmed recently by the Supreme Court of Appeal in *D & H Piping Systems (Pty) Ltd v. Trans Hex Group Ltd* 2006 3 SA 593 (SCA) para. 31.
830. *See D & H Piping Systems (Pty) Ltd v. Trans Hex Group Ltd* 2006 3 SA 593 (SCA), in which the Supreme Court of Appeal formulated a test to determine whether a seller indeed 'manufactured' the goods in question: the goods must differ in nature from the raw material from which they are made, and they must have commercial utility as a consequence of the manufacturing process – *see* para. 36 of the judgment.
831. *See* in general on this topic *Hackett v. G & G Radio & Refrigerator Corporation* 1949 3 SA 664 (A); *Kroonstad Westelike Boere-Ko-Operatiewe Vereniging Bpk v. Botha* 1964 3 SA 561 (A); *Holmdene Brickworks (Pty) Ltd v. Roberts Construction Co. Ltd* 1977 3 SA 670 (A).
832. Cf. *Consol Ltd t/a Consol Glass v. Twee Jonge Gezellen (Pty) Ltd* 2005 6 SA 1 (SCA).
833. *See Glaston House (Pty) Ltd v. Inag (Pty) Ltd* 1977 2 SA 846 (A); *Van der Merwe v. Meades* 1991 2 SA 1 (A); *Waller v. Pienaar* 2004 6 SA 303 (C); *Beyers NO v. Ackerman* [2007] 3 All SA 125 (C); *Ellis and Another v. Cilliers NO and Others* 2016 1 SA 293 (WCC). It will also not serve to exempt a seller from negligence or misrepresentation: *see Humphrys NO v. Barnes* 2004 2 SA 577 (C).
834. National Credit Act 35 of 2005, s. 90(2)(g).
835. Paragraphs 563 et seq.

§4. REMEDIES

559. In South African law, the seller has, in general, no special remedies when the purchaser breaches the contract by not paying the purchase price as agreed upon. However, in terms of insolvency legislation, certain special arrangements apply in cases of instalment sales.

560. Usually, the seller's remedies are construed in terms of the general principles of contract.[836] A brief summary of these remedies will suffice.

1. Before delivery: The seller may claim payment of the price against tender of delivery[837] plus damages, usually in the form of *mora* interest on the purchase price, but compensation for other damages, such as loss of profit, may also be claimed if it can be proven as a special loss. The seller may cancel the contract in the following circumstances: when the contract contains a cancellation clause; when cancellation is claimed in terms of the so-called double-barrelled procedure as an alternative to a claim for payment in case the purchaser does not comply with a court order to pay; when non-payment constitutes a breach that is serious enough – in the case of *mora debitoris*, when time is of the essence or is made of the essence; and in the case of repudiation when the repudiation relates to the whole or a substantial part of the duty to pay and the seller elects to cancel. The seller may also claim damages as set out above.
2. After delivery: The remedies for the unpaid seller aimed at fulfilment and at cancellation as set out above also apply here. When the seller cancels the sale, he or she will in addition be entitled to the return of the thing sold and delivered. When the sale is for cash and ownership has not passed, despite delivery, or when ownership has been reserved for the seller, he or she will obtain return by instituting a *rei vindicatio*,[838] even against persons other than the purchaser. In other circumstances, the seller may obtain return by way of a general duty of restitution, which is a consequence of cancellation. This entails the return of the price or any part of it that has been received by the seller, subject to any valid forfeiture clause that might be a part of the contract.[839]

561. In terms of the Insolvency Act 24 of 1936 (as amended), the common law right of the seller of goods for cash to vindicate his or her property has basically

836. But cf. the provisions of the National Credit Act 35 of 2005 on remedies for breach of an instalment-sale by a consumer: ss 129 et seq.

837. Sale is of course a reciprocal contract. When the seller reasonably believes that the purchaser will be unable to pay the price, he or she may, in the absence of security to be provided by the purchaser, well be justified in refusing to take the necessary steps to enable him or her to deliver. Cf. *Hayne v. Narun Bros* 1926 OPD 207; *Moodley v. Moodley* 1990 1 SA 427 (D). This possibility will not be construed in terms of a lien in favour of the seller.

838. Delay in instituting the claim may create an estoppel against the seller.

839. *See Botha and Another v. Rich NO and Others* 2014 4 SA 124 (CC) for an example of a forfeiture clause that was held to be unconstitutional and unenforceable on the grounds that it would constitute a penalty that was disproportionate to the breach. In this case, the clause would have required the purchaser, who had paid more than 75% of the purchase price of land in terms of an instalment sale, to forfeit all payments already made.

been re-enacted for situations in which the purchaser receives delivery but becomes insolvent before having paid the price in full (section 36). However, the seller must give written notice of his or her claim within ten days after delivery. In terms of section 84 of the Insolvency Act, when goods have been delivered in terms of an instalment-sale agreement, the agreement is regarded, upon the insolvency of the purchaser, as creating a hypothec over the property in favour of the seller, whereby the amount still due is secured. The seller may claim delivery of the goods to him or her, to hold as security for his or her claim.

In addition to the ordinary common law remedies available to purchasers and sellers, parties to a consumer contract of sale may seek recourse from the institutions created by the Consumer Protection Act and the National Credit Act, most importantly, the National Consumer Commission and the National Consumer Tribunal.

§5. Product Liability

562. As has been indicated above, South African law has developed an adequate arsenal of remedies enabling the purchaser to recover damage caused by a defective product, but only against the seller of the product.

563. In principle, South African law is well-equipped to develop *Aquilian* delictual liability as a basis for liability of a manufacturer for harm caused to a consumer or a third party by a defective product.[840] The courts' apparent reluctance to broaden liability for harm caused by defective products can be attributed to the fear of creating limitless liability and causing a multiplicity of actions.

564. Thus, to recover damage for loss (either physical or purely economic) caused by a defective product in terms of common law, a claimant would have to prove all the elements of a delict.[841]

The elements that are mostly at issue are the following:

1. Wrongfulness may be constituted by the production (and making available to the market) of a defective article that causes damage to any person. A product will be defective if it is unreasonably dangerous or does not meet the standards of safety reasonably expected with respect to such a product by consumers. The state of technical and scientific knowledge at the time of manufacture is a factor to be considered.
2. Fault, usually in the form of negligence, will be present when the damage was reasonably foreseeable and preventable by the manufacturer. Abnormal or

840. The problem of liability for pure economic loss negligently caused has ceased to exist since 1979 – *see Administrateur, Natal v. Trust Bank van Afrika Bpk* 1979 3 SA 824 (A); cf. also the development of liability for negligent misstatements *in contrahendo* referred to above.

841. *See* in general P.Q.R. Boberg, *The Law of Delict*, vol. 1, 193 et seq. (Juta 1984); J. Neethling, J.M. Potgieter & P.J. Visser, *Law of Delict* 322 et seq. (Butterworths 2001); *Bayer South Africa (Pty) Ltd v. Viljoen* 1990 2 SA 647 (A); *A Gibb & Son (Pty) Ltd v. Taylor & Mitchell Timber Supply Co. (Pty) Ltd* 1975 2 SA 457 (W).

careless use of the product by the consumer excludes fault.[842] An inference of fault by making use of the principle of *res ipsa loquitur* is also possible in South African law, but this is subject to policy considerations and will be applied restrictively only when the facts of the case give rise to an inference of fault – the presumptions against the manufacturer that exist in Anglo-American law do not arise, nor is the onus of proof shifted in any other way.

3. The usual test for causation discussed elsewhere in this work, namely a factual test supplemented by a legal test that limits liability for factual consequences (eventually perhaps by means of the requirement of reasonable foreseeability), will be applied in this context.

No special periods of prescription apply: the usual time limit within which a claim for damages will prescribe is three years from the date when the debt becomes due, that is, when the claimant acquires knowledge of the identity of the debtor and of the facts from which the claim arises.

565. The legislature has recently taken steps to extend product liability so as to protect consumers from 'hazards to their well being and safety'.[843] Thus, the Consumer Protection Act 68 of 2008 grants consumers a right to 'fair value, good quality and safety', which includes liability for damage caused by goods. The Act extends liability not only to producers, but also to importers, distributors, retailers, and suppliers of services who install or give access to goods.[844] Such parties will be strictly liable[845] for harm caused wholly or partly by supplying unsafe or defective goods,[846] product failure, defects or hazards, or inadequate instructions or warnings.[847] The harm in question includes death, injury, illness of a person,[848] loss or damage to any property, and economic loss resulting from any of these.[849] Liability is excluded in certain circumstances, for example, where the lack of safety did not exist at the time of delivery of the goods in question, or where it would be unreasonable to expect the distributor or retailer to have found out about the lack of safety.[850]

842. In *A Gibb & Son (Pty) Ltd v. Taylor & Mitchell Timber Supply Co. (Pty) Ltd* 1975 2 SA 457 (W), the duty to inspect the goods was, in the circumstances, held to rest on the consumer and not on the supplier – the damage was thus not reasonably foreseeable and preventable.

843. *See* the Preamble to the Consumer Protection Act 68 of 2008. On the general purposes of the Act and its scope of application, *see* para. 233 above.

844. Section 61(1) and (2).

845. And jointly and severally liable if there is more than one party: s. 61(3).

846. This includes used goods: *Vousvoukis v. Queen Ace CC t/a Ace Motors* 2016 3 SA 18 (ECG).

847. Section 61(1).

848. According to the court in *Halstead-Cleak v. Eskom Holdings Ltd* 2016 2 SA 141 (GP), protection under the Act extends not only to consumers who have a contractual relationship with the supplier, but also to injured third parties; in this case a cyclist who suffered injury when he collided with the supplier's low-hanging live power line.

849. Section 61(5).

850. Section 61(4).

§6. SALE ON INSTALMENTS

566. The sale of goods on instalments[851] is regulated in South Africa by common law and the National Credit Act 34 of 2005, which came into operation in stages between June 2006 and June 2007.

567. The National Credit Act, which repealed the Credit Agreements Act[852] and the Usury Act,[853] applies to credit transactions, which by definition include instalment-sale transactions.[854] An instalment-sale agreement is defined by the National Credit Act[855] as an agreement in terms of which movable goods are sold in exchange for the payment of a price (all or part of which is deferred) in periodic instalments, and payment of interest or other charges. In addition, the parties must agree that the consumer will be given possession immediately, and ownership will either be transferred to the consumer immediately, provided that in such a case the credit provider will have a right to repossess the property if the consumer breaches any financial obligations, or only when the consumer has complied with all the terms of the agreement.

The Act applies to all instalment sales except those concluded by the State, an organ of the State or a juristic person with an asset value or annual turnover of ZAR 1 million or more; those for whom the credit provider is the Reserve Bank; and certain 'large agreements' (i.e., with a principal debt of ZAR 250,000 or more)[856] concluded by a consumer who is a juristic person.[857]

In general, credit providers must register with the National Credit Regulator to validly enter into instalment-sale agreements;[858] an instalment-sale agreement concluded by an unregistered credit provider will be unlawful,[859] and a court is obliged to declare it void with retrospective effect.[860] As a consequence of such a declaration, the credit provider would have to return any payments already made by the consumer, together with interest. In contrast, the credit provider will have no right to reclaim any money or goods from the consumer unless the court decides that this would 'unjustly enrich' the consumer, in which case the money or goods must be forfeited to the State.[861]

Except where the consumer is a juristic person,[862] a credit provider must not conclude a credit agreement until he or she has taken 'reasonable steps' to assess the consumer's 'general understanding and appreciation of the risks and costs of the

851. The sale of land on instalments is regulated by ch. 2 of the Alienation of Land Act 68 of 1981.
852. Act 75 of 1980.
853. Act 73 of 1968.
854. Section 8(4).
855. Section 1 q.v. *See Voltex (Pty) Ltd v. Chenleza CC* 2010 5 SA 267 (KZP); *Ribeiro and Another v. Slip Knot Investments 777 (Pty) Ltd* 2011 1 SA 575 (SCA).
856. Section 9(4) read with Government Notice 713 of 1 Jun. 2006.
857. Section 4, read with Government Notice 713 of 1 Jun. 2006.
858. Section 40(1). *See*, for example, *Paulsen and Another v. Slip Knot Investments 777 (Pty) Ltd* 2014 4 SA 253 (SCA).
859. Section 89(2)(d).
860. Section 89(5).
861. Section 89(5).
862. Section 78(1).

proposed credit, and of the rights and obligations of a consumer under a credit agreement', his or her previous credit record, and his or her present creditworthiness. If the credit provider does not take these steps, he or she will be guilty of granting 'reckless credit', and the consumer's rights and duties under the contract may be set aside or the entire credit agreement may be suspended.[863]

Also prior to concluding a credit agreement, the credit provider must give the consumer certain documents, disclosing, *inter alia,* any payments to be made by the consumer, including payment of interest and other charges.[864] The credit provider is not allowed to charge for these or for any other documents that he or she is obliged to provide to the consumer.[865]

Once the agreement has been concluded, the credit provider must provide the consumer with a free copy of the credit agreement in writing, either on paper or in printable electronic form.[866] This written document must contain certain information, such as the personal particulars of the parties, a detailed breakdown of the consumer's financial obligations in the form of a table, and various statutory rights and duties.[867] Subject to certain exceptions, the consumer has a right to receive this document (as well as any other information provided by the credit provider) in the official language of his or her choice,[868] and the document must be expressed in plain and understandable language.[869] Failure to comply with these requirements, however, apparently does not affect the validity of the contract and does not amount to an offence.[870]

The inclusion of certain clauses is prohibited by the National Credit Act. For example, the parties may not include a clause exempting the seller from liability for latent defects, for eviction,[871] for misrepresentation,[872] or for the acts, omissions, or representations of its representatives.[873] Certain forfeiture clauses[874] are prohibited, as are clauses that require a consumer to deposit any of his or her identity documents or a bank card with the credit provider.[875] Similarly prohibited are clauses that have the aim or effect of defeating the purpose or policies of the Act or of deceiving the consumer,[876] clauses that purport to deprive a consumer of his or her

863. *See* ss 80 et seq.
864. Section 92.
865. Section 65(3).
866. Section 93(1).
867. *See* s. 93(2) and Regulations 30 and 31 of 31 May 2006. Also see T. Naudé, *Law of Purchase and Sale*, Annual Survey S. African L. 239, at 242 (2006).
868. Section 63.
869. Section 64. It has been held that interpreting sections 63 and 64 strictly does not assist an illiterate consumer and that they should therefore be interpreted purposively to mean that the consumer should be 'informed by reasonable means of the material terms of the documents he signs': *Standard Bank of South Africa Ltd v. Dlamini* 2013 1 SA 219 (KZD).
870. T. Naudé, *Law of Purchase and Sale*, Annual Survey S. African L. 239, at 242 (2006).
871. Section 90(2)(g).
872. Section 90(2)(h)(i).
873. Section 90(2)(g).
874. Section 90(2)(i).
875. Section 90(2)(l).
876. Section 90(2)(a).

statutory rights or certain of his or her common law rights,[877] and clauses that purport to evade the credit provider's statutory duties or any other provision of the Act.[878] All such unlawful clauses are void.[879] A court faced with a credit agreement containing any such clause must either sever it from the agreement or modify it so as to render it lawful, or it must declare the entire agreement to be unlawful.[880]

The National Credit Act also grants consumers certain statutory rights. For example, the Act also provides for a 'cooling-off' period when the contract was signed by the purchaser at a place other than the seller's place of business. Accordingly, the purchaser may, within five days after the conclusion of the contract, cancel the contract unilaterally by notice.[881] Further examples include the consumer's right to settle a debt in advance[882] or to surrender the goods for sale in settlement of any outstanding debt.[883]

The Act sets out detailed rules regarding the remedies[884] available to a credit provider in the case of a breach by a consumer. Thus, the credit provider must first notify the consumer of his or her default and advise him or her on steps that he or she could take to resolve the dispute. The credit provider cannot take steps against the consumer for at least ten days after delivery of the notice and for twenty days after the breach occurred.[885]

877. Section 90(2)(c).
878. Section 90(2)(b).
879. Section 90(3).
880. Section 90(4).
881. Section 121.
882. Section 125.
883. Section 127.
884. *See* T. Naudé, *Law of Purchase and Sale*, Annual Survey S. African L. 239, at 243 (2006), and J.M. Otto, *The National Credit Act Explained* 87–88 (Butterworths LexisNexis 2006).
885. Sections 129 et seq.

Chapter 5. Letting and Hiring of Work and Building Contracts

§1. Definition

568. In terms of a contract of letting and hiring of work (*locatio conductio operis*), a person (the *locator,* more usually called an 'independent contractor')[886] undertakes to perform a piece of work (*opus*) for another (the *conductor*, often, though less precisely, called the 'employer'), in exchange for remuneration by the latter.[887] The work may be physical or intellectual. Examples of such contracts are contracts to transport persons or goods,[888] to construct a building or a bridge, to repair a car or other property,[889] to connect electricity, and to audit a company's books.

§2. Letting and Hiring of Work Distinguished

569. The contract of letting and hiring of work should be distinguished from certain other specific contracts. It differs from the other two types of letting and hiring (*locatio conductio*) in regard to the subject matter of the contract, namely that which is 'let out'.[890] Unlike an employee in terms of a contract of employment, an independent contractor is not subject to the other contractant's control. Also, an employer is vicariously liable for the delict of his or her employees, but not for those of his or her independent contractors.[891] Although he or she occupies a position similar to that of an employee, an independent contractor is not, by virtue of the

886. On the definition of a subcontractor, *see Street Pole Ads Durban (Pty) Ltd v. Ethekwini Municipality* 2008 5 SA 290 (SCA) 298 G.

887. *See Wille's Principles of South African Law* 941–947 (F. du Bois ed., Juta 2007); *The Law of South Africa* vol. 2 part 1, paras 457 et seq. (W.A. Joubert ed., 2d ed., Butterworths 2003); P. Ramsden, *McKenzie's The Law of Building and Engineering Contracts and Arbitration* (Juta 2014).

888. In this regard, *see Wille's Principles of South African Law* 967–982 (F. du Bois ed., Juta 2007) and the sources cited there.

889. *See* the Consumer Protection Act 68 of 2008 for provisions that seek to protect an employer (who falls within the definition of a consumer) who concludes a contract for the repair or maintenance of his or her property. Section 15, for example, requires a contractor to provide a consumer in advance with an estimate of the costs involved, failing which the contractor will generally not be allowed to charge for the maintenance or repairs. The service provider may not charge for preparing the estimate unless he or she and the consumer have in advance agreed on a price for doing so. Having provided an estimate, the supplier may not charge a higher price unless the consumer has in advance agreed thereto. Section 57 imposes a warranty on the contractor for every new or reconditioned part installed during repair or maintenance work, and the labour required to install it, for a period of at least three months after the date of installation. This warranty is void if the consumer misuses or abuses the part or the property in which it was installed. It also does not apply to ordinary wear and tear and exists alongside any other implied or express warranty. According to s. 67, a contractor who is authorized to make repairs is generally obliged to return to the consumer any parts or components removed from the property in the course of the repairs, unless the consumer declined the return thereof.

890. *Locatio conductio operarum:* contract of employment; *locatio conductio rei*: contract of letting and hiring a thing. *See* R. Zimmermann, *Law of Obligations* 338 et seq. (Juta 1990).

891. *See*, for example, *Wille's Principles of South African Law* 941 (F. du Bois ed., Juta 2007); *Pienaar v. Brown* 2010 6 SA 365 (SCA).

contract of letting and hiring of work, an authorized representative of the other contractant. The parties could, however, agree that the contractor should also act as such.

§3. Building Contracts

570. The most common, and most highly developed, example of a contract of letting and hiring of work is a building contract.[892] This is a contract in terms of which a contractor is to construct a building or other 'works' for the other contractant or owner of the land in exchange for money.

Although it is not required by law that a building contract be in writing, unless the building is to be a dwelling in terms of the Housing Consumers Protection Measures Act,[893] parties almost always reduce their agreement to writing and require that it be signed. Architects' plans and specifications and quantity surveyors' bills of quantities are often made part of the contract.

The contract is governed by the general principles of the law of contract, and, apart from some implied terms,[894] the contents are determined by the parties. It has become customary, however, to include certain standard clauses in building contracts relating to large works. Examples include the following: that the work shall be done under the supervision of an architect or an engineer, or both; that the contractor will be entitled to be paid for the work only if the architect finds it satisfactory and indicates such satisfaction by issuing a certificate to that effect; that the contractor may refer to arbitration[895] a dispute that relates, for example, to the architect's withholding a certificate; that the work be completed within a specified time; that if, for reasons within the contractor's control, the work is not completed timeously, he or she will be liable for a specified amount of money per day or week after the due date.

571. The main duties of the *conductor* in terms of a building contract are to grant the contractor possession of the site until the work has been completed; to pay the contractor upon completion of the work, unless the parties have agreed otherwise;[896] and, if the parties have not specifically agreed on the amount of remuneration, to pay a reasonable price for the work.

---

892. *See* P. Ramsden, *McKenzie's The Law of Building and Engineering Contracts and Arbitration* (Juta 2014) for an example of a standard building contract as recommended by the different organized interest groups in the building industry. *See also* E. Finsen, *The New Building Contract* (Juta 1991); E. Finsen, *The Building Contract: A Commentary on the JBCC Agreements*, (2d ed., Juta 2006).

893. Act 95 of 1998.

894. *See* para. 577 below on the implied terms prescribed by the Housing Consumers Protection Measures Act.

895. For an account of the South African law of arbitration, *see* P. Ramsden, *McKenzie's The Law of Building and Engineering Contracts and Arbitration* (Juta 2014).

896. It is usual in most contracts, even with respect to small works, to provide for payment to the contractor upon completion of specified stages of the work. Cf., for example, *Graham NO v. Williams Hunt (Pty) Ltd* 1995 1 SA 371 (D) 374 C–D: in a contract of *locatio conductio operis*, '[p]ayment for the work is dependent upon its proper completion. Save to the extent that the contract otherwise provides, payment does not become due until completion of the works'.

When the contractor has performed defectively and he or she can satisfy the court that the other contractant is using the defective performance, and also that it would be equitable for the court to do so, the court may relax the principle of reciprocity and require the owner to pay the contractor a smaller amount than the amount originally agreed upon as remuneration. The payment of this smaller amount (which also has to be proven by the contractor with reference to the cost of rectifying the imperfect performance) is based upon the contract and not upon unjustified enrichment.[897]

572. The contractor's duties are to complete the work in accordance with the contract and any incorporated plans and specifications in a proper or good and competent manner,[898] applying reasonable skill and using materials of a reasonable quality or of the specified quality.[899] If the other contractant supplies the materials, the contractor will not be responsible for any defects in the materials, unless the other party sought his or her opinion as to their quality. In the latter case, the contractor will not be able to claim payment for the work, unless he or she can show that he or she informed the other contractant of the risk of using those materials.[900] Further, the contractor must complete the work timeously (by the date agreed upon by the parties or, in the absence of such an agreement, within a reasonable time) unless he or she is delayed by the other contractant or his or her agent, or by *vis maior* or *casus fortuitus*.[901] Finally, the contractor must deliver the work after completion, by restoring possession of the site to the other party. The contractor has a lien *(ius retentionis)* by which he or she can enforce payment of the full contract price – he or she can thus retain possession of the site until the contract price has been paid.[902]

573. Work performed by the contractor that does not comply with the standards and quality as required by the contract (in other words, defective work), amounts to breach of contract. In such a case, the other contractant can withhold (further) payment until the work is completed properly, subject to what was stated above in regard to the payment of a lesser amount. The usual remedies for breach of contract (positive malperformance in this case) are available to the other contractant. He or

897. *See BK Tooling (Edms) Bpk v. Scope Precision Engineering (Edms) Bpk* 1979 1 SA 391 (A) and the discussion of reciprocity and the *exceptio non adimpleti contractus* above.
898. If this duty is not expressly agreed upon by the contractants, it may well be that a tacit term to that effect can be inferred. In this respect the objective elements of the test for inferring a tacit term may more readily lead to such an inference. Any reference to the presence of an implied term (in the sense of being implied by law) does not seem to be supported by authority, and must probably be understood as referring to a tacit term. *See SM Goldstein and Co. (Pty) Ltd v. Cathkin Park Hotel (Pty) Ltd* 2000 4 SA 1019 (SCA) 1024 for a recent consideration by the Appeal Court of the duty to carry out the work with a view to safety.
899. The question whether the contractor is strictly liable under all circumstances, or whether he or she can ever rely on absence of fault does not appear to have been settled. For a discussion of the general considerations regarding this question, *see* the section on breach of contract and the requirement of fault.
900. *See The Law of South Africa* vol. 2 part 1, para. 474 (W.A. Joubert ed., 2d ed., Butterworths 2003).
901. *See The Law of South Africa* vol. 2 part 1, paras 471 et seq. (W.A. Joubert ed., 2d ed., Butterworths 2003).
902. *See The Law of South Africa* vol. 2 part 1, para. 486 (W.A. Joubert ed., 2d ed., Butterworths 2003).

she may cancel the contract and claim damages, or claim only damages, or, in certain limited circumstances, claim specific performance.[903]

574. The parties may regulate the allocation of risk[904] by an agreement. In the absence of a different agreement by the parties, the allocation of risk depends on whether the performances regarding the work are divisible or indivisible. If the performance of the work is divisible in the sense that the work is to be done by the contractor in stages or parts, the other contractant bears the risk of damage or loss regarding the completed parts of the work.

If the performance of the work is indivisible (even if the corresponding duty is to pay in instalments), the contractor bears the risk of any damage or loss, including the risk caused by *vis maior* that occurs before the work has been completed. The risk shifts to the owner upon completion of the work. In either case, if the parties have agreed that the contractor should maintain the completed work for a period, he or she bears the risk during that maintenance period.

575. No privity of contract exists between any subcontractors and the other contractant, who therefore has no contractual remedies against a subcontractor. Similarly, a subcontractor generally cannot sue the other contractant for payment of the contract price.[905]

576. The Housing Consumers Protection Measures Act[906] seeks to protect consumers who conclude contracts for the construction of homes. The Act provides for the establishment of a National Home Builders Registration Council so as to regulate the building industry,[907] to protect and promote the rights of 'housing consumers', and to assist with the resolution of disputes. A home builder cannot receive or claim payment[908] for constructing a dwelling, and is guilty of an offence, unless he was registered as a home builder with the National Home Builders Registration Council prior to commencement of construction.[909] The Act also prescribes formalities for the validity of building contracts, and states that certain warranties relating to quality will be deemed to be a part of every contract covered by the Act, and that such warranties may not be excluded by agreement.

---

903. In *Rens v. Coltman* 1996 1 SA 452 (A) (at 458 et seq.), it was held that, as it would be unfair to insist that the date for assessing damages should be the date of performance, particularly with regard to building contracts, the appropriate date should be the date on which it would have been reasonable for the plaintiff to have begun repairs.

904. On the question of risk, *see*, in general, *The Law of South Africa* vol. 2 part 1, para. 483 (W.A. Joubert ed., 2d ed. Butterworths 2003).

905. *See* the discussion above on privity of contract and subcontracting. *See also Minister of Public Works and Land Affairs v. Group Five Building Ltd* 1999 4 SA 12 (SCA).

906. Act 95 of 1998.

907. The Act provides, *inter alia*, for the registration of builders (s. 10). On the interpretation of the Act in this regard, *see Hubbard v. Cool Ideas* 1186 CC 2013 5 SA 112 (SCA) paras 13–14; *Cool Ideas 1186 CC v. Hubbard and Another* 2014 4 SA 474 (CC) paras 29–37.

908. Whether via the law of contract or the law of unjustified enrichment: *see Cool Ideas 1186 CC v. Hubbard and Another* 2014 4 SA 474 (CC) paras 38 ff.

909. *See Cool Ideas 1186 CC v. Hubbard and Another* 2014 4 SA 474 (CC) paras 29–37. The underlying building contract will nevertheless be valid, in order to protect the consumer and the builder regarding what has already been performed under the contract: *see* paras 47 ff.

Chapter 6. Lease

577. In terms of a contract of lease[910] (*locatio conductio rei*), one party (the lessor) agrees to provide another (the lessee) with temporary use and enjoyment of a thing, and the latter agrees to pay money in exchange for such use.

578. Although there are some special additional rules relating to particular kinds of lease (such as long leases and rural leases,[911] leases of dwellings,[912] and leases of movables),[913] the principles outlined below relate to all leases.

---

910. *See* in general, *The Law of South Africa* vol. 14, 1st re-issue, paras 154–217 (W.A. Joubert ed., Butterworths 1999);, *Wille's Principles of South African Law* 906–923 (F. du Bois ed., Juta 2007); G. Glover, *Kerr's The Law of Sale and Lease* (LexisNexis 2014); W.E. Cooper, *The South African Law of Landlord and Tenant* (Juta 1994).

911. With regard to the question whether urban tenants are, like rural tenants, prohibited from claiming a lien for improvements to leased property, *see Business Aviation Corporation (Pty) Ltd and Another v. Rand Airport Holdings (Pty) Ltd* 2006 6 SA 605 (SCA). Regarding labour tenants, *see* the Land Reform (Labour Tenants) Act 3 of 1996.

912. For example, certain formalities are required for a long lease of land to be effective vis-à-vis third parties: *see* the Formalities with respect to the Leases of Land Act 18 of 1969. Leases of property for housing purposes are covered by the Rental Housing Act 50 of 1999, which, *inter alia,* forbids the landlord to discriminate unfairly in advertising or negotiating a lease agreement (s. 4(1)), to invade the privacy of the tenant (s. 4(2–3)), or to terminate the lease except when such termination does not amount to an 'unfair practice' as defined in the Act (s. 4(5)). It also states that certain terms are deemed to have been included in any such lease (e.g., that the landlord will provide written receipts for payments received from the tenant; that the landlord and tenant must inspect the property prior to occupation and prior to termination with a view to ascertaining defects or damage; that the deposit must be deposited in an interest-bearing account at a financial institution and the balance thereof be repaid together with interest) (s. 5(3)). These terms cannot be waived by either party (s. 5(4)). It has been held that lessees of land are also protected as occupiers in terms of the Prevention of Illegal Eviction from and Unlawful Occupation of Land Act 19 of 1998 (*see Ndlovu v. Ngobo* 2003 1 SA 113 (SCA)); and, in the case of persons with a low income living on agricultural land, the Extension of Security of Tenure Act 62 of 1997 (*See*, for example, *Van Zyl v. Maarman* 2001 1 SA 957 (LCC) 963 E–G and 964 E–F; *Molusi and Others v. Voges NO and Others* 2016 3 SA 370 (CC)). It has been held that he owner of property, on the other hand, may be regarded as an unlawful occupier in terms of the the Prevention of Illegal Eviction from and Unlawful Occupation of Land Act 19 of 1998 if he or she occupies the property without the consent of the party who is 'in charge' of the property: *Hendricks v. Hendricks and Others* 2016 1 SA 511 (SCA). On the impact of the Constitution on lease agreements, *see Brisley v. Drotsky* 2002 4 SA 1 (SCA); *Mpange v. Sithole* 2007 6 SA 578 (W); *Malan v. City of Cape Town* 2014 6 SA 315 (CC); T. Roux, *Continuity and Change in a Transforming Legal Order: The Impact of s. 26(3) of the Constitution on South African Law*, S. African L. J. 121, 466 (2004).

913. The National Credit Act 34 of 2005 governs leases of movable property, which fall within the Act's definition of 'credit agreements'. As a consumer, a lessee of movables is thus afforded the general protection extended to consumers by the Act. In particular, such a lessee is entitled to insist on receiving a statement of account from the lessor at least every two months (s. 108); in cases in which a lease of movables is concluded anywhere other than at the lessor's business premises, the lessee has five days within which he or she may terminate the lease, either by notice to the lessor or by offering to return the leased goods (s. 121); and the lessee may terminate the lease of movables by written notice to the lessor, returning to the lessor the goods in question and paying any outstanding amounts demanded by the lessor (s. 122, read with s. 127). On the distinction between a lease and a credit agreement, *see ABSA Technology Finance Solutions (Pty) Ltd v. Michael's Bid A House CC and Another* 2013 3 SA 426 (SCA).

§1. EVIDENCE

579. Writing is not a requirement for the validity of a contract of lease,[914] but the parties may reduce the contract to writing so as to facilitate proof, or they may agree that writing will be a formal requirement for the validity of their contract.

§2. FORMATION OF A CONTRACT OF LEASE

580. To create a contract of lease, the parties must agree that the lessor will deliver to the lessee a corporeal thing (whether movable or immovable) that is identified or identifiable with sufficient certainty; that the lessee will be entitled to use and enjoy[915] the thing temporarily (until a certain or determinable date, or even indefinitely, but not in perpetuity); and that the lessee will pay rent in money[916] to the lessor.[917] The parties may expressly or tacitly agree on the amount, or they may agree upon a method for determining the amount (e.g., that a specified third party will decide the amount of rent to be paid).[918]

581. The terms set out above are essential terms for the creation of a lease as such. If the agreement does not contain all these terms, it may still be a contract, but it will not be a lease.[919] Thus, for example, if the parties omit an undertaking to pay rent, the contract could be one of loan for use (*commodatum*).

914. Unless it amounts to a credit agreement as defined in s. 8 of the National Credit Act 34 of 2005 (i.e., when it is a lease of movable property). Section 93 of the Act stipulates that, in such a case, the agreement must be written in the prescribed form, and it must be transmitted to the consumer on paper or in a printable electronic form. Should these provisions be contravened, the lease will not be void unless it is declared to be unlawful by a court (s. 164(1)). Also see s. 5 of the Rental Housing Act 50 of 1999: while leases of such premises need not be in writing, the landlord must reduce the agreement to writing upon the request of the tenant.

915. That is, the lessee will have the *ius utendi* and the *ius fruendi* but not the *ius abutendi* with respect to the property.

916. Except when the contract is a rural lease, in which case the rent may take the form of yield or produce of the property.

917. On the *essentialia* of a contract of lease, *see Ferndale Crossroads Share Block (Pty) Ltd and Others v. Johannesburg Metropolitan Municipality and Others* 2011 1 SA 24 (SCA). Leases, like all other contracts, are subject to the general requirement of legality. Thus a contract of lease that was concluded between parties with unequal bargaining power may be declared invalid if the situation of inequality was harmful to the public interest: *see Uniting Reformed Church, De Doorns v. President of the Republic of South Africa and Others* 2013 5 SA 205 (WCC) at 215E-F.

918. *The Law of South Africa* vol. 14, 1st re-issue paras 154–158 (W.A. Joubert ed., Butterworths 1999); *Wille's Principles of South African Law* 907 (F. du Bois ed., Juta 2007). *See*, for example, *Southernport Developments (Pty) Ltd v. Transnet Ltd* 2005 2 SA 203 (SCA).

919. Cf. *Southernport Developments (Pty) Ltd v. Transnet Ltd* 2005 2 SA 203 (SCA).

§3. Duties of the Lessor

582. The lessor is obliged by law (as natural consequences of the contract of lease) to deliver the leased property to the lessee, to maintain the property,[920] and to ensure undisturbed enjoyment by the lessee (or, as it is often put, to guarantee against eviction).[921]

The duty to deliver the leased property entails that the lessor (who may or may not be the owner of the property) must provide the lessee with *vacua possessio* or undisturbed occupation of the property, together with anything that is essential for its use and enjoyment.[922] The lessor is obliged to deliver the leased property in the condition in which it was when the parties entered into the agreement,[923] and he or she is obliged to maintain it in that condition for the duration of the lease.

The duty to ensure undisturbed enjoyment of the property by the lessee entails that the lessor himself or herself must not disturb the lessee's use or enjoyment of the property. It is, however, lawful to do so in order to inspect the property that is let[924] and in order to effect repairs that are reasonably necessary.[925]

The lessor must also protect the lessee from interference by any party who has a superior title to the lessor. If, however, the lessee's use or enjoyment is disturbed by a party who does not have a superior title to the lessor, the lessee is responsible for protecting himself or herself against such interference; for example, by using the remedies available to a possessor (such as an interdict or a spoliation order). If it becomes impossible to fulfil the duty to prevent eviction because of *vis maior* or *casus fortuitus*, the lessee's duty to pay rent is diminished proportionately.

A lessee who has been in occupation of the premises but who has not been afforded the full use and enjoyment of the premises may withhold the payment of rent.[926]

---

920. It appears that this obligation may be enforced by an order of specific performance: *see Mpange v. Sithole* 2007 6 SA 578 (W) (obiter).

921. For further detail, *see*, for example, *The Law of South Africa* vol. 14, paras 159 et seq. (W.A. Joubert ed., Butterworths 1999); A.J. Kerr, *The Law of Sale and Lease* 263 et seq (Butterworths 2004).

922. For example, the landlord has a duty to ensure that the premises are safe for human occupation: *see Swinburne v. Newbee Investments* 2010 5 SA 296 (KZD) at 312H.

923. It seems that the lessor also has a duty to compensate the lessee for any loss caused by defects in the property that were known to him or her or that should have been known to him or her, except in circumstances in which the lessee was aware of the defect(s) and accepted the risk of their causing loss – *see* A.J. Kerr, *The Law of Sale and Lease* 294–307 (Butterworths 2004).

924. Subject to the provisions of the Rental Housing Act 50 of 1999, especially s. 4, which protects the privacy of the tenant.

925. The lessee's right not to have its possession disturbed by the lessor may also be limited by agreement: *see*, e.g., *Sweets from Heaven (Pty) Ltd v. Ster Kinekor Films (Pty) Ltd* 1999 1 SA 796 (W); *Hyprop Investment v. Sophia's Restaurant* 2012 5 SA 220 (GSJ).

926. *See Ntshiqa v. Andreas Supermarket* 1997 3 SA 60 (Tk) and *Thompson v. Scholtz* 1999 1 SA 232 (SCA) 246 et seq.; cf. *Arnold v. Viljoen* 1954 3 SA 322 (C). This right derives from the *exceptio non adimpleti contractus*. The landlord may thus claim a reduced rental.

§4. Duties of the Lessee

583. The lessee is obliged by law to pay rent, to use the leased property in a proper manner, and to return the property upon expiry of the lease.[927]

In the absence of an agreement to the contrary by the parties, the rent is payable in arrears. The lessee must take reasonable steps to pay by the due date. The rent must be paid at the place stipulated by the parties or, if no place has been agreed upon, wherever the lessor is if a date for payment has been agreed upon, or wherever the lessee is if no date for payment has been agreed upon. The risk that the rent may be received after the due date because of failure of the means of transmission lies with the lessee, unless the lessor stipulated or consented to the means of transmission.[928]

584. One of the *naturalia* of a contract of lease is that the lessor has a tacit hypothec for the payment of rent.[929] The hypothec covers all movables (*invecta et illata*),[930] including those owned by a sub-lessee or other third parties in certain circumstances.[931] The hypothec only exists while rent is actually in arrears and if the movables are present on the property. It ceases to exist when the movables are removed from the property. The hypothec does not give rise to a real right, but, after attachment and sale of the movables in execution of a judgment by a court, the lessor has the status of a preferred creditor in regard to the proceeds.

585. Should the landlord of a dwelling demand an 'exploitative rental', the tenant may make a complaint to a rental-housing tribunal, which may order the landlord to discontinue this unfair practice.[932] The tribunal also has the power to make a ruling regarding the rental to be paid, taking into account all the relevant circumstances.[933]

586. The duty to use the leased property in a proper manner entails that it may be used only for the purpose for which it was expressly or tacitly leased. The lessee

927. For more detail, *see* A.J. Kerr, *The Law of Sale and Lease* 318 et seq. (Butterworths 2004). Should the lessee refuse to vacate the leased premises on cancellation of the lease, the lessor will be entitled to damages for the lessee's 'holding over'. Such damages need not be limited to market-related rental for such premises: *see Hyprop Investments Ltd and Another v. NCS Carriers and Forwarding CC and Another* 2013 4 SA 607 (SCA).

928. A lessor's claim for arrear rental is a claim for specific performance, not a claim for damages: *Director-General, Department of Public Works v. Kovacs Investments 289* 2010 6 SA 646 (GNP), 648G-I.

929. For further detail, *see*, for example, *The Law of South Africa* vol. 14, 1st re-issue paras 181 et seq. (W.A. Joubert ed., Butterworths 1999); A.J. Kerr, *The Law of Sale and Lease* 346 et seq. (Butterworths 2004). Regarding the lease of housing, cf. s. 4(3)(c) of the Rental Housing Act 50 of 1999, which grants the tenant the right not to have his or her possessions seized, 'except in terms of law of general application and having first obtained an order of court'.

930. Fruit and crops produced on land are also subject to the hypothec.

931. *See* J.S. McLennan, *A Lessor's Hypothec Over the Goods of Third Parties: Anomaly and Anachronism, S. African Mercantile L. J.* 16, 121 (2004); A.J. Van der Walt & N.S. Siphuma *Extending the Lessor's Tacit Hypothec to Third Parties' Property*, S. African L. J. 518 (2015).

932. Rental Housing Act 50 of 1999, s. 13(4).

933. Rental Housing Act 50 of 1999, s. 13(5).

must exercise the standard of care of a *bonus paterfamilias*. There is a rebuttable presumption that any damage caused to the property during the existence of the lease is a result of the lessee's negligence.

587. Upon expiry of the lease, the leased property must be returned in the condition in which it was at the beginning of the lease, except for reasonable wear and tear.

§5. Assignment, Cession, and Subletting

588. Assignment of a contract of lease[934] may only take place with the cooperation of the lessor. In the absence of an agreement to the contrary by the parties, the lessee is generally[935] permitted to cede his or her rights in terms of the contract or to sublet the property. If the lessee cedes his or her rights or concludes a sublease in contravention of a contractual prohibition, it amounts to a breach that would justify cancellation. Cession of the lessee's rights will not affect the duties that he or she owes to the lessor. A contract of sublease does not give rise to a contractual relationship between the original lessor and the sub-lessee.

§6. Duration of a Lease

589. In general, a lease may be terminated by the parties in the same way as any other contract. A lease may also come to an end automatically upon the date fixed for termination, or upon the expiry of the period of the lease on which the parties may have agreed. Under certain circumstances, a lease may be terminated by notice of termination given by either party,[936] as in the case of a lease that is to continue indefinitely and in terms of which the rent is paid periodically. The notice must be

934. That is, a cession of the lessee's rights and a delegation of his or her duties to a third party, effecting the substitution of a new lessee for the old one. The concepts of cession, delegation, and assignment are discussed in more detail earlier in this work.
935. Except when the lease is a rural one.
936. Also *see*, however, the sources referred to under para. 579 above. The Prevention of Illegal Eviction from and Unlawful Occupation of Land Act 19 of 1998 applies not only to persons who illegally occupy land, but also to those who were previously lawfully in possession (e.g., under a lease) but whose possession has become unlawful (e.g., through cancellation resulting from a breach of a lease agreement). A number of additional procedural requirements posed by the Act must therefore be met before a landlord may eject an occupier protected by the Act. Section 4 (5) of the Rental Housing Act 50 of 1999 also circumscribes the landlord's right to terminate the lease by notice: in this regard, *see Maphango v. Aengus Lifestyle Properties (Pty) Ltd* 2012 3 SA 531 (CC) and s. 4(5)(c) of the Act, which states that a landlord has the right to 'terminate the lease in respect of rental housing property on grounds that do not constitute an unfair practice and are specified in the lease'. The Extension of Security of Tenure Act 62 of 1997 imposes similar limitations on the landlord's right to terminate a lease of agricultural land by notice: *see*, for example, *Molusi and Others v. Voges NO and Others* 2016 3 SA 370 (CC). A lease of public housing may not be terminated on notice alone; it must be for good cause: *see Malan v. City of Cape Town* 2014 6 SA 315 (CC) para. 64.

communicated to the other party.[937] If no specific or determinable notice period was agreed upon, notice must be given for a reasonable time before the moment of termination indicated in the notice. The period of notice will be reasonable if it allows the other party sufficient time to make suitable alternative arrangements, and, as a rule, this will be accepted to be equal to the period with respect to which the periodic payment of rent must be made. There is, however, no general requirement that the termination itself should be fair or reasonable in the circumstances.[938]

590. An agreement in terms of which one party gives the other permanent use of property will not be a lease.

§7. Renewal of a Lease

591. The parties may expressly agree, prior to or upon termination of the lease in due course, that the lease will be 'renewed', that is, replaced by a new lease. This new lease may contain terms that differ from the terms of the previous lease. If the parties agree to extend their lease, without excluding any terms of the lease, terms that are 'collateral, and not incident to' the lease will also be extended, unless the terms are such that it is clear that the parties could not have intended their extension.[939] Where a lease has been renewed on a month to month basis, the question whether the lease will be terminated by giving a month's notice, or by giving reasonable notice, is a matter of interpreting the intention of the parties as expressed in the extension agreement.[940]

592. Even if the parties did not expressly agree on renewal, the lease may be renewed tacitly. Tacit renewal (or 'tacit relocation') may occur when, after expiry of the original lease, the lessee continues to occupy the property and to pay the rent,

937. But the notice could be communicated via a pleading or an application: *see Win Twice Properties (Pty) Ltd v. Binos and Another* 2004 4 SA 436 (W).

938. *Maphango v. Aengus Lifestyle Properties (Pty) Ltd* 2011 5 SA 19 (SCA), paras 22–25. It may, however, amount to an 'unfair practice' under the Rental Housing Act 50 of 1999: (*see Maphango v. Aengus Lifestyle Properties (Pty) Ltd* 2012 3 SA 531 (CC)) or, with respect to occupiers of agricultural land, the Extension of Security of Tenure Act 62 of 1997 (*see Molusi and Others v. Voges NO and Others* 2016 3 SA 370 (CC)). A court may order the eviction of unlawful occupiers in terms of s. 4(7) of the Prevention of Illegal Eviction from and Unlawful Occupation of Land Act 19 of 1998, provided that it is 'just and equitable' to do so, taking into account all the relevant circumstances. (*See*, for example, *Johannesburg Housing Corporation (Pty) Ltd v. Unlawful Occupiers, Newtown Urban Village* 2013 1 SA 583 (GSJ); *Arendse v. Arendse and Others* 2013 3 SA 347 (WCC)).

939. *Mokone v. Tassos Properties CC and Another* [2017] ZACC 25; 2017 (10) BCLR 1261 (CC); 2017 (5) SA 456 (CC) para. 36.

940. *Airports Company South Africa Soc Ltd v. Airports Bookshops (Pty) Ltd t/a Exclusive Books* [2016] ZASCA 129; [2016] 4 All SA 665 (SCA); 2017 (3) SA 128 (SCA).

and the lessor accepts this position. The new lease will be on the same terms as the original lease,[941] save that it will probably be regarded as continuing for an indefinite period.[942]

§8. Nature of the Lessee's Right

593. With respect to a lease of immovable property (land and anything attached to land), the lessee may acquire a real right with respect to the leased property.[943] The real right entitles the lessee to personally enforce his or her rights against anyone; for example, against a person who trespasses on the property, against anyone who has a personal right with respect to the property and who attempts to exercise his or her right in conflict with the lessee's rights in terms of the contract of lease, or against anyone who obtains a real right in the property after conclusion of the lease and who attempts to exercise his or her right in conflict with the lessee's rights in terms of the lease.

594. An example of the latter situation occurs when someone purchases leased immovable property from the original lessor and subsequently attempts to evict the lessee while the lease is still in operation. The rule *huur gaat voor koop* (lease prevails over sale), which has been inherited from Roman-Dutch law and is part of modern South African law, is applicable to this situation. The rule even applies in certain circumstances when the lessee was not in occupation of the property at the time of the sale.[944] The purchaser will be bound by the lease if he or she had actual notice of the lease,[945] or if the lease is registered against the title deed of the property in the office of the Registrar of Deeds. By virtue of the rule, the purchaser is substituted as lessor in the place of the seller-lessor, and he or she acquires the same rights and duties as the previous lessor. It follows that the mere fact that the lessor has sold the leased property does not give the lessee an option to terminate the lease for that reason only.[946]

941. Cf. *Mokone v. Tassos Properties CC and Another* [2017] ZACC 25; 2017 (10) BCLR 1261 (CC); 2017 (5) SA 456 (CC).
942. *See*, for example, A.J. Kerr, *The Law of Sale and Lease* 402–407 (Butterworths 2004). *See also* s. 4(5) of the Rental Housing Act 50 of 1999: 'If on the expiration of the lease the tenant remains in the dwelling with the express or tacit consent of the landlord, the parties are deemed, in the absence of a further written lease, to have entered into a periodic lease, on the same terms and conditions as the expired lease, except that at least one month's written notice must be given of the intention by either party to terminate the lease.'
943. In general, *see* F. du Bois, *Wille's Principles of South African Law* 908 et seq. (Juta 2007).
944. If the tenant is not in occupation of the premises, however, he has, not a real right, but merely a personal right against the landlord which will terminate if the premises are transferred to a bona fide purchaser: *see Metcash Seven Eleven (Pty) Ltd v. Pollev Property Holding and Investment CC* 2013 4 SA 506 (GSJ) at 512.
945. Even if the lessee was not in occupation of the leased premises: *see Metcash Seven Eleven (Pty) Ltd v. Pollev Property Holding and Investment CC* 2013 4 SA 506 (GSJ).
946. This is of particular importance when a lessor sells the leased property to a property developer who wishes to retain the lessee as such. *See Genna-Wae Properties (Pty) Ltd v. Medio-Tronics (Natal) (Pty) Ltd* 1995 2 SA 926 (A).

595. The lessee's real right does not arise from the contract of lease, which, like all contracts, creates only personal rights. The real right arises either from occupation of the property or from registration of the lease.[947]

Up to the first ten years of any lease of immovable property, a lessee acquires the real right as a consequence of his or her occupation of the leased property. A lease for ten years or more (a 'long lease') creates a real right for the lessee if the lease is registered. Registration is, however, not a requirement for the validity of the lease.

947. Cf. *Reddy v. Decro Investments CC t/a Cars for Africa* 2004 1 SA 618 (D).

Chapter 7. Compromise

596. Compromise, also called 'settlement' or *transactio*, has been defined as follows:

> Compromise ... is an agreement between the parties to an obligation, the terms of which are in dispute, or between the parties to a lawsuit, the issue of which is uncertain, settling the matter in dispute, each party receding from his previous position and conceding something, either diminishing his claim or increasing his liability.[948]

Compromise is thus an agreement[949] in terms of which the parties to a dispute recede from their original positions so as to settle a dispute. The compromise terminates any disputed obligation[950] already in existence.[951] It cannot, however, properly be construed as a form of novation.[952] According to the weight of legal opinion, a compromise in regard to a dispute that has become the subject of litigation has the effect of res judicata.[953] Accordingly, and also because a compromise is not based upon the existence of a valid original cause of action,[954] a party who is sued on a compromise may not raise a defence with respect to any original cause of action.[955]

948. *See Tauber v. Von Abo* 1984 4 SA 482 (E) 485. In general, *see also*, Van Huyssteen, Lubbe & Reinecke, *Contract General Principles* paras 13.45–13.51 (Juta 2016); J.C. de Wet & A.H. van Wyk, *Die Suid-Afrikaanse Kontraktereg en Handelsreg*, vol. 1, 5th edn (Durban: Butterworths, 1992), 266–272.
949. For a discussion of the law of reasonable reliance as it applies in this context, and the construction of payment of a cheque 'in full and final settlement' as an offer to compromise, *see Be Bop A Lula Manufacturing & Printing CC v. Kingtex Marketing (Pty) Ltd* 2008 3 SA 327 (SCA).
950. Whether arising from a contract or any other cause of action: *see*, for example, *Hamilton v. Van Zyl* 1983 4 SA 379 (E); *Road Accident Fund v. Ngubane* 2008 1 SA 432 (SCA).
951. *See* Van Huyssteen, Lubbe & Reinecke, *Contract General Principles* para. 13.49 (Juta 2016) (but see para. 13.47 n. 190 for an exception).
952. Because a valid original obligation is not a prerequisite for compromise and because, in view of the required uncertainty, it is doubtful whether *animus novandi* would be present: *see* Van Huyssteen, Lubbe & Reinecke, *Contract General Principles* para. 13.47 (Juta 2016). That a compromise does not constitute a novation of the original obligation is illustrated by *New Port Finance Co (Pty) Ltd and Another v. Nedbank Ltd* 2016 5 SA 503 (SCA), in which it was held that a compromise does not alter the original obligation (and therefore does not affect a surety's liability in relation to that obligation). But cf. *Wille's Principles of South African Law* 839 (F. du Bois ed., Juta 2007). *See also Karson v. Minister of Public Works* 1996 1 SA 887 (E); *Benefeld v. West* 2011 2 SA 379 (GSJ) at 383B-D.
953. Cf. Van Huyssteen, Lubbe & Reinecke, *Contract General Principles* para. 13.49, at n. 198 (Juta 2016).
954. *See*, for example, *Syfrets Mortgage Nominees Ltd v. Cape St Francis Hotels (Pty) Ltd* 1991 3 SA 276 (SE).
955. *See Road Accident Fund v. Ngubane* 2008 1 SA 432 (SCA); *Benefeld v. West* 2011 2 SA 379 (GSJ). In the latter case, the court stated (at 383C) that compromise 'is a substantive contract that exists independently of the original cause. In the case of a novation, the original invalid contract taints the novated contract, but a compromise is not affected by the validity of the original obligation'. The fact that the original contract was *contra bonos mores*, and therefore void, did not affect the validity of the compromise.

597. The general principles of the law of contract in regard to mistake, misrepresentation, duress, undue influence or other grounds for rescission, and breach of contract also apply to compromise.[956] Whether a mistake relating to a compromise is material and thus renders the compromise void for dissensus, or whether it is a mistake in motive that does not affect the creation of a valid compromise, is often a difficult factual question. For the mistake to be material, it must relate to the content of the agreement of compromise itself,[957] and not to the dispute that the parties intend to settle. However, it could well be that the parties to the compromise make some aspect of their dispute a common supposition upon which the compromise is based. If the supposition turns out to be ill-founded, the compromise fails and falls away.[958]

956. *See* the references cited in Van Huyssteen, Lubbe & Reinecke, *Contract General Principles* paras 13.48 and 13.51 (Juta 2016); *Wille's Principles of South African Law* 839 (F. du Bois ed., Juta 2007).

957. *See* J.C. de Wet & A.H. van Wyk, *Die Suid-Afrikaanse Kontraktereg en Handelsreg*, vol. 1 (Durban: Butterworths, 1992), 270, at n. 106; *Turbo Prop Service Centre CC v. Croock t/a Honest Air* 1997 4 SA 758 (W).

958. *See* Van Huyssteen, Lubbe & Reinecke, *Contract General Principles* para. 13.48, at n. 194(Juta 2016) and the sources referred to there.

Chapter 8. Suretyship

§1. Nature of Suretyship

598. Suretyship (*fideiussio*) is a contract in terms of which one party (the 'surety') agrees with the creditor of another (the debtor) that he or she (the surety) will fulfil the debtor's obligation to the creditor if the debtor fails to do so.[959] The debtor remains bound in terms of the original obligation (called the 'principal' obligation); the surety's obligation does not replace the principal obligation but is merely accessory to it.

The principal debtor is not a party to the contract of suretyship and may, in fact, have no knowledge of it. One can stand surety for a surety, by way of a so-called rear suretyship (*achterborg).*

§2. Requirements for Validity

599. A contract of suretyship must comply with all the general requirements for a valid contract.[960] In addition, the terms of the contract must be reduced to writing, and the contract must be signed by the surety or someone on his or her behalf.[961] The suretyship contract depends on the existence of a valid principal obligation;[962] the suretyship will thus be void if the principal obligation itself is void. The general

959. *See* in general *The Law of South Africa* vol. 26, 1st re-issue, paras 189 et seq. (W.A. Joubert ed., Butterworths 1997); *Wille's Principles of South African Law* 1018 et seq. (F. du Bois ed., Juta 2007); C.F. Forsyth & J.T. Pretorius, *Caney's The Law of Suretyship in South Africa* (Juta 2002); R. Zimmermann & D. Visser, *Southern Cross: Civil Law and Common Law in South Africa* 417 et seq. (Juta 1996).

960. Like any other contract, suretyship may be based on consensus, or on one party's reasonable reliance on the appearance of consensus (quasi-mutual assent): *see*, for example, *Slip Knot Investments 777 (Pty) Ltd v. Du Toit* 2011 4 SA 72 (SCA). Again like any other contract, a suretyship agreement is unaffected by any misrepresentation made by a third party (viz. anyone other than the surety or the creditor): *Slip Knot Investments 777 (Pty) Ltd v. Du Toit* 2011 4 SA 72 (SCA). Where the surety is married in community of property, his or her spouse must consent to the suretyship unless the suretyship was undertaken in the course of the surety's business, trade or profession: *see* s. 15 of the Matrimonial Property Act 88 of 1984; *Strydom v. Engen Petroleum Ltd* 2013 2 SA 187 (SCA).

961. *See* s. 6 of the General Law Amendment Act 50 of 1956, as amended. Amendments to the original deed must also comply with the formalities: *see African Life Property Holdings (Pty) Ltd v. Score Food Holdings Ltd* 1995 2 SA 230 (A). If the parties leave out an essential term, the contract will be void; if they leave a blank space in the document instead of a non-essential term, one must look to the intention of the parties; should they have deliberately omitted that term, the contract will be valid; should they have omitted an agreed term by mistake, the contract will be void for want of compliance with the formal requirements posed by s. 6 of the Act: *see Nedbank Ltd v. Wizard Holdings (Pty) Ltd* 2010 5 SA 523 (GSJ); *Airports Company South Africa Ltd v. Masiphuze Trading (Pty) Ltd and Others* [2018] ZAKZDHC 22.

962. *See Heathfield v. Maqelepo* 2004 2 SA 636 (SCA). The principal obligation may be a civil or a natural obligation: C.F. Forsyth & J.T. Pretorius, *Caney's The Law of Suretyship in South Africa* 187 et seq. (Juta 2002); *Wille's Principles of South African Law* 1018 (F. du Bois ed., Juta 2007).

requirement of legality, as expressed in terms of public policy and interest,[963] is of particular relevance to contracts of suretyship. There may often be a serious imbalance of bargaining power between the creditor and the surety that may lead to a contract that overprotects the interests of the stronger party to the unreasonable disadvantage of the weaker party.

A contract of suretyship falls within the definition of a 'credit guarantee' in terms of the National Credit Act[964] if the principal debtor amounts to a 'consumer', as defined by the Act, and the principal debt arises from a credit facility or credit transaction that is governed by the Act.[965] Sureties to such agreements are protected by the Act in various ways. For example, if a surety is regarded as having recklessly provided credit, a court may suspend or set aside his or her obligations.[966] Common law still governs all suretyship agreements that do not fall under the National Credit Act.

§3. Termination

600. Suretyship is terminated by the payment or prescription of the debt. The surety's obligation may also be terminated if the creditor materially alters the principal obligation to the prejudice of the surety.[967]

963. *See*, for example, the minority judgment of Olivier JA in *Eerste Nasionale Bank van Suidelike Afrika Bpk v. Saayman* 1997 4 SA 302 (HHA), and his judgment in *Brisley v. Drotsky* 2000 4 SA 1 (HHA). *See also Sasfin (Pty) Ltd v. Beukes* 1989 1 SA 1 (A) and the discussion on legality in Part I above.
964. Act 34 of 2005.
965. Section 8(5) of the Act. The Act therefore does not apply to an agreement in terms of which credit is granted to a juristic person with an annual turnover of more than ZAR 1 million, the state or an organ of state: *see*, for example, *Structured Mezzanine Investments v. Davids* 2010 6 SA 622 (WCC). If the parties mistakenly think that the Act applies to their agreement, where it is in fact inapplicable, their error will not render the Act applicable: *see RMB Private Bank (A Division of FirstRand Bank Ltd) v. Kaydeez Therapies CC (in Liquidation) and Others* 2013 6 SA 308 (GSJ) (but cf. *First National Bank, A Division of FirstRand Bank Ltd v. Clear Creek Trading 12 (Pty) Ltd and Another* 2014 1 SA 23 (GNP)).
966. Sections 80 and 81 of the Act.
967. *See Fry v. First National Bank of South Africa Ltd* 1996 4 SA 924 (C); *Jans v. Nedcor Bank Ltd* 2003 6 SA 646 (SCA); *Bilsbury v. Standard Bank of SA Ltd (Stannic Division)* 2006 3 SA 60 (E). But cf. *ABSA Bank Ltd v. Davidson* 2000 1 SA 1117 (SCA) 1124 I–J, in which it was held that 'prejudice caused to the surety can only release the surety (whether totally or partially) if the prejudice is the result of a breach of some or other legal duty or obligation'. A surety cannot be said to have been prejudiced, and therefore cannot rely on this defence, if he or she authorized the allegedly prejudicial conduct in question: *see Bock v. Duburoro Investments (Pty) Ltd* 2004 2 SA 242 (SCA) and J.T. Pretorius, *Prejudice and the Surety*, S. African Mercantile L. J. 17, 381 (2005). The liability of a surety is unaffected by any compromise entered into by the principal debtor (such as one entered into by a company in business rescue): *New Port Finance Co (Pty) Ltd and Another v. Nedbank Ltd* 2016 5 SA 503 (SCA).

§4. Effect of Suretyship Between the Creditor and the Surety

601. The surety is obliged to perform to the creditor only if the debtor fails to do so when performance falls due. When called upon to perform, the surety may claim the benefit of excussion (*beneficium excussionis sue ordinis*)[968] – that is, the creditor first exhausts any legal remedies that he or she has against the principal debtor. In certain circumstances, this benefit will not be available to the surety, for example, when he or she has renounced it, as is common practice.[969]

The surety may raise against the creditor any defences in rem (defences not personal to the debtor)[970] that the principal debtor could have used.

If there are several sureties with respect to the same debt, and only one is sued by the creditor, that surety may claim the benefit of division (*beneficium divisionis*) unless he or she has expressly or impliedly renounced it. The benefit of division implies that the surety will only be liable for a proportionate amount of the debt.

602. Further protection is provided to the surety in that a deed of suretyship is to be restrictively interpreted and that any ambiguity should be resolved in favour of the surety.[971]

§5. Effect of Suretyship on the Relationship Between the Debtor and the Surety

603. A surety who has performed has recourse against the principal debtor, whether or not the latter had knowledge of the suretyship and whether or not the surety performed voluntarily. The surety's claim against the principal debtor can include the amount of the surety's performance to the creditor, any expenses arising from the suretyship, and any loss suffered by the surety.

There are various mechanisms for enforcing this right of recourse. Thus, the surety may, in terms of the benefit of cession of actions (*beneficium cedendarum actionum*), claim from the creditor cession of the creditor's rights against the principal debtor, thereby obtaining the right to sue the debtor. Then again, the surety may bring against the debtor an action based on an implied mandate, provided that the debtor had consented to the suretyship, or, if the debtor had not given such consent, the surety may sue the debtor with an *actio negotiorum gestorum*.

968. Cf. *Asco Carbon Dioxide Ltd v. Lahner* 2005 3 SA 213 (N).
969. C.F. Forsyth & J.T. Pretorius, *Caney's The Law of Suretyship in South Africa* 125 (Juta 2002). When a surety accepts liability as 'surety and principal (co-principal) debtor', he or she renounces the benefit of excussion.
970. For an explanation of the distinction between defences in personam and defences in rem in this context, *see Investec Bank v. Bruyns* 2012 5 SA 430 (WCC), 435.
971. *See*, for example, *HNR Properties CC v. Standard Bank of SA Ltd* 2004 4 SA 471 (SCA).

§6. EFFECT OF SURETYSHIP BETWEEN CO-SURETIES

604. If one of several co-sureties is sued for payment of a debt, he or she may claim the *beneficium divisionis*, namely that his or her liability should be limited to a proportionate share of the debt. If a co-surety has already performed the entire debt, he or she may sue the other co-sureties for their proportionate shares. Normally, the co-surety may sue once he or she has obtained cession by virtue of the *beneficium cedendarum actionum*, or when the sureties had agreed on a right of recourse. There is, however, support for the view that a right of recourse may even be available to a paying co-surety in the absence of such cession or agreement when the sureties had guaranteed the debt in a single instrument or independently of one another, even when they were unaware of the fact that there were co-sureties. The basis for the right of recourse in such circumstances may be a tacit or even an implied term flowing from the guarantee, or more generally, that it is equitable in the circumstances so as to avoid unjust enrichment.[972]

972. *See The Law of South Africa* vol. 26, 1st re-issue, para. 190 (W.A. Joubert ed., Butterworths 1991); J.C. de Wet & A.H. van Wyk, *Die Suid-Afrikaanse Kontraktereg en Handelsreg*, vol. 1 (Durban: Butterworths, 1992), 400.

Chapter 9. Pledge

§1. Meanings of Pledge

605. The term 'pledge'[973] (*pignus*) has various meanings in South African law. It may refer to a *contract*, as a consequence of which a right of real security[974] is created with respect to a movable thing,[975] to the *movable property* in question, or to the *limited real right of security* thus created. The last meaning is the most common – the hypothecatory aspect of the relationship between the parties (which is dealt with as part of the law of property) is usually emphasized rather than the contractual aspect.

§2. Definition and Requirements of a Pledge Contract

606. In general, a pledge contract is an agreement in terms of which the owner of, or in some circumstances the holder of a limited real right in, a movable asset (the 'pledgor') undertakes to give possession of the asset to the pledgee, thereby creating real security for a valid obligation between the pledgee and the pledgor or a third party. The pledge contract is thus accessory to the principal obligation.

607. The distinctive and essential requirement of a contract of pledge (other than the general requirements for all contracts) is that the parties manifest the intention to create a real right of security in a movable asset for the performance of a principal obligation. It is not required that the contract be in writing.

§3. Duties of the Pledgor

608. The pledgor's primary duty arising by operation of law (as a *naturale*) out of a contract of pledge is to constitute the pledge. This is achieved by delivering the movable asset.[976] Although the subject matter of a pledge is usually a corporeal thing, personal rights as incorporeal assets may also be pledged by way of a cession *in securitatem debiti.* [977]

973. *See* in general *Wille's Principles of South African Law* 643–651 (F. du Bois ed., Juta 2007); *The Law of South Africa* vol. 17, paras 406 et seq., especially paras 417 et seq. (W.A. Joubert ed., 2d ed., Butterworths 2008).
974. As opposed to personal security by suretyship.
975. Real security with respect to immovable property is called mortgage.
976. The delivery may be either actual or constructive.
977. *See* the discussion earlier in this work on the question of the construction to be placed on cession to provide security.

§4. Who May Pledge?

609. In general, only the owner of the movable property in question may constitute a pledge to it, assuming that he or she has the capacity to act. Someone who has a limited real right with respect to property may pledge the property but may not grant a right greater than his or her own (*nemo plus iuris transferre potest quam ipse haberet*).

§5. Terms of a Pledge Contract

610. In principle, the terms of a contract of pledge depend on the agreement between the parties. With certain exceptions, the *naturalia* of a pledge may be varied by the parties by their agreement. For example, a clause in terms of which the ownership of the pledged property will pass to the pledgee automatically if the pledgor does not fulfil the principal obligation (called a *pactum commissorium*) will be invalid.[978] An example of a variation of *naturalia* that will be valid is a clause that creates a right for the pledgee to resort to a private sale of the pledged property to satisfy the principal obligation, without going through a court process. The normal rule (as a *naturale* of the contract) is that the pledgee may only sell the pledged property with the cooperation of the court.[979]

§6. Duties of the Pledgee

611. The pledgee has a duty to take care of the asset while it is in his or her possession.[980] Subject to an agreement to the contrary by the parties, the pledgee must act like a *bonus paterfamilias* with respect to the pledged property.

612. The pledgee must return to the pledgor the property and its fruits when the pledge is terminated by fulfilment of the principal obligation. He or she must also compensate the pledgor for any loss caused by the destruction or deterioration of the pledged assets due to his or her fault.[981]

§7. Rights of the Pledgee

613. Normally, the pledgee does not have the right to use and enjoy the property and its fruits, but the parties may agree to the contrary.

614. The pledgor remains the owner of the pledged property, but the pledgee is entitled to compensation for expenses incurred in maintaining the property.

978. *The Law of South Africa* vol. 17, para. 427 (W.A. Joubert ed., 2d ed., Butterworths 2008).
979. Such a clause would be invalid if it were contained in a mortgage bond.
980. *The Law of South Africa* vol. 17, para. 426 (W.A. Joubert ed., 2d ed., Butterworths 2008).
981. *Ibid.*

615. The pledgor may not grant other real rights with respect to the pledged property. If someone else subsequently acquires possession of the pledged property, the pledgee has a limited right to 'follow up on' the property. His or her right is limited by the rule *mobilia non habent sequelam ex causa hypothecae*, so that he or she may not follow up on the property if he or she has voluntarily relinquished possession in favour of another. He or she may, however, reclaim the property if he or she lost possession involuntarily.

616. The pledgee has the right to use the proceeds from the sale of the pledged property to settle the principal obligation. This claim with respect to the property has preference over the claims of other creditors.

§8. Termination of a Pledge

617. The main grounds for termination of the real right of a pledge are the extinction of the principal obligation, destruction of the pledged property, voluntary dispossession of the pledgee, and the sale in execution of the pledged property.

In recent years, it has become common for micro-lenders to insist that borrowers pledge a bank card or an identification document as security for a loan. Possession of a bank card, together with the personal identification code, enables the micro-lender to withdraw cash from the borrower's bank account in repayment of the loan. Without an identification document, it is difficult to claim State benefits, such as pension payments, or to conduct any transactions for which identification is necessary. The legislature has sought to stop this iniquitous practice by means of legislation. In terms of the National Credit Act[982] and the Consumer Protection Act,[983] it is thus unlawful for a consumer to agree (in terms of a credit agreement[984] or any other transaction or agreement)[985] to deposit with a credit provider or a supplier[986] 'an identity document, credit or debit card, bank account or automatic teller machine access card, or any similar identifying document or device'. If such a provision appears in a credit agreement, a court may sever or alter the offending clause or declare the whole agreement to be unlawful, and it may make any order that would be just and reasonable in the circumstances.[987] Should such a term appear in any other agreement, it will be void.[988]

982. Act 34 of 2005, s. 90(2)(l)(i).
983. Act 68 of 2008, s. 51(1)(j)(i).
984. Section 90(1) of the National Credit Act.
985. Section 51(1) of the Consumer Protection Act.
986. Or with any other person at the direction of the credit provider or supplier.
987. Section 90(4) of the National Credit Act.
988. Section 51(3) of the Consumer Protection Act.

Chapter 10. Loan

618. In South African law, there are two types of loans: a loan for use (*commodatum*) and a loan for consumption (*mutuum*). A loan for use arises when parties agree that one party (the lender) gratuitously gives temporary use of a thing to the other (the borrower), who later returns exactly the same thing to the lender.[989] A loan for consumption may be created when the lender gives ownership and possession of some fungible thing (a thing that is consumed by the use to which it is put) to the borrower, who later delivers to the lender a thing of the same kind, quantity, and quality.[990]

§1. Loan for Use

619. The two main distinguishing features of a loan for use are that the contract is always gratuitous, and that the thing itself must be returned after a fixed or determinable time. If it is not gratuitous, the contract is not a loan for use, although it may be a different class of contract, such as letting or hiring, or an innominate contract. If the parties do not expressly or impliedly agree upon a specific time during which the thing should be returned, or upon the purpose for which the thing is lent (which relates to a determinable time in that the thing should be returned once this purpose has been fulfilled), the borrower may keep the thing for a reasonable period.

620. For the duration of the loan, the lender may not interfere with the borrower's use of the thing. Interference would amount to breach of contract. If the borrower is evicted by a third party who has a stronger title with respect to the thing, and he or she suffers loss as a consequence, the lender is liable to compensate for such loss. If any loss is caused by defects in the thing, and the lender was aware but the borrower was unaware of the defects, the lender is similarly liable for the loss.

621. The borrower may only use the thing loaned for the purpose for which it was lent. During the period of the loan, the borrower is required to exercise the care of at least a *diligens paterfamilias* in caring for the thing. Therefore, the borrower will be liable if the thing is damaged, lost, or destroyed as a result of his or her negligence, although, in general, the lender bears the risk of such damage, loss, or destruction. If the borrower uses the thing in a manner different from that agreed upon, and the thing is, as a result, lost, destroyed, or damaged, he or she will be liable for such loss or damage.

622. Since the borrower has a duty to return the thing in the condition in which it was received, he or she must maintain the thing and is liable for all normal expenses regarding such maintenance. The lender bears any special expenses.

989. *See*, generally, *Wille's Principles of South African Law* 948–956 (F. du Bois ed., Juta 2007) and *The Law of South Africa* vol. 15 part 2, (W.A. Joubert ed., 2d ed. Butterworths 2008).
990. *See*, generally, du Bois, *ibid.* 957–961 and Joubert, *ibid.*

§2. Loan for Consumption

623. A loan for consumption entails the giving of possession and the transfer of ownership of *res fungibiles*, namely things that can be measured, counted, or weighed (the most common example being money). Because ownership of the thing lent is transferred to the borrower, he or she bears the risk of loss, damage, or destruction of the thing. The loan need not be gratuitous, although this is usually the case.

624. The borrower is obliged to return a thing of the same quantity, kind, and quality as the thing borrowed after a fixed or determinable time, if such a time is agreed upon by the parties. If there is no agreement as to the period of the loan, the borrower must return the subject matter of the loan within a reasonable time.

625. In the case of a loan of money, the amount to be repaid is the exact amount in numerical terms originally lent: South African courts generally apply the principle of nominalism.[991] In the absence of an agreement to the contrary, the repayment must be in the currency of the place of repayment. If the sum repaid is in a different currency from that of the sum borrowed, the relevant exchange rate will be the rate on the date of repayment, unless the parties have agreed otherwise.

§3. Loan on Interest

626. In the case of a money loan, the parties may agree (expressly or tacitly) that an interest shall be paid. The rate or amount payable can be agreed upon by the parties or implied by law. A contract of loan that confers on the lender an exclusive discretion to vary the interest rate from time to time is valid, but the lender must exercise this discretion *arbitrio bono viri*.[992]

991. There is (at this stage of the development of the law) only tenuous support for the view that a significant change in the value of money may lead to an application of the principle of valorism, on the basis of the requirements of good faith or legality.

992. *ABSA Bank Ltd v. Lombard* 2005 5 SA 350 (SCA); *NBS Boland Bank Ltd v. One Berg River Drive CC and Others, Deeb and Another v. ABSA Bank Ltd, Friedman v. Standard Bank of SA Ltd* 1999 4 SA 928 (SCA). In the latter case, which dealt with a clause granting a mortgagor the unilateral discretion to vary the interest rate, the court held that such a contract would be voidable at the instance of the mortgagee if the discretion were not exercised *arbitrio bono viri*. The court did not decide (para. 30) whether a clause conferring an unfettered discretion would be valid. In terms of s. 103(4) of the National Credit Act 34 of 2005, a loan governed by the Act 'may provide for the interest rate to vary during the term of the agreement only if the variation is by fixed relationship to a reference rate stipulated in the agreement, which reference rate must be the same as that used by that credit provider in respect of any similar credit agreements currently being issued by it'.: s. 103(4).

627. The loan in question may be subject to the National Credit Act.[993] The parties may not agree to a rate of interest higher than any maximum interest rate prescribed by the relevant Minister in terms of the Act.[994] Should the parties do so, a court may declare their agreement or the clause in question to be unlawful and therefore void.[995] The parties may expressly or tacitly agree to the payment of compound interest.

628. The rate of interest implied by law in the absence of an agreement by the parties is prescribed by the Minister of Justice in terms of the Prescribed Rate of Interest Act.[996]

629. According to the *in duplum* rule, the amount of interest payable at any time[997] may not exceed the unpaid capital sum.[998]

993. Act 34 of 2005; *Friend v. Sendal* 2015 1 SA 395 (GP). On the question whether the Act will apply to an agreement where the statute is in fact inapplicable but the parties erroneously believe that it is applicable, *see RMB Private Bank (A Division of FirstRand Bank Ltd) v. Kaydeez Therapies CC (in Liquidation) and Others* 2013 6 SA 308 (GSJ) and *First National Bank, A Division of FirstRand Bank Ltd v. Clear Creek Trading 12 (Pty) Ltd and Another* 2014 1 SA 23 (GNP)).
994. Section 105. *See*, for example, *Structured Mezzanine Investments v. Davids* 2010 6 SA 622 (WCC).
995. Section 164(1).
996. Act 55 of 1975; *Thoroughbred Breeders' Association v. Price Waterhouse* 2001 4 SA 551 (SCA).
997. *Margo v. Gardner* 2010 6 SA 385 (SCA). The total amount of interest paid in the end may therefore exceed the unpaid capital sum, provided that the creditor never allows the *unpaid* interest to exceed that amount.
998. *See*, for example, *LTA Construction Bpk v. Administrateur, Transvaal* 1992 1 SA 473 (A); *Commercial Bank of Zimbabwe Ltd v. MM Builders and Suppliers (Pvt) Ltd* 1997 2 SA 285 (ZH); *Leech v. ABSA Bank Ltd* [1997] 3 All SA 308 (W); *F & I Advisors (Edms) Bpk v. Eerste Nasionale Bank van SA Bpk* 1999 1 SA 515 (SCA); *Sanlam Life Insurance Ltd v. South African Breweries Ltd* 2000 2 SA 647 (W). For a list of circumstances in which the *in duplum* rule does not apply, *see Verulam Medicentre (Pty) Ltd v. Ethekweni Municipality* 2005 2 SA 451 (D). Until recently, the application of the rule was suspended pendente lite (cf. *Standard Bank of South Africa Ltd v. Oneanate Investments (Pty) Ltd (in Liquidation)* 1998 1 SA 811 (SCA); *Margo v. Gardner* 2010 6 SA 385 (SCA)). This was changed by the Constitutional Court in *Paulsen and Another v. Slip Knot Investments 777 (Pty) Ltd* 2015 3 SA 479 (CC): the institution of legal proceedings to reclaim the debt does not affect the application of the *in duplum* rule.

Chapter 11. Contracts with the State

630. In principle, the state and its organs[999] have the capacity to contract, which power derives from either specific enabling legislation or the common-law prerogative of the state.[1000] The contractual capacity of the state and its organs is limited by the principle that it cannot enter into a contract that is wholly incompatible with the discretion conferred on it,[1001] nor can it abdicate its discretionary powers to others.[1002] In general terms, agreements with the state or organs of the state (and, indeed, many agreements between state organs) are governed by the ordinary rules and principles of common law and, very importantly, the requirements of the Constitution. Contracts with the state are enforceable as such against the state in an ordinary court of law, and the state is generally in the same position as any other party to a contract.[1003] There is no special administrative court in South Africa.

631. Some general rules and principles of common law gain special importance in relation to contracts with the state. Most importantly, the requirement that an agreement may not be inimical to the public interest will be in the foreground and will be directly and indirectly influenced by the Constitution, as will be discussed below. Also, for example, applicable legislation will be incorporated into particular contracts by operation of law, such as the terms of an expropriation ordinance into a contract to pay compensation. Public authorities cannot agree in advance not to exercise their discretionary powers for the public good, and any contract to such effect would be void or at least unenforceable as being against the public interest, if not void for infringing upon the Constitution. Insofar as it would be against the public interest to bind someone to a representation made by him or her, the doctrine of estoppel by representation would not operate. In state contracts, the process of offer and acceptance by which an agreement is to be reached usually takes place through the mechanism of tender,[1004] which is now (at least for certain contracts) directly governed by the Constitution and other legislation, as is discussed below.

999. It appears that the concept of 'organ' is widely interpreted also to include a limited company that renders a general service to the public and in which the government owns all the shares. *See Transnet Ltd v. Goodman Brothers (Pty) Ltd* 2001 1 SA 853 (SCA), but cf. *Katshwa and Others v. Cape Town Community Housing Co (Pty) Ltd and Four Similar Cases* 2014 2 SA 128 (WCC). How far the courts will extend the concept is unclear.

1000. *See Minister of Home Affairs v. American Ninja IV Partnership* 1993 1 SA 257 (A).

1001. *See President of the Republic of South Africa v. South African Rugby Football Union* 2000 1 SA 1 (CC).

1002. *See Government of the Province of the Eastern Cape v. Frontier Safaris (Pty) Ltd* 1998 2 SA 19 (A).

1003. *See* s. 1 of the State Liability Act 20 of 1957. Also see Part 2 of the Institution of Legal Proceedings against Certain Organs of State Act 40 of 2002 for requirements as to notice of proceedings, and service of process. In this regard, *see Director-General, Department of Public Works v. Kovacs Investments 289 (Pty) Ltd* 2010 6 SA 646 (GNP); *Nicor IT Consulting (Pty) Ltd v. North West Housing Corporation* 2010 3 SA 90 (NWM) and *Thabani Zulu v. Minister of Water Affairs* 2012 4 SA 91 (KZD).

1004. The tender amounts to an offer, which must be accepted unconditionally, otherwise it will amount to a counter-offer: *see Command Protection Services (Gauteng) (Pty) Ltd t/a Maxi Security v. SA Post Office Ltd* 2013 2 SA 133 (SCA).

632. Depending on the nature of the right involved, the fundamental rights in the Constitution have indirect and, less often, direct application between individuals. However, the fact that the state is a party to a contract will probably be an important factor to frame the argument that, since such a contract very often relates to the public domain, the Constitution should have direct horizontal application to such a contractual relationship.[1005] Thus, for example, when a state department acts in a discriminatory manner when negotiating a contract (other than one for goods or services), it may be argued that that conduct is an administrative act and, as such, directly justiciable in terms of the Constitution, which requires just administrative action.[1006] The injunction on the courts to develop the common law in accordance with the spirit, purport, and objects of the Constitution may well in this context also lead to more general and widely ranging restrictions on contractual freedom and a policing of the bargaining process, such as a limitation on the right to withdraw from negotiations,[1007] the necessity to provide reasons for a particular decision, or the imposition of delictual liability.[1008]

When an organ of the state wishes to procure goods and services, the contractual process (most often a tender system) is directly subject to section 217 of the Constitution, which prescribes a system 'which is fair, equitable, transparent, competitive and cost-effective'. In addition, the Constitutional requirement of just administrative action and other legislation apply.[1009] If, therefore, there are procedural irregularities or unfairness in awarding a tender, a court may review the contract and grant an order of invalidity. It may refer the contract back to the authority in question,[1010] or, in cases of serious irregularities, 'order that the tender be awarded to the bidder to whom, in the court's view, it should have been awarded, had a proper process been followed'.[1011] The court may even hold the responsible officials liable for costs in their personal capacities.[1012]

633. Some agreements display a combination of features that are both contractual and administrative to such an extent that they may be classified as

---

1005. Cf. *Baloro v. University of Bophuthatswana* 1995 4 SA 197 (BSC) 238–240.
1006. Section 33.
1007. Cf., for example, *KOPM Logistics (Pty) Ltd v. Premier, Gauteng Province, and Others* 2013 3 SA 105 (GNP) at para. 14.
1008. Cf. *Transnet Ltd v. Goodman Brothers (Pty) Ltd* 2001 1 SA 853 (SCA); and *see* Van Huyssteen, Lubbe & Reinecke, *Contract General Principles* paras 3.65–3.69(Juta 2016).
1009. Section 33 of the Constitution, the Promotion of Administrative Justice Act 3 of 2000 and the Preferential Procurement Policy Framework Act 5 of 2000. Cf. also *Claude Neon Ltd v. Germiston City Council* 1995 3 SA 710 (W) in which the Court held that a certain undertaking given by a deputy town clerk was an administrative act and that a subsequent refusal by the municipality to consider a late tender amounted to a failure of administrative justice within the meaning of s. 24 of the Constitution; *Transnet Ltd v. Goodman Brothers (Pty) Ltd* 2001 1 SA 853 (SCA) and the authority referred to there.
1010. *See*, for example, *Westinghouse Electric Belgium SA v. Eskom Holdings (Soc) Ltd and Another* 2016 3 SA 1 (SCA).
1011. *Mogale City v. Fidelity Security Services and Others* 2015 5 SA 590 (SCA) para. 21.
1012. *Gauteng Gambling Board v. Silverstar Development Ltd and Others* 2005 4 SA 67 (SCA) paras 28–29 and 38–40; *Mogale City v. Fidelity Security Services and Others* 2015 5 SA 590 (SCA) para. 21.

administrative-law agreements.[1013] Important examples of such administrative-law agreements are collective labour agreements, town-planning schemes, some service agreements (e.g., electricity supply agreements), employment contracts between officials and the state, and insurance and provident agreements in which the state is involved. Here, the Constitution may well have direct application.[1014]

634. In principle, debts owed by and to the state prescribe according to the usual rules, but different periods of prescription apply for some debts, as discussed earlier in this work.[1015]

1013. *See* M. Wiechers, *Administrative Law* 117–121 (Butterworths 1985); G.E. Devenish, K. Govender & D.H. Hulme, *Administrative Law and Justice in South Africa* 66–67 (Butterworths 2001).

1014. Cf. *Transnet Ltd v. Goodman Brothers (Pty) Ltd* 2001 1 SA 853 (SCA) and the authority referred to there.

1015. *See* Part 1 of the Institution of Legal Proceedings against Certain Organs of State Act 40 of 2002.

Chapter 12. Partnership

§1. Definition

635. Partnership may be defined as 'a legal relationship based on a contract between at least two ... persons, in which the parties agree to carry on a lawful enterprise in common, to which each contributes something of commercial value, with the object of making and sharing profits'.[1016] In terms of section 30 of the Companies Act 61 of 1973, no partnership for the purposes of carrying on business for gain and consisting of more than twenty persons could be formed.[1017] According to South African common law (which the courts regard as consistent in most respects with the English law of partnership), a partnership does not have a legal personality.[1018] The term 'partnership' is used to refer to both the contract creating the relationship and the relationship itself.

§2. Requirements

636. To create a relationship of partnership, the contract must comply with the following distinct requirements:[1019] the parties must intend to give rise to a relationship of partnership; each party must contribute something or undertake to contribute something to the partnership (e.g., money, work, or skill); the partnership business or endeavour must be for the joint benefit of the parties; and the object of the partnership must be to make and share profits. A clause in terms of which one partner is to receive all of the benefits and the other to bear the losses (a 'leonine partnership' or *societas leonina*) will not be valid and may even invalidate the entire agreement.[1020] It is not necessary for the parties to agree specifically to share the losses, but the fact that it is the net and not the gross profits that are shared means

1016. *Wille's Principles of South African Law* 1004–1005 (F. du Bois ed., Juta 2007). *See also* in general *The Law of South Africa* vol. 19, 1st re-issue, paras 252–320 (W.A. Joubert ed., Butterworths 1997); H.S. Cilliers et al., *Entrepreneurial Law* 9–51 (Butterworths 2003); J.C. de Wet & A.H. van Wyk, *Die Suid-Afrikaanse Kontraktereg en Handelsreg Handelsreg* (reprint) (Durban: Butterworths, 1979). It is also possible to conclude a domestic partnership (a so-called universal partnership) where partners are married, engaged or merely co-habiting. The *essentialia* of such a universal partnership are the same as for an ordinary commercial partnership: *see*, e.g., *Butters v. Mncora* 2012 4 SA 1 (SCA); *Pezzuto v. Dreyer* 1992 3 SA 379 (A), 390; *Ponelat v. Schrepfer* 2012 1 SA 206 (SCA).

1017. This provision has been omitted from the Companies Act 71 of 2008, which repealed Act 61 of 1973 and which came into force on 1 May 2011.

1018. The courts have consistently held that the partnership nevertheless has no legal personality, even though the legislature has introduced some rules that might suggest a legal personality, such as allowing a partnership to sue in its own name. Cf., for example, the National Credit Act 34 of 2005 and the Consumer Protection Act 68 of 2008, both of which include partnerships within their definitions of a juristic person. A company may constitute a quasi-partnership; in other words, it may function as a partnership: *see*, for example, *Apco Africa (Pty) Ltd v. Apco Worldwide Inc* 2008 (5) SA 615 (SCA).

1019. *See*, for example, *The Law of South Africa* vol. 19, paras 260 et seq. (W.A. Joubert ed., 2d ed. Butterworths 2006).

1020. *See* E. Kahn et al., *Kahn's Contract and Mercantile Law: A Source Book* vol. 2, 417 (Juta 1985).

that the losses will, in effect, be shared. A contract to share gross profits, that is, not taking losses into account, will not be a partnership.

637. No formalities are required for the formation of a partnership. It may even come into being tacitly as a result of the conduct of the parties.

§3. EFFECT

638. Upon creation of the partnership, each of the partners, by operation of law, becomes an authorized representative of the 'partnership'. A partner has a duty to act with utmost good faith in any transactions on behalf of the partnership. He or she must perform a share of the duties, as determined in the agreement or by law. Because a partnership as such is not a legal person, property held or used for purposes of the partnership business is owned by the partners in undivided shares.[1021] While the partnership is in existence, each of the partners is liable for the debts of the partnership *in solidum,* but a creditor of the partnership can only sue all of the partners together. After dissolution of the partnership, a creditor may claim the partnership's debts from any partner individually.[1022] The profits and losses are shared by the partners in proportion to the amount that each contributed to the partnership, or as otherwise agreed upon.[1023] It may be agreed that, vis-à-vis the other partners, one partner will not have to share in the losses; such an agreement would not, however, affect the partnership's creditors' right to hold each member liable *in solidum* for the partnership's liabilities.

§4. TERMINATION

639. A partnership will terminate in the following circumstances:[1024] when the number of partners increases to more than twenty subsequent to its formation;[1025] when the partners so agree; when the period for which the partnership has been created has expired, if such a period was agreed upon; when the undertaking for which the partnership was created has been completed; by notice of termination given by

1021. Corporeal movables brought into the partnership by a partner, or acquired subsequently by the partnership, automatically become 'partnership property'. Immovable property must be registered in the names of all the partners.

1022. Should one of the former partners reach a final settlement with a creditor, the other members of the former partnership will still be jointly and severally liable for any outstanding partnership debts: *see Geldenhuys v. East and West Investments (Pty) Ltd* 2005 2 SA 74 (SCA).

1023. A former partner has no proprietary claim to an asset owned by a partnership upon dissolution of the partnership. At most, he or she would be able to claim a proportionate share of the proceeds of the sale of such an asset when it amounts to an indivisible object: *see Carmel Trading Co. Ltd v. Commissioner, South African Revenue Service* 2008 2 SA 433 (SCA) 438 E–F.

1024. *See The Law of South Africa* vol. 19, paras 310 et seq. (W.A. Joubert ed., 2d ed., Butterworths 2006).

1025. But cf. para. 635 n. 2 above.

one of the partners;[1026] upon a change of membership or death of one of the partners; by an order of a court, as applied for by one of the parties for just cause; upon the insolvency of the partnership or one of the partners; or, in a situation of war, if one of the partners is an alien enemy who resides in enemy territory.[1027]

1026. *See Espag v. Hattingh* 2010 3 SA 22 (SCA), in which it was held that where one partner is asked by the rest to withdraw from the partnership on the basis of misconduct (in accordance with the terms of their contract), his partners do not thereby breach their duty to act in good faith, and he is not entitled to the application of the *audi alterem partem* principle.

1027. The dissolution of a partnership only has an effect vis-à-vis third parties when they receive notice of the dissolution, and the partners have a duty to inform third parties of such dissolution: *Koekemoer v. Langeberg Stene Bpk* 1999 1 SA 361 (NC).

Chapter 13. Quasi-Contracts

§1. INTRODUCTION

640. As has been already explained, 'quasi-contract' is not a term of art in South African law.[1028] The main type of 'quasi-contract', unjustified enrichment, is dealt with as a distinct branch of the law of obligations. The specific actions[1029] by means of which a party can reclaim an amount by which another has been unjustifiably enriched will now be considered in more detail.

§2. *CONDICTIO CAUSA DATA CAUSA NON SECUTA*

641. The elements of this *condictio*[1030] are, first, that transfer of money or other property took place and, second, either that the transfer took place on the basis of an assumption regarding a future event that did not occur or that the transfer took place subject to a modal clause that was not complied with or that was frustrated.

If these elements have been complied with, the enriched person must return to the claimant the thing that was transferred to him or her; if he or she no longer possesses it, its value, as well as its fruits[1031] and accessions. The enriched person is probably able to claim compensation for any necessary expenses incurred with respect to the property and those useful expenses that have increased the value of the property, to the extent of the increase in value.

1028. *See* the discussion in ch. 1 §5 above, especially para. 74 (which deals with the question of a general enrichment action).

1029. Academic writers, most notably W. de Vos, *Verrykingsaanspreeklikheid in die Suid-Afrikaanse Reg* (Cape Town: Juta, 1987), have identified the general principles that underlie the specific actions, and the courts have on occasion acknowledged these general principles. However, until the courts or the legislature introduce a general enrichment action (*see McCarthy Retail Ltd v. Shortdistance Carriers CC* 2001 3 SA 482 (SCA) and the discussion about a general enrichment action in Part I above), parties will have to bring their claims within the ambit of the specific actions. As an example of a case in which a court allowed an enrichment action even though the case did not clearly fit into one of the traditional pigeonholes, *see Besselaar v. Registrar, Durban and Coast Local Division and Others* 2002 1 SA 191 (D). The recent approach of the courts in relation to the *condictiones* is to require proof of actual enrichment of the defendant, rather than mere proof of a transfer of money or property to the defendant: *see*, for example, *Trustees, Estate Whitehead v. Dumas and Another* 2013 3 SA 331 (SCA); *Absa Bank Ltd v. Lombard Insurance Co Ltd* 2012 6 SA 569 (SCA), but cf. *ST v. CT* 2018 (5) SA 479 (SCA).

1030. *See* the discussion in ch. 1 §5 above. *See* in general, *The Law of South Africa* vol. 9, paras 217–218 (W.A. Joubert ed., 2d ed. Butterworths 2005); *Wille's Principles of South African Law* 1067 and 1072 (F. du Bois ed., Juta 2007); W. de Vos, *Verrykingsaanspreeklikheid in die Suid-Afrikaanse Reg* (Cape Town: Juta, 1987), 10–20, 62–66 and 154–160; S. Eiselen & G. Pienaar, *Unjustified Enrichment: A Casebook* 141 et seq. (Butterworths 2008); D. Visser, *Unjustified Enrichment* 457 et seq. (Juta 2008); J.C. Sonnekus, *Unjustified Enrichment in South African Law* 97 et seq. (Butterworths 2008).

1031. Wherever mention is made in this chapter of a duty to restore the fruits of an enrichment, it denotes fruits less the cost of producing them. For the purposes of enrichment, interest earned on money is apparently not regarded as fruit. *See The Law of South Africa* vol. 9, para. 218 (W.A. Joubert ed., 2d ed. Butterworths 2005).

§3. *CONDICTIO OB TURPEM VEL INIUSTAM CAUSAM*

642. The elements of this *condictio*[1032] are that the defendant was enriched[1033] by a transfer of money[1034] or other property that took place in terms of an agreement that was void for illegality[1035] and in circumstances in which the claimant himself or herself was not *in delicto.*[1036] The claimant must also offer to return to the other any counter-performance that was made to him or her.[1037]

The requirement that the claimant himself or herself must not be *in delicto,* expressed in terms of the so-called *par delictum* rule (*in pari delicto potior est conditio defendentis/possidentis*),[1038] is not applied without exception. The courts will relax the rule when it is necessary to allow the *condictio* to achieve 'simple justice between man and man' and to promote public policy.[1039]

If these requirements have been satisfied, the enriched person must return to the claimant the thing that was transferred, or if he or she no longer has possession of it, then its full value, as well as its fruits and accessions. The enriched person is probably entitled to compensation for useful and necessary expenses in regard to the property.

1032. *See* the discussion in ch. 1 §5 above. *See* in general *The Law of South Africa* vol. 9, paras 214–216 (W.A. Joubert ed., 2d ed. Butterworths 2005); *Wille's Principles of South African Law* 1064–1065 (F. du Bois ed., Juta 2007); W. de Vos, *Verrykingsaanspreeklikheid in die Suid-Afrikaanse Reg* (Cape Town: Juta, 1987), 20–23, 66–68 and 160–171; S. Eiselen & G. Pienaar, *Unjustified Enrichment: A Casebook* 81 et seq. (Butterworths 2008); D. Visser, *Unjustified Enrichment* 414 et seq. (Juta 2008); J.C. Sonnekus, *Unjustified Enrichment in South African Law* 129 et seq. (Butterworths 2008).

1033. *Trustees, Estate Whitehead v. Dumas and Another* 2013 3 SA 331 (SCA); *Absa Bank Ltd v. Lombard Insurance Co Ltd* 2012 6 SA 569 (SCA).

1034. For a clear exposition of the law relating to transfer of money by way of *commixtio, see Trustees, Estate Whitehead v. Dumas and Another* 2013 3 SA 331 (SCA) at para. 13.

1035. *See* the discussion of legality in Part I of this work above. In *ST v. CT* 2018 (5) SA 479 (SCA) paras 115–116, a performance was made consequent upon an agreement that the majority of the court deemed void for contravening public policy. The court allowed the performing party's claim for enrichment, but assumed that it was a *condictio indebiti* rather than a *condictio ob turpem vel iniustam causam,* without considering the particular requirements of either action. Albeit this was a relatively minor matter in the case, it does illustrate how the courts now take a rather relaxed attitude towards the special requirements of the traditional enrichment actions.

1036. *See*, for example, *Watson NO v. Shaw NO* 2008 1 SA 350 (C); *Tecmed (Pty) Ltd v. Hunter* 2008 6 SA 210 (W). Prima facie, a claimant will be *in delicto* when he or she was party to an illegal agreement. *See* the discussion in Part I of this work.

1037. For a recent statement of these requirements, *see National Credit Regulator v. Opperman and Others* 2013 2 SA 1 (CC) at para. 15.

1038. *See*, for example, *Jajbhay v. Cassim* 1939 AD 537; *Visser en 'n Ander v. Rousseau en Andere NNO* 1990 1 SA 139 (A); *Henry v. Branfield* 1996 1 SA 244 (D).

1039. *See Jajbhay v. Cassim* 1939 AD 537 and the discussion in Part I of this work. It appears that the proper basis for relaxing the rule and granting a claim for return even when the claimant participated in an illegal agreement is indeed public policy. Factors that have been taken into account by the courts in this regard are the following: whether a fair result will be achieved between the parties by refusing or granting return; whether one of the parties had kept to the terms of the agreement; and the moral turpitude of the parties. *See also Henry v. Branfield* 1996 1 SA 244 (D); *Visser en 'n Ander v. Rousseau en Andere NNO* 1990 1 SA 139 (A) and *Afrisure CC v. Watson NO* 2009 2 SA 127 (SCA).

§4. *CONDICTIO INDEBITI*

643. To succeed with this *condictio*,[1040] the plaintiff must prove that there was a transfer of money or other property,[1041] and that this transfer was not in terms of any legal or natural obligation[1042] (except in the case of a minor who performs in terms of a natural obligation arising out of an 'unassisted contract').[1043] It must further be shown that the transfer was made in the erroneous belief that it was due, or was made under duress, or was made by a person who had limited capacity to act. The error in question must be excusable,[1044] and it seems that it may be one of fact or of law. If the plaintiff performed under duress, he or she may bring the *condictio*, provided that he or she can show that he or she protested or otherwise expressly reserved his or her rights at the time of performance.[1045]

The enriched person is required to return the thing that was transferred (or the equivalent amount of *res fungibiles*), or, if he or she no longer has possession of it, then its surrogate or value to the extent of which he or she is still enriched, as well as its fruits and accessions. The enriched person may claim reimbursement of expenditure with respect to the thing, but it is unclear whether this claim is limited to useful and necessary expenses.

1040. *See* the discussion in ch. 1 §5 above. *See* in general *The Law of South Africa* vol. 9, paras 211–213 (W.A. Joubert ed., 2d ed. Butterworths 2005); *Wille's Principles of South African Law* 1058–1064 (F. du Bois ed., Juta 2007); W. de Vos, *Verrykingsaanspreeklikheid in die Suid-Afrikaanse Reg* (Cape Town: Juta, 1987), 23–29, 69–71 and 171–209; S. Eiselen & G. Pienaar, *Unjustified Enrichment: A Casebook* 99 et seq. (Butterworths 2008); D. Visser *Unjustified Enrichment* 271 et seq. (Juta 2008); J.C. Sonnekus, *Unjustified Enrichment in South African Law* 227 et seq. (Butterworths 2008). This is the enrichment remedy most often granted by the courts, and numerous cases could be cited as examples: as recent examples, *see*, for example, *Willis Faber Enthoven (Pty) Ltd v. Receiver of Revenue and Another* 1992 4 SA 202 (A); *Bowman, De Wet and Du Plessis NNO and Others v. Fidelity Bank Ltd* 1997 2 SA 35 (A); *Watson NO and Another v. Shaw NO and Others* 2008 1 SA 350 (C); *Alphina Investments Ltd v. Blacher* 2008 5 SA 479 (C).

1041. This rule is subject to some exceptions: for example, the *condictio* may be brought when that, which was transferred, was possession rather than ownership; the thing 'transferred' could be a *res incorporalis* – *see The Law of South Africa* vol. 9, para. 212 (W.A. Joubert ed., 2d ed. Butterworths 2005).

1042. It is insufficient to prove merely that there was an undue transfer; it must in addition be shown that this transfer actually enriched the defendant: *MN v. AJ* 2013 3 SA 26 (WCC) para. 69. This is in accordance with the approach recently followed by the Supreme Court of Appeal in relation to the *condictio ob turpem vel iniustam causam: see Trustees, Estate Whitehead v. Dumas and Another* 2013 3 SA 331 (SCA); *Absa Bank Ltd v. Lombard Insurance Co Ltd* 2012 6 SA 569 (SCA); cf. *ST v. CT* 2018 (5) SA 479 (SCA) para. 116.

1043. It seems that it is not required in modern South African law that the transfer should relate to a *negotium*, in the sense of an antecedent legal relation or transaction, between the parties. *See* S. Eiselen & G. Pienaar, *Unjustified Enrichment: A Casebook* 69, 87 and 162 (Butterworths 2008).

1044. *See Willis Faber Enthoven (Pty) Ltd v. Receiver of Revenue* 1992 4 SA 202 (A); *Affirmative Portfolios CC v. Transnet Ltd t/a Metrorail* 2009 1 SA 196 (SCA); *MN v. AJ* 2013 3 SA 26 (WCC); cf. *Bowman, De Wet and Du Plessis NNO v. Fidelity Bank Ltd* 1997 2 SA 35 (A); cf. *ST v. CT* 2018 (5) SA 479 (SCA) paras 115–116, where the court classified the enrichment claim in question as a *condictio indebiti*, but did not consider the question of error.

1045. *Commissioner for Inland Revenue v. First National Industrial Bank Ltd* 1990 3 SA 641 (A); *Shuttleworth v. SA Reserve Bank and Others* 2015 1 SA 586 (SCA).

§5. *Condictio Sine Causa Specialis*

644. The *condictio sine causa specialis*[1046] is so-called to distinguish it from the *condictio sine causa generalis*, which is merely another name for any of the three *condictiones* mentioned above. As the requirements for the *condictio sine causa specialis* are tailored to fit the several types of situations in which it may be brought, it is preferable to deal with each of these situations in turn.

In the first situation, which relates to the possession of the property of another, the requirements are the receipt by the enriched person of possession of the property of another and the subsequent bona fide disposal or consumption of the property by the possessor.

The second situation is the receipt by the enriched person of possession of the money of another person[1047] *ex causa lucrativa* or on the basis of a *negotium*,[1048] and the subsequent bona fide disposal or consumption of the money by the possessor.[1049]

The third situation (in this context, the *condictio* is also called the *condictio ob causam finitam*) relates to the transfer of money or other property to the enriched person in terms of a *causa* that later falls away.[1050]

The fourth situation relates to the transfer of money or other property without there being a valid *causa* in a situation in which none of the other *condictiones* would be applicable.[1051]

The enriched person will be liable for the following: the value of the property, if he or she received only possession of it; the return of the property itself, together

---

1046. *See* the discussion in ch. 1 §5 above. *See* in general *The Law of South Africa* vol. 9, paras 219–221 (W.A. Joubert ed., 2d ed. Butterworths 2005); W. de Vos, *Verrykingsaanspreeklikheid in die Suid-Afrikaanse Reg* (Cape Town: Juta, 1987), 29–36, 71–83 and 209–213; S. Eiselen & G. Pienaar, *Unjustified Enrichment: A Casebook* 152 et seq. (Butterworths 2008); J.C. Sonnekus, *Unjustified Enrichment in South African Law* 329 et seq. (Butterworths 2008); *Rulten NO v. Herald Industries (Pty) Ltd* 1982 3 SA 600 (D); *First National Bank of Southern Africa Ltd v. East Coast Design CC and Others* 2000 4 SA 137 (D); *ABSA Bank Ltd v. Standard Bank of SA Ltd* 1998 1 SA 242 (SCA).

1047. This remedy should not be limited to situations in which only money has been acquired *ex causa lucrativa*, but should also apply when other property has been so received – *see* W. de Vos, *Verrykingsaanspreeklikheid in die Suid-Afrikaanse Reg* (Cape Town: Juta, 1987), 211–212.

1048. Regarding the question whether the payment of a cheque by a bank to a payee amounts to a *negotium*, *see B & H Engineering v. First National Bank of SA Ltd* 1995 2 SA 279 (A) 293 A.

1049. *See*, for example, *First National Bank of Southern Africa Ltd v. East Coast Design CC and Others* 2000 4 SA 137 (D); *ABSA Bank Ltd v. Standard Bank of SA Ltd* 1998 1 SA 242 (SCA).

1050. Cf., for example, *Jacquesson v. Minister of Finance* 2006 3 SA 334 (SCA). This action is not available when a contractual remedy exists. For example, in a case of cancellation for breach of a contract in terms of which a transfer was made, the *condictio* would not apply. *See Wille's Principles of South African Law* 1071 (F. du Bois ed., Juta 2007); W. de Vos, *Verrykingsaanspreeklikheid in die Suid-Afrikaanse Reg* (Cape Town: Juta, 1987), 158–159.

1051. There is still uncertainty as to the precise scope of the action in this type of situation. But see *First National Bank of Southern Africa Ltd v. East Coast Design CC and Others* 2000 4 SA 137 (D) 142 C–D; *First National Bank of Southern Africa Ltd v. Perry NO* 2001 3 SA 960 (SCA); *Nissan South Africa (Pty) Ltd v. Marnitz NO* 2005 1 SA 441 (SCA) (although the Court did not specifically state that the action in question was the *condictio sine causa specialis*, it appears that this is what the court had in mind: *see* D.P. Visser, *Unjustified Enrichment*, Annual Survey S. African L. 291, at 298 (2005).

with its fruits and accessions, if he or she received ownership and still has possession of the property; or its value, if he or she received ownership but no longer has possession of the property.[1052]

The enriched person may claim compensation for any necessary expenses incurred with respect to the property and those useful expenses that have increased the value of the property, to the extent of the increase in value.

§6. Action for Improvements

645. In general,[1053] a possessor or occupier[1054] who maintains or improves the property of another without the latter's express or implied consent may bring an enrichment action or raise an enrichment lien[1055] against the owner of the property.

The owner will only be liable when the expenditure was not luxurious, but necessary or useful. In the case of necessary expenses, the possessor may sue for the amount expended, because the other party has been enriched in that he or she did not have to pay these sums necessary for the preservation of his or her property. When the expenses were useful,[1056] the measure of the enrichment will be the amount by which the value of the property has been increased (by tangible improvements[1057]), or the amount of the expenditure, whichever is the lesser. In regard to useful expenses, the court has discretion to allow the owner to waive his or her right to the improvement and to allow the possessor to remove it, or to allow the owner to keep it and pay the possessor the value that it would have upon separation. When

1052. These rules, and those in the following paragraph, are extrapolated from those applicable to the other *condictiones* – *see The Law of South Africa* vol. 9, para. 221 (W.A. Joubert ed., 2d ed. Butterworths 2005).

1053. *See* the discussion in ch. 1 §5 above. *See* in general, *The Law of South Africa* vol. 9, paras 227 et seq. (W.A. Joubert ed., 2d ed. Butterworths 2005); *Wille's Principles of South African Law* 1074–1081 (F. du Bois ed., Juta 2007); W. de Vos, *Verrykingsaanspreeklikheid in die Suid-Afrikaanse Reg* (Cape Town: Juta, 1987), 48–59, 96–110 and 224–274; S. Eiselen & G. Pienaar, *Unjustified Enrichment: A Casebook* 211 et seq. (Butterworths 2008); D. Visser, *Unjustified Enrichment* 590 et seq. (Juta 2008); *Nortje en 'n Ander v. Pool NO* 1966 3 SA 96 (A); *Wynland Construction (Pty) Ltd v. Ashley-Smith en Andere* 1985 3 SA 798 (A). On the issue of 'indirect enrichment' in such cases, *see*, for example, *Buzzard Electrical (Pty) Ltd v. 158 Jan Smuts Investments (Pty) Ltd* 1996 4 SA 19 (A) and *Hubby's Investments (Pty) Ltd v. Lifetime Properties (Pty) Ltd* 1998 1 SA 295 (W).

1054. This includes lessees of urban immovable property: *see Business Aviation Corporation (Pty) Ltd v. Rand Airport Holdings* 2006 6 SA 605 (SCA); *De Aguiar v. Real People Housing (Pty) Ltd* 2011 1 SA 16 (SCA).

1055. *See*, for example, *Business Aviation Corporation (Pty) Ltd v. Rand Airport Holdings* 2006 6 SA 605 (SCA); *Goncalves and Another v. Weber and Another* [2018] ZAGPJHC 598. The possessor or occupier has to prove that the owner was actually enriched by the improvements in question: *see De Aguiar v. Real People Housing (Pty) Ltd* 2011 1 SA 16 (SCA).

1056. According to the weight of academic opinion, expenses are useful when they enhance the market value of the property and are regarded as useful in light of the social and economic values of the community – *see The Law of South Africa* vol. 9, para. 229, at n. 3 (W.A. Joubert ed., 2d ed., Butterworths 2005).

1057. *See Nortje v. Pool* 1966 3 SA 96 (A).

a claim exists, there will also be a right of retention until such claim is satisfied.[1058] A court has the discretion to order the possessor to give up possession in exchange for the provision of adequate alternative security for the enrichment debt. The court may order that this security be provided by the owner of the property, or a third party such as the purchaser of the property.[1059]

646. The above position applies to bona fide *possessors*, that is, possessors who believe that they are the owners of the property in question.[1060] Except for fiduciaries, usufructuaries, and lessees, *lawful occupiers* (those who do not believe that they are owners but have the right to occupy the property)[1061] are in a similar situation to bona fide possessors, except that an amount may be subtracted from their claim with respect to their use of the property. Bona fide *occupiers* (occupiers who mistakenly believe themselves to be lawful occupiers) are treated in the same way as lawful occupiers. *Mala fide possessors* (possessors who know that they are not owners but act as if they were) and *mala fide occupiers* (occupiers who know that they are not lawful occupiers but act as if they were) are probably also in the same legal position as bona fide possessors, except that such possessors of movable property (thieves) will not be able to sue for enrichment.

§7. Claim Against a Minor

647. Persons of limited capacity to act, such as minors, may not be held liable in terms of any agreement that they conclude without the assistance of a parent or legal guardian.[1062] The other party[1063] to such an 'unassisted contract' can, however, bring an enrichment action to claim back a performance made in terms of the agreement. The action will be for the return of the performance or the amount by which the minor is still enriched.

§8. Alienation of Land: Statutory Enrichment Action

648. Contracts for the alienation of land (sale, exchange, or donation, whether conditional or not) must, in terms of the Alienation of Land Act 68 of 1981,[1064] be

1058. *See*, for example, *Business Aviation Corporation (Pty) Ltd v. Rand Airport Holdings* 2006 6 SA 605 (SCA).
1059. *Pheiffer v. Van Wyk and Others* 2015 5 SA 464 (SCA).
1060. For this definition and the following definitions, *see* W. de Vos, *Verrykingsaanspreeklikheid in die Suid-Afrikaanse Reg* (Cape Town: Juta, 1987), 245–247.
1061. *See*, for example, *St Helena Primary School v. MEC, Department of Education, Free State Province* 2007 4 SA 16 (O).
1062. *See* the discussion in ch. 1 §5 above. *See* in general *The Law of South Africa* vol. 9, paras 225–226 (W.A. Joubert ed., 2d ed. Butterworths 2005); W. de Vos, *Verrykingsaanspreeklikheid in die Suid-Afrikaanse Reg* (Cape Town: Juta, 1987), 46, 95–96 and 219–224; S. Eiselen & G. Pienaar, *Unjustified Enrichment: A Casebook* 167 et seq. (Butterworths 2008); *Edelstein v. Edelstein NO and Others* 1952 3 SA 1 (A).
1063. This is assuming that he or she has the full capacity to act.
1064. *See* the discussion in ch. 1 §5 above.

contained in a written deed of alienation, signed by the parties or their agents authorized to do so in writing.[1065] If this formality is not complied with, the contract will be unenforceable at the least[1066] and may even be declared void.[1067]

The Alienation of Land Act laid to rest the uncertainty that previously prevailed regarding the position of a party who performed in terms of a contract that did not comply with the required formalities. In terms of this legislation, such a person may recover his or her performance, whether it was full or partial.

In addition, the *alienee* may claim interest at the prescribed rate with respect to any money that he or she paid in terms of the contract, for the period between payment and recovery. The alienee is also entitled to 'reasonable compensation' for any necessary expenses in regard to the maintenance or improvement of the property and for improvements that increase the market value of the land, provided that the alienator consented to them.

If the relevant party was the *alienator*, he or she may, in addition to reclaiming the property, claim 'reasonable compensation for the occupation, use or enjoyment' of the land and compensation for any damage to the land caused by the alienee.

If both parties perform fully in terms of a contract for the alienation of land that does not comply with the formalities, the contract will be valid *ab initio* for all purposes.[1068]

§9. Claim for Reduced Performance

649. As explained above,[1069] the court may, in the exercise of its discretion, allow a party to sue for a reduced performance in terms of a reciprocal contract when the other party has retained his or her performance because of the former's insufficient performance.[1070] This claim for a reduced performance, which was previously called a claim for *tantum quantum meruerit* (a claim quantum meruit), is based on the contract and not on enrichment.[1071]

An enrichment action will arise, however, when the performance was so seriously defective that the other party was entitled to cancel the contract but is unable to return the defective performance. The claim will be for the amount by which the cancelling party has been enriched due to the inadequate performance of the other. Thus, for example, if a contractor agrees to erect a garage but does nothing other

1065. Section 2(1).
1066. Section 2(1).
1067. Section 24(1)(c).
1068. Section 28(2).
1069. *See* the discussion in the General Introduction of this work and on the right to withhold and the *exceptio non adimpleti contractus*.
1070. *See The Law of South Africa* vol. 9, paras 243–244 (W.A. Joubert ed., 2d ed. Butterworths 2005) and S. Eiselen & G. Pienaar, *Unjustified Enrichment: A Casebook* 316 et seq. (Butterworths 2009).
1071. *See BK Tooling (Edms) Bpk v. Scope Precision Engineering (Edms) Bpk* 1979 1 SA 391 (A) and *Thompson v. Scholtz* 1999 1 SA 232 (SCA).

than prepare the foundation and the flooring, the other contractant would be entitled to cancel the contract but would nevertheless be enriched by those parts of the work that have been completed.

§10. *NEGOTIORUM GESTIO*

I. *Negotiorum Gestio* in General

650. If a person (*negotiorum gestor*[1072]) voluntarily administers the affairs of another (*dominus negotiorum*) without the latter's knowledge or consent, the quasi-contract of *negotiorum gestio* will arise. *Negotiorum gestio* is generally regarded as a quasi-contract, properly so-called, in that rights and duties arise from a source other than a consensus or unjustified enrichment. The contract that it most closely resembles is a mandate. It is distinguished from a mandate, however, in that the mandatary has a duty to perform the mandate as a consequence of the agreement between himself or herself and the mandator.

II. Requirements

651. The requirements for *negotiorum gestio* are the following:

1. The *negotiorum gestor must* administer the affair or affairs of another (the *dominus negotiorum*). If, for example, the *gestor* manages his or her own affairs but thinks that they are another's, there will be no *negotiorum gestio.*
2. The *dominus* must either be absent or unaware that his or her affairs are being administered by another – there must be no authorization whatsoever of the management by the *dominus*. If there is, the relationship may be one of a mandate, not *negotiorum gestio.*
3. The *gestor* must have the intention to administer the affairs of another (the *animus negotia aliena gerendi*); if, for example, he or she has the intention of benefiting himself or herself rather than the *dominus*, no *negotiorum gestio* will arise.
4. The *gestor* must also have the intention to recover from the *dominus* any expenses incurred while administering his or her affairs; if the *gestor* does not intend to recover his or her expenses because, for example, he or she has the

1072. *See* the discussion in ch. 1 §5 above; *Odendaal v. Van Oudthoorn* 1968 3 SA 433 (T); *Standard Bank Financial Services Ltd v. Taylam (Pty) Ltd* 1979 2 SA 383 (C); *ABSA Bank Ltd t/a Bankfin v. Stander t/a CAW Paneelkloppers* 1998 1 SA 939 (C); S. Eiselen & G. Pienaar, *Unjustified Enrichment: A Casebook* 181 et seq. (Butterworths 2008); D. Visser, *Unjustified Enrichment* 565 et seq. (Juta 2008); J.C. Sonnekus, *Unjustified Enrichment in South African Law* 151 et seq. (Butterworths 2008). *See The Law of South Africa* vol. 17 part 1, (W.A. Joubert ed., 2d ed. Butterworths 2009), for a very useful account of the law relating to *negotiorum gestio*. For more details, *see* D.H. van Zyl, *Negotiorum Gestio in South African Law: An Historical and Comparative Analysis* (Butterworths 1985).

intention of donating his or her services, there will be no *negotiorum gestio stricto sensu*, although there may be an enrichment action.

5. The *gestor* must, at the beginning of the administration of the affairs of the *dominus*, act in a useful or reasonable manner – his or her management must be *utiliter coeptum*. The ultimate success or otherwise of the endeavour is irrelevant. The approach to be taken in deciding whether the *gestor's* conduct was carried out *utiliter* is objective: if the *dominus* himself or herself would have followed the same course of action in light of all the circumstances, the *gestor's* conduct will most probably satisfy the requirement that the administration be *utiliter coeptum*.

III. Duties of the Gestor

652. If all of the above requirements have been satisfied, certain duties on the part of the *gestor* arise. He or she must, for example, act as an 'ordinarily prudent' person in administering the affairs of the *dominus*. He or she will thus be liable for any damage suffered by the *dominus* as a consequence of the *gestor's* fault while managing the affairs of the *dominus*. In addition, he or she must complete whatever he or she has undertaken, even if the *dominus* dies before completion of the *gestio*. The *gestor's* estate may be sued for completion if the *gestor* dies before completion. Moreover, the *gestor* must return anything that he or she has acquired as a consequence of the administration of the affairs of the *dominus* and render to the *dominus* an account of the *gestio*.

IV. Rights of the Gestor

653. Conversely, the *gestor* will also have certain rights, for example, the right to be compensated for any necessary and useful expenses incurred by him or her while managing the affairs of the *dominus*, including interest and a right of retention (or lien) on any property of the *dominus* that he or she has in his or her control, until he or she has been reimbursed for his or her expenses.

V. Names and Nature of Actions

654. The action of the dominus is called the actio negotiorum gestorum directa, and that of the gestor is called the actio negotiorum gestorum contraria.

655. In certain instances, the action of the *negotiorum gestor* will be an enrichment action, in that the amount of the claim will be limited to the amount by which the other party has been enriched.

656. The action of the *gestor* (*actio negotiorum gestorum contraria*) functions as an enrichment action, in terms of which the *dominus* is only liable to the extent that he or she remains enriched, in the following four situations:

1. The *gestor* managed another's affairs, bona fide believing that they were his or her own.
2. The *gestor* managed the affairs of another against the latter's expressed wishes, provided that it is shown that there is some just cause for ignoring the wishes of the *dominus*.
3. The *gestor* managed another's affairs *mala fide* and for his or her own benefit, that is, *sui lucri causa*.
4. The *gestor* managed the affairs of a minor.

Selected Bibliography

§1. Encyclopaedic Works and Annual Reviews

Annual Survey of South African Law, Cape Town: Juta.
Joubert, W.A. (founding editor). *The Law of South Africa*. Durban: Lexis Nexis:
Vol. 1 'Agency and Representation' 3rd edn (2014) by M Dendy.
Vol. 2 'Arbitration' 3rd edn (2015) by D.W. Butler.
Vol. 2 Part 1 'Building and Engineering Contracts' (2003) by P.M. Nienaber.
Vol. 2 Part 1 'Carriage' 2nd edn (2003) by I.B. Moss.
Vol. 2 Part 2 'Cession' 2nd edn (2003) by P.M. Nienaber.
Vol. 5 Part 1 'Consumer Credit' 2nd edn (2010) by M. Kelly-Louw.
Vol 5 Part 1 'Consumer Protection' 2nd edn (2010) by E. van Eeden.
Vol. 7 'Damages' 2nd edn (2005) by P.J. Visser.
Vol. 8 Part 1 'Deposit' 2nd edn (2005) by C.J. Pretorius.
Vol. 9 'Contract' 3rd edn (2015) by R. D. Sharrock.
Vol. 9 'Enrichment' 2nd edn (2005) by F.D.J. Brandt.
Vol. 9 'Estoppel' 2nd edn (2005) by H. Daniels.
Vol. 10 Part 2 'Gambling, Gaming, and Lotteries' (2005) by M. Carnelley.
Vol. 14 Part 2 'Lease' 2nd edn (2007) by A.J. Kerr & G. Glover.
Vol. 15 Part 2 'Loan' 2nd edn (2008) by J.J. Henning.
Vol. 17 Part 1 'Mandate and Negotiorum Gestio' 2nd edn (2009) by D.H. van Zyl.
Vol. 17 'Part 2 Mortgage and Pledge' 2nd edn (2008) by T.J. Scott.
Vol. 19 'Obligations' 2nd edn replacement vol. (2016) by L.T.C. Harms.
Vol. 19 'Partnership' 2nd edn replacement vol. (2016) by J.J. Henning.
Vol. 24 'Sale' 2nd edn (2010) by A.J. Kerr & and G. Glover .
Vol. 25 Part 2 'Shipping' 2nd edn replacement vol. (2016) by G.B. Bradfield.
Vol. 26 'Suretyship' 2nd edn replacement vol. (2015) by K.L. Mould.
Vol. 32 'Indigenous Law' 2nd edn (2009) by J. Church, N.J.J. Olivier, R.B. Mqeke, L. Mwambene, J.C. Bekker, W.H. Olivier, W. du Plessis & C. Rautenbach.

§2. Books and Chapters or Sections in Books

Aronstam, P.J. *Consumer Protection, Freedom of Contract and the Law*. Cape Town: Juta, 1979.
Bamford, B.R. *The Law of Partnership and Voluntary Association in South Africa*. 3rd edn. Cape Town: Juta, 1982.
Boberg, P.Q.R. *The Law of Delict*. Vol. 1. Cape Town: Juta, 1984 (revised reprint 1989).

Selected Bibliography

Bradfield, G. B. *Christie's Law of Contract in South Africa.* 7th edn. Durban: Lexis Nexis, 2016.

Brand, H. *Gambling Laws of South Africa.* Cape Town: Juta, 2013.

Cameron, E., et al. *Honoré's South African Law of Trusts.* 5th edn. Cape Town: Juta, 2002.

Caney, L.R. *A Treatise on the Law Relating to Novation, Including Delegation, Compromise and* Res Judicata. 2nd edn. Cape Town: Juta, 1973.

Christie, R.H. 'The Law of Contract and the Bill of Rights'. In *Bill of Rights Compendium.* Durban: Butterworths, 1998.

Cilliers, H.S., et al. *Entrepreneurial Law.* 2nd edn. Durban: Butterworths, 2000.

Cockrell, A. 'Private Law and the Bill of Rights: A Threshold Issue of "Horizontality"'. In *Bill of Rights Compendium.* Durban: Butterworths, 1998.

Cooper, W.E. *Landlord and Tenant.* 2nd edn. Cape Town: Juta, 1994.

Cornelius, S.J. *Principles of the Interpretation of Contracts in South Africa.* 2nd edn. Durban: LexisNexis, 2007.

Davis, D.M. *Democracy and Deliberation: Transformation and the South African Legal Order.* Cape Town: Juta, 1999.

De Vos, W. *Verrykingsaanspreeklikheid in die Suid-Afrikaanse Reg.* 3rd edn. Cape Town: Juta, 1987.

De Wet, J.C. & A.H. van Wyk. *Die Suid-Afrikaanse Kontraktereg en Handelsreg.* Vol. 1. 5th edn. Durban: Butterworths, 1992.

De Wet, J.C. & A.H. van Wyk. *Die Suid-Afrikaanse Kontraktereg en Handelsreg.* Vol. 2: *Handelsreg.* 4th edn (reprint). Durban: Butterworths, 1993.

Diedrich, F. (ed) *Ubuntu Good Faith & Equity: Flexible Legal Principles in Developing a Contemporary Jurisprudence.* Cape Town: Juta, 2011.

Du Bois, F., et al. *Wille's Principles of South African Law.* 9th edn. Cape Town: Juta, 2007.

Du Plessis, A. (ed.). *Environmental Law and Local Government in South Africa.* Cape Town: Juta, 2014.

Du Plessis, J.E. *The South African Law of Unjustified Enrichment.* Cape Town: Juta, 2012.

Du Plessis, J. E. & Lubbe, G. (eds) *A Man of Principle/'n Man van Beginsel.* Cape Town: Juta, 2013.

Eiselen, S. & G. Pienaar. *Unjustified Enrichment: A Casebook.* 3rd edn. Durban: Butterworths, 2008.

Finsen, E. *The Building Contract: A Commentary on the JBCC Agreements.* 2nd edn. Cape Town: Juta, 2006.

Forsyth, C.F. & J.T. Pretorius. *Caney's the Law of Suretyship in South Africa.* 6th edn. Cape Town: Juta, 2010.

Glover, G. *Kerr's The Law of Sale and Lease.* 4th edn. Durban: LexisNexis, 2001.

Gluckman, M. *The Ideas in Barotse Jurisprudence.* Manchester: Manchester University Press, 1972.

Grové, N.J. & J.M. Otto. *Basic Principles of Consumer Credit Law.* 2nd edn. Cape Town: Juta, 2002.

Hackwill, G.R.J. *Mackeurtan's Sale of Goods in South Africa.* 5th edn. Cape Town: Juta, 1984.

Hahlo, H.R. & E. Kahn. *The South African Legal System and Its Background.* Cape Town: Juta, 1968.
Hahlo, H.R. & E. Kahn. *The Union of South Africa: The Development of its Laws and Constitution.* Cape Town: Juta, London: Stevens and Sons, 1960.
Hawthorne, L. & C.J. Pretorius. *Contract Law Casebook.* 3rd edn. Cape Town: Juta, 2010.
Hosten, W.J., et al. *Introduction to South African Law and Legal Theory.* 2nd edn. Durban: Butterworths, 1995.
Hutchison, D. 'Good Faith in the South African Law of Contract'. In *Brownsword, Hird, Howells, Good Faith in Contract: Concept and Context.* Aldershot: Ashgate Publishing Co., 1999.
Hutchison, D., et al. *The Law of Contract in South Africa.* 3rd edn Cape Town: Oxford University Press Southern Africa, 2017.
Joubert, D.J. *Die Suid-Afrikaanse Verteenwordigingsreg.* Cape Town: Juta, 1979.
Joubert, D.J. *General Principles of the Law of Contract.* Cape Town: Juta, 1987.
Kahn, E. & K.M. Kritzinger. *Principles of Mortgage, Pledge and Lien.* Cape Town: Juta, 1999.
Kahn, E., C. Lewis & C. Visser. *Kahn Contract and Mercantile Law: A Source Book.* Vol. 1: *General Principles of Contract, Agency and Representation.* 2nd edn. Cape Town: Juta, 1988.
Kahn, E., et al. *Kahn Contract and Mercantile Law through the Cases.* Vol. 2: *Specific Contracts and Mercantile Law; Security.* 2nd edn. Cape Town: Juta, 1985.
Kerr, A.J. *The Law of Agency.* 4th edn. Durban: Butterworths, 2006.
Kerr, A.J. *The Principles of the Law of Contract.* 6th edn. Durban: Butterworths, 2002.
Lambiris, M.A. *Orders of Specific Performance and Restitutio in Integrum in South African Law.* Durban: Butterworths, 1989.
Lehmann, K. & G. Bradfield. *Principles of the Law of Sale and Lease.* 2nd edn. Juta: Cape Town, 2010.
Lotz, D.J. & C.J. Nagel. *Specific Contracts in Court.* 3rd edn. Durban: Butterworths, 1999.
Loubser, M.M. *Extinctive Prescription.* Cape Town: Juta, 1996.
Lowe, M.J., et al. *Elliott's the South African Notary.* 6th edn. Cape Town: Juta, 1987.
Lubbe, G.F. & C.M. Murray. *Farlam and Hathaway's Contract: Cases, Materials and Commentary.* 3rd edn. Cape Town: Juta, 1998.
Millard, D. *Modern Insurance Law in South Africa.* Cape Town: Juta, 2013.
Naude, T. & Eiselen, S. (eds) *Commentary on the Consumer Protection Act.* (loose-leaf service). Cape Town: Juta, original service 2014.
Neethling, J., J.M. Potgieter & P.J. Visser. *Law of Delict.* 6th edn. Durban: LexisNexis, 2009.
Newman, E. & D.J. McQuoid-Mason. *Lee and Honoré's the South African Law of Obligations.* 2nd edn. Durban: Butterworths, 1978.
Olivier, P. A., et al. *Trust Law and Practice.* (Loose-leaf service). Durban: Lexis Nexis.
Prinsloo, M.W. & L.P. Vorster. *Indigenous Contract in Bophuthatswana.* Pretoria: Centre for Indigenous Law University of South Africa Pretoria, 1990.

Rabie, P.J. & J.C. Sonnekus, *The Law of Estoppel in South Africa.* 2nd edn. Durban: Butterworths, 2000.
Ramsden, P. *McKenzie's The Law of Building and Engineering Contracts and Arbitration.* 7th edn. Cape Town: Juta, 2014.
Ramsden, P. *The Law of Arbitration.* Cape Town: Juta, 2009.
Ramsden, W.A. *Supervening Impossibility of Performance in the South African Law of Contract.* Cape Town: Juta, 1985.
Reinecke, M.F.B., et al. *South African Insurance Law.* Durban: Lexis Nexis, 2013.
Saner, J. *Agreements in Restraint of Trade in South African Law.* Durban: Butterworths, 1999.
Scholtz, J.W. *Guide to the National Credit Act.* Durban: Butterworths, 2008.
Scott, S. *The Law of Cession.* 2nd edn. Cape Town: Juta, 1991.
Scott, S. *Cession for Students.* 2nd edn. Cape Town: Juta, 2013.
Scott, T.J. & S. Scott. *Wille's Law of Mortgage and Pledge in South Africa.* 3rd edn. Cape Town: Juta, 1987.
Silke, J.M. *De Villiers' and Macintosh's the Law of Agency in South Africa.* 3rd edn. Cape Town: Juta, 1981.
Sonnekus, J.C. *The Law of Estoppel in South Africa.* 3rd edn. Durban: Butterworths, 2013.
Sonnekus, J.C. *Unjustified Enrichment in South African Law.* Durban: Butterworths, 2008.
South African Law Commission. *Unreasonable Stipulations in Contracts and the Rectification of Contracts.* Pretoria: Government Printer, 1998, R/P 133/1998.
South African Yearbook 1994, Pretoria: South African Communication Service Pretoria, 1994.
Tennant, S-L. *The National Credit Act and Consumer Protection Act: A Guide for Credit Providers and Suppliers.* Cape Town: Juta, 2011.
Theal, G. McC. *Records of the Cape Colony.* Public Record Office, 1905.
Van der Merwe, C.G. *Sakereg.* 2nd edn. Durban: Butterworths, 1989.
Van der Merwe, F. E. *Notarial Practice.* Durban: Butterworths, 2001.
Van der Ross, R.E. *Myths and Attitudes an Inside Look at the Coloured People.* Cape Town, Tafelberg, 1979.
Van Huyssteen, L.F. *Onbehoorlike Beinvloeding en Misbruik van Omstandighede in die Suid-Afrikaanse Verbintenisreg.* Cape Town: Juta, 1980.
Van Huyssteen, L. F., Lubbe, G. F. & Reinecke M.F. B. *Contract; General Principles.* 5th edn. Cape Town: Juta, 2016.
Van Zyl, D.H. *Negotiorum Gestio in South African Law: An Historical and Comparative Analysis.* Durban: Butterworths, 1985.
Visagie, G.G. *Regspleging en Reg aan die Kaap van 1652 tot 1806.* Cape Town: Juta, 1969.
Visser, D. (ed.) *The Limits of the Law of Obligations.* Cape Town: Juta, 1997.
Visser, D. *Unjustified Enrichment.* Cape Town: Juta, 2008.
Visser, J.P. & J.M. Potgieter. *Law of Damages through the Cases.* 3rd edn. Cape Town: Juta, 2004.
Woker, T. *The Franchise Relationship under South African Law.* Cape Town: Juta, 2012.

Woolman, S., T. Roux & M. Bishop. *Constitutional Law of South Africa*. Cape Town: Juta, 2002.
Zeffertt, D.T. & A. Paizes. *Parol Evidence with Particular Reference to Contract*. Johannesburg: Centre for Banking Law Rand Afrikaans University, 1986.
Zeffertt, D. et al *The South African Law of Evidence*. Durban: LexisNexis 2017.
Zulman, R.H. & G. Kairinos. *Norman's Law of Purchase and Sale in South Africa*. 5th edn. Durban: Butterworths, 2005.
Zimmermann, R. *The Law of Obligations: Roman Foundations of the Civilian Tradition*. Cape Town: Juta, 1990.
Zimmermann, R. & D. Visser. *Southern Cross: Civil Law and Common Law in South Africa*. Cape Town: Juta and Oxford: Oxford University Press, 1996.

§3. Articles and Notes

Aquilius. 'Immorality and Illegality in Contract'. *South African Law Journal* (1941): 337; *South African Law Journal* (1942): 16.
Beinart, B. 'The English Law Contribution in South Africa: The Interaction of Civil and Common Law'. *Acta Juridica* (1981): 7.
Bhana, D. 'The Law of Contract and the Constitution: Napier *v.* Barkhuizen (SCA)'. *South African Law Journal* (2007): 269.
Bhana, D. 'The Role of Judicial Method in Contract Law'. *South African Law Journal* (2015): 122.
Bhana, D. & M. Pieterse. 'Towards a Reconciliation of Contract Law and Constitutional Values: Brisley and Afrox Revisited'. *South African Law Journal* (2005): 865.
Boberg, P.Q.R. 'Back to Winterbottom v Wright? – Not quite!'. *South African Law Journal* (1985): 3.
Bolton, P. 'Government Dealings and the Intention to Create Legal Relations'. *South African Mercantile Law Journal* (2004): 196.
Bonthuys, E. 'Reciprocity in Relation to the *Exceptio non Adimpleti Contractus*: The Intention of the Parties?'. *Tydskrif vir die Suid-Afrikaanse Reg* (2001): 180.
Brand, F.D.J. 'The Role of Good Faith, Equity and Fairness in the South African Law of Contract: The Influence of the Common Law and the Constitution'. *South African Law Journal* (2009): 71.
Brand, Fritz 'The Role of Good Faith, Equity and Fairness in the South African Law of Contract: A Further Instalment'. *Stellenbosch Law Review (*2016): 238.
Cockrell, A. 'Substance and Form in the South African Law of Contract'. *South African Law Journal* (1992): 40.
Cockrell, A. 'Reliance and Private Law'. *Stellenbosch Law Review* (1993): 41.
Cockrell, A. 'The Hegemony of Contract'. *South African Law Journal* (1998): 286.
Coetzee, J. 'The Convention on the Use of Electronic Communications in International Contracts: Creating an International Legal Framework for Electronic Contracting'. *South African Mercantile Law Journal* (2006): 245.
Cornelius, S. 'Rectification of Contracts and Evidence of Prior Oral Agreements'. *Tydskrif vir die Suid-Afrikaanse Reg* (2000): 563.
Cornelius, S. 'Bepaalde Verskyningsvorme van Goeie Trou in die Kontraktereg'. *Tydskrif vir die Suid-Afrikaanse Reg* (2001): 241.

Selected Bibliography

Cornelius, S. 'The Unexpressed Terms of a Contract'. *Stellenbosch Law Review* (2006): 494.
De Vos, W. 'Mora Debitoris and Rescission'. *South African Law Journal* (1970): 304.
De Waal, M.J. 'Anomaliëe in die Suid-Afrikaanse Trustreg'. *Tydskrif vir Hedendaagse Romeins-Hollandse Reg* (1993): 1.
Du Plessis, A. 'Pre-Contractual Misrepresentation, Contractual Terms, and the Measure of Damages when the Contract is Upheld'. *South African Law Journal* (2008): 413.
Du Plessis, H. 'Display of Goods for Sale, Advertisements and the Consumer Protection Act'. *South African Law Journal* (2015): 150.
Du Plessis, J.E. 'Towards a Rational Structure of Liability for Unjustified Enrichment: Thoughts from Two Mixed Jurisdictions'. *South African Law Journal* (2005): 142.
Eiselen, G.T.S. 'Herlewing van die Algemene Verrykingsaksie'. *Tydskrif vir Hedendaagse Romeins-Hollandse Reg* (1992): 124.
Eiselen, S. 'Adoption of the Vienna Convention for the International Sale of Goods (The CISG) in South Africa'. *South African Law Journal* (1999): 323.
Eiselen, S. 'Adopting the Vienna Sales Convention: Reflections Eight Years Down the Line'. *South African Mercantile Law Journal* (2007): 14.
Floyd, T.B. 'Die Voorkoopreg'. *Tydskrif vir Hedendaagse Romeins-Hollandse Reg* (1986): 253.
Floyd, T. 'The Capacity of Government to Conclude Contracts: Still an Unlimited Power?'. *South African Public Law* (2005): 378.
Glover, G. 'The Inducement of a Contract by "Duress of Goods": A Reappraisal'. *South African Mercantile Law Journal* (2006): 175.
Glover, G. '"Methinks He Doth Protest Too Much?" Recovering Unjustified Payments Made under Duress and Protest'. *Tydskrif vir Hedendaagse Romeins-Hollandse Reg* (2006): 135.
Glover, G. 'The Test for Duress in the South African Law of Contract'. *South African Law Journal* (2006): 98.
Glover, G. 'Lazarus in the Constitutional Court: An Exhumation of the Exceptio Doli Generalis?'. *South African Law Journal* (2007): 449.
Harms, L.T.C 'The Puisne Judge, the Chaos Theory and the Common Law'. *South African Law Journal* (2014): 3.
Hawthorne, L. 'The Principle of Equality in the Law of Contract'. *Tydskrif vir Hedendaagse Romeins-Hollandse Reg* (1995): 157.
Hawthorne, L. 'The Principle of Equality Impacts on the Classical Law of Contract'. *Tydskrif vir Hedendaagse Romeins-Hollandse Reg* (1999): 596.
Hawthorne, L. 'Closing of the Open Norms in the Law of Contract'. *Tydskrif vir Hedendaagse Romeins-Hollandse Reg* (2004): 294.
Hawthorne, L. 'The development clause section 39 (2) of the Constitution and the law of contract'. *Tydskrif vir Hedendaagse Romeins-Hollandse Reg* (2018): 81.
Hefer, J.J. 'Billikheid in die Kontraktereg'. *Tydskrif vir Regwetenskap* (2004): 1.
Henning, J.J. & J.J. Du Plessis. 'Kontraksluiting namens 'n Vennootskap: 'n Ondernemingsregtelike Perspektief'. *Tydskrif vir Hedendaagse Romeins-Hollandse Reg* (1993): 339.

Hutchison, A. 'What's So Wrong with Williams v Evans: An Examination of the Concept of the Supposition in Futuro'. *South African Law Journal* (2008): 441.

Hutchison, A. 'Liability for Breaking off Contractual Negotiations?' *South African Law Journal* (2012): 104.

Hutchison, A. 'Remoteness in Contract: Under Revision in the House of Lords too?' *South African Law Journal* (2012): 199.

Hutchison, A. & Hutchison, D. 'Simulated Transactions and the Fraus Legis Doctrine' *South African Law Journal* (2014): 69.

Hutchison, D.B. & B. Van Heerden. 'Mistake in Contract: A Comedy of (Justus) Errors'. *South African Law Journal* (1987): 523.

Hutchison, D.B. & D.P. Visser. 'Lillicrap Revisited: Further Thoughts on Pure Economic Loss and Concurrence of Actions'. *South African Law Journal* (1985): 587.

Hutchison, D. 'Non-variation Clauses in Contract: Any Escape from the *Shifren* Straitjacket?'. *South African Law Journal* (2001): 720.

Hutchison, D. 'Back to Basics: Reliance Damages for Breach of Contract Revisited'. *South African Law Journal* (2004): 51.

Joubert, D.J. 'Die Verswëe Prinsipaal en Formele Kontrakte'. *Tydskrif vir Hedendaagse Romeins-Hollandse Reg* (1992): 363.

Kahn, E. 'Some Mysteries of Offer and Acceptance'. *South African Law Journal* (1955): 246.

Kerr, A.J. 'Some Questions Relating to Fraud in Agency'. *South African Law Journal* (1994): 291.

Kerr, A.J. 'Dangers in the Use of Synonyms to Describe Different Categories of Contractual Provisions: "Implied" and "Tacit"'. *Tydskrif vir Hedendaagse Romeins-Hollandse Reg* (1994): 279.

Kerr, A.J. 'The Warranty against Eviction in Contracts of Sale'. *South African Law Journal* (1999): 455.

Kerr, A.J. 'Implied Provisions in Contracts: Is There to Be a New Role for the Hypothetical Bystander? Conflicting Supreme Court of Appeal Decisions'. *South African Law Journal* (2006): 195.

Kerr, A.J. & B.G. Glover. 'May Essential Provisions of a Contract Be Determined by One of the Parties Alone?'. *South African Law Journal* (2000): 201.

Kleyn, D. 'The Reality of Real Contracts'. *Tydskrif vir Hedendaagse Romeins-Hollandse Reg* (1995): 16.

Kritzinger, K.M. 'The Irrevocable Offer'. *South African Law Journal* (1983): 441.

Legwaila, T. 'An Introduction to the Rental Housing Act 50 of 1999'. *Stellenbosch Law Review* (2001): 277.

Lewis, C. 'The Demise of the *Exceptio Doli*: Is There Another Route to Contractual Equity?'. *South African Law Journal* (1990): 26.

Lubbe, G. 'Taking Fundamental Rights Seriously: The Bill of Rights and Its Implications for the Development of Contract Law'. *South African Law Journal* (2004): 395.

Lubbe, G.F. '*Bona Fides*, Billikheid en die Openbare Belang in die Suid-Afrikaanse Kontraktereg'. *Stellenbosch Law Review* (1990): 7.

Lubbe, G.F. 'Die Oordrag van Toekomstige Regte en die Aanwending van Retensiegeld ter Versekering van Skuld'. *Tydskrif vir die Suid-Afrikaanse Reg* (1999): 561.

Lubbe, G. & S. van der Merwe. 'Apportionment of Loss in Contractual Claims for Damages at Common Law'. *Stellenbosch Law Review* (1999): 141.

McLennan, J.S. 'Positive and Negative Damages for Breach of Contract: The Confusion of Labels'. *South African Law Journal* (1999): 521.

McLennan, J.S. 'Tacit Terms and Common Mistake in Contract'. *South African Law Journal* (2000): 219.

McLennan, J.S. 'Specific Performance and Impossibility of Performance of Contracts'. *South African Law Journal* (2001): 245.

McLennan, J.S. 'A Lessor's Hypothec over the Goods of Third Parties: Anomaly and Anachronism'. *South African Mercantile Law Journal* (2004): 121.

Myburgh, F. 'The South African Approach to the Rectification of Agreements subject to Constitutive Formalities: One Step too Many?' *South African Law Journal* (2016): 787.

Nagel, C.J. 'Die Regsposisie van 'n Verkoper waar Uitwinning Dreig'. *South African Mercantile Law Journal* (2005): 375.

Naudé, T. 'Rights of First Refusal or Preferential Rights to Contract: A Historical Perspective on a Controversial Legal Figure'. *Stellenbosch Law Review* (2004): 66.

Naudé, T. 'The Rights and Remedies of the Holder of a Right of First Refusal or Preferential Right to Contract'. *South African Law Journal* (2004): 636.

Naudé, T. 'Unfair Contract Terms Legislation: The Implications of Why We Need It for Its Formulation and Application'. *South African Law Journal* (2006): 461.

Naudé, T. 'Enforcement Procedures in respect of the Consumer's Right to Fair, Reasonable and Just Contract Terms under the new Consumer Protection Act in Comparative Perspective'. *South African Law Journal* (2010): 515.

Naudé, T. & G. Lubbe. 'Cancellation for "Material" or "Fundamental" Breach: A Comparative Analysis of South African Law, the UN Convention on Contracts for the International Sale of Goods (CISG) and the UNIDROIT Principles of International Commercial Contracts'. *Stellenbosch Law Review* (2001): 371.

Naudé, T. & G.F. Lubbe. 'Exemption Cluases: A Rethink Occasioned by Afrox Healthcare Bpk v Strydom 2002 (6) SA 21 (SCA)'. *South African Law Journal* (2005): 22.

Neels, J.L. 'Die Aanvullende en Beperkende Werking van Redelikheid en Billikheid in die Kontraktereg' *Tydskrif vir die Suid-Afrikaanse Reg* (1999): 684.

Nienaber, P.M. 'Enkele Beskouinge oor Kontrakbreuk in Anticipando'. *Tydskrif vir Hedendaagse Romeins-Hollandse Reg* (1963): 19.

Nortje, M. 'Of Reliance, Self-reliance and Caveat Subscriptor'. *South African Law Journal* (2012): 132.

Otto, J.M. 'Unilateral Determination of Interest Rates by Creditors: The Supreme Court of Appeal (Almost) Settles the Matter'. *South African Law Journal* (2000): 1.

Otto, J.M. 'Verskuilde Borgstellings en Standardkontrakte en Iustus Error'. *Tydskrif vir die Suid-Afrikaanse Reg* (2005): 805.

Pistorius, T. 'From Snail Mail to E-Mail: A South African Perspective on the Web of Conflicting Rules on the Time of e-Contracting'. *Comparative and International Law Journal of South Africa* (2006): 178.

Pretorius, C-J. 'The Basis of Contractual Liability in English Law and Its Influence on the South African Law of Contracts'. *Comparative and International Law Journal of South Africa* (2004): 96.

Pretorius, C-J. 'The Incorporation of Contractual Terms and Reliance'. *Tydskrif vir die Suid-Afrikaanse Reg* (2004): 416.

Pretorius, C-J. 'Reasonable Reliance on the Duty to Enquire'. *Tydskrif vir Hedendaagse Romeins-Hollandse Reg* (2005): 122.

Pretorius, C-J. 'The Basis of Contractual Liability (1): Ideologies and Approaches'. *Tydskrif vir Hedendaagse Romeins-Hollandse Reg* (2005): 253.

Pretorius, C-J. 'The Basis of Contractual Liability (2): Theories of Contract (Will and Declaration)'. *Tydskrif vir Hedendaagse Romeins-Hollandse Reg* (2005): 441.

Pretorius, C-J. 'The Basis of Contractual Liability (3): Theories of Contract (Consideration, Reliance and Fairness)'. *Tydskrif vir Hedendaagse Romeins-Hollandse Reg* (2005): 575.

Pretorius, C-J. 'The Basis of Contractual Liability (4); Towards a Composite Theory of Contract'. *Tydskrif vir Hedendaagse Romeins-Hollandse Reg* (2006): 19.

Pretorius, C-J. 'Caveat Subscriptor and Iustus Error: Brink v Humphries & Jewell (Pty) Ltd'. *Tydskrif vir Hedendaagse Romeins-Hollandse Reg* (2006): 675.

Pretorius, J.T. 'Prejudice and the Surety'. *South African Mercantile Law Journal* (2005): 381.

Price, A. 'The Influence of Human Rights on Private Common Law' *South African Law Journal* (2012): 330.

Rautenbach, I.M. 'The Bill of Rights applies to Private Law and Binds Private Persons'. *Tydskrif vir die Suid-Afrikaanse Reg* (2000): 296.

Roux, T. 'Continuity and Change in a Transforming Legal Order: The Impact of Section 26(3) of the Constitution on South African Law'. *South African Law Journal* (2004): 466.

Scott, S. 'Die Rol van Kennis van Sessie aan die Skuldenaar'. *Tydskrif vir die Suid-Afrikaanse Reg* (2007): 813.

Snyman-van Deventer, E. & J. Henning. 'Is die Essentialia van die Vennootskap Onderskik aan die Bedoeling van die Partye? 'n Oorsig oor die Suid-Afrikaanse Reg'. *Tydskrif vir Hedendaagse Romeins-Hollandse Reg* (2007): 87.

Steyn, L. 'The Inclusion of "Additional" Terms or "Standard Terms and Conditions" in a Contract: The Significance of the "Ticket" Cases, Caveat Subscriptor and the Application of the Reliance Theory'. *South African Mercantile Law Journal* (2004): 106.

Sutherland, P.J. 'Ensuring Contractual Fairness in Consumer Contracts after Barkhuizen v Napier 2007 5 SA 323 (CC): Part 1'. *Stellenbosch Law Review* (2008): 390.

Sutherland, P.J. 'Ensuring Contractual Fairness in Consumer Contracts after Barkhuizen v Napier 2007 5 SA 323 (CC): Part 2'. *Stellenbosch Law Review* (2009): 50.

Trakman, L.E. 'The Effect of Illegality in South African Law: A Doctrinal and Comparative Study'. *South African Law Journal* (1977): 327, at 468.

Van Aswegen, A. 'The Implications of a Bill of Rights for the Law of Contract and Delict'. *South African Journal on Human Rights* (1955): 50.

Van Aswegen, A. 'The Future of South African Contract Law'. *Tydskrif vir Hedendaagse Romeins-Hollandse Reg* (1994): 448.

Van der Merwe, S., G.F. Lubbe & L.F. van Huyssteen. 'The Exceptio Doli Generalis: Requiescat in Pace: Vivat Aequitas'. *South African Law Journal* (1989): 235.

Van der Merwe, S. & L.F. van Huyssteen. 'Reasonable Reliance on Consensus, *Iustus Error* and the Creation of Contractual Obligations'. *South African Law Journal* (1994): 679.

Van der Merwe, S. & L.F. van Huyssteen. 'The Force of Agreements: Valid, Void, Voidable, Unenforceable?'. *Tydskrif vir Hedendaagse Romeins-Hollandse Reg* (1995): 549.

Van der Merwe, S. & L.F. van Huyssteen. 'A Perspective on the Elements of Estoppel by Representation'. *Tydskrif vir die Suid-Afrikaanse Reg* (1988): 568.

Van der Merwe, S. & L.F. van Huyssteen. 'Estoppel by Representation: The Ambiguity of an "Unambiguous Representation"'. *Tydskrif vir die Suid-Afrikaanse Reg* (1990): 86.

Van der Merwe, D. 'Constitutional Colonization of the Common Law: A Problem of Institutional Integrity'. *Tydskrif vir die Suid-Afrikaanse Reg* (2000): 12.

Van der Walt, A.J. & Siphuma, N.S. 'Extending the Lessor's Tacit Hypothec to Third Parties' Property', *South African Law Journal* (2015): 518.

Van der Walt, C.F.C. 'Die Huidige Posisie in die Suid-Afrikaanse Reg met Betrekking tot Onbillike Kontraksbedinge'. *South African Law Journal* (1986): 646.

Van der Walt, C.F.C. 'Kontrakte en Beheer oor Kontrakteervryheid in 'n Nuwe Suid-Afrika'. *Tydskrif vir Hedendaagse Romeins-Hollandse Reg* (1991): 367.

Van Huyssteen, L.F. & S. van der Merwe. 'Good Faith in Contract: Proper Behaviour amidst Changing Circumstances'. *Stellenbosch Law Review* (1990): 244.

Van Huyssteen, L.F. 'Some Notes on Roman-Dutch Law at the Cape under British Rule: Evaluation of a Few General Principles of the Law of Contract as applied by the Court of Justice between 1806 and 1827'. *Tijdschrift voor Rechtsgeschiedenis* (1994): 357.

Van Huyssteen, L.F., S. van der Merwe & J.H. Herbots. 'Onzorgvuldige en Onjuiste Informatie bij de Contractsluiting in het Zuidafrikaans Recht'. *Tijdschrift voor Privaatrecht* 1 (1993): 61.

Van Huyssteen, L.F. 'The Horizontal Application Theory and Its Influence on Freedom of Agreement in the Law of Contract – A South African Perspective'. *Law Democracy and Development* 2 (1998): 209.

Van Niekerk, J.P. 'An Unintended Amendment of the Common Law? The National Gambling Act and the Enforceability of Gaming and Wagering Agreements'. *Juta's Business Law* (2005): 70.

Van Rensburg, A.D.J. 'Formaliteitsvoorskrifte, Voorkoopregte en Opsies'. *Tydskrif vir Hedendaagse Romeins-Hollandse Reg* (1986): 208.

Visser, D.P. 'Error of Law and Mistaken Payments: A Milestone'. *South African Law Journal* (1992): 177.

Wallis, M. 'Commercial Certainty and Constitutionalism: Are they Compatible?' *South African Law Journal* (2016): 545.
Zimmermann, R. 'Synthesis in South African Private Law: Civil Law, Common Law and *Usus Hodiernus Pandectarum*'. *South African Law Journal* (1986): 259.

Selected Bibliography

Table of Cases

Table of Cases

Index

The numbers here refer to paragraph numbers.

Index

Index

Index

Index

Index

Index